Testimonials

"An authoritative guide and must-buy for anyone who lives
in the area and owns a mountain bike,"
—MOUNTAIN BIKE MAGAZINE

"In the world's busiest mountain bike playground,
Delaine Fragnoli's guide is an indispensable way to finding and
riding the good, the rad and the gnarly. Even though I've spent 10 years
of riding all over Southern California, I use it regularly,"
—DAN KOEPPEL, COLUMNIST, MOUNTAIN BIKE MAGAZINE

"Too often guidebooks are an exercise in poaching that leads
to disastrous results such as sending people places where they shouldn't be.
This author list reads like a who's who of Southern California mountain
bike notables. That feels right morally and gives the reader complete
faith that the rides are accurate, legal, and proven."
—DON CUERDON, MOUNTAIN BIKE MAGAZINE

"Delaine is a great traveling companion and her insight
into the trails of Southern California is a worthwhile investment
for any mountain biker,"
—MARTI STEPHEN, MOUNTAIN BIKE EDITOR, VELONEWS

"Great information and inspiration to try new trails!
With trail access under attack, it's great to see a guidebook with all
the classics as well as some new surprises,"
—CHRIS HATOUNIAN, SENIOR EDITOR, MOUNTAIN BIKING MAGAZINE

Rest stop along the Kern Canyon Trail, Sequoia National Forest.

MOUNTAIN BIKING
Southern California's
BEST 100 TRAILS

Second Edition

Edited by Delaine Fragnoli & Don Douglass

MOUNTAIN
BIKING
PRESS™

FINE EDGE
Productions

IMPORTANT LEGAL NOTICE AND DISCLAIMER

Mountain biking is a potentially dangerous sport, and the rider or user of this book accepts a number of unavoidable risks. Trails by nature have numerous natural and man-made hazards; they are generally not signed or patrolled and they change with time and conditions.

While substantial effort has been made to provide accurate information, this guidebook may inadvertently contain errors and omissions. Any maps in this book are for locator reference only. They are not to be used for navigation. Your mileages will vary from those given in this book. Contact land managers before attempting routes to check for suitability and trail conditions.

The authors, editors, contributors, publishers, distributors, and public and private land managers accept no liability for any errors or omissions in this book or for any injuries or losses incurred from using this book.

Credits:
book design: Melanie Haage
copy editing: Réanne Hemingway-Douglass & Cindy Kamler
diagrams: Sue Irwin, Faith Rumm
cover photos: © Tony Quiroz
all other photos by the authors, except as noted

Library of Congress Cataloging-in-Publication Data

Mountain biking southern California's best 100 trails / edited by Delaine Fragnoli & Don Douglass. —2nd ed.
  p.   cm.
Includes bibliographical references (p.   ) and index.
ISBN 0-938665-53-7
  1. All terrain cycling—California, Southern—Guidebooks.
  2. California, Southern—Guidebooks.   I. Fragnoli, Delaine, 1962–
Douglass, Don, 1932–
GV1045.5.C22S685   1998   97-37592
917.94'90453-dc21   CIP

Address requests for permission to
Mountain Biking Press™
Fine Edge Productions; Route 2, Box 303, Bishop, CA 93514
www.fineedge.com

TABLE OF CONTENTS

Chapter 1: San Diego County
By Delaine Fragnoli

Chapter 2: Orange County
By Robert Rasmussen

Chapter 3: Coachella Valley/Riverside County
By Paul Maag

Chapter 4: San Bernardino Mountains
By Robert Shipley and Allen Thibault

Chapter 5: Angeles National Forest
By Mike Troy, Kevin Woten and Delaine Fragnoli
Mt. Baldy District:

Arroyo Seco District:
Saugus District:
Valyermo District:

Chapter 6: Santa Monica Mountains
By Jim Hasenauer and Mark Langton

Chapter 7: Ventura County and the Sespe
By Mickey McTigue

Chapter 8: Santa Barbara County
By Mickey McTigue and Don Douglass

Appendices

Delaine Fragnoli

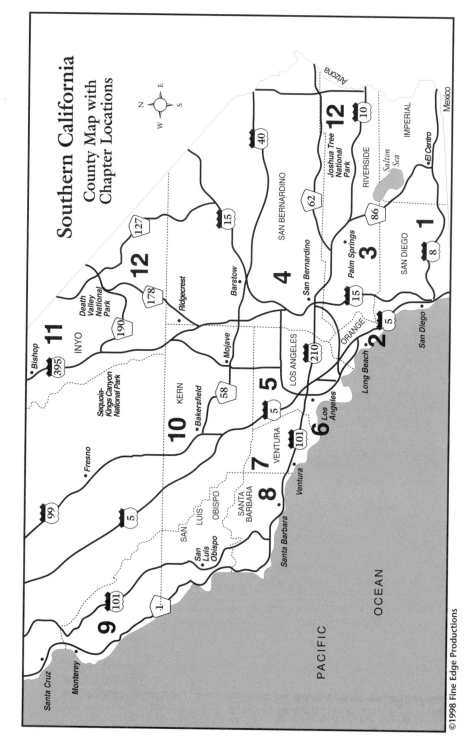

Southern California
County Map with
Chapter Locations

©1998 Fine Edge Productions

10

Acknowledgments

I wish to express my gratitude: to the authors involved in this project for their knowledge, insight and perseverance; to the many United States Forest Service, Bureau of Land Management, National Park, State Park and other land management personnel at all levels for their cooperation and encouragement during a time of increased demand for recreation and decreased funding to meet those demands; to Réanne Douglass for her invaluable direction in pulling the many parts of this project together under a very tight deadline; to map designers, Sue Irwin and Faith Rumm, for outstanding dedication and skill; to book designer Melanie Haage for her vision and quick work; to the "Gnarly Girls" (Liz, Jeanine, Li, Roxie, Beth, Karen) for their friendship on the trail, and especially to Jamie, Jan and gnarly boy Ben; and, most of all, to Jim for understanding that riding/writing this book was indeed work.

Delaine Fragnoli
Altadena, California
February 1998

Safety and Precautions

One of the joys of mountain biking on dirt is the freedom to experience nature. However, mountain biking in the backcountry involves unavoidable hazards and risks that each cyclist accepts when leaving the pavement behind. You can increase your safety by being aware of potential dangers, preparing ahead and respecting and remaining alert to the environment in all its variety and changes. Just because a trail is described in this book does not mean it will be safe or suitable for you.

Trails in this book cover an unusually wide range of terrain, elevation, and weather patterns that require different levels of skill and conditioning. A route that is safe for one rider may not be safe for another. It is important that you know and heed your own limitations, that you condition properly both physically and mentally, and that you give thought to your equipment as well as to trail and weather conditions.

En route, take appropriate action, including turning back at any time your judgment and common sense dictates. This book is not a substitute for detailed mountain survival or for cycling texts or courses. We recommend that you consult appropriate resources or take courses before you attempt the more strenuous or remote routes. When you have a question about route suitability or safety, consult local bike shops and land management offices.

This warning and the legal disclaimer herein are not given to discourage your enjoyment, but to remind you to take responsibility for yourself so your feeling of satisfaction comes truly from being independent and self-sufficient.

SPECIAL NOTE: FOREST ADVENTURE PASS

As of June 1997, the four Southern California National Forests (Angeles, Cleveland, Los Padres, San Bernardino) have instituted a demonstration user-fee project. Called a Forest Adventure Pass, the program amounts to a parking fee. Any vehicle parked within one of these forests must display the Forest Adventure Pass. If you drive into a U.S. Forest, park and ride your bike, your vehicle must display one of these passes. If, on the other hand, you park outside the U.S. Forest, and ride your bike in, you do not have to have a pass. Note that all or part of chapters 1, 2, 3, 4, 5, 7 and 8 of this book describe rides located in the U.S. Forests affected by this program.

You can purchase a $5/one-day pass or a $30/annual pass at forest headquarters or at local sporting goods or outdoor supply stores. If you buy one annual pass, it's valid for all four areas. If you have already paid a facility fee (i.e. paid to camp at a Forest Service campground), you do not have to buy a Forest Adventure Pass in addition. Residents and those using an educational or organizational camp or facility are also exempt.

When and how vigorously the program will be enforced is unclear. What citations and fines may be issued also remain to be seen. Note that the project is a "demonstration" project, meaning it may or may not become permanent.

The fees were initiated as part of a larger program to raise revenues for budget-crunched federal land management agencies. Other federal agencies (National Park Service, Fish and Wildlife Service, Bureau of Land Management) are also developing recreation user-fee programs and selecting test sites for the programs, so you may find yourself paying fees elsewhere as well. Supposedly the majority (80% or more) of the funds raised will go directly back into maintaining and building recreational facilities in the area where the fees were collected.

Reaction from the outdoor community to the programs has been mixed. For more details on the pros and cons of the issue, contact IMBA; or for more information on user-fees in your area, call the appropriate land management agency. (See "Agencies and Visitor Centers" in the back of this book for numbers and addresses.)

Pasadena Mountain Bike Club gathers at Red Box, Angeles National Forest.

Tony Quiroz

FOREWORD

Over the last eight years, I have traveled to many domestic and international destinations to race mountain bikes. But my favorite rides are my training rides in Southern California. Here, I can enjoy scenic landscape almost year-round under usually sunny skies. Only in Southern California can I experience desert, sea-kissed coastline, mountains and alpine lakes. With the expert tour guides in this book, you too can discover California's great scenic wild places.

I knew Don Douglass was one of those expert route finders when I first met him in 1986. He was hosting a challenging 50-mile mountain bike race known as the Sierra 7500. Most of the original race course is described in this book, modified and improved as the Coyote High Sierra Traverse. With an average elevation of 10,000 feet, the marvelous views of the Sierra Crest to the west and Owens Valley to the east make this ride one of the most outstanding in the country.

I personally covered the original Sierra 7500 race course in six hours, one minute, and without a seat for 98% of the time. My seat post broke off a mile into the race, and I was stuck with giving up or trying to finish. The big question was, Could I ride 49 miles without impaling myself on the jagged seatpost?

I decided to go for it and managed to finish first—before the reigning women's national champion—and found that Don's course had changed my life. Certain inner qualities came out in me that day that might still lie dormant had I stayed home or turned back.

In your journeys, too, you will tap your inner strength, determination and fervor as you travel the various routes described in this book. Don't worry, you can take your pick of short, easy rides for families and beginners, as well as challenging backcountry classics. And you can use a seat and not hurry!

Don and Delaine have selected well-known authors from different regions of Southern California to describe in detail their cherished local rides. Accurate descriptions of trail data were meticulously gathered to help you prepare and enjoy your backcountry adventures. Throughout your travels you will experience the best in trails, vegetation, wildlife, views, thrills and spills.

Each time I ride off-road in beautiful backcountry I feel a sense of peacefulness and happiness. I am always amazed at how much terrain my bicycle and I can cover and how quickly the time passes. I appreciate being a fit athlete so I can thoroughly enjoy my mountain bike experiences, and I urge you to discover your own potential so you can feel as thankful and blessed as I do.

Whether you choose to ride in the desert, the mountains, or along the coast, this field guide is a must and will provide you with the information you need to explore Southern California's beauty. *Go for it!*

Cindy Whitehead, Slalom, Downhill, and
Cross-Country Mountain Bike Champion
and Inductee in the Mountain Bike Hall of Fame

A Letter from the Bureau of Land Management

United States Department of the Interior

BUREAU OF LAND MANAGEMENT
California State Office
2800 Cottage Way, Room E-2845
Sacramento, California 95825-1889

IN REPLY REFER TO:

Welcome to some of the best mountain biking country in the United States ... the Public Lands of Southern California. From the subtle to the sublime, vivid and exciting riding opportunities await your exploration. Thrill your senses to the variety of environments that include desert mountain ranges and a valley so deep that it seems to disappear below the towering Sierra Nevada.

The Bureau of Land Management administers millions of acres of Public Land. A few of these areas are described in this book. Imagine the remoteness and majesty that these lands have to offer. Imagine yourself and your family exploring the panoramic roads of the Santa Rosa Mountain National Scenic Area. No matter what your experience level is, you will find a myriad of roads and trails that will challenge and enlighten.

During the past several years I have had the pleasure of working with many in the mountain biking community. I have watched the evolution and growth of the industry and activity. I have discovered that mountain bikers care deeply about the environment and have a tremendous volunteer ethic. Don and Reanne Douglass, pioneers of the mountain bike movement, have contributed greatly to raising public awareness of access and other related needs. Most importantly, they have worked tirelessly to codify the International Mountain Bike Association (IMBA) Rules of the Trail for bikers to aspire to. The IMBA Rules have become a well-known standard of courtesies supported by industry, public agencies and mountain bikers.

Apply these courtesies to others you encounter on the trail. It will increase the acceptance of you and your fellow mountain bikers in the community of recreationists that we serve. Through these efforts and your sensitivity to others, I embrace your cause and invite you to some of the best riding in California.

Contact us at any of our offices throughout the state for information on specific trail restrictions, information on recreation opportunities or on becoming a partner in our programs. Your interest and involvement in your Public Lands is invaluable.

Ed Hastey

Ed Hastey
State Director
State of California

A Letter from the U.S. Forest Service

United States Department of Agriculture	**Forest Service**	**Inyo National Forest**	**873 N. Main St. Bishop, CA 93514 (619)873-2400**

Dear Mt. Bike Enthusiast:

Mountain biking is one of the fastest growing recreational activities on public lands today. It is a recreational use that is generally "light on the land" and considered to be appropriate in most places. We recognize that some of the very best mountain bike riding in California exist within national forests. I encourage you to use and enjoy the routes that have been included in this publication.

I applaud the efforts of the publishers, the editors and the authors of *Mountain Biking California's Best 100 Trails,* in educating the public to a wide range of recreational opportunities, as well as stressing the need for responsible riding habits. During all your rides, please practice good mountain bike ethics by following the **IMBA Rules of the Trail,** particular by staying on existing and open roads and trails, being considerate of other users, leaving gates as you find them, controlling your speed, and packing out your trash. You are generally responsible for your own personal safety, which includes knowing what hazards might exist and using proper safety procedures and equipment to minimize the inherent risks associated with mountain biking.

If you are unfamiliar with an area, we recommend that you study existing guidebooks and topographical maps to plan your trip. Please contact the nearest ranger station for local trail information and/or regulations before you start your ride. Since we care about what you think of management of your national forests, I encourage you to share with us your ideas on how we can improve our services and facilities.

Sincerely,

Bill Bramlette

BILL BRAMLETTE
Recreation Officer
Inyo National Forest

      Caring for the Land and Serving People

IMBA RULES OF THE TRAIL

1. **Ride on open trails only.** Respect trail and road closures (ask if not sure), avoid possible trespass on private land, obtain permits and authorization as may be required. Federal and State wilderness areas are closed to cycling.

2. **Leave no trace.** Be sensitive to the dirt beneath you. Even on open trails, you should not ride under conditions where you will leave evidence of your passing, such as on certain soils shortly after a rain. Observe the different types of soils and trail construction; practice low-impact cycling. This also means staying on the trail and not creating any new ones. Be sure to pack out at least as much as you pack in.

3. **Control your bicycle!** Inattention for even a second can cause disaster. Excessive speed maims and threatens people; there is no excuse for it!

4. **Always yield trail.** Make known your approach well in advance. A friendly greeting (or bell) is considerate and works well; startling someone may cause loss of trail access. Show your respect when passing others by slowing to a walk or even stopping. Anticipate that other trail users may be around corners or in blind spots.

5. **Never spook animals.** All animals are startled by an unannounced approach, a sudden movement, or a loud noise. This can be dangerous for you, others, and the animals. Give animals extra room and time to adjust to you. In passing, use special care and follow the directions of horseback riders (ask if uncertain). Running cattle and disturbing wild animals is a serious offense. Leave gates as you found them, or as marked.

6. **Plan ahead.** Know your equipment, your ability, and the area in which you are riding — and prepare accordingly. Be self-sufficient at all times, wear a helmet, keep your machine in good repair, and carry necessary supplies for changes in weather or other conditions. A well-executed trip is satisfying to you and not a burden or offense to others.

WELCOME TO MOUNTAIN BIKING
SOUTHERN CALIFORNIA

Southern California offers mountain bikers year-round opportunities and challenges found nowhere else . . . from urban, palm-lined beaches to remote desert canyons and gorges, from thick pine and fir forests to the alpine zones in the High Sierra and White Mountains, from gently rolling oak-covered hills for the family to twisting gnarly singletrack for the technical expert. Ride below sea level in Death Valley National Park or climb 14,200-foot White Mountain. This is mountain biking at its best!

We assembled the who's who of mountain biking authors in Southern California and asked them for their favorite rides. This book is a result of their collective efforts. You will benefit from their years of experience and know-how as they share with you areas and rides—from the well known to the not-yet-discovered that have helped make mountain biking America's fastest growing sport.

The authors—experts in their own areas—include a founder of the International Mountain Biking Association, its former president, the founders and directors of a number of successful regional mountain biking clubs, numerous federal, state, and local trail advisory group members across Southern California, two editors of mountain biking magazines, and a Mountain Bike Hall of Fame inductee. Their collective experience is a history of the activity to which they are dedicated.

HOW TO USE THIS BOOK

With so many great trails to choose from, selecting the best was difficult. Obviously "best" means different things to different people. Some rides were included for their outstanding scenic value, others for their historical significance, others simply for their high fun factor. A few were included because they were quintessentially Californian in some way. We have also attempted to represent a variety of terrain and levels of difficulty.

We have organized all this information in an easy-to-use way. Each chapter is dedicated to a particular area, usually a county or national forest. The chapters are organized in a loop, beginning in San Diego and traveling north to Monterey County, northeast to Owens Valley and the Eastern Sierra Nevada, and south to the California desert. Within each chapter we have tried to group rides in the same vicinity.

At the beginning of each ride you will find capsule information to let you decide quickly if a ride is for you or not. Ride distance is included as is a rating of difficulty. Mileages shown are approximate and may vary among riders and odometers. We rated the rides for strenuousness (from easy to very strenuous) and for technical difficulty (not technical to extremely technical). The ratings are a subjective assessment of what the average fit rider (acclimatized to elevation) might consider the route. If you are a racer you may find some of our difficult rides to be moderate. If you are new to the sport you may find our mildly technical rides challenging. Know your limits and be honest in evaluating your skill level. We also recommend that you check with local bike shops and land managers for their evaluation of your fitness for a particular ride. We do not know

Tony Quiroz

Mountain biking high above Los Angeles.

your skill level and consequently cannot be responsible for any losses you may incur using this information. Please see the important legal notice and disclaimer.

For elevation we include whatever elevation information seems pertinent to that particular ride. Rides with lots of elevation gain and loss will give you that information. Rides at high elevations will include such information. Ride Type lets you know if the ride is a loop, an out-and-back trip, a multiple-day tour or if it requires a car shuttle. It also tells you the trail surface; for example, fire road loop with singletrack return. Unless otherwise noted, maps refer to USGS 7.5-minute topos. Last, we suggest the best season for riding each route. If after reading the capsule information you are not sure if a ride is for you, the text of each ride description should give you additional information with which to make a decision.

Please note that the routes described in this book are not patrolled and contain natural hazards. Trail conditions and surfaces are constantly changing. Check with local land managers for latest trail and access conditions. Pertinent phone numbers are included in the appendix "Agencies, Visitor Centers, and Mountain Bike Clubs."

Throughout we have tried to be consistent in presentation. We have tried, however, to retain some of the character and tone of each individual author. Mountain biking is a very individualistic sport, and we think that should be reflected in any writing about the sport. Remember also that each author's odometer gives different results and yours may vary.

We hope you think of this book as a group of friends getting together to tell you about their favorite bicycling spots. We believe our authors' enthusiasm for their areas will be contagious.

Enough talk. Get on your bike and start riding! You've got 100 trails to explore and the best trail guides around.

SPECIAL CONSIDERATIONS

To enhance your pleasure and safety we ask that you observe the following Special Considerations:

1. **Courtesy.** Extend courtesy to all other trail users and follow the golden rule. Observe the IMBA Rules of the Trail. The trails and roads in Southern California are popular with many user groups: hikers, equestrians, fishermen, ranchers, 4-wheel drive enthusiasts, hunters, loggers, and miners. Mountain bikers are the newest user group, so set a good example of courtesy and respect.

2. **Preparations.** Plan your trip carefully; develop and use a check list. Know your abilities and your equipment. Prepare to be self-sufficient.

3. **Mountain Conditions.** Be sensitive at all times to the natural environment: the land, beautiful and enjoyable, can also be frightening and unforgiving. The areas covered by this book often provide extremes in elevation, climate and terrain. If you break down, it may take you longer to walk out than it took you to ride in! Check with your local Red Cross, Sierra Club, or mountaineering textbooks for detailed mountain survival information. Know how to deal with dehydration, hypothermia, altitude sickness, sunburn and heatstroke. Always be prepared for:

Intense Sun: Protect your skin against the sun's harmful rays by wearing light colored long-sleeved shirts or jerseys and a hat with a wide brim. Many of the rides in this book are at relatively high altitude, and the higher you go, the more damaging the sun becomes. Use sunscreen with a sufficient rating. Wear sunglasses with adequate protection. Guard against heatstroke by riding in early morning or late afternoon when the sun's rays are less intense.

Low Humidity: East-facing slopes and high elevation usually have low humidity. To avoid headaches or cramps, start each trip with a minimum of two or more large water bottles. (Gallons of water may not be sufficient for really hot weather or hard rides.) Force yourself to drink before you feel thirsty. Carry water from a known source, or treat water gathered from springs, streams and lakes. Untreated drinking water may cause Giardiasis or other diseases.

Variations in Temperature and Weather Conditions: Carry extra clothing—a windbreaker, gloves, stocking cap—and use the multi-layer system so you can quickly adapt to different weather conditions. Afternoon thundershowers occur frequently in the high country, so keep an eye on changing cloud and wind conditions and prepare accordingly.

Fatigue: Sluggish or cramping muscles and fatigue indicate the need for calories and liquids. Carry high-energy snack foods such as granola bars, dried fruits and nuts to maintain strength and warmth. To conserve energy, add layers of clothing as the temperature drops or the wind increases.

Fire Closures: Many mountain and foothill areas are closed to the public during times of high fire danger. Please check ahead of time with local authorities, and observe such fire closures. Always be extremely careful with fire.

Smog Alerts: Although most of the rides in this book are outside the Los Angeles Basin, if you cycle within the Basin during the summer we recommend that you listen to the smog forecasts over local radio stations. If you know the zip code for your riding area, you can get a smog report by dialing 800/242-4022. Heavy exercise is unwise at midday or during smog alerts.

4. Maps and Navigation. The maps in this book are not intended for navigation but as guides to the appropriate forest or USGS topographic maps which we recommend you carry and use. Have a plan ready in advance with your cycling group in case you lose your way (it's easy to do!). En route, record your position on the trip map(s), noting the times you arrive at known places. Be sure to look back frequently in the direction from which you came, in case you need to retrace your path. Do not be afraid to turn back when conditions change, or if the going is tougher than you expected. Before you leave on a ride, tell someone where you're going, when you expect to return, and what to do in case you don't return on time. Ask that person to call the proper officials if you are more than six hours overdue, giving full details about your vehicle and your trip plans. (At the end of each chapter you will find the author's local book cited. For more detailed information concerning local conditions and specific safety hazards, please consult the individual book.)

5. Horses and Pack Animals. Some of the trails in Southern California are used by recreational horse riders as well as cyclists and hikers. Horses can be spooked easily, so make them aware of your presence *well in advance of an encounter.* A startled horse can cause serious injuries both to a rider and to itself. If you come upon horses moving toward you, yield the right-of-way, even when it seems inconvenient. Carry your bike to the downhill side and stand quietly, well off the trail in a spot where the animals can see you clearly. If you come upon horses *moving ahead of you in the same direction,* stop well behind them. Do not attempt to pass until you have alerted the riders and asked for permission. Then, pass on the downhill side of the trail, talking to the horse and rider as you do. It is your responsibility to ensure that such encounters are safe for everyone. Do not disturb grazing sheep or cattle.

6. Respect the Environment. Minimize your impact on the natural environment. *Remember: Mountain bikes are not allowed in Wilderness Areas and in certain other restricted areas.* You are a visitor, so ask when in doubt. Leave plants and animals alone, historic and cultural sites untouched. Stay on established roads and trails, and do not enter private property. Follow posted instructions and use good common sense. If you plan to camp, you may need a permit. Contact the nearest land management agency for information.

7. Control and Safety. Crashes usually don't cause serious injury, but they occasionally can and do. Stay under control and slow for the unexpected. Wear protective gear—helmet, gloves, and glasses to protect yourself from scrapes and impacts with rocks, dirt, and brush. Guard against excessive speed. Avoid overheated rims and brakes on long or steep downhill rides. Lower your center of gravity by lowering your seat on downhills. Lower your tire pressure on rough or sandy stretches. In late summer and fall, avoid opening weekend of hunting season, and inquire at local sporting goods stores as to which areas are open to hunting. Carry first aid supplies and bike tools for emergencies. *Avoid solo travel in remote areas.*

8. **Trailside Bike Repair.** Minimum equipment: pump, spare tube, patches and 2 tubes of patch glue or glueless patches, 6" adjustable wrench, Allen wrenches, chain tool and spoke wrench. Tools may be shared with others in your group. Correct inflation, wide tires, and avoiding rocks will prevent most flats. Grease, oil, and proper adjustment prevent most mechanical failures. Frequent stream crossings wash away chain grease; carry extra.

9. **First Aid.** Carry first aid for your body as well as your bike. If you have allergies, be sure to bring your medicine, whether it's for pollen or bee stings. Sunscreen saves your skin, and insect repellent increases your comfort in many seasons. Bring bandages and ointment for cuts and scrapes, and aspirin for aches that won't go away. Additional first-aid items you might want to carry in your kit are antiseptic swabs, moleskin, a single-edged razor blade, a needle, an elastic bandage, and waterproof matches. For expedition trips, consult mountaineering texts on survival for additional suggestions.

Tony Quiroz

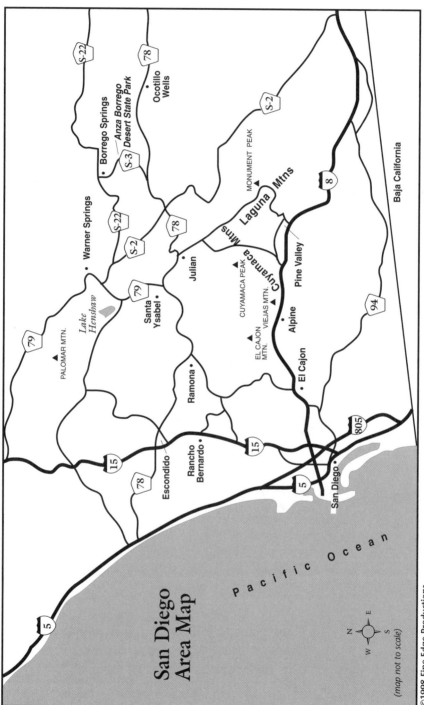

San Diego Area Map

Pacific Ocean

(map not to scale)

©1998 Fine Edge Productions

CHAPTER 1

San Diego County

By Delaine Fragnoli

Smaller and less famous than Los Angeles to the north, San Diego has many of the virtues of her sister city, but few of her vices. Like L.A., San Diego enjoys a warm and sunny climate most of the year, and thus makes a year-round vacation spot. While she lacks the glitz of Hollywood, she holds her own with cultural attractions: the San Diego Zoo, Balboa Park with its many museums, several missions, and fine examples of Spanish colonial and Victorian architecture. Good restaurants and hotels are easy to find, as are fine shops and coffee houses. In short, San Diego has all the amenities of a large city.

What San Diego doesn't have is L.A.'s smog, bumper-to-bumper traffic or hectic pace. Everything is a little more relaxed in San Diego. Dress is casual, people are mellow and everything moves a half-step slower. San Diego is not immune to growth—population is now around 3 million. But she has done a better job of managing growth than L.A. has, having learned from her northern neighbor's uncontrolled urban sprawl. A Stop-Los-Angelization-Now movement has sprung up to control growth. The city and county have wisely set aside much of their open space, and a full one-third of the land in San Diego County has been dedicated to public use. This includes county parks as well as state parks and recreation areas. In fact, San Diego boasts one of the largest urban parks in the country—Mission Trails Regional Park.

All this land for public recreation makes for many and varied recreational opportunities. What this means for fat-tire fanatics is trails, trails and more trails. Take your pick of beaches, foothills, mountains and desert—all within two hours' drive of the city of San Diego. The county also boasts 2,000 species of wild plants and abundant wildlife.

Near the coast you can enjoy canyon and mesa landscapes, formed by a terraced plain with steep-sided canyons and arroyos. The riding here is pleasant for the beginning/intermediate rider—unless you decide to try those canyons. Then it's decidedly difficult.

To the east, the peninsular ranges rise up to challenge your climbing skills. A series of parallel mountain ranges that run roughly northwest-southeast with high, narrow valleys between them, cut across the county and constitute the majority of its land. The Laguna and Cuyamaca mountains offer the most challenging and scenic mountain biking in the county. The granny-gear climbs and technical singletrack to be found here make this a mecca for the intermediate/advanced rider. Never fear—beginning riders will still find plenty of scenic, nicely wooded rides. Both areas are a little over an hour's drive from San Diego, and they are among the highest points in San Diego County. Chaparral covers the lower slopes of these mountains but gives way to black oaks and various wild oaks on the higher slopes. Ponderosa pine forest blankets the upper reaches of the area's peaks, while pinyon pine and California juniper thrive on the drier east-facing slopes. By water-starved Southern California standards, these mountains are lush.

Cuyamaca Rancho State Park borders Cleveland National Forest and the Laguna Mountain Recreation Area. With about 30,000 acres (13,000 of which are wilderness and closed to bikes), Cuyamaca is one of California's largest state parks. Its beauty and proximity to the city of San Diego make it very popular. West of the Lagunas, the Cuyamacas are wetter and lusher. Numerous springs and creeks trickle through cool, shady forests of willow, sycamore and alder. Three peaks dominate the area—North, Middle and Cuyamaca peaks. Cuyamaca Lake lies to the north. Over 100 miles of trail, about half of which are open to bikes, tantalize bicyclists, hikers and equestrians alike.

The mountains get their name from the Kumeya'ay tribe, who summered in these mountains. The name has been translated as "the place where it rains." Native American artifacts, such as bedrock morteros, can be found throughout the park. The park itself was part of an 1845 Mexican land grant called Rancho Cuyamaca. In 1933 the state acquired the property for use as a park.

Pick up a free information sheet on mountain bike rides at park headquarters, which gives brief descriptions of seven rides and spells out bicycling regulations in the park. All singletrack in the park is closed to bikes, and there is a 15-mph speed limit. You can also get water at park headquarters.

The Lagunas, farther east and therefore drier than the Cuyamacas, are included within Cleveland National Forest, although the higher regions are part of the Laguna Mountain Recreation Area administered by the Forest Service as a high-use, multiple-use area. Over 50 miles of hiking trails, numerous picnic areas, campgrounds and nature trails dot the area. The Pacific Crest Trail zigzags through the Lagunas and is strictly off limits to bikes. The other roads and trails are open. With the best singletrack in San Diego County, indeed some of the best in all of Southern California, the Lagunas are an advanced rider's nirvana. The east side of the range is a dramatic meeting of mountain and desert.

The best base for exploring here is the town of Julian, nestled between the Cuyamaca and Volcan mountains at the junction of Highways 78 and 79. A gold rush town, Julian was a rough-and-tumble place 100 years ago. Today it's a rustic retreat for city-weary San Diegans, and the biggest event of the year is the fall apple festival.

Today, antique shops, restaurants and bed and breakfasts beckon to visitors. Main Street is lined with buildings with wooden facades. You can sample Julian's justly famous apple pie, apple cider, apple-you-name-it, and buy any kind of apple knickknack imaginable. (I like Mom's Apple Pie, next to Jack's Market on Main Street.)

Farther east is another "hot" spot for San Diego mountain bikers—the Anza Borrego desert. About 90 miles northeast of San Diego, this rugged desert region is a unique environment. Expect the bizarre and unusual when you ride in Anza Borrego Desert State Park. Along with the expected rocky washes and sparse vegetation, the park contains one-of-a-kind desert plants such as the California fan palm and other-worldly geological formations: wind caves, fossil shell reefs, rock slots, mudhills, sandstone cliffs and folded rock anticlines. The park is also home to the endangered desert bighorn sheep. Spring, when flowers are in bloom, is a good time to visit. Rainy years are best for spring wildflower shows.

The park is partly named for Spanish explorer Juan Bautista de Anza, who in 1774 created a route across the desert to link Sonora, Mexico, with areas of Northern California. The other half of the park's name comes from the Spanish word for the desert bighorn sheep, *borrego*. The Anza trail was soon replaced by a better route called the Southern Emigrant Trail. Today County Road S2 follows it closely. This route was used extensively during the Mexican War. After the war it was turned into the first wagon route into Southern California, the one that thousands of gold-crazy prospectors traveled during the state's gold rush. Stage routes followed, but soon ended when the Civil War began. After the war, they were rendered obsolete by the transcontinental railroad.

Today's mountain-biking route finders can explore 500 miles of dirt roads, most of which are open to bikes, in this 600,000-acre desert. Most of the trails in the area are soft dirt or sand, so bring your fattest tires and run them with less air pressure than normal for better traction. Many of the roads are open to 4WD vehicles, too, so be on the alert. Bring plenty of water, especially if you plan to camp. Figure on 2 gallons per person per day.

The town of Borrego Springs, located off County Highway S22, is a good jumping off spot for exploring the park, especially the northern end. Travelers will find accommodations and facilities, including the park's Visitor Center, on Palm Canyon Road. Two miles north of the Visitor Center is Borrego Palm Canyon Campground.

View of Lake Hodges from Elfin Forest.

Entrance to Elfin Forest.

1 Elfin Forest Recreational Reserve Loop

Distance: 9 miles
Difficulty: Strenuous, technical
Elevation: Over 1,500' gain/loss
Ride Type: Lollipop loop on singletrack and dirt roads
Season: Year-round; summer can get hot
Map: Elfin Forest Recreational Reserve, available at trailhead
Comments: The Reserve has several bicycling regulations. There's a 15 mph speed limit, 5 mph within 100 feet of hikers or horses. Bicyclists must dismount in the immediate vicinity of equestrians. A special use permit is required for group use of the reserve. A group is defined as 8 or more persons, 8 or more horses, *4 or more bicycles.*

Overview: The 800-acre Elfin Forest Recreational Reserve has 17 miles of multi-use trails. About 10 miles are open to and appropriate for mountain biking. The reserve encompasses a stretch of Escondido Creek in San Elijo Canyon, an oak valley and several surrounding ridges. What this means is that the riding is up and over the ridges, down and back out of the canyons and valleys, making

for some steep climbing and descending. Trails surfaces are hard-packed, rutted, rocky and almost always technically challenging. This is not a place to take beginning riders.

A cooperative effort of the Olivenhain Municipal Water District and the Bureau of Land Management, the reserve combines the goals of domestic water supply development, natural resource management and recreation-

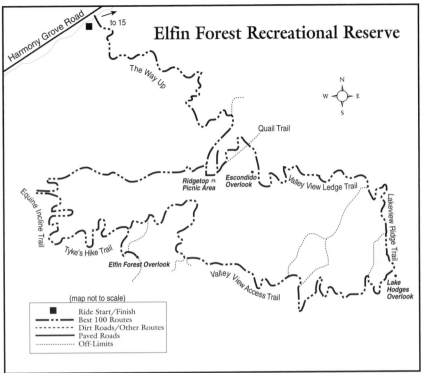

©1998 Fine Edge Productions

al opportunities. They've done a good job on the recreational part of it. The trails are generally well marked and signed; the parking area and trailhead are clean and have all the amenities—pay phone, port-a-potties and water fountains.

The recreational opportunities are certainly enhanced by the natural resource management. Here you will find great examples of several southern California habitats, including oak riparian, oak woodland, coastal sage scrub and chaparral. The term "Elfin Forest" refers to the low-growing laurel sumac, black sage and manzanita plants of the chaparral.

The loop described here takes in most of these habitats while leading you to three vista points—one of Lake Hodges. Despite the limited

mileage, this ride is a physical and technical workout. This is THE place to work on switchback-riding technique. I lost count after awhile, but the whole loop must contain over 50 switchbacks!

Getting There: From Interstate 15 near Escondido, take the 9th Street exit and go west. Stay on 9th as it jogs and becomes Hale Avenue. Turn left on Harmony Grove Road and follow it to the Elfin Forest Recreational Reserve on the south side of the road. The reserve is well signed and has a gated road (open during daylight) at its entrance.

Route: The trailhead starts near the port-a-potties beside the information displays. From the trailhead, go left.

Then turn right, following signs for The Way Up Trail. Cross a concrete bridge that spans the cool, oak- and sycamore-shaded Escondido Creek. The trail curves right and begins climbing. Steeply. Let's just say the trail's name is quite literal. A hard left-hand switchback soon gives you a taste of things to come.

At 0.2 mile there's a cool rock outcropping on your left and the grade eases a bit. At 0.3 mile you hit a trail intersection. The Botanical Trail goes left (closed to bikes). You go right to stay on The Way Up. It soon gets steep again as you tackle the first of 14 tough (rocky and rutted) switchbacks. Most of us will have to push at least a couple of these.

After a mile you reach a flat spot. This is a good spot to regroup. You have a view of the valley behind you. Proceed up a rocky pitch. An expansive view opens on the left. The trail Ts into a dirt road. Go right to stay on The Way Up. I should say that almost all of these intersections are clearly signed. Just beyond, at 1.3 miles, pass Equine Incline Trail forking right. You fork left. (We return on the Equine Incline Trail at the end of the loop.)

At 1.5 miles you reach a major intersection. It's quite sandy here, but at least you're done climbing for the moment. The Quail Trail goes left. Straight ahead 0.1 mile is the Ridgetop Picnic Area (picnic tables, port-a-potties, water). A maintenance road goes to the right.

Go left on Quail Trail for some more climbing. You see what looks like a death climb in front of you, but you take the trail to the left at 1.6 miles. Make a rocky climb and hit another intersection at 1.8 miles. The left road leads outside the park. The right road drops down the death climb you just skirted.

You go straight onto Valley View Ledge Trail. In 0.1 mile you come to the first vista point, Escondido Overlook. From here you can see Escondido and, on the horizon, the San Bernardino Mountains.

Continue down on what is immediately a sketchy patch of trail. Then the trail becomes fun and rolling, and nearly always rocky. At 2.6 miles the trail you're on crosses a road (Saddle Up Trail). Continue on the singletrack on the other side of the road. You have a steep climb up about three switchbacks.

You top out at 3.0 miles. A sign says you're now on Lakeview Ridge Trail (avoid the alternate route to the right). After more steep down and up, you reach the Lake Hodges Overlook at 3.3 miles. The lookouts all have maps, shaded stone benches and signage, and make for great rest stops.

Leaving the overlook you begin a fun, technical downhill. Watch for rutted switchbacks and be sure to obey the 15 mph speed limit. At 4.0 miles you come to a road (Oak Valley Loop Trail). Continue across it; there is a patch of gravel here. You soon T into another road (the end of the Oak Valley Loop Trail). Go left. Then, less than 100 yards later, branch right onto Valley View Access Trail (more like a road) and begin climbing.

You reach Hidden Oaks Picnic Area at 4.7 miles—another good rest spot. An equestrian-only trail goes right. You continue to the left and up. Less than 0.1 mile later, take a hard right onto singletrack Tyke's Hike Trail. Begin a steep, rocky climb with some of the sharpest switchbacks yet.

At 5.0 miles, go right briefly onto the maintenance road and then left back onto the trail. If you've had enough, you could stay on the maintenance road, which would take you back to the Ridgetop Picnic Area.

If you continue on the trail, less than 0.1 mile later you hit another intersection. A right will once again return you to the Ridgetop Picnic Area. Straight leads onto the Equine Incline Trail. Take Equine Incline Trail to continue the loop. Bear with me as things get a little confusing through here since many trails criss-cross the area. At 5.2 miles there's yet another intersection. The trail crosses the road; continue straight on it. (The decision is really made for you since all other routes are signed as closed to bikes.)

At the next Y, fork left to climb up to the third and last vista point, the Elfin Forest Overlook, at 5.5 miles. On the way up you join an equestri-an-only trail. From here to the over-look is OK for bikes. Once you get to the overlook, Tyke's Hike Trail drops off the far side. You can take it back down to the maintenance road and then to the Ridgetop Picnic Area. Or,

for more singletrack fun, go back the way you came. Bypass the horse trail and drop to the Y; go left to continue on Equine Incline.

This is one of the ride's best downhill sections, full of fun, rocky, totally rideable switchbacks. Of course, you have to climb again to get back up to the ridge that sepa-rates Escondido Creek from the rest of the reserve. After you climb through several switchbacks the grade eases and you pass through a flat area with oaks. A final couple of switchbacks takes you to a Y-intersec-tion at 7.6 miles.

Take the left fork. A little later the trail joins a road. Go left. Soon you find yourself back at the top of The Way Up. Now you get to ride down all those switchbacks you suffered up. They're much easier to descend. Enjoy. You earned it. But watch your speed as this trail is the major access route into the reserve and thus sees lots of use.

2 Los Peñasquitos Canyon Preserve

Distance: 12 miles
Difficulty: Easy, mildly technical
Elevation: 450' gain/loss
Ride Type: Out-and-back on dirt roads
Season: Year-round, summer can get hot
Map: Del Mar

Overview: When we put together the first edition of this book, we left Los Peñasquitos Canyon out be-cause, at the time, it looked as if the whole preserve would be closed to bikes. Fortunately it wasn't. But bikes are now limited to the canyon's main through-road, a couple of des-ignated connector trails and a parallel road in the canyon's eastern half. The

thoroughness with which virtually every singletrack in the preserve has been signed as closed to bikes attests to the fervor of the anti-bike advo-cates. Kinda scary. Be on your best behavior here. Yield the "trail" (road) and observe the ludicrously slow 10-mph speed limit. (I'm sorry, but I could do that on most of the canyon's climbs.)

Getting There: From I-805 take Mira Mesa Boulevard east. Turn left on Vista Sorrento Parkway and parallel the freeway. Turn right onto Sorrento Valley Boulevard for 1 mile to a preserve parking lot on the right.

The preserve can be accessed from the eastern end as well. From I-15 in Mira Mesa take Mercy Road west for 2 miles. There's a parking lot and equestrian staging area for the preserve at the intersection of Mercy and Black Mountain Road.

The route described here begins at the western end. Just reverse the directions to start at the eastern end.

Route: Access the preserve's main road via the trailhead at the east side of the parking lot. You immediately come to Y-intersection. There's a display here with park rules and information. Go left. (There's a small trail sign and an arrow.) Go through an underpass and up a short, rocky climb.

Go right at the next junction (also signed). Here you are in grassy, open landscape, except for the tract homes that crowd the preserve's border to your right. At 1.0 mile begin another short, steep climb. At the Y after that you can go either way—they loop back together. Just past here, a couple of beautiful sycamore specimens on your left cast welcome shade on a hot summer evening.

Continue up-canyon. Lots of trails take off from the road—all vigorously signed as closed to bikes. The road through here is hard-packed with some brief sandy sections and some rocky climbs. Keep on the main route by staying high. This area is good for beginning riders since it gives a taste, but not too much, of several different trail surfaces.

At 2.7 miles you reach an interesting rock outcropping on your left. The turn-off to some waterfalls is here. There are racks for you to park your bike. You can hike down to the stream, a good place

Waterfall and swimming hole area of Los Peñasquitos.

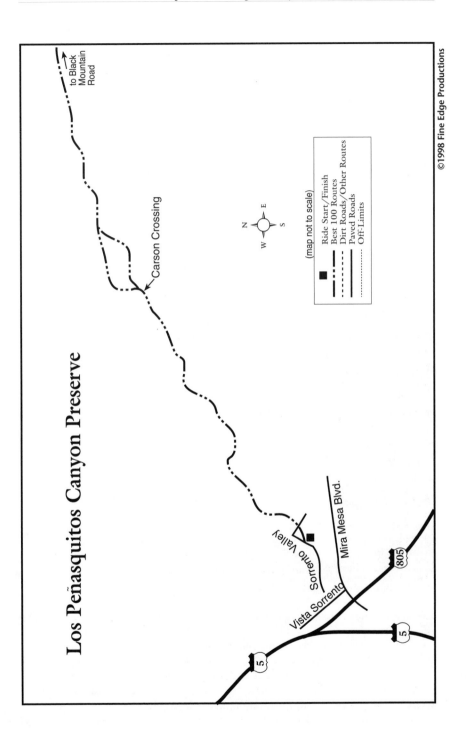

Los Peñasquitos Canyon Preserve

to Black Mountain Road

Carson Crossing

(map not to scale)

Ride Start/Finish
Best 100 Routes
Dirt Roads/Other Routes
Paved Roads
Off-Limits

N
W — E
S

Sorrento Valley
Mira Mesa Blvd.
Vista Sorrento

5
805
5

for a refreshing dip on a hot day. The falls run during winter and spring, but the wet environment makes a nice stop even when they're dry. The amazing thing is that you would never know these pools of water were here. You can't see the drop down to the stream from the road.

Some people make the falls their destination and head back from here for a 5.5-mile out-and-back ride. To continue, keep pedaling up-canyon. There are wooden mileage markers along the road, but they read a mile high of what my computer recorded. Just past the 4.5-mile marker—3.6 miles on my odometer—you come to Carson Crossing, a designated spot where cyclists can cross the creek. There's a sign indicating bikes are OK. There's a gorgeous oak stand here, and plenty of poison oak. It's worth a stop even if you choose to stay on the south side of the creek.

From here you can continue up-canyon on the south side of the creek, or you can cross the creek and con-

tinue up-canyon on the north side of the creek. At the east end of the canyon, about 2.5 miles away, you can connect these two roads, so you can loop up one and back on the other. Take your pick.

The landscape along the north-side road is more open. Cloned homes crowd against the preserve boundary, and numerous spurs here lead to one housing tract or another. The main through-route is always obvious. There are patches of pavement along here, and near the end of the preserve, the road bends south (right) and joins the south-side road.

In contrast, the south-side road feels more "natural." There are more trees closer to the road, and what housing developments are on this side sit on a mesa above the canyon.

When you've looped up to the east end and back to the crossing, simply retrace your route to your car. The way back is almost all gradually downhill except for a few short climbs near ride's end.

3 Mission Trails Regional Park

Distance: 9.2 miles
Difficulty: Strenuous, technical; easier options possible
Elevation: High point 1,291'; gain/loss 980'
Ride Type: Loop on singletrack and dirt roads
Season: Year-round
Map: Pick up a map at the Visitor Center

Overview: Like the previous ride, this is a good choice for those of you stuck in the city. Just 8 miles from downtown San Diego, this 5,700-acre tract is one of the largest urban parks in the country. It's excellent for intermediate riders, but advanced riders can challenge themselves by climb-

ing the various peaks in the park.

Much has changed at this park in the last few years. First, Highway 52 has been completed, slicing through the middle of the park. More facilities have been added, including a visitor center and more trail signs.

Three areas are worth riding here.

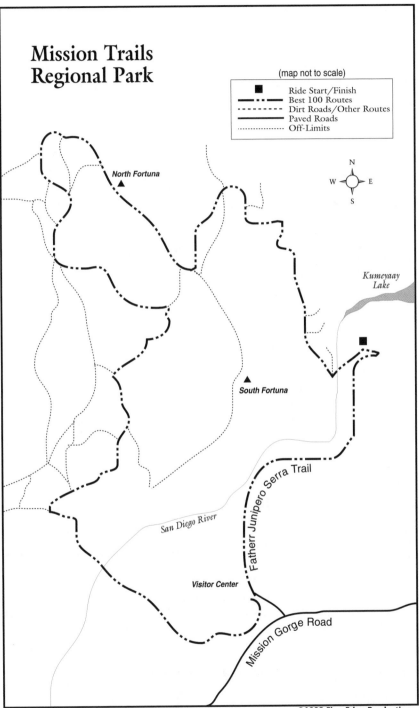

Mission Trails Regional Park

(map not to scale)

- ■ Ride Start/Finish
- ━▪━ Best 100 Routes
- - - - Dirt Roads/Other Routes
- ━━━ Paved Roads
- ········ Off-Limits

N
W ✦ E
S

North Fortuna ▲

Kumeyaay Lake

South Fortuna ▲

Father Junipero Serra Trail

San Diego River

Visitor Center

Mission Gorge Road

©1998 Fine Edge Productions

View from Fortuna Saddle looking east to Grasslands and Kumeyaay Lake.

Jim MacIntyre

Beginners should stick to the grasslands area near Oak Canyon and Kumeyaay Lake, or to the paved Father Junipero Serra Trail, which has a bike lane and follows the scenic San Diego River. Intermediate riders can check out the Rim Trail and Suycott Wash. Advanced riders can tackle the very steep and technical ascent and descent of North Fortuna Mountain (described here) or Fortuna Saddle. North and South Fortuna Mountains basically form a steep ridge through this part of the park. Climbing up and over them from any direction is quite a workout.

Getting There: Take I-8 east from San Diego and exit at Mission Gorge Road. Continue east to Father Junipero Serra Trail (FJST). You can park at the Visitor Center, but the gate there is locked at 5 p.m. It's better to continue another 2 miles to the Old Mission Dam Historical Area and park there. That area closes at 7 p.m., April through September, and 5 p.m., October through March. Night riders need to park outside the park. Note that vehicle traffic on FJST is one-way from the Visitor Center to the dam site.

Route: FJST is named for a Spanish priest who was one of the founders of the California mission system. Begun in 1810, the Old Mission Dam, a nationally registered historic site, was the first water supply project in what is now the western United States. Spanish missionaries from Mission San Diego de Alcala used Native American labor to build the adobe tile-lined flume that carried water 5.5 miles to the mission to irrigate crops and provide drinking water. Take time to check out the dam before or after your ride.

Take the paved road 1.8 miles to the Visitor Center. Enjoy the bike-only lane (how enlightened!) as you follow the San Diego River through the rugged cliffs of Mission Gorge. A lush riparian habitat of willow, cottonwood and sycamore trees thrives along the river banks. It's also home to the endangered least Bell's vireo.

At the Visitor Center take the trail to the left of the gate. You actually hang right like you're going to the center, but 15 feet later you go left at the gate. This is a moderate, rolling singletrack. At 2.1 miles make a right turn and head downhill onto a fire road where there's a trail marker and map.

At 2.4 miles cross a stream and go straight. Just 0.1 mile later you come to a small sign for Fortuna Mtn./Suycott Wash and begin a steep but not technical fire road climb. At 2.9 miles bear right at the fork.

At 3.0 miles you top out and take a singletrack on the right, signed *Fortuna Mtn./South Suycott Wash*. This is a steep, rocky, technical downhill. At 3.3 miles bear right at the junction, then left, following signs. You are loosely following a dry streambed upwards.

At 3.7 miles you regain a fire road and veer right. Sign says *Fortuna Mtn./East Suycott Wash*. At 3.8 miles go right at the Y and make a moderate fire road climb following the power lines. There are many intersecting trails in the park, but the power lines, which go through Fortuna Mountain, make a good landmark to help you keep your bearings.

At 4.1 miles go left, then straight, then left (4.2 miles) at sign for North Suycott Wash, West Fortuna Mtn., Shepherd Canyon on a steep and rolling singletrack. At 4.5 miles continue straight (signed *West Fortuna Mtn./Shepherd Canyon*). This is a very steep uphill—you may need to push your bike.

At 4.8 miles go right at the fire road (signed) and continue the climbing. At 4.9 miles go right at the Y, signed *West Fortuna Mtn*. After a brutally steep doubletrack climb, turn left at 5.1 miles. It's signed for Shepherd Canyon; West Fortuna Mtn. is straight. Highway 52 is visible here to your left—another good landmark to help you keep your bearings.

At 5.3 and 5.4 miles continue straight, paralleling Highway 52. At 5.9 miles go right at "Trail" sign (left dead-ends). Half a mile later—half of which you may have to walk—you finally summit North Fortuna Mountain, 1,291 feet. Rest and take in the view, you've certainly earned it.

Descend steeply toward Fortuna Saddle for 0.5 mile. Go left, heading east/northeast and down. At 7.4 miles at the bottom of the steep, rutted fire road, go straight. It's signed *Oak Canyon/Old Mission Dam*. This is a moderate fire road climb. At 7.9 miles go right at the T-intersection. Left is signed *Oak Canyon* and right is signed *Grasslands Trails/Old Mission Dam*. Beyond this intersection is a fast, blissfully smooth dirt road descent.

The fun continues when, at 8.3 miles, you turn right onto a fun, swoopy singletrack. At 8.4 miles stay left; a closed singletrack is on the right. At 8.7 miles you come to the Old Mission Dam Vista Point—a nice stopping place. From here, drop down to the right side of the river and follow it downstream to a technical and rocky, but fun, singletrack.

At 8.9 miles cross the narrow pedestrian bridge and head upstream to the dam, reached at 9.1 miles. From the dam proceed back to the parking area for a total of 9.2 miles.

Cuyamaca Rancho State Park

4 Cuyamaca Rancho State Park: East Loop

Distance: 12.5 miles
Difficulty: Moderate, mildly technical
Elevation: 1000' gain/loss
Ride Type: Fire road loop
Season: Fall and spring best, but rideable most of the year
Map: Tom Harrison's Trail Map of Cuyamaca Rancho State Park

Overview: Riders of various ability levels can enjoy this loop. A variety of trail surfaces and the climb up Soapstone Grade Fire Road are challenges for your legs, while the meadows and Lake Cuyamaca are sights for your eyes.

The route also gives you the option of exploring one of the historic mine sites near Julian, the Stonewall Mine. In the 1860s gold was discovered in the Julian area. By 1872 the town of Cuyamaca had sprung up around the Stonewall Mine, named for Stonewall Jackson. The "Jackson" was eventually dropped to appease anti-Southern sentiments in the area. The most extensively developed mine in the region, it employed 200 men during its peak years 1886 to 1891. Owned by California governor Robert W. Waterman, the mine yielded over $2 million in gold (gold prices at the time were between $16 and $20 an ounce) before its main shaft was sealed in 1892.

Getting There: From Julian, take Highway 79 south for 10 miles. Park at the dirt parking area (east side of the road) across from the Boy Scout Camp. From I-8, take Highway 79 north 14 miles to the parking area.

Route: Head south on Highway 79 for half a mile. Turn left onto a paved road. This is easy cruising along here. At 1.5 miles, just before a gate, a spur to your left leads to the Stonewall Mine. The mine is just south of Lake Cuyamaca, called The Lake That Dries Up by the Spanish because it dries up almost to the point of disappearing in the summer. You can explore the mine now or on your return route.

Back on the main road you pass the gate and head south. About 0.3 mile later, fork left (east) onto a trail. (The road continues to the right and leads to a campground.) A mile later you reach the junction of Soapstone Grade Fire Road to the left and Stonewall Creek Fire Road to the right.

From here you can loop around in either direction. I prefer to go down Stonewall Creek and back up Upper Green Valley Fire Road and Soapstone Grade. The climb up Upper Green Valley is very moderate, and then you have a tough, rocky 0.5-mile climb along Soapstone Grade. Going in the opposite direction, down Soapstone and Upper Green Valley and up Stonewall, involves a shorter but more consistently steep and rocky climb. Pick your poison.

To head down Stonewall Creek, go right. You have a 2.5-mile downhill before you reach the junction with

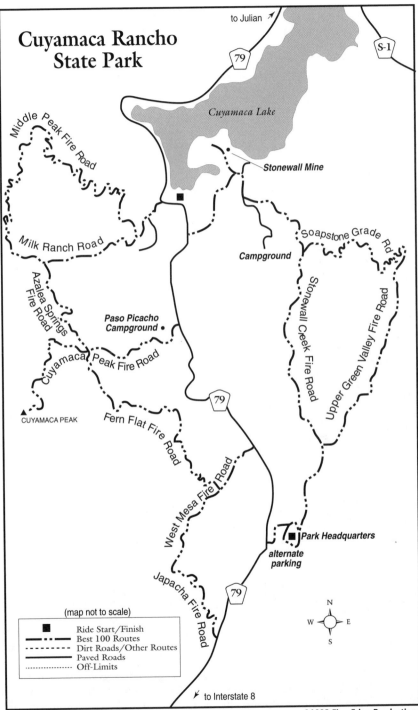

Cuyamaca Rancho State Park

to Julian

79

S-1

Cuyamaca Lake

Middle Peak Fire Road

Stonewall Mine

Milk Ranch Road

Soapstone Grade Rd

Campground

Azalea Springs Fire Road

Paso Picacho Campground

Stonewall Creek Fire Road

Upper Green Valley Fire Road

Cuyamaca Peak Fire Road

79

CUYAMACA PEAK

Fern Flat Fire Road

West Mesa Fire Road

Park Headquarters

alternate parking

Japacha Fire Road

79

(map not to scale)

N
W   E
S

■ Ride Start/Finish
—··—··— Best 100 Routes
------- Dirt Roads/Other Routes
———— Paved Roads
··············· Off-Limits

to Interstate 8

©1998 Fine Edge Productions

Upper Green Valley Fire Road, a left turn. Going straight and continuing onto pavement through the School Camp will take you to park headquarters. A good place for a rest break; headquarters has restrooms and water.

To continue the loop, make the left onto Upper Green Valley Fire Road and begin a 2.5-mile climb to the junction with Soapstone Grade. Soapstone is rockier and more exposed and gets quite steep for half a mile.

Go right and head downhill at the Y with Stonewall Creek at 9.3 miles. Backtrack the way you came past Stonewall Mine. A right turn on the highway takes you back to your car.

Option: This loop can also be done starting from park headquarters. From there it's about 8.5 miles without a trip to Stonewall Mine, which would add another 3 miles. From park headquarters take the main road east to a gate labeled "Authorized Vehicles Only." Go around the gate and proceed through the school camp. Pass the Cold Stream Trail to the left and then the Harvey Moore Trail on the right in less than 0.5 mile. Just beyond here Stonewall Creek goes left (sign indicates Cold Stream Trail, 1.5 miles) and Upper Green Valley goes right. You can loop around either way.

5 Cuyamaca Rancho State Park: West Loop

Distance: 13.5 miles or 17 miles, depending on return option
Difficulty: Moderate, mildly technical
Elevation: 1,500'
Ride Type: Loop on fire road and pavement
Season: Fall and spring best, but rideable all year
Map: Tom Harrison's Trail Map of Cuyamaca Rancho State Park

Overview: Deer. Springs. A 5-mile downhill. Some of San Diego's largest trees. A look at Cuyamaca Park's west and east sides. Need I say more? Well, I guess I should point out that there's lots of climbing involved. Hey, sometimes you have to pay to play!

Getting There: Follow the directions for the previous ride and park in the same spot. As with the previous ride, you could start at park headquarters. Starting there would allow you to get the pavement climb over with at the beginning of the ride.

Route: Cross the highway and take the paved road toward the Boy Scout

Camp. When it forks, take Milk Ranch Road to the right. (To the left is the camp.) The road turns to dirt and there is a gate just beyond here. Soon after, Middle Peak Fire Road takes off to your right. If you want extra climbing, you can take Middle Peak, loop around the mountain of the same name and rejoin the route at Azalea Springs Fire Road. This would add about 5 miles to the ride. The rest of us will stay on Milk Ranch Road and begin a very moderate climb to Azalea Springs Fire Road at 1.8 miles.

Go left and continue climbing until you reach Azalea Springs at 2.5 miles. Singletracks crisscross this whole area. Stay off them since they are all closed to bikes. At 3.0 miles you cross the paved Cuyamaca Peak Fire Road. If you want to bag the highest peak in San Diego County, turn right and make the very steep 1,200-foot climb to the peak with its radio towers. The view is worth the work, especially if it's a clear day. Stay in control on the descent—you can work up some serious speed and go into some of the tight corners too hot. The detour will add almost 4 miles to your ride. If, on the other hand, you're gagging when you reach Cuyamaca Peak Fire Road, you can turn left and bail out to Highway 79, where another left would return you to your car.

Now comes the fun part. To continue the main loop, take the Fern Flat Fire Road on the other side of the Peak Road to begin a 5-mile downhill. At 5.5 miles you come to a T with West Mesa Fire Road on your left (another bail-out point back to the highway) and Japacha Fire Road on your right. Continue downhill on Japacha. This is one of the most heavily wooded and pleasant areas of the park. It's also a great descent. It would be easy to exceed the park's 15-mph bike speed limit along here.

At just under 8 miles Japacha Fire Road ends at a gate at the highway. Head north (left) on Highway 79 for a mile to the park headquarters on your right. This makes a nice rest stop where you can contemplate your return options.

You could continue up Highway 79 for 4.5 miles to your car, for a total of 13.5 miles. This would involve about 3 miles of climbing and 1.5 miles of descending on the narrow, winding highway.

Your second option, and the one I recommend if you have the energy, is to combine this ride with the previous ride, using the directions at the end for starting from headquarters. You could opt to climb either Stonewall Creek Fire Road or Upper Green Valley Fire Road. Going up Upper Green Valley Fire Road and Soapstone Grade would deposit you 0.5 mile south of your car and would make for a 17-mile loop.

Trail sign for Noble Canyon (Ride 6).

Laguna Mountain Recreation Area

 Noble Canyon

Distance: 19 miles
Difficulty: Strenuous, very technical
Elevation: 2,500' gain/loss
Ride Type: Loop on fire road, paved road and singletrack; can be done as a shuttle
Season: Fall and spring best; expect snow in winter; can be crowded on weekends
Map: Tom Harrison's Recreation Map of the San Diego Backcountry

Overview: This tough ride is a local favorite for its scenery and challenge. Control your speed on the 9 miles of singletrack since the Noble Canyon trail is also popular with hikers.

Getting There: From San Diego take I-8 east. Exit at Pine Valley Road and go north. Turn left on Highway 80. Turn right 1 mile later onto Pine Creek Road (a very sharp turn). It's another mile to the Noble Canyon Trail sign on your right. There's a dirt lot right there or you can continue up the road to a developed parking area, complete with restrooms. Bring all the water you will need.

From Julian, go south on Highway 79. Head east on Old Sunrise Highway through Guatay to Pine Creek Road and go left to the Noble Canyon Trail sign on your right.

Route: Head north on Pine Creek Road, which turns into Deer Park Road. Often described as "dirt," it's actually more like gravel. This is not as ugly as it sounds. The gravel is generally well packed and causes little problem.

At 1.1 miles stay right onto Deer Park Road. After some moderate climbing, the road rises more steeply, reaching about a 20 percent grade at one point. After a paved stretch and a cattleguard, turn right. This road is signed "Pine Creek Road," but maps label it

"Laguna Meadow Road." Whatever. It winds pleasantly around several hills before crossing Noble Canyon Trail for the first time. If you're whipped, you can head down from here.

It's more fun if you continue on the main road, turning left at 6.2 miles toward Filaree Flat. Once you reach Sunrise Highway (paved), head right just over 0.5 mile to the Noble Canyon trailhead and turn right down the trail. At the parking area here you'll probably see mountain bikers being deposited by their friends for the downhill only. Real bicyclists ride up and down! To be fair, some ride the downhill first and finish by coming up the mountain.

At the top of the trail you are in pines. The trail drops and swerves gently. At 8.0 miles you cross Big Laguna Trail (see the following ride description); continue straight. You then cross Laguna Meadow Road three times in quick succession, always picking up the trail on the other side. At 10 miles Indian Creek Trail Ts in on the right; you continue straight. A final crossing of Laguna Meadow Road occurs a mile later. From this point on finding the route is easy. Stay on the obvious Noble Canyon Trail.

Don't let the beginning of the trail lull you into complacency. Once you hit the first of about four tight switchbacks, you're heading into the

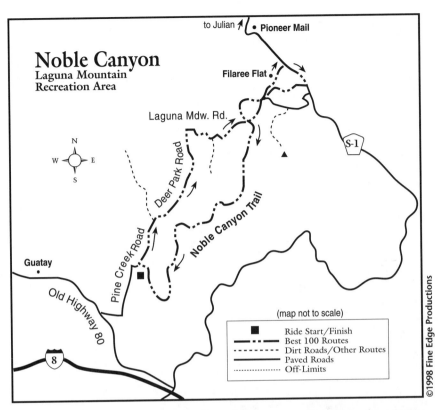

Noble Canyon
Laguna Mountain
Recreation Area

roughest part of the ride. From here on the trail gets more technical—and rocky. Fortunately there are a few smooth sections for respite and a few stream crossings.

The trail drops into oak-shaded canyons before breaking out onto a rocky ledge. Small jagged rocks and a cliff make this potentially the most dangerous section. Once past it you have to do a little bit of climbing. There's also some sand at the bottom of the canyon. The very end of the trail becomes virtually unrideable thanks to some boulder fields—unless you're a trials rider. The trail finally deposits you at your car in the parking area at 19 miles.

7 Indian Creek/ Big Laguna Meadow Loop

Distance: 14 miles
Difficulty: Moderate, some technical sections
Elevation: 1,100' gain/loss
Ride Type: Loop with lots of singletrack, some pavement
Season: Fall and spring; in winter expect cold weather and possible snow; can be crowded on weekends
Map: Tom Harrison's Recreation of the San Diego Backcountry (Note that Big Laguna Trail does not appear on any maps.)

Overview: In the same area as Noble Canyon, the Indian Creek and Big Laguna Meadow trails can be fashioned into a 14-mile loop that is all singletrack except for the 4-mile pavement return along Sunrise Highway. The ride begins with a climb up the Indian Creek Trail and a portion of Noble Canyon Trail, and continues with a rolling traverse alongside Big Laguna Meadow.

The ride offers scenery to die for and miles of winding singletrack. Spring is the best time to ride, when Big Laguna Meadow is bursting with wildflowers. To complete the picture, the route has stream crossings, rocky descents and enough technical sections to keep your bike dancing as you pass through pines and oak habitat.

For a shorter (7-mile), easier loop, you could start at the top of Noble

Canyon Trail (near mile marker 27.5 on Sunrise Highway) and take Noble Canyon Trail 0.1 mile to Big Laguna Trail and turn left to join the loop. This would eliminate the climb of Indian Creek Trail and would shorten the pavement return. Or, like many people, you could opt to ride back the way you came for an all-single-track ride (10.4 miles). Returning the way you came is an option for the longer loop as well; this would make for a 19.6-mile ride.

Getting There: From San Diego take I-8 east to Highway 79 north. Follow Highway 79 north for 17 miles to the Mt. Laguna turnoff (Sunrise Highway). Take Sunrise Highway 8.5 miles to Pioneer Mail picnic area and park. Pioneer Mail is just past the National Forest entrance sign near mile marker 29.5.

From Julian take Highway 79 south for 6 miles to the Mt. Laguna turnoff (Sunrise Highway). Follow Sunrise Highway 8.5 miles to Pioneer Mail picnic area and park.

Route: Begin by backtracking to the highway and going right. Almost immediately, at a crosswalk, turn left onto a gated (open) paved road. Head downhill and pass through a barbed wire gate. The road turns to dirt here, and there's a Y (0.2 mile). Go right.

Continue on the main road, keeping the meadow on your left. Soon you start climbing. At the Y at 1.2 miles go left. Just over the top you begin a short, steep, rocky, and quite gnarly descent. At

Trail sign: "Indian Creek/Big Laguna Meadow"

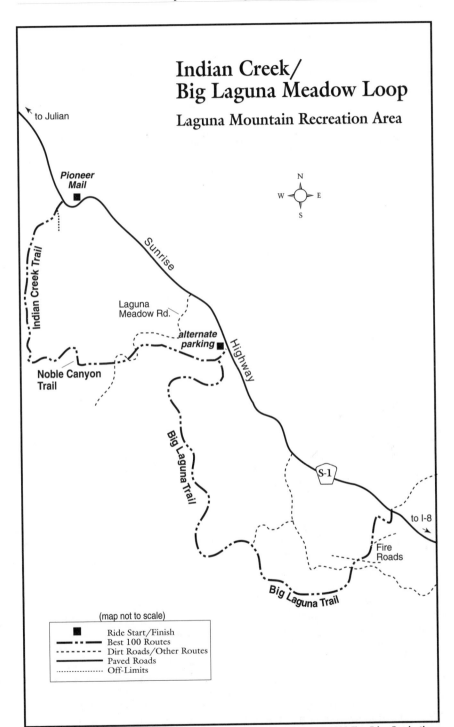

Indian Creek/
Big Laguna Meadow Loop

Laguna Mountain Recreation Area

to Julian

Pioneer Mail

N
W — E
S

Sunrise

Indian Creek Trail

Laguna Meadow Rd.

alternate parking

Highway

Noble Canyon Trail

Big Laguna Trail

S-1

to I-8

Fire Roads

Big Laguna Trail

(map not to scale)

■ Ride Start/Finish
—·—·— Best 100 Routes
- - - - - Dirt Roads/Other Routes
——— Paved Roads
·············· Off-Limits

©1998 Fine Edge Productions

Big Laguna Lake

the bottom go right and cross the small stream. You will probably have to portage here as it is quite overgrown. A trail rises steeply from the stream bed up a hillside beside an oak tree. The rough trail contours along the hillside and drops back to the stream at 1.6 miles.

On the other side of the stream and meadow, a trail with a brown post rises to your right (an alternate and more difficult route to this point). You stay straight, keeping the stream on your right. The trail climbs steeply in front of you. You will probably have to carry or push your bike here. The trail continues steep and rocky around a left-hand switchback. After this corner the grade eases, the trail surface smoothes out somewhat, and you can resume riding.

Continue climbing to 1.8 miles. Here a signed trail junction indicates that a left turn takes you back to Pioneer Mail, while a right turn takes you to Noble Canyon Trail. Go right.

More gradual climbing takes you past some great oak trees until you intersect Noble Canyon Trail at 2.5 miles. Go left on Noble Canyon toward Sunrise Highway (you are going up the beginning of the previous ride's downhill). A mile later the trail crosses Laguna Meadow Road, then crosses again 0.1 mile later. Go right onto the road, cross the cattleguard and immediately swing left back onto the trail. Almost immediately you cross the road for a third time.

The trail climbs more steeply here before mellowing into a rolling ride. At 4.7 miles you reach the junction with Big Laguna Trail in the middle of a lovely oak grove—a good rest stop. Turn right onto Big Laguna Trail. Soon you pass through a horse gate.

The trail rolls along pleasantly here and you enter more open terrain. Just under 6.0 miles you pass a trail sign for Old Sunset Trail on your right and you enter Big Laguna Meadow. In the spring the long, narrow meadow is a carpet of yellow and purple wildflowers.

The trail continues to follow the side of the meadow, which is to your right. At 7.0 miles you reach a sign declaring Big Laguna Lake, which is more like a really wet meadow. At 7.1 miles stay straight when another smaller trail forks right. You pass a couple of other spurs, but you stay on the well-worn main trail.

You reach a fence and a gate at 7.4 miles. Do not pass through the gate. Instead, turn right and follow the fence line. You soon pass a trail sign on your right. Continue straight in the direction of the Pacific Crest Trail. The trail gets a little more technical here with a few rocky sections. In general it rolls up and down, closely paralleling the fence.

At 8.0 miles you come to a gate in the fence. A trail continues to the right. Go straight through the gate. Beginning here, the trail is marked with brown trail signs. Soon you begin a tough, rocky climb that will

take some skill to "clean".

At 8.7 miles you cross through another horse gate. Just past here, 8.9 miles, the trail crosses a dirt road. Continue on the trail, marked by a brown trail sign and a wooden post with an arrow. Almost immediately the trail crosses a second dirt road. Here the trail turns into a dirt road itself. Continue straight. You pass a *Not a Through Road* sign on your right. Proceed uphill—the grade is pretty moderate—to 9.5 miles, where a wooden post and a partially obscured brown trail sign mark the trail on your left. Go left and enjoy the smooth, somewhat sandy single-track as it swoops and winds its way to Sunrise Highway at 9.8 miles.

Turn left onto the highway for an almost all downhill cruise back to Pioneer Mail, 4.2 miles away. Or, you could turn around and go back the way you came. The trail is very different in the opposite direction.

Anza Borrego Desert State Park

8 Pinyon Mountain Road and Fish Creek Wash to Split Mountain

Distance: 30 miles
Difficulty: Difficult because of length and long initial climb; technical in spots
Elevation: Begins 2,000'; climbs to 3,980'; descends to 650'
Ride Type: One-way on dirt and sand roads, car shuttle required; either end of the route can be done as an out-and-back
Season: Winter is best, but spring and fall are possible.
Map: Tom Harrison's Recreation Map of the San Diego Backcountry
Comments: You need to be self-sufficient for this rugged ride. Take as much water as you can carry, food for 5 or 6 hours, good topo maps, extra tubes, pump, and tools.

Overview: Granted, setting up the shuttle for and then doing this ride requires a very long day. But the scenery and the riding experience are worth the effort. Beginning at about 2,000 feet, the road climbs to 3,980 feet before starting a 3,300-foot descent to near sea level. You roll through spectacular ocotillo cactus and pinyon pine before dropping to wind- and water-scarred fossil shell reefs and wind caves. After the initial climb, the route is mostly a downhill cruise, although sand, rocks, washboard and motorized vehicles make it far from effortless.

Pinyon Mountain Road climbs up the Pinyon Mountain Valley, sandwiched between the Pinyon Mountains (the geographic heart of Anza Borrego) to the north and the higher Vallecito Mountains to the south, before dropping into Fish Creek Wash and traversing the geologic marvel of Split Mountain.

Speaking of "borrego," these mountains harbor a herd of bighorn sheep, despite a lack of a known year-round water source. In the past 25 years water tanks have been installed in a couple of spots to help improve the bighorn habitat.

If you're not up to the whole ride, you could do the western portion of the route up to The Drop-Off and return; or you could do the eastern portion up Fish Canyon as far as you like. The route is marked on maps as one-way from west to east starting at Squeeze Rock, but there are no signs to this effect.

Getting There: Leave one car at ride's end at Fish Creek Wash. From Julian, take Highway 78 east for 30 miles to Ocotillo Wells. Turn right onto Split Mountain Road. Fish Creek intersection is 8 miles south. Park here. (You could shorten the ride by driving up Fish Creek Wash as far as road conditions and your vehicle allow.)

To get to the ride's start, go back the way you came until you hit the junction of Highway 78 and Highway S2. Turn left and continue for 5 miles until you pass the Anza Borrego Desert State Park sign. Just opposite of it on your left (east) is the Pinyon Mountain sign. Drive up this dirt road 0.1 mile to a wide area at the junction of North Pinyon Mountain Road and Pinyon Mountain Road (both signed). Park here.

Route: Pedal east on Pinyon Mountain Road, avoiding the left fork which climbs North Pinyon Mountain. This is a wide, mildly sandy, somewhat washboarded road that climbs steadily into the mountains, more like boulder piles, ahead of you.

At 2.2 miles the first interesting rock outcroppings begin to appear. At first you are in a relatively wide valley among creosote and yucca. As you gain elevation, more and more ocotillo appear, some of which are quite impressive, their thin tendrils reaching 15 feet or more into the air. The canyon also narrows the higher you go, and the effect is of being in a wonderful cactus garden.

Around the 3-mile mark, the road begins to climb more steeply. It's worth stopping to look at the valley views behind you. At 3.7 miles the canyon grows more narrow and rockier. After 4 miles of climbing you get a brief flat spot and even a little downhill. A road joins from the right, but you continue east on the main road. During the next half mile there are quite a few spurs which lead to camping spots. Stay on the obvious main road, always heading east. Along here you begin to pass pinyon pines, unexpected greenery.

You resume climbing until 5.7 miles, where you top out among more spurs and camping spots. Once again, continue straight on the main road, heading east. There's a cool

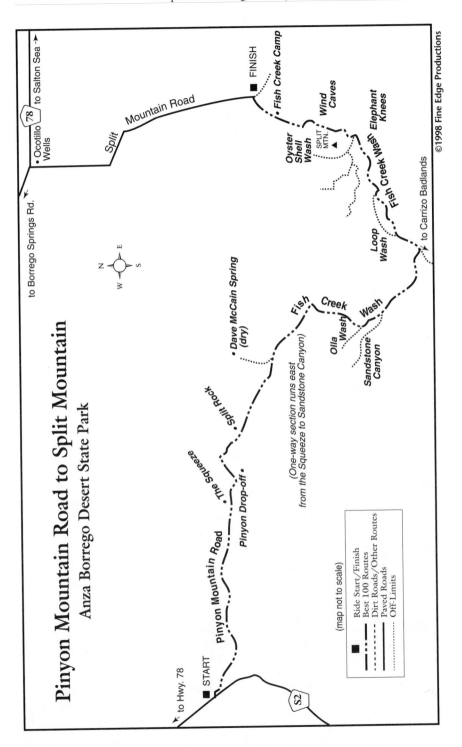

Pinyon Mountain Road to Split Mountain
Anza Borrego Desert State Park

to Salton Sea →
• Ocotillo Wells
78
Split Mountain Road
FINISH
Fish Creek Camp

Wind Caves
SPLIT MTN. ▲
Oyster Shell Wash
Elephant Knees
Fish Creek Wash
to Carrizo Badlands

Loop Wash

to Borrego Springs Rd.

• Dave McCain Spring (dry)

N
W — E
S

Fish Creek Wash
Olla Wash
Sandstone Canyon

(One-way section runs east from the Squeeze to Sandstone Canyon)

• Split Rock

The Squeeze

Pinyon Drop-off •

Pinyon Mountain Road

(map not to scale)

	Ride Start/Finish
	Best 100 Routes
	Dirt Roads/Other Routes
	Paved Roads
	Off-Limits

to Hwy. 78 ←
■ START

S2

©1998 Fine Edge Productions

view off to your left here. Beyond this you start descending. The road gets rockier and narrower.

About 7 miles into the ride you come to Squeeze Rock, a narrow boulder-filled slot about 8 feet wide through solid rock. A sign here declares *Severe Drop-Off One Mile Ahead*. The passage is so narrow that Jeeps often scrape on their way through. All but the hardiest 4-wheelers turn around at the Squeeze. Even with your fattest tires you shouldn't have any trouble fitting through, although the rocky exit is a technical challenge.

Less than half a mile later you come to a Y. Go right. (The left fork soon ends at a vertical drop. If you're curious, you can go take a look.) The right fork goes immediately up a steep, rocky climb. Hike-a-bike time

for most of us. A downhill, a very brief uphill with a right-hand turn at the top, and a sharp left bring you to the top of The Drop-Off.

Stop here. Why? First, because if you look to the northeast, you can see the Salton Sea. Second, because this is definitely gnarly. You are literally dropping off Pinyon Mountain Road and toward Fish Creek Wash. About 40 yards in length, this pitch is very steep and choked with big boulder-drops followed by extremely deep sand. If you are not a very skilled rider, do not attempt it. If you are skilled, scout first and think twice. The last time I was there, the line to the right looked like the best bet.

At the bottom the road bends left and climbs briefly before dropping again. A mile from The Drop-Off stay right on the main road. Begin the 1-mile climb to Hapaha Flat. From here you begin to follow Fish Creek Wash past several other washes, most of which are signed.

First you pass a hiking trail to Dave McCain Spring on your left. Beyond here the wash, which has been heading southeast, turns due south. A little over 4 miles from the spring trail, you pass Olla Wash on your right.

Less than a mile later you pass Sandstone Canyon on your right. Often called the most spectacular small wash in the whole park, Sandstone Canyon features 200-foot high walls. As the name implies, the walls are beige and brown sandstone. The real marvel is how narrow the canyon is—the walls are about 9 feet apart at their base. Desert shrubs and cat-

Jim MacIntyre

From the top of the Dropoff looking toward Fish Creek Wash (Ride 8).

claw—not a friend to Lycra or tires—are among the few plants that survive here. It's worth temporarily abandoning your bike to hike up the canyon.

About 0.7 mile farther you swing left as Arroyo Seco del Diablo (about as unfriendly a name as I've ever heard) enters from the right. You are now heading northeast. Pass Loop Wash on the left. Some 4.5 miles from Arroyo Seco del Diablo you come to Mud Hills Wash on the right, followed shortly by Wind Caves also on your right. Both of these make interesting side trips if you have the time and energy at this point of the game. The Mud Hills appear to shimmer; the gleam is the result of gypsum chips in the rock. The Wind Caves are sandstone rocks that have been so worn by wind that they now have caves and alcoves in them. Just beyond these detours you pass the North Fork of Fish Creek Wash on your left.

You immediately come to the ride's final highlight—a 2.5-mile trip through Split Mountain, which does indeed look like a mountain that has been rent in two. It actually consists of two stacks of sedimentary rock, mostly sandstone and fanglomerate—a conglomerate of rock and sand that was once part of an alluvial fan. Remarkable rock contortions here are the result of faulting.

Exiting Split Mountain, you pass Fish Creek Primitive Camp to your right. From here, it's two miles back to paved Fish Creek Road and your car.

9 Jasper Trail/Grapevine Canyon

Distance: 13 miles
Difficulty: Moderate, mildly technical
Elevation: Net loss of 2,600'
Ride Type: One-way downhill on dirt and sand roads; requires car shuttle
Season: Fall, winter, spring
Map: Tom Harrison's Recreation Map of the San Diego Backcountry

Overview: An excellent winter ride, this route drops from the juniper, yucca, pinyon and chaparral of the high desert to the willow, creosote and agave of the low desert. Mostly downhill, it features sandy and occasionally rocky terrain. Several springs and deep-walled canyons add to its appeal.

If you want to explore this area but can't arrange a shuttle, you can ride the eastern end of Grapevine Canyon as an out-and-back venture.

Be aware that the route is open to motorized vehicles, so expect 4-wheelers and motorcyclists on weekends and holidays.

Getting There: This ride begins about 10 miles southwest of Borrego Springs near the town of Ranchita. To arrange the car shuttle: Take Highway 78 east from Julian. Park one car at Tamarisk Campground near the junction with S3. Take the other car back down Highway 78 to S2 and go right. Turn right again on Highway S22. After you cross the Anza Borrego Desert State Park boundary, look off the right-hand side of the

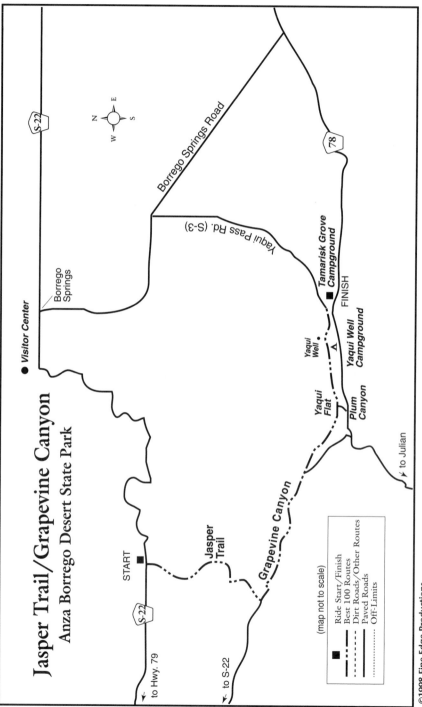

Jasper Trail/Grapevine Canyon
Anza Borrego Desert State Park

S-22

Borrego Springs Road

78

N
W E
S

Borrego Springs

Yaqui Pass Rd. (S-3)

Tamarisk Grove Campground

FINISH

• Visitor Center

Yaqui Well

Yaqui Well Campground

Yaqui Flat

Plum Canyon

to Julian

Grapevine Canyon

START

Jasper Trail

S-22

(map not to scale)

■ Ride Start/Finish
▪▪▪ Best 100 Routes
••• Dirt Roads/Other Routes
── Paved Roads
···· Off-Limits

to Hwy. 79

to S-22

©1998 Fine Edge Productions

road for the hard-to-spot Jasper Trailhead. It's between mile markers 6 and 7.

Route: Proceed south on the Jasper Trail. (Although called a trail, it's actually a road.) The soft trail rolls through sparse vegetation, mostly desert brush and cacti, for the first couple of miles. At 0.5 mile you pass a trail on your left. Continue south and cross Culp Valley Road at 1.4 miles.

At 2.2 miles fork right. At this point you encounter the ride's only climbing. It's steep and it's followed by an equally steep downhill. Breathe easy, your work is already done for the day as the rest of the ride is a continuous downhill.

On your way to the junction with Grapevine Canyon at 5 miles, you pass through a sheer-walled canyon sure to make it hard to keep your eyes on the road. The canyon gradually widens into a flat area, grows sandier for a stretch and then leads into Grapevine Canyon. Turn left.

The road through Grapevine Canyon is much smoother going and a lot less steep than the Jasper Trail as it makes its way east. (Jasper Trail drops 1,500 feet in 5 miles, whereas Grapevine Canyon descends a mere 1,300 feet in 8 miles.) At 5.4 miles you pass the first of two springs, signed *Stuart Spring,* on the left. At 6.7 miles you pass the second spring, Angelina Spring. This stretch of road is pretty willow-filled riparian habitat. Stay left as the road rises; the right fork continues by the water but soon peters out.

At 9.0 miles bear left; the right heads toward Highway S-2 and Plum Canyon, an early bail-out point. Two miles later you reach a second bail-out on the right to Plum Canyon. Yaqui Well is to your left at 12.5 miles. This oasis is one of San Diego County's best birdwatching spots. The area is also known for its stands of cholla cactus. It's worth dismounting your bike and walking the self-guided nature trail. Or, you could continue to Tamarisk Grove Campground (0.5 mile away), lock your bike in your waiting car and backtrack to Yaqui Well.

10 Coyote Canyon Shuttle

Distance: 18.5 miles
Difficulty: Strenuous, technical because of variety of trail surfaces
Elevation: Net loss of 3,000'
Ride Type: One-way downhill on dirt roads, sand and streambeds; requires long car shuttle
Season: Fall, winter, spring; the canyon is closed from June 16 to September 15 to protect the watering of bighorn sheep.
Map: Tom Harrison's Recreation Map of the San Diego Backcountry
Comments: You need to be self-sufficient for this rugged ride. Take as much water as you can carry, food for 5 or 6 hours, good topo maps, extra tubes, pump, and tools.

Overview: This mostly downhill ride is an epic and a classic. Unfortunately it involves an equally epic car shuttle. Once you drive from the end point to the start point and then back to the start point you spend over 3 hours driving. Obviously this ride isn't something you're going to do very often, or on the spur of the moment. I recommend tackling it with a group of friends as part of a long weekend (or longer) at Anza Borrego.

As a once-in-a-lifetime (or once-every-few-years) adventure, however, it can't be beat. This is desert riding at its best: rocky, sandy, and wet. (Yes, wet! Upper, Middle, and Lower Willows have water year-round.) These lush, riparian habitats are fragile enough that in 1996 the section of canyon between Middle and Lower Willows was closed to motorized traffic. (You may still encounter motorized vehicles doing the top or bottom of the canyon as an out-and-back.) You may see *Not a Through Road* signs in the canyon. Don't worry, it is a through route. These signs and the closure do not apply to mountain bikes.

The route is of historical interest as well. It follows part of Juan Bautista de Anza's pioneering route through the area. Along the way you will see several historical markers commemorating the trail's past.

Speaking of the past, MGE Racing of San Diego used to organize the Coyote Clunker Classic during the late 1980s and early 90s. At the time it was one of the Southland's premier mountain bike events. The entry fee covered transportation to and from the start/end point (worth the cost by itself) and a barbecue at the end. But due to bad weather and other problems, the event has not run for several years now. If it's ever resurrected, it's probably the least hassle for arranging the ride's logistics.

Getting There: Leave one car at your end point at Desert Gardens picnic area, just inside the south entrance of the park. From Borrego Springs, take Di Giorgio Road north. This paved road turns to dirt and enters the park.

Desert Gardens is just ahead on your right. This is all well signed. You could leave your car somewhere in town, but that would add 8 to 10 miles to an already long, tough ride.

This ride actually begins in Riverside County. From Borrego Springs, take Highway S-22 to Highway S-2 to Highway 79 to Aguanga, where you turn north on Highway 371. Fifteen miles later you reach Anza (named for Juan Bautista de Anza). Go 1.5 miles and turn south on Kirby Road. Continue for 4.5 miles to the intersection of Terwilliger Road and Coyote Canyon Road on your left. A white post serves as a road sign. Head east on Coyote Canyon Road and follow it for 2 miles before it bends south (right). About 2 miles later you reach a gate and a sign for Anza Borrego Desert State Park. This is your starting point.

Route: Go south on Coyote Canyon Road. Despite the trail name, you are not actually in Coyote Canyon. At this point you are in Nance Canyon, from which you descend into Coyote Canyon. At 0.5 mile, you cross the Pacific Crest Trail (closed to bikes). A half-mile later you begin to lose elevation in earnest on a rutted, cobby, rocky descent. Indeed, you lose almost half of the ride's elevation in this first descent. The downhill culminates in some steep, rutted switchbacks. At 2.8 miles, the plunge ends at Turkey Track, where you cross a stream coming out of Tule Canyon.

Turkey Track, marked on most maps, is an odd name, but it refers to a confluence of canyons. As you reach the bottom of Nance Canyon, Tule Canyon is on your right; just a bit later Horse Canyon sits to your left (due north, and marked by a sign post). Once past Horse Canyon things go

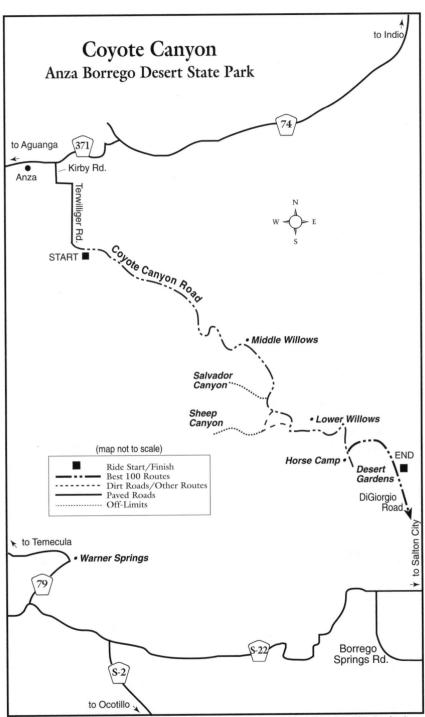

Coyote Canyon
Anza Borrego Desert State Park

to Indio

74

to Aguanga

371

Kirby Rd.

Anza

Terwilliger Rd.

START

Coyote Canyon Road

N
W   E
S

• Middle Willows

Salvador Canyon

Sheep Canyon

• Lower Willows

Horse Camp •

END

Desert Gardens

DiGiorgio Road

to Salton City

(map not to scale)

■   Ride Start/Finish
▬ · ▬ · ▬   Best 100 Routes
- - - - -   Dirt Roads/Other Routes
▬▬▬▬   Paved Roads
· · · · · · · ·   Off-Limits

to Temecula

• Warner Springs

79

S-22

S-2

Borrego Springs Rd.

to Ocotillo

©1998 Fine Edge Productions

from rocky to sandy. You are now in Coyote Canyon proper, following the course of Coyote Creek.

At 5.7 miles you pass a road (signed) on your right (west) that leads up Alder Canyon. At 6.5 miles you come to a stone cabin, corral, and old water tank. This is Bailey's Cabin. From here, the road squiggles northward to Upper Willows before bending south again.

Just under a mile later, you pass a stone historical marker commemorating Anza's expedition. A mile beyond that (about 9.5 miles total) you begin riding down a streambed. The road is the stream at this point—Middle Willows—and you continue in Coyote Creek for about a mile. Water level will vary, but it can be quite high in spring. Middle Willows also marks the Riverside County/San Diego County line—not that that means much out here!

When you hit the T-intersection at 12.2 miles, go left into Collins Valley. (A right turn would lead to Salvador Canyon, signed.) A mile later you hit another intersection, a Y. The right fork goes to the primitive Sheep Canyon camp. You go left. Stay left again at the intersection at 14.5 miles. This right fork also loops around to Sheep Canyon camp.

Continue to head southeast. You begin to see signs *To Borrego.* That's where you want to go. At 15.2 miles you pass Santa Catarina Spring and another stone monument. At 15.5 miles you must take the Lower Willows By-Pass Road. Ten years ago park officials, concerned about the heavy recreational use of the area, decided to route the main Coyote Canyon Road around Lower Willows to protect the wildlife which waters there. About a mile long, the bypass drops off a ridge—steep and rocky—and into a sandy wash.

After the bypass, about 16.3 miles total, you make the first of three stream crossings. (The water can be over 18 inches deep in the winter!) After the first one, stay to the right on the main road, heading south. To your left is Ocotillo Flats, full of the spindly-armed namesake cactus.

Pass through the gate at 16.5 miles. A half mile later you make the second water crossing. Just under 18 miles head east (left) to Di Giorgio Road. (The signed right fork leads to Whitaker Horse Camp.) You make a third water crossing, and half a mile later, 18.5 miles total, you're back at your car at Desert Gardens.

CHAPTER 2

Orange County

By Robert Rasmussen

Orange County, located midway between San Diego and Los Angeles, has never been mentioned in the same breath with America's great mountain biking spots. Most people are unaware the area has any good riding. In fact, the county's most well known "peak" is Disneyland's Matterhorn, hardly a boost to the public's perception of Orange County's mountain biking potential.

Many folks think of this area as a resort: four-star hotels, elegant restaurants, ocean and miles of beautiful beaches (the Orange Coast). Newport Harbor, in Newport Beach, is the world's largest small boat harbor. Dinghies to million-dollar yachts share the harbor's water for most of the year.

Tony Quiroz

Group rides provide camaraderie.

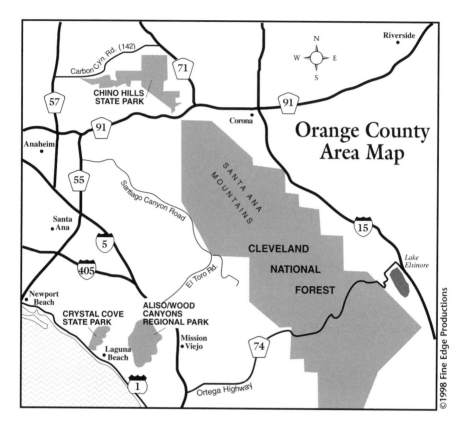

The remainder of the county, the place most locals know, is table flat. The land is covered by freeways and housing tracts. It is the last place you'd dream of finding good mountain biking territory.

Well, forget the common wisdom. Forget what you thought you knew about Orange County. The fact is there's plenty of good riding here, much of it within thirty minutes to one hour of most Orange County urban centers.

Most of the northern county is a level plain. The south is more mountainous. Inland from the coast, gentle rolling hills rise up from the flatlands. These hills and canyons were the grazing lands of early California's ranchos. Soon the hills soar into mountains 3,000 to 5,000 feet in elevation. These high ridges and peaks form the heart of Cleveland National Forest in isolated high country known as the Santa Ana Mountains. The range runs roughly north to south over 30 miles, forming the eastern border of Orange County. You can ride this entire distance atop the Santa Anas. There are also other United States Forest Service roads and trails to explore throughout Cleveland National Forest's 50,000-acre Trabuco District.

The valleys of the Santa Ana Mountains are narrow. Small seasonal creeks lined with oak and sycamore trees run through these canyons. Poison oak thrives here too, along with the occasional rattlesnake, making cautious off-trail walking a must.

The mountainsides above the valleys are steep and covered with impenetrable brush. In full sun (especially from June through October), the areas above tree line can be unbearably hot. Fall and winter are the best times to ride the Santa Anas. Two to three quarts of water per person are needed while riding under these conditions.

The beauty of this backcountry is stunning. The higher elevations offer vistas of the Santa Ana Mountain canyons and foothills. Beyond (depending upon location) you can see several thousand square miles of land over five counties (including several major mountain ranges). The distant snow-capped peaks of winter are a delight to see. West, across the channel, lies Catalina Island, its rugged contours visible most of the year from the Santa Ana range.

In addition to the mountainous terrain of Cleveland National Forest, there are other areas open to mountain biking in Orange County. The State of California and County of Orange maintain several "wilderness" parks that offer a wide variety of mountain biking experiences.

One small corner of peace remaining in a too-fast world, Chino Hills State Park is like all the other gorgeous oak-dotted hill country you've ever seen in California—the kind of place that makes you want to jump on your bike and ride off into the sunset.

Chino Hills is a land of gold and brown most of the year; a world green in winter and spring, the optimum seasons for riding, when temperatures are moderate and air quality is usually good. In summer and fall—when daytime temperatures are extremely high and when smog can obscure the views or be physically harmful—it's best to ride in early morning or evening.

Air quality permitting, views across the north and south ridges are spectacular when snow covers the local mountains—Mt. Baldy to the north and Saddleback to the south.

So, forget Disneyland. The best rides in the county are on a bicycle in the hills and valleys of Orange County's outback.

11 Crystal Cove State Park: Moro Ridge Route

Distance: 6 miles
Difficulty: Moderate, steep, technical
Elevation: 900' gain
Ride Type: Loop on dirt roads and singletrack
Season: Year-round
Map: Laguna Beach

Overview: The very last stretch of open coastal land in Orange County's San Joaquin Hills is a part of Crystal Cove State Park. The area consists of a series of lush valleys and rolling hills high above the Pacific between Lag-

una Beach and Corona Del Mar. Year after year, the surrounding open areas are transformed piecemeal into suburbia. However, Crystal Cove State Park has saved several priceless coastal areas for public use. Among them is a

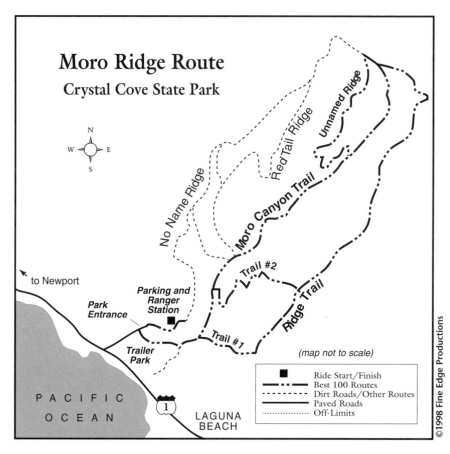

Moro Ridge Route

Crystal Cove State Park

to Newport

Park
Entrance

Parking and
Ranger
Station

Trailer
Park

PACIFIC
OCEAN

LAGUNA
BEACH

No Name Ridge

Red Tail Ridge

Unnamed Ridge

Moro Canyon Trail

Trail #2

Ridge Trail

Trail #1

(map not to scale)

■	Ride Start/Finish
—·—·—	Best 100 Routes
- - - -	Dirt Roads/Other Routes
———	Paved Roads
·········	Off-Limits

©1998 Fine Edge Productions

3,000-acre paradise called Moro Canyon. In the stillness of the coastal canyons and the shade of the tall trees you can imagine what this land was like not so long ago.

The canyon areas of the park comprise four main ridges and two valleys, running primarily north and south. Abundant plant life and seasonal streams combine to make a lovely place with just about every kind of mountain biking terrain imaginable. The major valley, Moro Canyon, is the main route north and south through the preserve. From Moro Canyon you can intersect with the many connecting trails, going anywhere into the park backcountry.

The early Spanish mapmakers called this place Lomarias de la Costa (ridge of hills on the coast). It was a part of Rancho San Joaquin, one of the many land grant cattle ranches that dominated early California. Jose de Sepulveda, the original grantee, received about 20,000 acres from the California governor in 1836. The land was sold to James Irvine in the 1860s; he purchased nearly half of modern-day Orange County for about 50 cents an acre.

The lands around Moro Canyon were used for farming and grazing from the early Spanish/Mexican days until late into the 20th century. The forested valley and chaparral-covered hills offer beauty and challenge to the mountain cyclist.

You can create many combinations of trails in Moro Canyon. Although small, this area combines both physical and technical challenge with great natural beauty. It also packs in a lot of fun and is probably the most popular mountain bike riding site in Orange County.

Getting There: From the 405 Freeway, take Laguna Canyon Road exit into Laguna Beach. Laguna Canyon dead-ends into Pacific Coast Highway. Turn right, heading north on Pacific Coast Highway 2 miles or so to the El Moro Canyon sign. Turn right. (There's a school on the corner.) Head up the small road and into the park. Park your car here and pay the State Park fee of $5 (there's a vending machine just outside the Ranger Headquarters). There are restrooms and a nature center here as well as a campground. Ranger headquarters is your only source of water.

Route: Ride south from the parking lot toward the park entrance. Turn left on the dirt road that parallels the trailer park. The road drops 60 feet over the space of a couple hundred yards. Extreme beginners may wish to dismount and walk their bikes to flatter terrain below. Just a hundred yards or so past the trailer park is the first connector trail heading right to Moro Ridge. Previously closed to the public, Trail #1 was re-opened in September 1992.

Once on Moro Ridge, point your bike up (northward), then walk n' ride a gnarly 0.3 mile or so. Farther up the ridge, the elevation becomes more gradual and you begin a long ascent. You travel from the 300-foot range to over 1,000 feet elevation at the far

north end of the park. It is a good workout with great views. The trip down is fast and fun, and the track is solid and relatively clean of debris.

You can also reach Moro Ridge on a more gradual route. Ride up Moro Canyon about 1 mile from the trailer park and turn right on the second Moro Ridge connector trail. This gradual trail follows the contours of the land and is "do-able," but strenuous. The trail can make you hot and sweaty and cause you to breathe hard, but the ride down is electrifying.

Atop the ridge, looking to the north end of Moro Canyon, you find one of the park's more distinctive features: a stretch of narrow singletrack for those who enjoy this type of ride.

Approximately 200 to 300 yards before reaching the northern end of Moro Ridge Trail, leave the main road through an entry in a wire fence onto a foot-trail. Follow that trail to the top of the hill (elevation 1,000+ feet) and down the other side to a fence line. The trail then continues for about a mile, twisting and turning, climbing and diving along the northern park boundary fence.

This singletrack lies on the high main ridge of the San Joaquin Hills. Among the coastal scrub and cactus there are views west and east along the ridge and down Moro Canyon.

The challenge of this ride is undeniable as the view switches from panoramic to the immediate area around the front wheel of your bike. Sharp turns, steep drops, roots, rocks, spiny cactus, and unstable soil combine to demand all your attention and skill. This is first and foremost a technical ride.

Occasionally, you may lose the trail in a small chunk of dirt road. Always bear to the right. Go for the fence line until the end. This 1-mile trail takes you across three of the four major ridge lines and their interconnecting trails.

On these hillsides there used to be just a little cactus that grazing cattle ate for brunch, keeping it in check. Now, however, it's spread everywhere and often grows quite close to the trail. Since this is a State Park, all plant species are protected. I urge you to ride cautiously, lest you knock down these cactus plants, damaging their tender spines and ravaging their flesh with your big strong bodies.

About 0.5 mile after entering the singletrack, the path dumps out onto the Moro Canyon Trail. To return to the parking lot you have two options: (1) A left turn takes you down a steep, hard, eroded surface (like riding down a washboard with ball bearings on it)—use extreme caution. This trail eventually takes you back to your car.

(2) A right turn from where the singletrack enters the same road will take you uphill a hundred yards or so to a junction of three trails—a much less treacherous route. Turn left and a dirt road gently descends a half-mile along an unnamed ridge line. At the southern tip of this ridge, the road drops abruptly, beginning a steep descent to Moro Canyon Trail on the valley floor. This is the route that returns you to the parking lot. The canyon road drops ever so gently through lovely shaded oak groves and grasslands. This portion of the ride is visually pleasant and blessedly downhill!

12 Aliso/Wood Canyons Regional Park: Rock-It/Cholla Loop

Distance: 7.1 miles or 10.2 miles
Difficulty: Intermediate, technical
Elevation: Begin/end 1,036'; low point 200'+
Ride Type: Loop on dirt trails
Season: Year-round
Maps: Laguna Beach, San Juan Capistrano

Overview: One of Orange County's most popular riding spots, Aliso/Wood Canyons Regional Park—part of Laguna Niguel Regional Park—lies hidden between Laguna Beach and Laguna Hills. It is a unique combination of city and county land. The western portion is part of Laguna Beach Greenbelt, whose high, lush ridges have been secured as a source of open space and recreation. A series of trails and roads crisscross this area above Laguna Canyon Drive, and from the ridge, four other trails drop down into the park. Together, these two parcels form an adult playground of over 5,000 acres.

In 1842, Juan Avila received this tract as part of a 13,000-acre land grant (Rancho Niguel). The land was used for farming and cattle grazing through the 1980s. Since then, suburban development has taken over.

Getting There: This ride can be done either from the Laguna Beach side or the Laguna Hills side. From Pacific Coast Highway in downtown Laguna Beach, turn onto Laguna Avenue (across from the old Laguna Hotel, one of the city's most famous landmarks). Head inland, and after

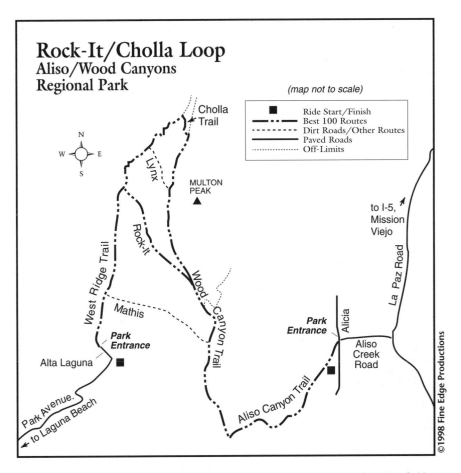

Rock-It/Cholla Loop
Aliso/Wood Canyons
Regional Park

(map not to scale)

Cholla Trail

Lynx

MULTON PEAK ▲

Rock-It

Wood Canyon Trail

West Ridge Trail

Mathis

Park Entrance

Alta Laguna ■

Park Avenue.
to Laguna Beach

Aliso Canyon Trail

Park Entrance

Alicia

Aliso Creek Road

La Paz Road

to I-5, Mission Viejo

■ Ride Start/Finish
— · — Best 100 Routes
- - - - Dirt Roads/Other Routes
——— Paved Roads
········· Off-Limits

©1998 Fine Edge Productions

one block, Laguna Avenue becomes Park Avenue. Park Avenue leads through the city, high into the hills directly to Alta Laguna Boulevard where you turn left and go 200 yards. On your right is a park. The ridge bike path begins at the street's dead-end. The highest point in Laguna Beach lies within the park: locals call it Top of the World, and the view is fabulous. Water is available only at this entry to Alta Laguna Park.

To ride from the Laguna Hills side, from I-5 in Laguna Hills take La Paz Road south to Aliso Creek Road and go right. Turn left on Alicia. The park entrance is immediately to the right.

Route: From the dead end of Alta Laguna, begin your long descent atop the West Ridge Trail. At 1.6 miles you see a water tank and facilities to your left. Turn right on a road that intersects nearby. You're now on the Rock-It Trail.

I'm not sure how the trail received its name. But there's a lot of rock everywhere, offering all the excitement of rock n' roll as the steep terrain makes for rocket-like acceleration—more than you need or want.

This downhill is a thoroughly challenging trail: steep drops, rocky paths and eroded soil. As the trail approaches the lower end of the ridge you see a path to the left and another to the right at the beginning of a large meadow. Take the left path; the right is for hikers only.

Cross through the grassy meadow which has immense old trees. After about 0.25 mile you enter a steep creek embankment. On the other side, turn left onto Wood Canyon Trail, the dirt road that runs prominently through the valley.

Continue through the valley another few miles until you see Cholla Trail on your left; it is well marked by brown park signs.

After you reach the Laguna Ridge again, turn left from Cholla Trail onto the main trail to return to your car. It's uphill all the way (about 400 feet)—time to pay for all the fun you had!

You can fashion a similar route by starting from the Alicia park entrance. Take the trail alongside Awma Road from the parking lot 1.5 miles to the gate at Wood Canyon Road. Go through the gate and up Wood Canyon Road through the lush grass-lands. Continue past the entry to Mathis Canyon (on your left) and, after 1 mile, ride into the main area of Wood Canyon. Keep left on the main trail. On warm days, this canyon provides welcome relief; the many trees shade you as you slowly gain more than 300 feet in elevation up to the turnoff to Cholla Trail.

Go left on the well-signed Cholla Trail and begin to work in earnest. It's steep but thankfully it doesn't last for long. Watch out for the trail's namesake cactus. When you reach the top of the Laguna ridge line, turn left to begin a mile-long descent. Just past a water tank on your right, Rock-It Trail begins as a doubletrack on the left. You won't see the trail sign until you go down a bit.

Bounce through the rocky, technical trail on your way down to Wood Canyon. Toward the end of the trail, take the left fork. A steep down and up through a stream crossing brings you back to Wood Canyon. Go right and retrace your path to the parking lot.

Cleveland National Forest

13 Silverado Canyon to Santiago Peak

Distance: 22 miles (or turn back at any point)
Difficulty: Easy to strenuous depending on options; not technical
Elevation: Begin/end 1,800' (possible to begin lower); high point 5,687'
Ride Type: Out-and-back on dirt roads (or pavement)
Season: Year-round
Maps: Santiago Peak, Corona South

Overview: Silverado Canyon was known by the early Hispanic settlers as Cañada de la Madera (Timber Canyon). The trees in the valley and on the mountain above were cut to form the structural elements of Mission San Juan Capistrano and other early California buildings.

The canyon was renamed Silverado in 1877 after silver was discovered

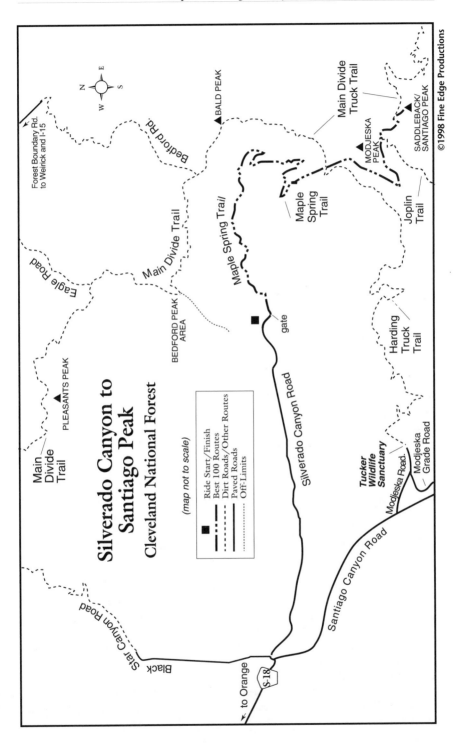

© 1998 Fine Edge Productions

Silverado Canyon to
Santiago Peak

Cleveland National Forest

(map not to scale)

- Ride Start/Finish
- Best 100 Routes
- Dirt Roads/Other Routes
- Paved Roads
- Off-Limits

and mined there. More trees were felled to build mine shafts and support a thriving city of 1,500 people. The valley boomed. Regular stage transport ran between Los Angeles and Santa Ana. After a few years, however, the silver ore played out and the glory days of Silverado came to a close.

Climbing steadily through Silverado Canyon you pass shady glens, pleasant creeks and pine forests—the latter not immediately associated with this arid coastal region. Finally, you find panoramic beauty atop the highest ridges of the Santa Ana Mountains.

Getting There: From the City of Orange and the 55 Freeway, take Chapman Avenue east. Chapman becomes Santiago Canyon Road after 5 miles. Continue another 5 miles to Silverado Canyon Road and make a left.

From the I-5 Freeway in the Mission Viejo area, take El Toro Road east 7.6 miles to the fork. Go left onto Santiago Canyon Road. Drive north 5 miles to the Silverado Canyon exit and turn right.

Follow Silverado Canyon Road until it turns to dirt at a metal pipe Forest Service gate. Park here.

Beginning riders can get in a pleasant 15- to 16-mile ride by parking in one of the numerous spots along the highway and riding up the pavement to the gate and beyond. The climb gets much steeper 2 to 3 miles past the gate. Turn around when you've had enough.

Regardless of where you start, you can get water at the U.S. Forest Service Stations at the beginning of Silverado Canyon.

Route: Head up Maple Spring Road (5S04) which begins at the gate as a dirt road. Beyond this spot there are no homes, the canyon narrows, and

the oak trees grow tall and thick along Silverado Creek. The road curves its way gently through the valley, and the sounds of birds and the creek predominate.

The ride continues in this way for another 2 to 3 miles past the gate. You cross a creek, make a sharp right turn and begin a steep climb. Beginners can turn around here; more experienced riders continue up 5S04 to the Main Divide Truck Trail (3S04) and a four-way trail junction.

Ascend a slight incline and make a quick right onto the Main Divide Truck Trail. Ride south toward Santiago Peak, the highest part of Saddleback Mountain. Four miles and about 1,000 feet more of elevation gain puts you atop Santiago Peak, up a short spur from the Main Divide Trail.

Depending upon air quality, the views are spectacular. Walk around the peak. Note Catalina Island across the way. Orange County, Los Angeles and Riverside counties lie before you. Drink to replace lost fluids, and eat to regain used nutrients.

Return to Silverado Canyon by the same route. Coming down off the peak, be sure to take the left fork of 3S04. (A right turn would drop you off on the wrong side of the mountain and you'd have to retrace your route uphill.)

Continue to the four-way trail junction and turn left onto Maple Spring Trail. Go straight downhill toward the stands of pine trees. Avoid road hazards on the descent. Seven miles and seemingly a few moments later you reach your car.

Note that you could combine this ride with the following ride by going down Joplin Trail and then down Santiago Truck Trail. This would be a 22-mile route, and you would need to shuttle between the start and end points.

14 Santiago Truck Trail with Joplin Trail Option

Distance: 15 miles; 20 miles with option
Difficulty: Moderate, not technical; strenuous, technical with option
Elevation: Begin/end 1,600'; high point 3,400'; high point 4,900' with option
Ride Type: Out-and-back on dirt roads with singletrack option
Season: Year-round; in dry season Santiago Truck Trail may occasionally be closed by the Orange County Fire Marshal. (You can't miss the sign if it is.) Call 714-736-1811 or 714-649-2645 for fire information.
Map: Santiago Peak

Overview: Modjeska Canyon is another of Orange County's cozy riparian valleys. It is named for Helena Modjeska—a Polish immigrant actress who found success on the American stage. Madame Modjeska purchased several hundred acres in the canyon and built an estate named "Arden" after Shakespeare's forest of Arden in *As You Like It*. Her home is currently undergoing restoration as an historic monument. The life of the free-spirited actress is honored today by a group called the Daughters of Helena Modjeska.

Getting There: From the 55 Freeway in Orange, take Chapman Avenue east. Chapman becomes Santiago Canyon Road after 5 miles. Continue 9.1 miles to Modjeska Grade Road, turn left and find a metal gate on your right in about a quarter mile.

From I-5 in Mission Viejo take El Toro Road 7.6 miles east to the fork. Go left onto Santiago Canyon Road, and in 0.9 mile turn right at Modjeska Grade Road. The gate is on the right about a quarter mile up. Park your car along the blacktop. Do not park in the trailhead driveway; your car will be ticketed or towed.

Route: Enter the gate, take the dirt road to your right, and ride up into

the hills. The road snakes up the contours of the hill. Look above and to your left where you can catch glimpses of the Harding Truck Trail climbing steadily above you toward Saddleback Mountain. The Santiago Truck Trail climbs the high ridge above Mission Viejo. The views below expand with your upward progress, with suburban and canyon views becoming grand, scenic vistas.

At 6.5 miles you come to the Joplin Road which drops sharply downhill and dead-ends. Don't make the mistake of taking it. There is no exit.

Two miles later you reach a fork in the road; take the left fork. The road drops into a small river valley, the site of Old Camp, reputedly an ancient hunting camp used by Native Americans.

If you've had enough for one day, turn around here and retrace your route. If you're up for a challenging singletrack trail, follow the road into a small clearing. Look left across the clearing to the opposite hillside. (The hillside is part of a valley dropping into Old Camp from above.) Find and take a small footpath (there are no signs) that leads you up the valley 2.2 miles to the Main Divide Truck Trail (3S04).

The path is steep. Expert riders will streak upward; intermediate riders will "walk 'n ride" steadily to the

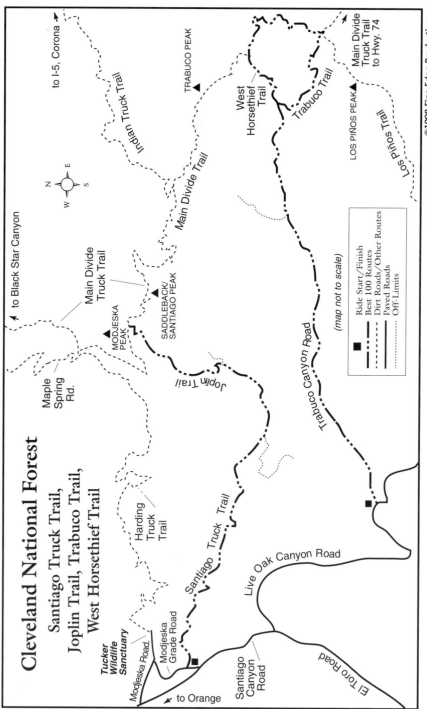

Cleveland National Forest

Santiago Truck Trail,
Joplin Trail, Trabuco Trail,
West Horsethief Trail

©1998 Fine Edge Productions

to I-5, Corona

Indian Truck Trail

TRABUCO PEAK

West Horsethief Trail

Trabuco Trail

Main Divide Truck Trail to Hwy. 74

LOS PIÑOS PEAK

Los Piños Trail

Main Divide Trail

N
E
S
W

to Black Star Canyon

Main Divide Truck Trail

MODJESKA PEAK

SADDLEBACK/ SANTIAGO PEAK

Maple Spring Rd.

Joplin Trail

Trabuco Canyon Road

(map not to scale)

Ride Start/Finish
Best 100 Routes
Dirt Roads/Other Routes
Paved Roads
Off-Limits

Tucker Wildlife Sanctuary

Harding Truck Trail

Santiago Truck Trail

Live Oak Canyon Road

Modjeska Road

Modjeska Grade Road

Santiago Canyon Road

El Toro Road

to Orange

top. Not only is Joplin Trail beautiful, but you'll be pleased to note that few people use it. The day you ride here, it will probably be your own private park.

Returning to your car from the top of Joplin Trail is its own reward. You bob, weave and brake down this entire narrow ribbon of trail. Joplin Trail is "E ticket" all the way. On completing the trip down, the only question in your mind will be, "When can I return?"

From Old Camp on the Santiago Truck Trail, return 7.7 miles to your car.

15 Trabuco Trail/ West Horsethief Trail

Distance: 11.5 miles
Difficulty: Moderately strenuous, technical
Elevation: Begin/end 1,900'; high point 4,200'
Ride Type: Loop on singletrack
Season: Year-round
Maps: Santiago Peak, Alberhill

Overview: The highlights of this loop are the heavily forested Trabuco Trail and the technically challenging West Horsethief Trail. Wet and lush, Trabuco Canyon was used by horse thieves escaping Orange County with stolen stock—thus the Horsethief Trail name. (Bring plenty of water; there is none en route.)

Getting There: Take I-5 to Mission Viejo. Exit on El Toro Road and head 7.6 miles east to where the road forks. Go right onto Live Oak Canyon Road (S19). Approximately 2 miles later you pass O'Neill Regional Park and find an open creek bed to your left. A dirt road enters the creek's flood plain area. This is the entrance to Trabuco Canyon. If your car has low clearance, park at the canyon entrance.

Provided your vehicle has adequate clearance, drive up Trabuco Canyon and park your car 1 mile beyond Holy Jim Canyon at road's end (plenty of parking).

Route: Ride the rocky trail 1.8 miles to the junction of West Horsethief Trail and Trabuco Trail. Take the right fork; it is much better for uphill travel than West Horsethief Trail which is too steep and has soil conditions that make riding extremely difficult.

The lower portion of Trabuco Trail is very rocky. You ascend a small canyon and enter some of the lushest woodlands in the Santa Ana Mountains. Large bushes grow over the trail in many areas, forming "Hobbit Tunnels" for you to glide through in the gloom of the darkened forest. The trails improve substantially the higher you climb toward Los Piños saddle and the Main Divide Truck Trail.

You emerge from the forest onto 3S04 at Los Piños Saddle, 2.7 miles from the lower trail junction on Trabuco Creek. Turn left. In 3 miles of elevation gains and losses you find West Horsethief Trail (5401) on your left which begins as a firebreak and becomes a footpath. At 1.9 miles down the mountain, you struggle with an unending series of switchbacks, twisting and sliding on unstable shale soil. You might ask yourself, "Am I riding or skiing?" and you answer "Both" until you finally reach the valley bottom linking you with Trabuco Canyon Trail. From here you have a serene ride back to your car at the end of Trabuco Road.

16 San Juan Trail to Blue Jay Camp

Distance: 22 miles; 11-mile shuttle
Difficulty: Strenuous, technical
Elevation: Begin/end 800'; high point 3,300'
Ride Type: Out-and-back on singletrack; car shuttle possible
Season: Year-round
Maps: Cañada Gobernadora, Alberhill

Overview: Undoubtedly Orange County's premier singletrack, the San Juan Trail is pure fun. It is the fastest of all the regional National Forest trails but still packed full of challenging obstacles. *Be careful:* More than a few people have had to be rescued on this trail. While advanced riders ride up and down the singletrack, intermediate riders may want to arrange a shuttle.

Getting There: Take I-5 to San Juan Capistrano. Exit on Highway 74 and drive east 12.5 miles. You'll see a sign for San Juan Hot Springs and notice some Forest Service buildings. Turn left here and drive down the canyon 1 mile to the trailhead. (There is plenty of parking in a grove of trees to the left.)

To arrange a shuttle, leave one car at San Juan Hot Springs. Return to Highway 74, turn left, and proceed up for about 9.5 miles. Turn left on Long Canyon Road (signed for Blue Jay Campground) and follow it for 2.5 miles. Stay left and park in a small lot to your right. The trail starts here.

Route: The trail begins as a series of switchbacks going straight up the mountainside. Daunting as it looks, the trail is well-engineered and the grades are within the abilities of "mere mortals."

Approximately 3 to 4 miles from the entrance of the trail you begin passing high ridges and mountain tops. The great valleys lie here and there. You see Highway 74 as a tiny line stretched across the mountains. The climb is sometimes steep and at other times gradual, but always relentless to 3,000+ feet. I caution you to take the greatest care when you ride this route, especially on the downside. Every gnarly rock, root, and pitfall imaginable exists on this wonderful trail. You'll note the path has lots of foot-traffic, especially on weekends.

At mile 5.4 the trail forks, with an eroded old road (Route A) to the left and a continuation of the footpath

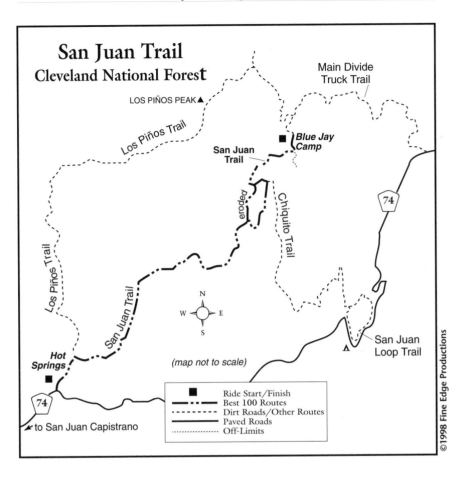

San Juan Trail
Cleveland National Forest

LOS PIÑOS PEAK ▲

Los Piños Trail

Main Divide
Truck Trail

San Juan
Trail

Blue Jay
Camp

eroded

Chiquito Trail

74

Los Piños Trail

San Juan Trail

N
W ⊕ E
S

Hot
Springs

San Juan
Loop Trail

(map not to scale)

74

to San Juan Capistrano

■ Ride Start/Finish
▬ ▪ ▬ Best 100 Routes
- - - - - Dirt Roads/Other Routes
▬▬▬ Paved Roads
.... Off-Limits

©1998 Fine Edge Productions

(Route B) to the right. Both paths wind up at Blue Jay Camp.

Route A: At the San Juan Trail junction, bear left on the deteriorated road. Follow this about 4 miles to a meadow area. You'll cross over another path and climb up a steep hill. (The soil is rocky and unstable.) Near the top of the hill is another footpath. Turn right and ride a mile or so to Blue Jay Camp.

Route B: At the San Juan Trail junction, bear right. After riding the footpath to mile 9, you pass by Chiquito Trail on the right. Bear left on the path skirting the bottom of a hill. At the bottom you cross over an old road and take the gentle switchbacks up the hill to Blue Jay Camp. The camp area, which affords shade and usually has water, is a great spot to rest before your return.

The trip back down is a riot! At the end you have an optional hot tub soak at San Juan Hot Springs. How thoughtful!

Chino Hills State Park

17 Aliso Valley

Distance: 8 miles
Difficulty: Beginner, not technical
Elevation: Begin/end 700'; end of canyon 400'
Ride Type: Out-and-back on dirt road
Season: Year-round
Map: Prado Dam

Overview: In terms of work and visual beauty, this is an ideal mountain bike ride for beginners. You can find water at the picnic tables near park headquarters.

Getting There: From north Orange County, take the 55 Freeway to the 91 Freeway and head east toward Corona. At Prado Dam take the off-ramp for Highway 71 north (toward Pomona). Continue north on this busy, narrow road and exit at Butterfield Ranch Road. Go left to Soquel Canyon Parkway and go left again. About a half-mile later, go left on Elinvar. Elinvar turns into Sapphire Road and leads into the park on your right. In a mile you'll reach the boundary of the park. Continue through a gate and gently descend through Bane Valley.

At the end of Bane Valley you pass the campground up around a hill. In another quarter mile or so is the Ranger Headquarters with plenty of public parking.

A treat to see, the headquarters is the old Rolling M Ranch whose buildings have been converted for use as public facilities. The former ranch house is the park office; the former barn is used as a work area. The windmill water pumps still stand as reminders of the area's rich ranching history.

Route: From Park Headquarters, take your bike south on the blacktop road. Just after leaving the ranch area you pass a dirt road on your right, the trailhead for Telegraph Canyon Trail. In another 100 yards you pass a second dirt road on the right, the beginning of South Ridge Trail, the park's longest trail.

Keep following the blacktop street around a hill and down toward the campground. Turn right into the camping area and ride the dirt road to a metal gate. Take your bike through the special opening in the gate and begin your ride.

Entering Aliso Canyon (south) is a visual experience. Vast expanses of the valley bottom are filled with lush fields of wild oats and large oak trees, gnarled and very old. The entire scene is strikingly beautiful, open and wide.

The main Aliso Valley Trail (north and south) is intersected by trails at many points. The trails from the east side of the valley all dead-end into private land—do not ride these trails. Trails from the west side of the canyon are okay to ride.

Half a mile from the camp area is the first connector trail which leads to Water Canyon, Scully Ridge Trail, and Bobcat Ridge Trail. Pass by this first set of trails and continue south into Aliso Canyon. As you ride you may notice small roads dead-ending into gullies and at the base of hills. Often there are manhole covers at the end of the roads—water wells tended by the local water district. Beneath Chino Hills State Park is a rich aquifer whose waters supply Orange County.

Riding down the valley 1.8 miles from the campground entry you'll pass a second connector trail on the right. This is Brush Canyon Trail, one large switchback climbing to the top of the western ridge. (With over 400 feet of elevation gain, I recommend this climb to all muscle freaks and other like-minded mortifiers of the flesh. As you'd expect from such a steep trail the downhill run is hot, the kind that broken bones are made of. *Caution advised:* 15 mph limit.)

Riding farther south through Aliso Canyon, at 2.6 miles from the campground you pass Scully Hill Trail on your right which rises abruptly to the Scully Ridge Trail with over 500 feet of elevation gain. Yes, it's definitely a challenging ride both up and down the Western Ridge.

Moving south from this last connector trail, you come to the end of Aliso Valley at a well-marked metal gate. To return to the ranch area, retrace your steps up the valley. The elevation gain on your 4-mile return is 300 feet, so gradual as to be nearly unnoticeable.

It's possible to link up with the Scully Ridge Trail from Aliso Valley beyond the park's southern boundary. Ride through the park entry gate down a dirt road for about a hundred yards until you come to a second dirt road. Turn right and ride a short distance to a stock gate. The gate opens out onto a large meadow. (Cyclists have permission to cross this land. Since horses are sometimes grazed here, you must re-lock each opened gate to prevent the loss of animals.) In less than half a mile the road passes south through the large meadow. The dirt road winds around the end of the West Ridge a short distance from some railroad tracks. On the right you'll find a blacktop road descending from the West Ridge above. Ride up the blacktop which gives way to dirt higher up—the south end of the Scully Ridge Trail.

Alone or in a group, mountain biking in Southern California is an adventure.

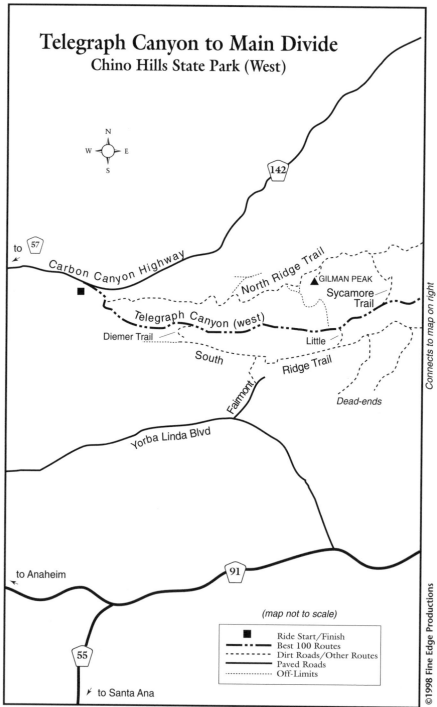

Telegraph Canyon to Main Divide
Chino Hills State Park (West)

N
W E
S

142

to 57

Carbon Canyon Highway

North Ridge Trail

GILMAN PEAK

Sycamore Trail

Telegraph Canyon (west)

Diemer Trail

Little

South

Ridge Trail

Dead-ends

Connects to map on right

Fairmont

Yorba Linda Blvd

to Anaheim

91

(map not to scale)

55

to Santa Ana

■   Ride Start/Finish
— · · — Best 100 Routes
- - - - - Dirt Roads/Other Routes
——— Paved Roads
· · · · · · Off-Limits

©1998 Fine Edge Productions

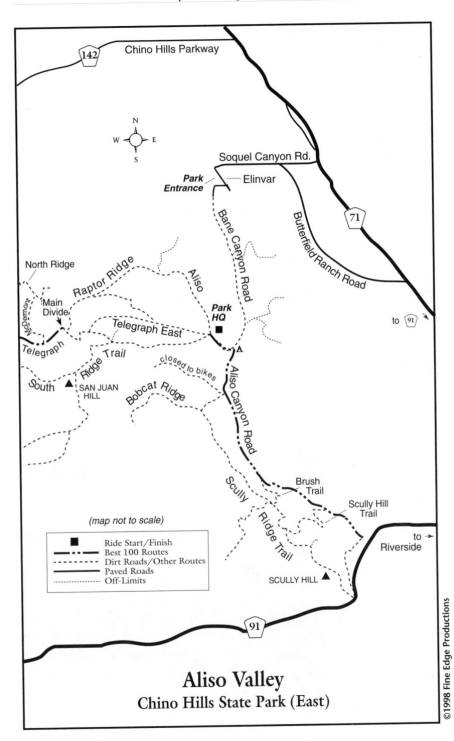

Aliso Valley
Chino Hills State Park (East)

142
Chino Hills Parkway

N
W   E
S

Soquel Canyon Rd.

Park Entrance — Elinvar

71

to 91

North Ridge

Raptor Ridge

Aliso

Bane Canyon Road

Butterfield Ranch Road

McDemont

Main Divide

Park HQ

Telegraph East

Telegraph

Ridge Trail

South

closed to bikes

SAN JUAN HILL

Bobcat Ridge

Aliso Canyon Road

Scully

Ridge Trail

Brush Trail

Scully Hill Trail

to →
Riverside

(map not to scale)

■	Ride Start/Finish
▪▪—▪▪—	Best 100 Routes
- - - -	Dirt Roads/Other Routes
———	Paved Roads
....	Off-Limits

SCULLY HILL ▲

91

©1998 Fine Edge Productions

18 Telegraph Canyon Trail to the Main Divide

Distance: 12 miles
Difficulty: Easy, not technical
Elevation: Begin/end 500', high point 1,500'
Ride Type: Out-and-back on dirt road
Season: Year-round
Maps: Yorba Linda, Prado Dam

Overview: Just as the previous ride outlined the main route into the park's east side, this route describes the main access to the park's west side. Thanks to some lovely oak and sycamore trees, Telegraph Canyon can be cool and shady. Because the climb gets steeper the farther you go, the route is a good choice for beginners who can turn around whenever they've had enough.

Getting There: This ride begins on the west side of Chino Hills State Park. In the Brea area of Orange County, traveling on the 57 Freeway, exit at Lambert. Drive east until the street becomes Brea Canyon Drive. After 2.2 miles you'll see Carbon Canyon Regional Park on your right.

Carbon Canyon Regional Park is the best place to park for your trip into the western Chino Hills. It's patrolled, cheap and easy to get in and out of (just bring two crisp Yankee Dollars, four dollars on weekends, to feed the android lot "attendant").

Route: Leave Carbon Canyon Park at the entrance and turn right, riding past an orchard. At a metal gate pass around and onto a blacktop road. The road dips into a creek bed. Most of the time there's water running in the creek, quite a bit in wintertime. The creek has a firm bottom so don't be afraid to roll on through. You rise out of the creek bed onto the other side and come upon another fence. Note the open entry and pass through. At this point you'll see one

Streamside riding offers a respite from summer heat.

dirt road going right and another left. Take the right-hand road. The left road climbs into the hills to become the North Ridge Trail.

Continue on the right-hand trail a few yards until another dirt road breaks off to the left near some park displays. Turn left and begin the Telegraph Canyon Trail (west).

Telegraph Canyon Trail begins in a very narrow valley that follows the bed of a seasonal creek. The canyon widens as it twists its way deeper into the hills. At first the canyon is largely grasslands with a few scattered bushes and trees. Later this gives way to larger stands of oak and huge sycamore trees that dominate the landscape. The entire ride through Telegraph Canyon has a nearly imperceptible elevation gain. In 5.5 miles you climb approximately 1,000 feet, but you hardly notice it due to its gradual nature.

There are many trails leading out of Telegraph Valley to other locations within the park. As you pedal up the valley road, you see the following connector trails:

Diemer Trail (named after the treatment plant up the hill on the right) leads from Telegraph Valley to the top of South Ridge. It begins on your right 1.5 miles from Carbon Canyon parking lot and climbs steeply up South Ridge. Little Canyon Trail, 1.8 miles beyond Diemer Trail, drops steeply from the South Ridge, connecting with Telegraph Canyon. Continue past this road. Sycamore Trail intersects Telegraph Canyon Trail from the left 0.5 mile beyond Little Canyon Trail. From the top of North Ridge it drops almost 500 feet in a very short distance, making it a downhill to remember. McDermont Trail comes in from the left 0.5 mile

beyond Sycamore Trail and leads up to the top of North Ridge at the very end of the North Ridge Trail. A few hundred yards beyond McDermont Trail is a crossroads of trails leading to various areas of the park. This is the Main Divide area. Marked by a well-used picnic table, it makes a perfect turnaround point or a great rest stop for those continuing to other areas of the park.

What exactly is the Main Divide? It is a north-south ridge, approximately 1,500 feet at its high point, that roughly separates the east and west sides of Chino Hills State Park, composed primarily of ridges and valleys running east-west.

From the Main Divide, if you continue east, you drop steeply toward park headquarters, with no easy way back. At the Divide there is a dirt road to your left (a dead-end). Next to it is the Raptor Ridge singletrack, a fast, seriously fun trail which deposits you at park headquarters. From there it's a grunt up Telegraph Canyon East or South Ridge Trail back to the Main Divide.

Or, from the Main Divide, you can take the footpath on your right marked South Ridge. This is probably the easiest way to get to one of the ridges. Once at the ridge, you can go left and climb San Juan Hill or go right for a rolling descent back to your car.

There are plenty of other options, too. Only three trails are closed to bikes: Gilman Peak (drops from the North Ridge into Telegraph Canyon), Water Canyon (drops from the South Ridge near San Juan Hill into Water Canyon) and Easy Street (parallels part of Telegraph Canyon). They may or may not be signed, but stay off of them.

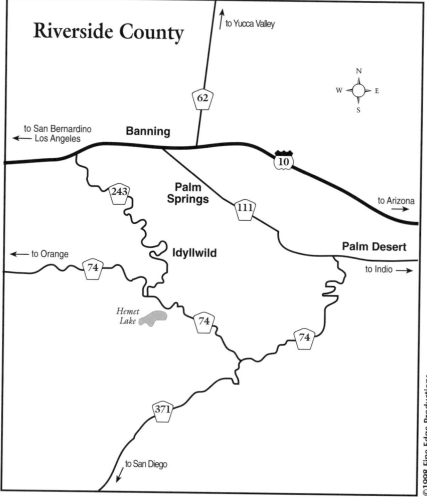

CHAPTER 3

Coachella Valley/
Riverside County

By Paul Maag

Great mountain bike riding can be found in the mountains south of Palm Springs and in the general vicinity of Idyllwild, an area of striking transition from low Colorado desert to high alpine terrain. The region has been known for years to a small group of locals and pro riders, including Cindy Whitehead and other well-known early mountain bikers. The San Jacinto and Santa Rosa Mountains offer some of the finest riding in the nation, especially in the winter months. When the north country is locked in snow and even the Southern California coast is locked in fog and drizzle, Coachella Valley offers clear blue skies and warm temperatures.

The lower Santa Rosa Mountains near Palm Springs are rugged, rolling hills with rocky, loose trail features. Most of the trails were built by equestrians, and many steep trails offer a gripping challenge for the mountain bicyclist. In very dry and hot years, the landscape may look foreboding, something like a moonscape. Springtime riding along the ridges of the Santa Rosa Mountains can be most rewarding with wonderful bursts of desert wildflowers.

The upper Santa Rosa Mountains and the San Jacinto Mountains offer a range of terrain and vegetation from brushy chaparral to cool pine forests. These higher ranges offer spectacular views from many of the trails described in this chapter. The singletrack trails here rate as high as those in Moab, Utah, or California's Sierra Nevada. Best of all, these trails are not crowded with other users. On many of them it is common not to encounter anyone else. This is a true mountain biking paradise!

Make sure you bring lots of water any time you ride in the desert; three jumbo water bottles sometimes last just an hour or two. Many cyclists have found just the insulated water carriers to be beneficial, in addition to the standard two or three water bottles. You can never take too much water on a ride in this kind of climate, especially in warm months.

The weather changes quickly in both the higher mountains and the desert.

The top of Mount Santa Rosa can be 40 degrees cooler than the desert below. Prepare for such changes with appropriate clothing, water, and sun block.

The Coachella Valley Cycling Association (see appendix for phone number) offers weekly rides in the Santa Rosa Mountains. If you are not familiar with the area or are alone, we recommend that you hook up with the group rides. Members can give you knowledge about additional trail routes, times for travel, tips for bettering your skills and some good camaraderie along the trail.

The Santa Rosa Mountains National Scenic Area (SRMNSA) just south of Palm Springs is not all federal land. The SRMNSA is a checkerboard of private, public and Agua Caliente tribal allotee lands. Land management policies and consequently biking access are under constant review.

Please check with the appropriate government office or land owner for current information. See "Agencies, Visitor Centers and Mountain Bike Clubs" in the Appendix.

19 Murray Peak

Distance: 12 miles
Difficulty: Strenuous, very technical
Elevation: 2,000'; high point 2,100'
Ride Type: Loop on dirt roads and trails
Season: Fall, winter, spring
Maps: Cathedral City, Palm Springs

Overview: Murray Peak, the highest peak in the area, gives you one of the finest views of Coachella Valley and southward over Dunn Road. Birds always circle the peak to pick up thermals, and in fact, local hang gliders often fly to the peak to pick up extra lift to continue on to Mt. San Jacinto.

Please be advised to remain on established routes only. Don't start a new trail by riding cross-country in this area. Even though the open, hardpan soil may look inviting, your tracks can damage the fragile desert environment.

Getting There: Take Highway 111 to Cathedral City and turn north on Bankside Drive. Park here.

Route: Ride your bike half a block west on Highway 111 and turn left through the opening in the water control fence. Follow the broken pavement road to its end at an old building pad site. Continue via the singletrack to the left. The singletrack follows 0.5 mile to doubletrack. An old dozer track continues west for 1 mile to the Eagle Canyon Wash. A network of trails here is referred to by locals as the Goat Trails.

From this point, continue west past the wash by portaging your bike down the dry waterfall or by swinging back to Highway 111 by a side trail. To continue west, ride up the dozer track approximately 100 yards and make a hard right. Continue on

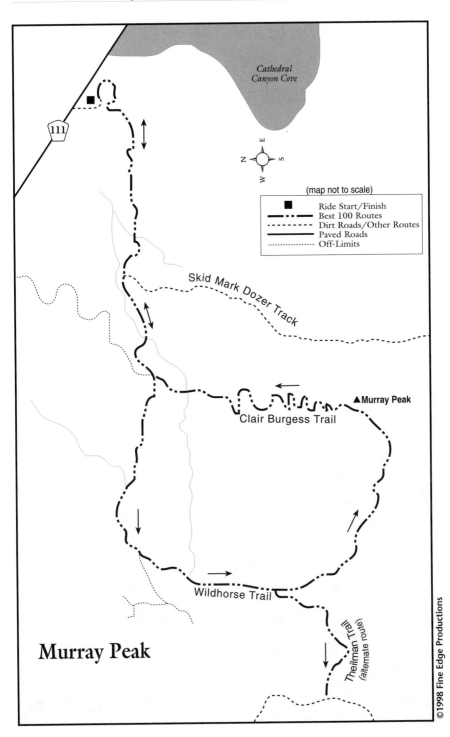

Cathedral
Canyon Cove

(map not to scale)

■   Ride Start/Finish
▬·▬· Best 100 Routes
---- Dirt Roads/Other Routes
―――― Paved Roads
······· Off-Limits

Skid Mark Dozer Track

▲Murray Peak

Clair Burgess Trail

Wildhorse Trail

Theilman Trail
(alternate route)

Murray Peak

©1998 Fine Edge Productions

through a series of turns and grunt climbs 0.3 mile to an intersection. A right turn heads back to Highway 111. Continue straight to explore more trail.

At 3.0 miles you come to a Y in the dozer track. Turn left and ride approximately 125 yards and turn right (west) on another dozer track. The doubletrack becomes singletrack and continues to an intersection. Turn left on the doubletrack and at 100 yards turn right (west) on another doubletrack. Continue riding 0.3 mile and turn left on a side trail (in a dip) and follow the singletrack to the trailhead of the Wildhorse Trail.

There are great views of Palm Springs here, and it is a good place for less ambitious riders to turn around and return the way they came. You could also exit the mountains via the Thielman Trail (unmarked) which heads directly west down the mountains to Palm Springs. This trail is unmaintained and very rocky with difficult drop-offs. Veer left on the doubletrack and head out to the Andreas Hills development and then to Palm Springs. Loop back via city streets to your car.

To reach Murray Peak continue up the steep switchbacks to the cairns on Wildhorse Mountain. Follow down the ridge, which can be lush with wildflowers in the spring, 1.0 mile to cairns marking the Clair Burgess trail. Take the Clair Burgess trail east. It continues east and then south through a series of switches and rollers. You then come to a saddle at the foot of Murray Peak. Ascend the peak via 6 switches. The very pinnacle of Murray Peak is less than 1,500 square feet, giving you the feeling of being on top of the world!

To descend, follow the steep switchbacks down the north face. Most of the beginning switches are difficult to ride without a dab. Don't be embarrassed if you have to get off

A spectacular view from Murray Peak; Dunn Road and Cathedral City in the background.

the bike and turn it around at the tight switchbacks (120° to 170° angles). *Warning!* The trail on the north face of Murray Peak is very steep, especially off the side of the mountain where the trail makes its tight turns. A mistake at the switchbacks can mean a long flying descent without your bike! Try these turns on your bike only if you are an experienced mountain biker with good working brakes and equipment.

At the bottom you intersect the goat trails just east of the Cathedral Canyon Wash. Turn east (right) and proceed back to your starting point.

20 Pinyon/Palm Canyon Loop

Distance: 14.5 miles
Difficulty: Moderate, technical
Elevation: 1,200' gain; 4,600' high point
Ride Type: Loop on singletrack, some pavement
Season: Year-round
Maps: Toro Peak, Butterfly Peak

Overview: This is one of the most enjoyable rides in this chapter. Be sure to bring extra water, especially in summer, and extra tubes or Slime.

Getting There: Drive 20 miles south from Palm Desert on Highway 74. Turn right on Alpine Drive (across from an old gas station and a development on the side of the mountain). Drive down the paved road and park at the end of the pavement.

Route: Ride about 150 yards on the dirt road to a trailhead on your right. It is marked, but it is a difficult sign to read. Take this doubletrack, Palm Canyon Trail, and follow it as it switches down the side of the mountain for a mile.

The doubletrack ends, and you must turn left on a steep singletrack on the left. Continue down this steep trail to a dirt road. Follow the dirt road south (straight ahead) and cross the low barbed-wire fence. Continue on the doubletrack to its end and take the singletrack on the right up the mountain. After a short climb you are on top of a ridge. Continue down the singletrack and through a couple of climbs. Then descend, switching down to Palm Canyon.

When you reach the bottom of the canyon, 5.3 miles, look across Omstot Creek (dry much of the year) and find the trail going up the side of the hill. This is the Pinyon Flats Trail. Follow the trail southeast up to the ridgetop. From here you have great views back toward Palm Canyon and the San Jacinto range.

Continue riding through a number of small washes. At 8.5 miles you come to a fork in the trail. Continue right on the main trail for another 2 miles. Cross Palm Canyon Drive and continue on the singletrack to Pinyon Drive, the entrance to the Pinyon Flats Forest Service Campground. Turn right on Pinyon Drive and ride 300 yards to Highway 74.

Turn right at Highway 74 and head east for 4.3 miles. Turn right on Alpine Drive to your car. Be extremely careful on the highway—it is very narrow and can be scary. If you would like to avoid the cars, bring two vehicles and park one at the Palm Canyon trailhead and one near the campground.

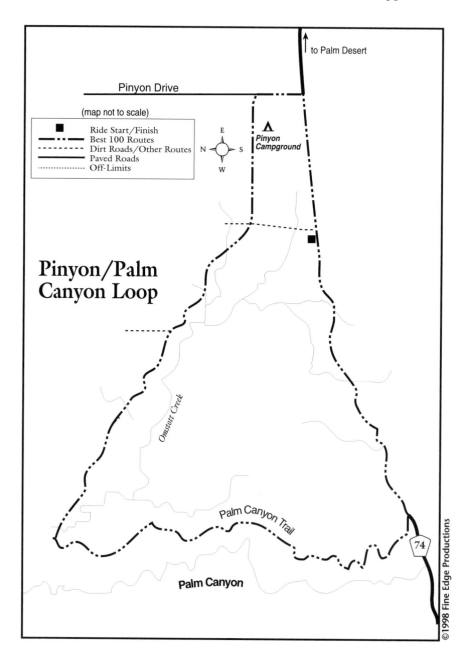

©1998 Fine Edge Productions

21 Pinyon Flats

Distance: 4 to 12 miles
Difficulty: Easy, not technical
Elevation: 500' gain
Ride Type: Loop on dirt roads
Season: All year
Map: Toro Peak

Overview: With lots of flat or nearly flat riding, this is a great area for beginners to practice their skills. The scenery is delightful among the pinyon pines and chaparral. There are constant views of Toro Peak and Mt. San Jacinto. Good camp spots are available at the Pinyon Flats Campground.

Getting There: To reach Pinyon Flats, drive 17.3 miles from Palm Desert on Highway 74 (south) to Palm Canyon Drive. Turn right (north) and park at the dozer pad behind the mailboxes.

Route: Begin by riding your bike 1.8 miles on Palm Canyon Drive before turning right (east) on Alpine Drive. Then ride 0.7 mile and turn left (north) on Jeraboa Street. Ride 0.5 mile to the road end and continue up the twisting doubletrack trail 0.5 mile to its end where you have great views. Ride back down the way you came and continue down Jeraboa Street 1.0 mile and turn left (east) on Pinesmoke Street.

Ride Pinesmoke 0.8 mile and turn right (south) on Stonecrest Street. Ride 0.6 mile and turn right (east) on an unmarked road (Juniper). Then go

Climbing the Clair Burgess Trail (Ride 19); Mount San Jacinto in the background.

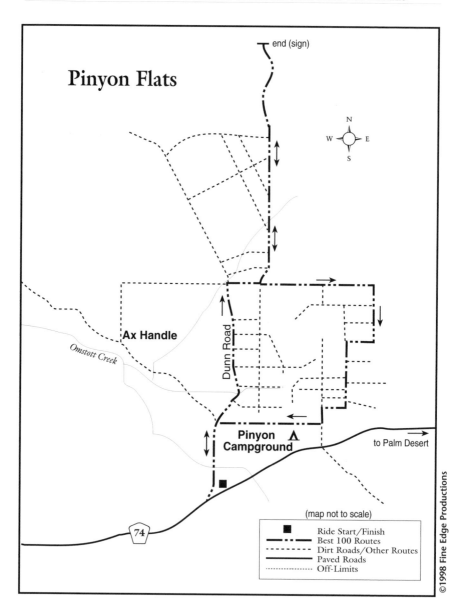

0.3 mile and turn left (south) on Santa Rosa Road. Continue 0.3 mile and turn right (east) on Indio Avenue. Ride 0.2 mile and turn left on Pinyon Drive. It's 0.1 mile to the Pinyon Flats Campground.

Turn right just after the entrance on the Pinyon Flats doubletrack and ride 0.7 mile to Palm Canyon Drive. Turn left (south) and continue 1.0 mile to the parking area.

Other routes abound. Just keep oriented to the location of your vehicle. Happy riding!

Riding in tandem on the approach to the Clair Burgess Trail (Ride 19).

22 Mt. Santa Rosa Road

Distance: 26 miles
Difficulty: Moderate, not technical
Elevation: 4,200' gain; high point 8,700'
Ride Type: Out-and-back on dirt road
Season: Late spring, summer, early fall
Maps: Butterfly Peak, Toro Peak

Overview: Mt. Santa Rosa Road makes for great mountain biking. Long, and with great vistas, it provides the rider with a medium incline. This is also a good climbing ride for those who don't like the radical, yet the downhill can be fast and wide open.

Getting There: Drive 18 miles from Palm Desert on Highway 74 and turn left on Mt. Santa Rosa Road.

There is limited parking here or you can park 200 yards up the road in a turnout.

Route: Begin riding up the road. Views will become apparent at about 1.0 mile as you look north toward Haystack Mountain and Mt. San Jacinto in the distance. Continue riding the road to reach a spring-fed creek and pine trees at 4.0 miles, a good resting spot. The road then begins to ascend the mountain in a series of switchbacks. At 8.0 miles you reach a short turnoff to Santa Rosa Spring, a good place to fill your water bottles. This is usually the point where intermediate riders start the return to their car.

Continue up the road until you reach viewpoints at 9.0 miles, just after a turnout to a communication tower. Pinyon Flat, Mt. San Jacinto and even Mt. San Gorgonio can be seen from here, as well as the switchback logging road far below. Continue riding past the upper Mt. Santa Rosa Camp-ground. At 12.0 miles, take the nar-rower and rocky road to the right, reaching a gate at 12.8 miles. Con-tinue as far as you can ride or until you reach the summit of Toro Peak which has a communication tower on top. Here, at 8,716 feet elevation and 13 miles out, you have a tremendous 360-degree view over all of Southern California—truly one of the finest viewpoints in all of the Southland.

To return to your car, go back the way you came being careful to watch your speed. On some weekends there are many cars and trucks on this road. Watch for them!

23 Sawmill Trail

Distance: 22.5 miles
Difficulty: Strenuous, technical
Elevation: 4,000' gain; 8,000' high point
Ride Type: Loop on pavement, dirt roads and singletrack
Season: Late spring, summer, fall
Maps: Butterfly Peak, Toro Peak

Overview: This is definitely the epic ride of the chapter. For many years locals wanted a connector trail between two roads—Mt. Santa Rosa Road and Sawmill Road—on Santa Rosa Mountain. Thanks to a grant from Shimano America, the United States Forest Service, and funds from Riverside County, the dream trail was constructed in 1997.

Getting There: Drive 16.5 miles from Palm Desert to Pinyon Drive and turn right. Park along the road across from the Forest Service camp-ground. You may want to bring a second car for this next leg of the route to avoid riding on Highway 74 since it is extremely narrow with fast moving vehicular traffic. Ride or drive 3 miles west (right) on the highway and turn left on Santa Rosa Road.

Route: Begin by riding Santa Rosa Road for 9 miles (see previous ride description). At 9 miles there's a road on your left with a cable across it. The Sawmill singletrack is 50 feet to the right of this road. The road takes a turn right at this intersection. As of June 1997, the trail had not yet been marked. If you miss it, you start see-ing good views of Coachella Valley and the desert below.

Now starts the best part of the ride. Descend the singletrack, follow-ing through very tight switchback

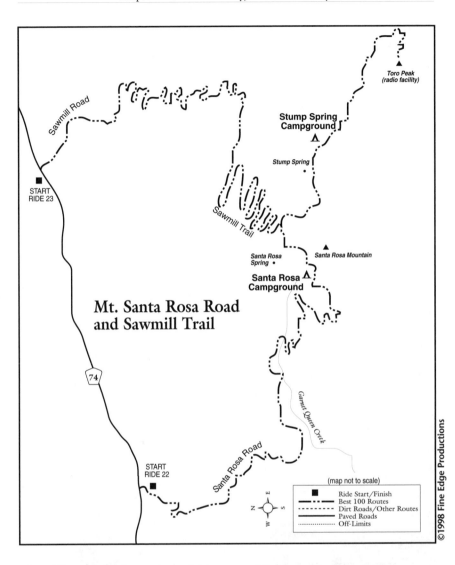

Sawmill Road

START
RIDE 23

Sawmill Trail

Mt. Santa Rosa Road
and Sawmill Trail

74

Toro Peak
(radio facility)

Stump Spring
Campground

Stump Spring

Santa Rosa
Spring

Santa Rosa Mountain

Santa Rosa
Campground

Garnet Queen Creek

START
RIDE 22

Santa Rosa Road

(map not to scale)

■ Ride Start/Finish
–··–·· Best 100 Routes
········ Dirt Roads/Other Routes
——— Paved Roads
········· Off-Limits

© 1998 Fine Edge Productions

turns. The trail continues through big trees and some great views. At 11.5 miles you cross a little creek, a good spot to stop.

Continue on into chaparral and out to a doubletrack. Turn right (east) and follow the rocky, rolling old fire track through some tough, short climbs to a muddy little stream crossing and a view of an old chimney. Continue down the road 6 miles to Highway 74. Be careful here on the old Sawmill Road. It is extremely rocky and fast—a good place for dual suspension. If you don't have it, make it easy on yourself and take a break halfway down.

You make a short, sandy climb at the end of Sawmill Road. Turn left on Highway 74 and pedal 0.5 mile to Pinyon Drive. Turn right to your car. Now that's a mountain bike ride!

24 Thomas Mountain Loop

Distance: 14 miles
Difficulty: Moderate, somewhat technical
Elevation: 1,700' gain; high point 6,200'
Ride Type: Loop on dirt road and singletrack
Season: Spring, summer; fall as snow permits
Maps: Anza, Butterfly Peak

Overview: This is one of the most popular rides in the San Jacinto mountain area. It offers a moderate climb along a Forest Service road and a wonderful 5.5-mile descent from Thomas Mountain via great singletrack.

Getting There: Drive 23 miles from Palm Desert on State Highway 74 and turn left (west) on Thomas Mountain Road.

From Idyllwild, go 12 miles on State Highway 74 (approximately 3 miles past Lake Hemet) and turn right (west) on Thomas Mountain Road. Park here.

Route: Ride on the paved road two long city blocks and turn left on Hop Patch Springs Road. Continue riding on pavement until it turns into a well graded dirt road. The road continues on flat and then rolling terrain through sugar pines. It then begins a relatively short but aerobic climb to a vista overlooking the town of Anza to the west. This is a good place to turn around if you find the first climb very difficult.

The entire Coachella Valley can be seen from Murray Peak (Ride 19).

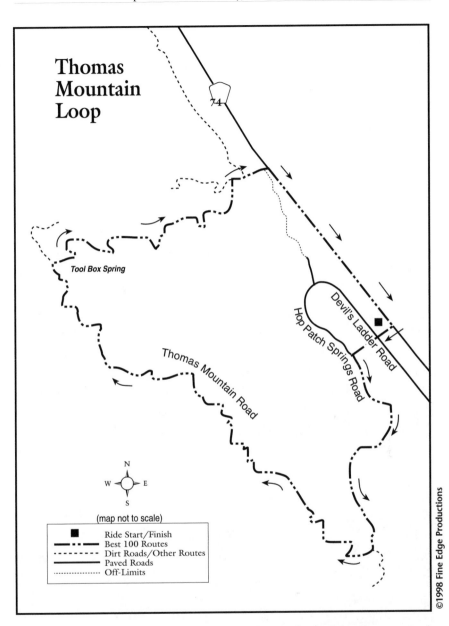

Thomas Mountain Loop

Tool Box Spring

Devil's Ladder Road

Hop Patch Springs Road

Thomas Mountain Road

N
W — E
S

(map not to scale)

■   Ride Start/Finish
━ ·· ━   Best 100 Routes
‑ ‑ ‑ ‑   Dirt Roads/Other Routes
━━━━   Paved Roads
·········· Off-Limits

©1998 Fine Edge Productions

The road now turns due north and continues a moderate but constant climb through chaparral with occasional shade. Watch for views of the Anza Valley to the west and the San Jacinto ridge line to the north. Toro Peak can be seen from behind to the south. At 5.0 miles you reach Tool Box Springs Camp among tall pine trees. Turn right and follow the spur road downhill to Tool Box Spring—a good place to fill water bottles.

Ride north on the road 100 yards

to its end to start the Ramona Trail (unmarked). Watch for some short drop-offs at the beginning (keep that weight back). The trail starts by switchbacking through sugar pines and alder. This is singletrack paradise! Some of the switchbacks are technical, but with a little brake action you can make them!

The trail descends into chaparral without shade as it becomes rockier. Some turns are sharp with lots of small boulders and rock water bars. Continue along more sandy trail on a ridge line and out to the trail end. Follow the primitive dirt road east to State Highway 74, making sure you close the gate.

Turn right on the highway and follow it 3.5 miles. Turn right on Thomas Mountain Road and return to your vehicle.

The primitive backcountry of Palm Canyon Trail (Ride 20) provides a wonderful ride.

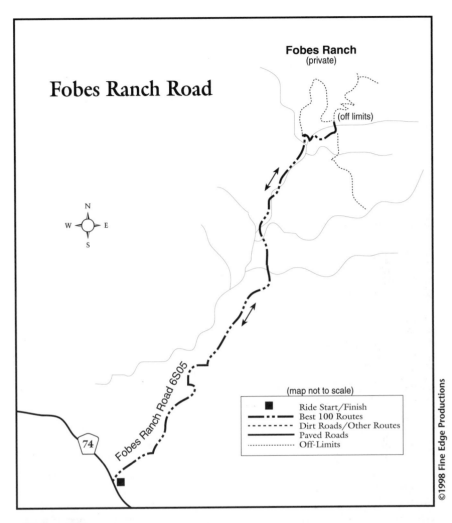

Fobes Ranch Road

Fobes Ranch
(private)

(off limits)

Fobes Ranch Road 6S05

74

(map not to scale)

■ Ride Start/Finish
–··–··– Best 100 Routes
--------- Dirt Roads/Other Routes
Paved Roads
················· Off-Limits

©1998 Fine Edge Productions

25 Fobes Ranch Road

Distance: 10 miles
Difficulty: Moderate, not technical
Elevation: 800' gain/loss
Ride Type: Out-and-back on dirt road
Season: Spring, summer; fall as snow permits
Maps: Idyllwild, Palm View Peak

Overview: This is a great ride for views of Garner Valley and the vast desert of Coachella Valley.

Getting There: To reach the trailhead drive 26 miles from Palm Desert on State Highway 74 and turn right (east) on Fobes Ranch Road (dirt).

From Idyllwild, drive 9.5 miles on State Highway 74 to the turnoff. Park at the beginning of the dirt road.

Route: Ride 0.3 mile and veer left at the intersection. Continue on, always taking a look back at Thomas Mountain and Mt. San Jacinto. The road continues as a medium climb on hard pack dirt for 4 miles. Turn right on the spur road (do not take the road to Fobes Ranch—*private property*) and follow it to another intersection in 0.75 mile. As you approach the road's end, you have views of Garner Valley, Thomas Mountain, and Mt. San Jacinto. A singletrack takes off 400 feet from here, but it is closed to bikes.

To return to your vehicle, retrace your route.

26 Black Mountain Road

Distance: 12 to 24 miles
Difficulty: Moderate, not technical
Elevation: 2,000' gain; 7,600' high point
Ride Type: Out-and-back on dirt road
Season: Late spring, summer, early fall
Maps: Lake Fulmor, San Jacinto Peak

Overview: Black Mountain Road is an excellent ride in beautiful forest, a good pick when other areas are too hot for riding since there is shade for the majority of the route. The road gains 2,000 feet in a short 5 miles. It is well constructed, with switchbacks up the side of the mountain with a good constant grade. Some of the road has been paved to reduce dust from motorized vehicles to the advantage of cyclists. The descent is fast and furious but don't forget that there are vehicles on the road! The views are spectacular from about 6.5 miles. Mt. San Gorgonio looks magnified from the Black Mountain Rim.

Getting There: Drive State Highway 243 from Banning 18 miles or drive 8 miles north of Idyllwild, reaching a wide dirt turnout with a sign that reads *Black Mountain Road 5.5 miles.* Park here.

Route: Start your ride through cool forest with partial sun and intermixed dirt and paved road. The road switches constantly, but the climb is never too extreme. At 2.5 miles you have good views toward the southeast and the city of Idyllwild. You also get good views of the east face of Mt. San Jacinto and Taquitz Peak.

Keep on, and soon you reach Cinco Poses Spring, a good place to fill water bottles with ice cold mountain water. At 5 miles you come to the turnoff to Boulder Basin Campground and Black Mountain Fire Lookout—a pleasant side trip for spectacular views.

Continue on past this junction for your first downhill, a welcome relief from the climb. You ride up and down through old forest past Black Mountain Group Camp. At 6 miles you reach the Black Mountain vista point and some of the most fantastic

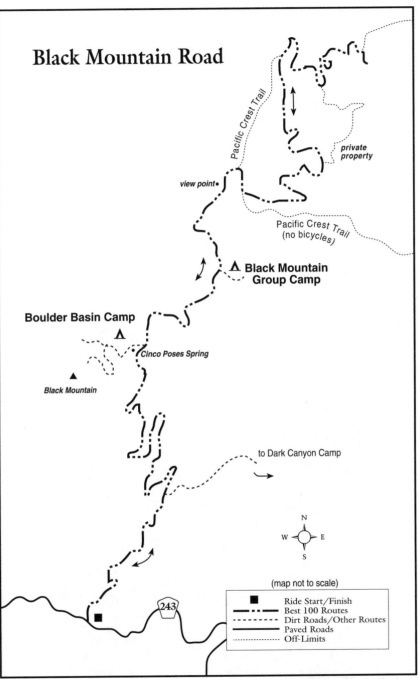

Black Mountain Road

Pacific Crest Trail

private property

view point•

Pacific Crest Trail (no bicycles)

△ **Black Mountain Group Camp**

Boulder Basin Camp

△

•*Cinco Poses Spring*

▲

Black Mountain

to Dark Canyon Camp

N
W —◆— E
S

(map not to scale)

243

■   Ride Start/Finish
▬▬   Best 100 Routes
----   Dirt Roads/Other Routes
——   Paved Roads
········   Off-Limits

©1998 Fine Edge Productions

views of Mt. San Gorgonio and Banning Pass. On very clear days Mt. Wilson and Mt. Baldy can easily be seen. This is a good place to turn around if you feel tired from the climb. The return down the road is very fast. Approach the switchback turns with caution. Weekend motorized traffic can be a hazard.

Those who don't turn back here can continue past the lookout and start a slow descent on the Black Mountain Rim, passing the Pacific Crest Trail in 0.75 mile (no bikes allowed). Follow the road downhill, crossing many small seeps, and heading out to a small, sloping valley. The road switches on hardpack and soft dusty soil to the road end and the start of the north section of the Pacific Crest Trail at 6,400 feet (mile 10). To return, follow the road back up to the rim and out to your starting point at State Highway 243.

Water crossing on the upper Palm Canyon Trail (Ride 20) after heavy winter rains.

CHAPTER 4

San Bernardino Mountains

By Robert Shipley and Allen Thibault

The San Bernardino Mountains are a truly wonderful playground, and the mountain bike has given us access to almost every stream and peak, meadow and trail sprinkled throughout the magnificent San Bernardino National Forest. Discover for yourself what thousands of Native Americans, prospectors, ranchers, hikers and vacationers have known for countless decades—the call to explore.

You'll come to know all types of terrain from the high desert at 3,500 feet to spectacular mountain peaks above 9,000 feet. You'll amble along rivers, pedal around high mountain lakes, splash across countless streams, clamber up to active fire lookout towers, whisper along more than 40 miles of singletrack and ponder dozens upon dozens of breathtaking vistas.

The principal riding areas in this chapter are around Silverwood Lake, Big Bear Lake and along the Santa Ana River Canyon north of Angelus Oaks. Along the western edge of this national forest is Silverwood Lake State Park, with a casual paved bike path bordering half its shoreline. There are excellent recreational opportunities here for the entire family, including swimming, boating, fishing, hiking, picnicking and of course, memorable bike riding.

By far the most popular mountain biking area in the entire forest lies around Big Bear Lake. On the north side of the lake is the ghost town of Holcomb Valley and the quaint community of Fawnskin. Butler Peak and Snow Slide Road offer challenges and views you won't forget. On the south side of the lake, you have to experience the no-effort ride on the chair lift to the top of Snow Summit! Once you get to Skyline Road you gain access to mile after mile of incomparable roller coaster riding.

If you lust for real trail riding, you'll find the longest singletrack in the forest along the Santa Ana River Canyon. You can choose among five options for this ride, with skill levels from beginner to advanced gonzo. From tight hairpins clinging to sheer cliffs to deep river crossings, you'll know you've tested your

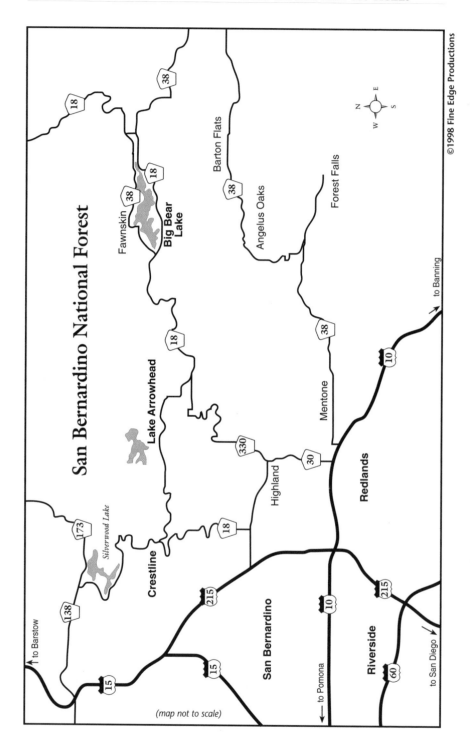

San Bernardino National Forest

©1998 Fine Edge Productions

(map not to scale)

abilities and will be hot to tell the disbelievers back home of your exploits.

If you'd like to camp on your vacation, there are numerous campgrounds in the forest. Among the most convenient are Barton Flats, Coldbrook, Green Valley, Hanna Flats, Holcomb Valley, Pineknot, San Gorgonio, Serrano and South Fork. Fees range from $6 to $15. Serrano is the only campground with showers. For a complete listing, see the American Automobile Association (AAA) map of Central and Southern California Camping.

27 Silverwood Lake Bike Path

Distance: 12.5 miles
Difficulty: Easy, not technical
Elevation: 3,400'
Ride Type: Paved bike path, out-and-back
Season: Spring, summer, fall
Map: Silverwood Lake

Overview: This is an excellent destination for the entire family because of the extensive recreational facilities at the lake shore. You can windsurf, swim, fish, launch your own boat or just walk the dog. There is something here for everyone. In fact, it's so popular, I recommend you do this ride before Memorial Day or well after Labor Day, and avoid the weekend crowds in particular.

A roller coaster, paved, smooth (sort of), two-lane bike path follows the shore. In some spots the path is badly eroded, making it more challenging as well as unsuitable for the skinny tired bikes for which it was probably first built. Unfortunately, the path doesn't circle the lake; this is an out-and-back ride. For more experienced riders, there is a rather technical, sometimes ugly singletrack at the end of the paved path on the north side of the lake. Beginners need not apply (at least for the dirt part).

Getting There: Take I-15 north of San Bernardino to Highway 138 east

to Silverwood Lake Park entrance. There's a day use fee ($6/car) but it's well worth the price. Plan on taking a picnic, arriving early and making a full day of the outing. There's water available at the picnic area. Nearest services are in Crestline or Summit. Drive to Lot #1. Park and ride to the bike path, which goes in both directions around the lake.

Route: This bike route takes you east, returns you to the lot, heads west and returns again to the lot. You can find the path by heading toward the lake behind the restrooms—turn right beyond the boat launch and continue past the east edge of the parking lot. You'll see a paved path climbing up the slope.

After 0.6 mile of steep climbing you come to a junction and a small restroom building. Turn left up the slope to the gate. This is a typical gate designed to allow passage of bikes (and people). A lot of people don't like to use this gate so they have worn a path around it. The choice is yours.

Turn left and coast down the hill to another gate. The twisting, swooping path crosses numerous wooden bridges as it hugs the shoreline. Through the trees you can catch fleeting glimpses of ducks, gulls, bald eagles in the winter, and people fishing from boats and along shore.

At 2.1 miles the path crosses a steel grate and concrete apron where the East Fork of the West Fork of the Mojave River enters the lake basin. The path loops to the north of the lake and heads west. Move through (or around) another gate at 2.3 miles, go up onto the paved road (not down to the dirt path to the left of the gate) and ride east. At 2.5 miles there is another restroom, a sign indicating Serrano Beach, and the return of the bike path just beyond a wood bridge.

Rolling fire roads abound near Big Bear Lake.

After 3.0 miles the paved portion of the path ends. Beginners should turn around here and retrace their route. Experienced riders can elect to continue on the singletrack leading off the end of the cul-de-sac. But if you get queasy clinging to sheer drop-offs, don't bother. For about 0.3 mile the path is rideable, but barely, in spots. It gradually climbs up the face of the slope, giving you a progressively better view of the lake. This path looks for all the world like a burro track and it probably should have stayed that way. But gonzo bike riders being what they are . . .

At 5.5 miles (if you didn't ride the singletrack) turn right at the top of the paved road to return through the locked gate. If you miss this turn you can still find your way back to your car by following the road down toward the lake. At 5.8 miles you will be back to your car.

You can end your cycling here, but if you have the time and energy for more, continue west on the bike path as it winds its way through several picnic areas.

After the path dumps you into

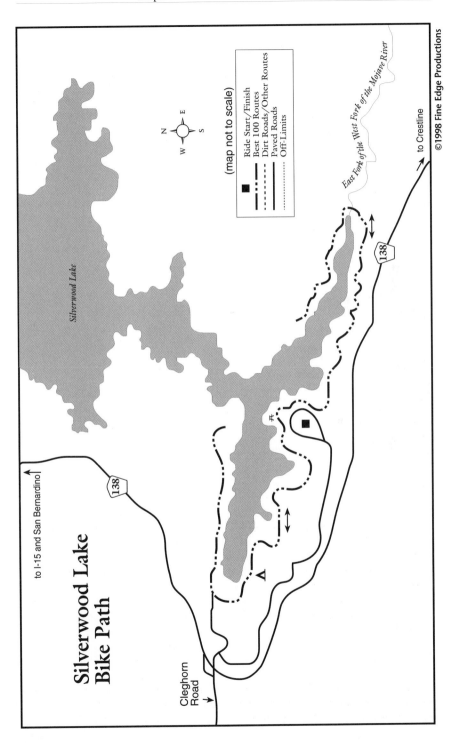

Silverwood Lake
Bike Path

(map not to scale)

■ Ride Start/Finish
━━ Best 100 Routes
-·-·- Dirt Roads/Other Routes
━━ Paved Roads
······ Off-Limits

Silverwood Lake

East Fork of the West Fork of the Mojave River

to I-15 and San Bernardino

to Crestline

Cleghorn Road

©1998 Fine Edge Productions

another parking lot, it turns right through a locked gate. Follow the path down and then up a slope to a Y. Take the left branch and continue up the hill to an attractive, somewhat remote campground. The path continues just a few feet to the right of where you enter the lot. Take this down the hill, around the campground back toward the lake. At the gate, turn right and head east. You can take the bike path on the far side of the road or ride the road to the picnic and beach area.

At the next parking lot take the path along the beach and then through the next locked gate up the side of the hill to the overlook. This is the other end of the paved bike path. The Los Animas hiking trail takes off from this cul-de-sac. Bicycles are not permitted on this trail.

Turn around and retrace your route. Go straight through the first gate, turn left to go through the second gate and stay to your left on the path as it hugs the shoreline. At 12.5 miles you are back at your car.

28 Pilot Rock/Miller Canyon

Distance: 11.8 miles
Difficulty: Moderately strenuous, mildly technical
Elevation: Start/end 3,400'; 340' gain/loss
Ride Type: Loop on fire roads
Season: Spring, summer, fall
Maps: Silverwood Lake, Lake Arrowhead

Overview: Almost all of the climbing on this ride occurs during the first 3 miles. The rest of the ride roller coasters in a general descent back to the start. There are a few challenging sections but nothing really difficult or technical. *Caution:* These roads tend to be popular with motorcycle riders and 4WDs, so you may want to avoid summer weekends. It can get pretty warm here in the middle of summer, too, so be sure to bring at least 2 water bottles and food on this ride. An even safer plan is to avoid it altogether during the heat of the summer between Memorial Day and Labor Day.

Getting There: From I-15 north of San Bernardino, take Highway 138 to Silverwood Lake. Continue east past

the park entrance staying on 138 to the Miller Canyon Unit turnoff and go down to the entrance (fee station) to the picnic area. There is an entry fee. The entrance to the conservation camp is to the right. Park here. Water is available at Silverwood Lake beach/picnic area. The nearest services are in Crestline or Summit Valley.

Route: Ride back up the paved road 0.1 mile and turn left on Miller Canyon Road (if you get all the way to the highway, you went too far). The road follows the south boundary of the correctional facility (minimum security prison), crosses Houston Creek and ends at the junction of 2N36 and 2N37 (0.9 mile from start). Take 2N36 to the left. At 2.9 miles, 2N36 ends at 2N33. Take the

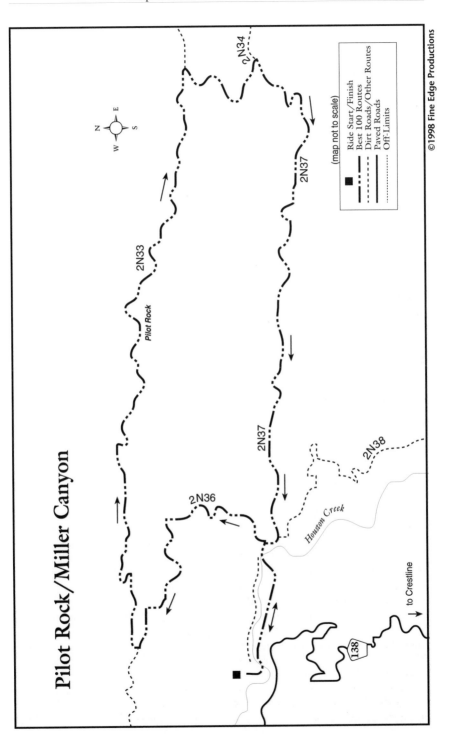

Pilot Rock/Miller Canyon

(map not to scale)

Ride Start/Finish
Best 100 Routes
Dirt Roads/Other Routes
Paved Roads
Off-Limits

2N34

2N37

2N33

Pilot Rock

2N37

2N38

2N36

Houston Creek

to Crestline

138

©1998 Fine Edge Productions

right branch of the junction heading east.

There are a few steep, technical sections but they are short and fun. The views of the Mojave River basin, Hesperia and Silverwood Lake are spectacular. Take time to stop and gaze down on the high desert.

At 4.1 miles 2N17X takes off to the left. Continue past this side road. You come to a gate at 6.7 miles, just before the junction of 2N33 and 2N34. Turn right onto 2N34 to ride an enjoyable rolling road through pines, oak, sage, and manzanita. At

7.3 miles turn right again onto 2N37. This is Miller Canyon Road. There are some short, steep, winding, rocky sections here that will challenge beginners. Take it slowly and you'll have no problem. After 8.7 miles you come to a junction where you take the right branch down the hill.

At the junction of 2N37 and 2N38 turn right for 0.1 mile to the junction of 2N37 and 2N36. Turn left onto the road you came in on. Continue past the conservation camp to the pavement. Turn right and ride down the hill back to your car.

29 Keller Peak/ National Children's Forest

Distance: 12.5 miles
Difficulty: Moderate only because of the long climb, not technical
Elevation: Start 6,080'; gain/loss 1,882'
Ride Type: Out-and-back on paved road and dirt fire road
Season: Spring, summer, fall
Map: Keller Peak

Overview: This out-and-back ride climbs a steep, smooth, paved, two-lane road from 6,000 feet to 7,882 feet at the top of Keller Peak. In some spots the road is just wide enough for two cars to pass, so be sure to stay to the right, especially on the curves. The view from the peak is breathtaking and easily worth the climb, not to mention the white-knuckle swooping downhill back to your car. Another wonderful part of this ride is the National Children's Forest, a unique forest-fire study area dedicated to thousands of children nationwide who have helped reforest our country's burned timber. No water is available at the ride start. Nearest services are in Running Springs.

Getting There: From Highway 18 at the east end of Running Springs, turn right onto 1N96. After 0.2 mile there are two small parking areas. Park in one of these. *Note:* If you don't want to bicycle up the paved road to the beginning of the dirt section below the peak, drive the 4.2 miles to the intersection described in the next paragraph to begin your bike ride.

Route: Begin your climb from the parking lots. At 2.5 miles there's a turnoff to a primitive campground. You reach the junction to Keller Peak at 4.2 miles. Turn to the right for the dirt road climb to the lookout tower. The road levels out around 5.4 miles and you get a fantastic view of the

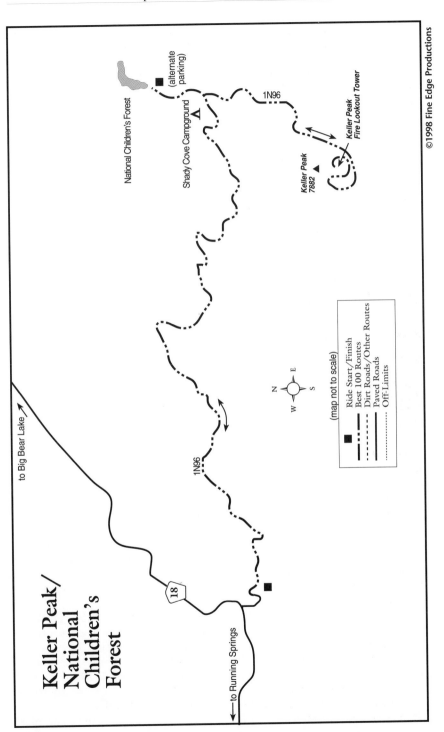

Keller Peak/
National
Children's
Forest

to Big Bear Lake

to Running Springs

18

1N96

National Children's Forest

(alternate parking)

Shady Cove Campground

1N96

Keller Peak
7882

Keller Peak
Fire Lookout Tower

(map not to scale)

N
W   E
S

Ride Start/Finish
Best 100 Routes
Dirt Roads/Other Routes
Paved Roads
Off-Limits

©1998 Fine Edge Productions

Santa Ana River basin below and the San Bernardino/Redlands/ Yucaipa areas farther to the southwest. You can also see the Morton Peak fire lookout above Mentone. Near the Santa Ana River you can see miles and miles of good dirt roads snaking along the slopes.

The road continues west to wind around the peak, climbing again to the top, 6.0 miles from the start of the ride. In addition to the fire lookout, you can see a vast array of broadcasting towers and microwave antennae bristling from the massive boulders. If the gate to the fire lookout tower is open, ride up to the base of the tower, park your bike, climb the stairs and say hi to the ranger. He or she will probably give you a short, fascinating tour of the tower and explain what a fire lookout does.

From this vantage point you can see the top of the chairlift at Snow Valley, Lake Silverwood to the west, and the towns of Hesperia and Apple Valley to the north.

When you've finished your snack and explored the peak, ride back down the dirt road to the junction and turn right. Ride 0.2 mile up a short hill to the parking lot of the National Children's Forest. Park your bike and take the short walk along the Phoenix Trail; this is an excellent interpretive tour through a once-burned forest. Under no circumstances may you ride your bike on the narrow, paved walking path. One of the reasons is that many blind people walk this interpretive trail and the sound of a bike close to them could be frightening. After your walk, collect your bike and return down the hill to your car.

30 Snow Slide Road/Green Valley Lake with Butler Peak Option

Distance: 30.4 miles; Butler Peak adds about 6 miles
Difficulty: Strenuous, not technical
Elevation: Start/end 6,744', high point 7,520'; Butler Peak 8,535'
Ride Type: Out-and-back with little loop on fire roads
Season: Spring, summer, fall
Maps: Keller Peak, Butler Peak, Fawnskin

Overview: On this ride you crank and coast through hilly, heavily forested, remote country and cross several streams trickling from springs. It's a wonderful forest jaunt that takes you from one quaint little town (Fawnskin) to another (Green Valley Lake).

You also have the option of climbing to Butler Peak. The highlight of this option is the fabulous view from the fire lookout on top.

Getting There: Park behind Fawn

Lodge in the town of Fawnskin (on Highway 38 on the north shore of Big Bear Lake). The lodge is on Navajo Street across from the fire station.

Route: Turn left onto Navajo Street. Then turn right, heading northwest, onto Rim of the World Drive in front of the State of California fire station. The road is paved and begins climbing. At 0.5 mile the road turns to dirt and 3N14 begins. It is open to vehicles so be sure to stay to the right,

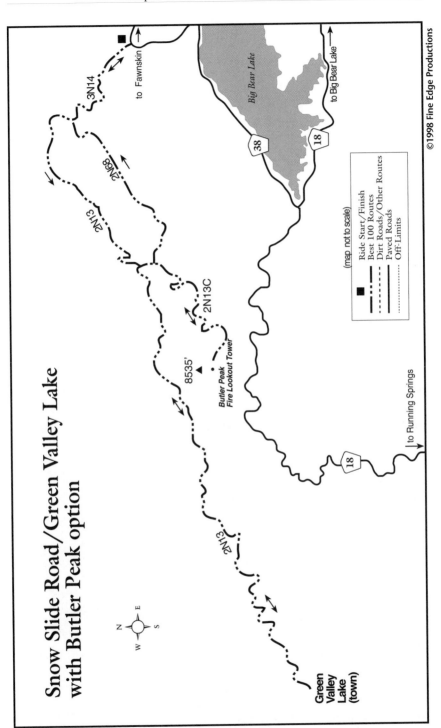

Snow Slide Road/Green Valley Lake with Butler Peak option

©1998 Fine Edge Productions

especially as you approach the curves.

Continue climbing. After 1.4 miles you come to the junction of 3N14 and 2N68. Stay to the right on 3N14 toward the YMCA Camp Whittle. At 1.8 miles 3N12 branches to the right but you continue on 3N14. Immediately after the driveway into Camp Whittle take 2N13 to the left. Continue on through the open gate and stay on 2N13 past the junction with 2N13A. Continue on 2N13, ignoring the lesser trails branching off to the left. The road is in good condition and allows a brisk ride through the undulating terrain. As you pass unmarked junctions with lesser roads, continue on the more heavily-traveled road. At 4.0 miles, 2N13C cuts to the left.

Butler Peak option: If you're not up for the whole ride to Green Valley Lake, you can turn left on 2N13C through the open gate and begin the long, rocky climb to Butler Peak. At the junction with 2N68Y stay right on 2N13C. After almost 3 miles of climbing you round a bend to be greeted by a breathtaking view of the Inland Empire—more than 7,000 feet below and 30 miles away—as well as the slopes of Snow Valley near Running Springs and Keller Peak to the south.

Around the next bend you suddenly see your destination: the fire lookout tower precariously perched atop a massive rock outcropping. The road gets steep and rocky, and it may be rutted. Ride past a spur off to the left and continue up to the parking area below the tower.

Park your bike. Please observe and respect the notice about visitors before you hike up the short trail (right side of the propane tank) to the tower. On the tower you have an absolutely fabulous view of Keller Peak to the south, Mt. Baldy in the San Gabriels to the west, San Gorgonio Mountain to the southeast, Big Bear Lake, Silverwood Lake, Apple Valley and (if the air is clear) Lake Perris. If you're shaky about heights, you may not want to climb up here. Imagine what it must have taken to build this tower on these rocks some 60 years ago.

Return back down to the junction and turn right onto 2N68Y at 9.6 miles. Turn left onto 2N68, continue past Graves Peak Group Camp and pass 2N80. At 3N14 turn right to coast back down to your car. This makes about a 14-mile loop.

If you want to continue to Green Valley Lake, from the junction of 2N13 and 2N13C stay right on

Enjoying a well-earned descent.

Tony Quiroz

2N13 as it becomes steep, a bit rocky and eroded, then level and delightful.

At 5.6 miles you crest a summit to view Mt. Baldy in the San Gabriel Mountains some 45 miles to the west and Cajon Canyon closer in. You begin a long, rocky, sandy descent, crossing Avalanche Spring and then climbing a short, steep grade through stands of Douglas fir and ponderosa pines.

After crossing Snow Slide summit you begin the challenging drop toward Green Valley Lake at 6.8 miles. At 8.0 miles continue straight past a spur to the right, then onto 2 miles of outstanding roller coaster riding through the forest. At 10 miles 2N13I cuts hard to the right and 2N13 curves left. Take a break and go straight ahead up a short slope to an overlook near an old concrete water tank. Have a drink and a snack as you survey the hills and canyons around you. Look back along the road that brought you here and contemplate your achievement.

Scoot back down to 2N13 and continue southwest. At 10.6 miles, enter a clearing where Craft Peak, Snow Slide and Middle Earth cross-country ski trailheads begin. Turn right and ride down the road among the massive ponderosas to the junction with 2N54 at 10.9 miles. Stay to the left on 2N13 for another 0.7 mile where you hit the pavement of Green Valley Road. Go right again and coast into the town of Green Valley Lake.

This is your turnaround point, but first take time to explore the town. Park your bike and pop into the Green Valley Lake Market across from the lake for a drink and snack. After your rest, head back up the paved road past the Lodge Steak House. Make a left turn onto 2N13 (dirt) and toward Fawnskin just under 15 miles away. Stay right at the junction with 2N54, left at the ski trailhead area (2N13), right at the junction below the concrete water tank.

When you get back to the junction of 2N13 and 2N13C, turn right on 2N13C. You can head back to your car by riding through the gate and turning left onto 2N68Y. Or, you can stay on 2N13C and make the climb to Butler Peak. (See the Butler Peak option described earlier.)

To return to your car, from 2N68Y turn left onto 2N68. Continue past Graves Peak Group Camp and pass 2N80. At 3N14 turn right to coast back into Fawnskin.

31 Big Bear Lake Circuit

Distance: 18 miles
Difficulty: Easy, not technical
Elevation: Start/end 6,800'; 80' gain
Ride Type: Loop on highway and paved bike path
Season: Late spring, summer, fall
Maps: Big Bear Lake, Fawnskin

Overview: You certainly don't need a mountain bike for this ride, but if you do use one, pump your tires to their maximum rated pressure to minimize your effort. This pleasant 18-mile ride takes you into part of the business district of Big Bear Lake, through the intriguing residential districts of the south shore and Boulder Bay, to Fawnskin, and on a delightful bike path along the north shore. Summer weekend traffic tends to be heavy but not fast. Be sure to stop in the rustic town of Fawnskin for a food and drink break.

Getting There: Drive to Big Bear Lake on Highway 18 from Running Springs or on Highway 38 from Angelus Oaks. Park in the Vons shopping center at the east end of the town of Big Bear Lake on Highway 18. There are two bike shops on the route if you need supplies—Big Bear Bikes and Bear Valley Bikes.

Route: From the Vons parking lot, turn right onto Big Bear Boulevard heading west. At the third signal, continue straight onto Lakeview Drive (Big Bear Boulevard turns left at this signal and heads into the main business district). Turn right, staying on Lakeview Drive. Turn left at Edgemoor Drive, right on Big Bear Boulevard, and left onto Cienega Road, which becomes Waterview Drive. Continue through this peaceful residential district, where you can see that most of the homes on your left have appealing lake views.

Turn left on Blue Jay Road, right on Catbird Lane, left on Landing Road, right on Blue Jay Road, and right on Big Bear Boulevard. This portion takes you through the neighborhood called Boulder Bay, and from the rock formations you'll see why. Now you enter the only hilly part of this ride. The climb is short, the road is winding, and there may be a good bit of traffic here. Then

the road drops back down to the lake and crosses the dam. At the junction with Highway 38 turn right.

You are now heading east. If it is afternoon you will probably be pushed along by a delightful tail wind. The road winds along the north shore of Big Bear Lake, affording you a wonderful view of San Bernardino peak to your right. If it is early in the year there will probably be a lot of snow on the mountains. The brisk tail wind, the gorgeous lake and the snow-covered mountains in the distance make for nearly ideal cycling.

Next you cruise through picturesque little Fawnskin, a fine spot for "refueling." There are several places to eat, including a restaurant and a small grocery. You can also picnic on the fire station lawn and use the restroom.

The ride continues east on Highway 38. Watch for the North Shore turnoff. Turn right on North Shore Drive toward the observatory. After about one block turn left onto the bikeway.

This is a Class 1 paved bikeway. It winds through the trees with a large picnic area and campground on your left and the lake on your right. The bikeway crosses the entrance to the Serrano Campground, then it crosses the highway, so watch for traffic. It then follows the lake shore in a curving, roller coaster ride for several miles. The bikeway ends across from the entrance to the North Shore Elementary School. Turn right on Standfield Cutoff and cross the landfill at the east end of Big Bear Lake. Turn right on Big Bear Boulevard and into the town of Big Bear Lake. Continue on to the parking lot and your car.

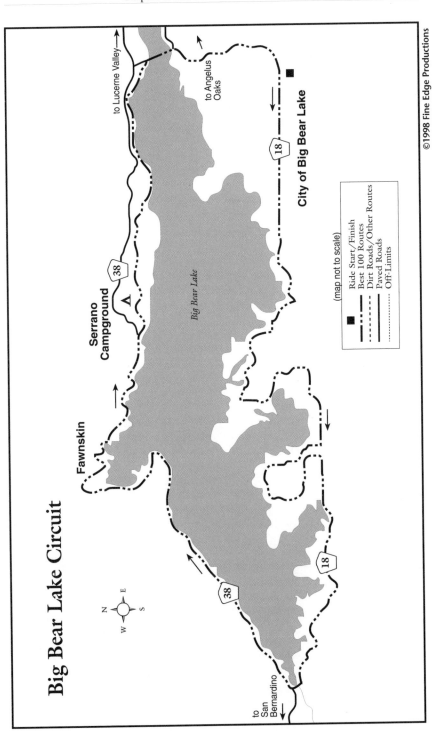

Big Bear Lake Circuit

to Lucerne Valley

to Angelus Oaks

City of Big Bear Lake

18

Serrano Campground

38

Fawnskin

Big Bear Lake

18

38

to San Bernardino

N
E
S
W

(map not to scale)

Ride Start/Finish
Best 100 Routes
Dirt Roads/Other Routes
Paved Roads
Off-Limits

©1998 Fine Edge Productions

32 Holcomb Valley Historic Settlement

Distance: 13.8 miles
Difficulty: Moderate, not technical
Elevation: 6,800' to 8,120'; 1,320' gain/loss
Ride Type: Out-and-back on fire roads and pavement
Season: Late spring, summer, fall
Maps: Fawnskin, Big Bear City

Overview: This trip visits the beautiful, historic Holcomb Valley. If you are at all adventurous, not afraid of ghosts wielding picks and shovels, have plenty of water and food and a few hours, consider exploring side roads in addition to the route listed here. There are many miles of Forest Service roads leading to old mining claims, picnic spots and just plain interesting places to explore.

Getting There: Park at the North Shore School parking lot (on the north shore of Big Bear Lake). *Note:* If you start your ride at the end of the pavement on Van Dusen, subtract 2.0 miles from each of the distances given in this description.

Route: To begin your ride, turn right (east) on Highway 38. Ride 2.0 miles and turn left (north) on Van Dusen Canyon Road. At the end of the pavement the road becomes 3N09. The road climbs gradually and is in good condition. It may be heavily traveled by vehicles, especially on weekends during the summer, so stay to the right.

At 5.6 miles turn left at the T with 3N16. Pass the Holcomb Valley Campground. Turn right at 3N05 (sign of the pick and shovel) at 5.9 miles to begin the ride through the remains of the historic settlement. At each of the markers ride through the opening in the split rail fence and slowly cruise past each of the ruins. Be careful not to disturb them, interfere with hikers, or stray from the established paths. Local sights include what's left of Two Gun Saloon, Jonathan Tibbets Grasshopper Quarts Mill and Hangman's Tree (be wary of the four aggressive ghosts at the base of the tree).

Turn left on 3N16 at 7.0 miles. Be sure to check the Original Diggings. Continue east (left) on 3N16 to 7.4 miles and turn left to the old log cabin. Park your bike here. Explore the cabin on foot and try to imagine what it was like to live here during gold mining days, especially during a hard winter without TV and an electric blanket.

This is the turnaround point. When you've finished exploring and having a snack, reclaim your bike from the ghost miner by the railing. Take a right on 3N16, turn left on 3N09 and ride back down to Highway 38. Turn right on the highway for the 2.0 miles to your car in the school parking lot.

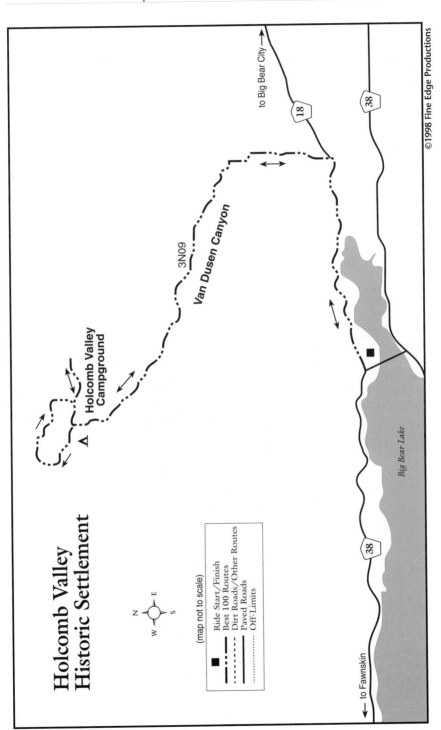

Holcomb Valley
Historic Settlement

(map not to scale)

■ Ride Start/Finish
━ ・ ━ Best 100 Routes
- - - - Dirt Roads/Other Routes
━━━ Paved Roads
······· Off-Limits

3N09

Van Dusen Canyon

Holcomb Valley
Campground

to Big Bear City →

18

38

Big Bear Lake

38

to Fawnskin

©1998 Fine Edge Productions

33 Skyline Drive via Sky Chair

Distance: 9 miles
Difficulty: Moderate, mildly technical
Elevation: 6,960' to 8,120'; 1,180' gain by chairlift
Ride Type: Loop on fire roads and singletrack
Season: Late spring, summer, fall
Map: Big Bear Lake

Overview: Skyline Drive is an ideal ride for the beginning mountain bike rider who wants a few thrills, a fairly short ride, a little climbing, a lot of downhill and fabulous mountain views high in the forest. Except for a few roller coaster sections, the ride is mostly downhill—virtually all of the elevation gain is achieved with the chairlift. This may be a bit scary for someone who has never ridden one, but it's totally safe. The lift takes you and your bike (in separate chairs) to the top of the ski run. To ride the lift, obtain your ticket ($7/one ride; $18/all day) and sign a waiver in the Team Big Bear bike shop at the foot of the lift. You can also rent a bike and a helmet here, but I recommend that you bring your own.

Getting There: Park in the Snow Summit lot at the upper end of Summit Boulevard in the town of Big Bear. Find the Team Big Bear bike shop, buy your lift ticket and take your bike to the bottom of the lift. Step off the lift at the top, retrieve your bike.

Route: Start your odometer and head east on the trail marked for bikes. It descends quickly, turns south and

Snow Summit Ski Area offers lift-assisted riding.

Tony Quiroz

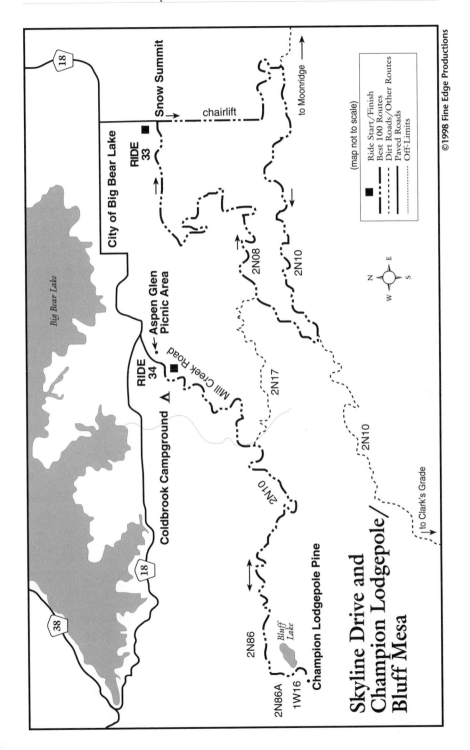

Skyline Drive and
Champion Lodgepole/
Bluff Mesa

©1998 Fine Edge Productions

(map not to scale)

■ Ride Start/Finish
▬ ▬ Best 100 Routes
– ▪ – Dirt Roads/Other Routes
▬▬ Paved Roads
…… Off-Limits

then hits 2N10 (Skyline Drive) just after you go around the locked gate. Turn right. *Caution:* This is a regularly used Forest Service vehicle road, so be sure to stay to the right, especially as you career downhill through the left-hand turns. To your left across the Santa Ana River canyon, you can see San Gorgonio Mountain (highest in Southern California) and to the southwest—thousands of feet below and some 60 miles away—the Pacific Ocean.

At 1.7 miles continue straight at the junction with 2N51Y (it may not be marked). Stay on 2N10 past the next spurs on the left. At about 2.7 miles, looking due west, you can see Butler Peak with its lookout tower perched on a massive rock outcropping. At 3.8 miles angle right at the junction onto 2N08. Just before you hit 2N08, a singletrack to a lookout

(Grand View) climbs to the left and another singletrack takes off to the right. At 4.6 miles go right on 2N08 where it joins 2N17 and begin a great downhill ride. When you reach the unmarked junction at 6.3 miles continue straight on 2N08. Then at 7.6 miles watch for a trail taking off between two large boulders on your right as the road sweeps around to the left. (If you miss the turn you hit pavement in 0.2 mile. Just turn around and go back up the hill, looking for the singletrack entrance on your left.)

This is the Town Trail back to Snow Summit, and it's a great roller coaster ride through quick turns, around rock outcroppings, and over streams. Go past the gate at the end of the buildings and cruise into the "bike jungle" outside Team Big Bear's shop where you started this escapade.

34 Champion Lodgepole/ Bluff Mesa

Distance: 10.4 miles
Difficulty: Moderately strenuous, mildly technical
Elevation: 6,870' to 7,600'; 730' gain/loss
Ride Type: Out-and-back on fire roads, singletrack and pavement
Season: Late spring, summer, fall
Map: Big Bear Lake

Overview: On this trip, you see what is believed to be the largest lodgepole pine standing guard over a serene mountain meadow. The route is hilly, remote and heavily forested in spots. It courses past beautiful rock formations on the way to the tree. The ride includes 2 miles of an easy, delightful singletrack. This is a two-water-bottle ride. Be sure to carry food.

Getting There: Park your car at Aspen Glen Picnic Area on Mill Creek

Road just off of Bear Boulevard on the west end of the lake.

Route: Begin your ride by turning left on Mill Creek Road. Ride 0.2 mile, turn left at the junction of Mill Creek and Tulip and begin climbing on 2N10. The road is paved, steep and winding. Be careful to stay to the right. You pass small, old wood cabins set well back from the road; they are privately owned but on land leased from the Forest Service.

Because of the large lots, these owners enjoy far more privacy than do most of the residents in Big Bear.

Just before the pavement ends after 0.8 mile, there is a junction. Stay left; the branch to the right goes to the Cedar Lake Christian Camp. Where the dirt road begins, you pass through an open gate. Remember, this is a regular Forest Service road used by cars and trucks, so stay alert and ride as close to the right as is safe. There are many good views of Big Bear Lake to your right as you climb up from the valley.

At the next junction, 1.3 miles from the start, 2N17 to Skyline Drive begins; you continue straight ahead on 2N10. You pass through a beautiful grove of old growth ponderosa pines as you continue to climb. You begin seeing lesser dirt roads branching off 2N10, but don't take any of them unless you feel adventurous. At the next junction, 2N52Y goes left, but you continue to the right around the bend. At the next junction 2N10B goes right, but once again, continue straight on 2N10.

After 2.6 miles of steady climbing with only a few level sections, you finally reach the top of the majority of the steep sections. Now there are several well-earned descents through the forest and past extensive rock formations. Except for some washboard sections, the road is in fine condition, and you can maintain a pretty good speed along the right hand side. To the right you can catch glimpses of the lake and valley through the thick stands of trees. The road levels out and even takes you on some descents. After 3.6 miles you come to a junction with 2N86. Look for the sign *Bluff Lake YMCA Camp, 2 miles,* and *Lodgepole Pine, 3 miles,* both to the left. Take 2N86 to the right. It's a dead-end road, but you turn off before it ends.

On both sides of the road are massive boulder formations that invite exploration. If you look closely you can see numerous small double-tracks (jeep roads) meandering into the forest among these formations. If you have the time and inclination, explore these roads but be sure to stay on them. Don't cut new trails here or anywhere else. At the junction of 2N86A and 2N86, continue left on 2N86A. After 0.1 mile, bear right at the unmarked Y. At 4.2 miles look for a small sign on your left indicating Bluff Mesa Trail, Champion Lodgepole Pine, 1 mile. Turn left off the road onto Trail 1W16.

This is a fun, beautiful, and only slightly technical singletrack. It should be no problem even for a beginning mountain bike rider. Watch for hikers and be ready to yield to them. Coast down to a small stream and cross a narrow, short wooden bridge. Immediately turn right where you can see a beautiful meadow ringed by trees and large rock formations. On your left is a split rail fence encircling the base of the Champion Lodgepole.

Park your bike and take a respectful walk around the fence to ponder the height and beauty of this spectacular conifer. If you brought along a picnic lunch, this is the perfect place to eat it. The meadow is a peaceful, spiritual place that deserves quiet and appreciation for its natural beauty.

After your pause here, the route returns to the starting point at Aspen Glen Picnic Ground. You can continue past the Champion Lodgepole either to the east or to the west. The Siberia Creek Trail begins here. The trail to the west (left) takes you either to the Bluff Mesa YMCA camp or out to 2N10, depending on which branch you take.

To return to Aspen Glen retrace your route. Take the singletrack back to 2N86A, turn right, stay to the left at the next unmarked junction and at the junction with 2N10. Stay right at the junction with 2N85 and continue on 2N10 (past the junction with 2N17) through the open gate and onto pavement (requires good bike handling on the steep descents). When you get to the pavement be sure to control your speed. The steep, sharp turns can lead you right into oncoming traffic if you aren't careful to stay right of the center line. At the T, turn right to return to the campground and your car.

35 Santa Ana River Trail

Distance: See listed options
Difficulty: See listed options
Elevation: 5,000' to 6,200'; gain 1,200'. *Note:* The elevation refers to the trail elevation from the parking area to Highway 38. Actual elevation gain/loss will vary with the different options.
Ride Type: Depends on option taken
Season: Late spring, summer, fall
Maps: Big Bear Lake, Moonridge

Overview: This is the longest single-track in the forest and it's one of my favorites. (It's also part of the Santa Ana River Corridor Trail System that starts in Heart Bar and—when completed—will eventually go all the way to the ocean.) You have the option of doing this ride as an out-and-back trip or as four different loops. In fact, since every option is a great ride, consider doing each one during the course of the season. You catch magnificent vistas of the Santa Ana River valley and mountain ranges, cross several streams and cruise through small meadows. You ride through miles of beautiful ponderosa pine, lodgepole pine, California black oak and Engleman oak forest. The downhills are fast and exciting while some of the climbs are short and steep but not difficult. Take plenty of food and at least two water bottles for these rides.

Caution: The trail options listed below are thrilling and just a touch risky in spots. This trail was designed and built for hikers and horses—very slow movers! Portions of the single-track twist sharply while clinging to the sides of very steep slopes. In addition, during the fall, many of these same sections are carpeted with acorns. Ever ridden on marbles? Here's your opportunity! So, if these turns are taken at more than a mere crawl, or if you slip, you may be launched into space. It's a long way down and I see no way for you to get yourself *and* your bike up to the trail—even if you wanted to.

Getting There: From Angelus Oaks (nearest services) on Highway 38, drive down toward Seven Oaks via Middle Control Road (dirt starts 0.5 mile east of Angelus Oaks). Following are the ride descriptions for the beginning of all the options. Park off the road on either side of the river (popular parking area for fishermen).

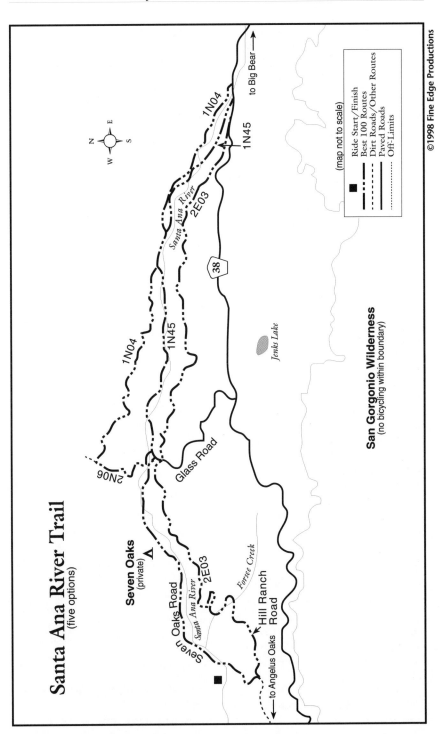

Santa Ana River Trail
(five options)

to Big Bear →

1N04

1N45

2E03

N
W   E
S

38

Jenks Lake

1N04

1N45

(map not to scale)

■ Ride Start/Finish
Best 100 Routes
Dirt Roads/Other Routes
Paved Roads
Off-Limits

San Gorgonio Wilderness
(no bicycling within boundary)

2N06

Glass Road

Seven Oaks
(private)

Santa Ana River

Forsee Creek

2E03

Seven Oaks Road

Hill Ranch Road

to Angelus Oaks →

©1998 Fine Edge Productions

Route: Start by riding back up Middle Control Road. At 0.9 mile look for a dirt road angling back to the left. Take this up to and over the locked gate. This is Hill Ranch Road or 1N07 (formerly Forsee Creek Road). At 2.7 miles there's a spur taking off to the left that dead-ends at the top of a plateau. If you feel like a short hike, this is perfect. If not, continue around to the right, down a short slope to the Santa Ana River Trail marker, 2E03, branching left. Drop onto the trail here to begin your singletrack adventure.

The trail crosses Forsee Creek (look for the log). The flow could be heavy and deep, depending on the snow runoff and time of year. At 3.2 miles, Seven Oaks Resort is to your left at the bottom of the canyon. Look for manzanita (Spanish for little apple—the red berries are edible in the fall and taste like apple), desert sage, and occasional holly. You also ride through small stands of incense cedar (red, stringy, gnarly bark) and past many pines that have been killed by the bark beetle. The infestation became epidemic after years of drought weakened the trees. At 4.0 miles, you cross two streams (they can be deep) and then cross Glass Road at 5.4 miles.

You have a number of options with this ride. (The mileages given here are ride totals.)

OPTION 1:

9.6-mile loop; easy, not technical

Turn left onto the pavement (watch for cars coming down the road!). Turn left again at the junction with Seven Oaks Road. Continue on Seven Oaks Road to the resort. If you have the time, stop in for refueling. This is a quaint old place and well worth a visit. Take Seven Oaks Road back down to your car.

OPTION 2:

23 miles out-and-back; moderately strenuous, technical

The trail picks up on the other side of the road about 60 feet down the pavement and continues east. At 7.0 miles the trail bends sharply to the right as it clings to the sheer, exposed slope with an open vista to the left. At 8.9 miles continue straight through an unmarked junction. (The branch to the right heads up 1 mile, goes over the ridge and drops into Barton Flats Campground. The left branch drops 1 mile to the Santa Ana River and 1N45.) Continue the roller coaster, hill-hugging escapade another 2.6 miles to the pavement and a small parking area adjacent to Highway 38 and opposite the South Fork Campground. This is the turnaround point for two of the five optional return routes. Retrace your route, getting back on 2E03, staying on the singletrack until it joins Hill Ranch Road (after crossing Forsee Creek). Take the old road back to and around the locked gate, turn right on Middle Control Road and ride 0.9 mile back down to your car.

OPTION 3:

21 miles out-and-back with loop; moderately strenuous, technical

From the turnaround point in Option 2, retrace your route just to Glass Road (at 17.2 miles from the start). Turn right on the pavement. Then bear left at the junction with Seven Oaks Road. Continue on Seven Oaks Road to the resort and then to your car.

OPTION 4:

20.4-mile loop; moderately strenuous, technical

This is particularly attractive on a hot

day when you'd like to get wet! From the turnaround point in Option 2, return on the pavement, 1N45, but do not get back onto the single-track. The road soon becomes dirt. For the next 5.5 miles you parallel and cross the river four times, passing a few cabins and private camps for the next several miles. Many of these cabins are on government leased land. You also see several rugged old stone homes built from native rock some 60 or more years ago. After 12.5 miles, just before the river crossing, there's at least one trail to the right that leads to well shaded, stream-side picnic spots and good swimming holes.

Making tracks through the pines.

At 14.0 miles, the road splits. Take the left branch, 1N45. At 14.4 miles, the road crosses the river. Another 0.4 mile takes you across the river again. At 16.2 miles, cross the river the last time. This becomes Seven Oaks Road and is paved. At 16.6 miles, 2N06 takes off to the right. Continue straight 0.1 mile (note the massive old incense cedar on the northwest corner). Turn right at the junction with Glass Road, heading toward Seven Oaks Resort and back to your car.

OPTION 5:

24.1-mile loop;
moderately strenuous, technical

If you want to stay dry and you have the energy to climb a little, return via 1N04 and Converse Station. Ride out of the parking area to the highway and cross the highway. Turn left, and then cross the bridge over the Santa Ana River. Watch for traffic as you cross the highway again to the left. Enter 1N04 (0.2 mile from the parking area on the other side of the river). Ride west on a gentle climb on 1N04 to its junction with 1N45 at 14.2 miles. At the next junction turn right onto 1N04 again and continue the climb to 6,000 feet. At 18.0 miles, turn left at the unmarked junction (Radford Road). If you miss this you quickly come to another junction, which is 2N06. Turn left here. Either road will get you to Converse Station and the beginning of a paved downhill cruise.

At the bottom of Radford Road turn right onto Seven Oaks Road. Bear right at the junction with Glass Road, past Seven Oaks Resort (stop for refueling if you want). In another 1.5 miles you're back to your car.

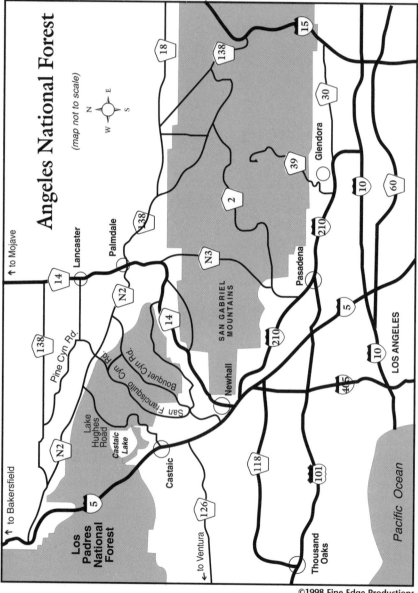

Angeles National Forest

(map not to scale)

©1998 Fine Edge Productions

CHAPTER 5

Angeles National Forest

By Mike Troy, Kevin Woten, and Delaine Fragnoli

Imagine yourself at 6,000 feet elevation in the San Gabriel Mountains, just an hour above Los Angeles, one of the largest cities in the United States. To the horizon, peak after peak of craggy mountains gives way to rugged canyons. Lying west to east along the northern boundary of the Los Angeles Basin, the San Gabriels offer recreational opportunities to millions of people. Your mountain bike can take you to a place where you can forget the rush and noise of the sprawling city far below.

Although the San Gabriels provide some of the most strenuous and technical biking in Southern California, they hold something for every level of mountain cyclist. What's your preference? An easy cruise up the beautiful and historic lower Arroyo Seco or a 9-mile climb to the top of Mt. Wilson? Something in between? It's here.

For over 100 years, people have visited these mountains to seek solitude and recreation. They came first on foot, then by horse and mule or wagon; later by railroad (yes, railroad!) and automobile. Now, the rugged and sophisticated mountain bicycle provides a near-perfect vehicle for exploration and quiet, non-polluting, low impact recreation.

Today the highways, roads and trails that crisscross the area make visiting the forest an easy task. There is plenty of room for exploration and enough space to find solitude if that's what you're seeking. Thousands of acres to pedal will challenge, thrill, and reward you for years to come.

The Arroyo Seco front range, easily accessible and very scenic, contains some of Southern California's most challenging climbs and best singletrack. It is also dotted with the ruins of historic hotels and lodges. The Arroyo Seco backcountry, on the northern side of the mountains, is less crowded but still accessible. Its higher elevations and cleaner air make it a good choice in the hot summer months.

Those who enjoy desert environments will want to visit the Valyermo District.

Its relatively small network of roads is uncrowded and offers some of the best riding in Angeles National Forest.

The northernmost section of Angeles National Forest, the Saugus District, has a different character than the rest of the Angeles—rounder and not so rocky and rugged, and lacking the elevation of the San Gabriels to the southeast. Still, the Saugus District has much to offer the mountain cyclist. The lesser elevations generally make for easier climbs and the area is far less traveled than the heavily-used San Gabriels.

The northern tip of this range, Liebre Mountain (the name comes from the Spanish word for cottontail), shoulders fine stands of black oak woodland and is especially rewarding to ride in the fall when the leaves turn color and carpet the forest floor.

The Angeles National Forest is urban mountain biking at its best!

Mt. Baldy District

36 West Fork to Monrovia Peak

Distance: 13 to 31 miles
Difficulty: Easy-to-strenuous, not technical
Elevation: 3,500' (full loop)
Ride Type: Loop on pavement and fire roads; can be done as a shorter, easier, out-and-back
Season: Year-round
Maps: Fine Edge Productions' San Gabriel Mountains Recreation Topo Map; Tom Harrison's Trail Map of the Angeles High Country

Overview: A beautiful ride, this loop travels along the scenic West Fork of the San Gabriel River before climbing over Cogswell Dam, where you have views of the San Gabriel Wilderness. A great choice for families, the initial paved part of this ride makes a pleasant, easy 13-mile out-and-back trip for those not up to the challenge of the whole loop. More conditioned cyclists who opt for the full loop are rewarded with an 8-mile downhill at the end, one of the best fire road descents in the area. Bring plenty of water as there's none en route.

Getting There: From the 210 Freeway in Azusa, take Highway 39 north. Continue up the canyon about 10.5 miles from the Forest Service parking kiosk, past the turn-off to the East Fork, past the OHV area and 1.0 mile past the Rincon Ranger Station. A roomy parking area is on your left—that's the west side of the highway. There are bathrooms and plenty of graffiti.

Route: Backtrack down the highway over the bridge. Immediately on your right, 0.1 mile, is a gated paved road (2N25), which actually looks more like a bike path. Make your way through the turnstile or over the gate.

The going here is easy but you are gaining elevation, albeit very gradually. Although the first part of this ride is marred by trash and graffiti, you quickly outdistance it. Soon you have just the West Fork of the San Gabriel River and a few fishermen to keep you company.

After a mile, you pass the junction for the Bear Creek Trail. Just past it the river forks and you cross a bridge. You continue to parallel the West Fork until, at 1.7 miles, you cross another bridge back to the shady south side of the stream. Under a canopy of alder, maple, oak and spruce, you continue to gain altitude gradually.

You pass Big Mermaids and Little Mermaids canyons to the north (on your right). At about 4.0 miles, the canyon begins to narrow. Steep rock walls rise up on either side of you, and you pass several waterfalls trickling down mossy cliffs. If you need a restroom there's an outhouse on the left at 4.5 miles.

At 6.5 miles you reach Glenn Trail Camp, with its sycamore-shaded picnic spaces and pit toilets. No water, however. This makes a pleasant lunch or food stop and a convenient turn-around point for those not up to the whole loop. If you have any energy left at all, however, it's worth the work to ride/push another mile up to Cogswell dam.

To continue, saddle up and prepare to suffer. At 7.0 miles you begin a nasty little climb, still paved but very steep, to Cogswell Dam. Dedicated in 1933, the dam is named after Prescott Cogswell, a Los Angeles County Supervisor who was very involved in flood control matters. Thankfully the climb tops out at 7.5 miles. Continue on the middle route, past the private driveways (signed as such) to the left and right. It's worth

your time to spin out to the dam itself and take a look up-canyon on one side and down-canyon on the other. To the west you can see the back of Mt. Wilson; that white dome you see is the observatory's 100-foot telescope.

From the dam, continue on the road you came in on, veering left around a switchback and past a final residence. Just past here at almost

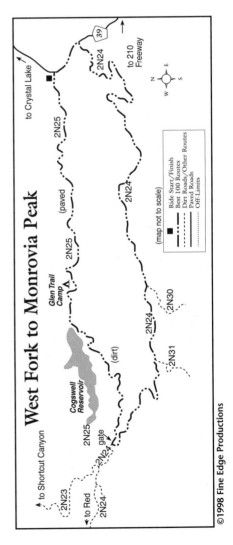

©1998 Fine Edge Productions

8.0 miles, the pavement turns to dirt. Keep climbing and climbing and climbing—for another 6.0 miles. The grade isn't too bad, although the road surface can be shale in places. But it's generally shady and you do have views of Mt. Wilson to the west and of the reservoir down below you.

At 14.0 miles you reach a gate. You've gained almost 2,000 feet since you left Glenn Trail Camp, so you deserve a break. Soak in the views and munch a Powerbar. You'll need it because the climbing isn't quite over yet. If you've had enough, you can turn around here for a downhill spin back to Highway 39.

From the gate, make a hairpin left turn onto 2N24/Red Box-Rincon Road. At about 16.8 miles you come to gated Clamshell Road (2N31) on

your right. Continue on 2N24, contouring around the north face of Monrovia Peak. Bear left at 19.2 miles when you pass gated 2N30 on your right. At 22.3 miles, fork right to avoid the turnoff (gated) to Pine Mountain (a 0.8-mile climb to the summit). Continue to head east and down, down, down—for 8.0 miles! This is a screaming, steep, switchbacked descent—a just reward for all your effort. *But do be careful and stay in control.*

The high-speed frolic ends at 30.3 miles at the Rincon Ranger Station, where 2N24 hits Highway 39. There is a gate at the bottom of the fire road; don't go crashing into it at high speed! Turn left onto the highway for a short pavement spin back to your waiting car.

Arroyo Seco District

37 Mt. Wilson Toll Road Climb

Distance: Varies. 5.5 to 18 miles
Difficulty: Very long and strenuous, fairly technical due to steep grade on the return
Elevation: 4,500' gain maximum
Ride Type: Out-and-back on fire road
Season: Year-round, but there can be snow in winter
Map: Fine Edge Productions' San Gabriel Mountains Recreation Topo Map

Overview: The Mt. Wilson Toll Road is a classic hill climb and a benchmark for anyone wanting to test his or her fitness against a consistently steep grade. If you love to climb, this is your ride. If you don't, you may find this ride hot, brutal, and not particularly scenic.

Fortunately the climb is not an all-or-nothing proposition. Many riders make Henninger Flats Campground

(water available) their goal and leave the summit to hardier folks. No matter how far you go, this is not the ride to do on a hot, smoggy day.

Please note that the Toll Road is *heavily* used by hikers, joggers, dog walkers, equestrians and bicyclists. Control your speed on the long, steep descent—there is a posted 15 mph speed limit. Be particularly careful below Henninger Flats as this is the most traveled part of the road.

One final note: The Toll Road was the center of a major wildfire in the fall of 1993. You will see the effects of the fire as you make your way up to and through Henninger Flats. Following the fire, the Toll Road was closed for many months, as Forest Service work crews used the road to truck out debris. No sooner had the Toll Road been opened for recreational use than a huge landslide just above the Eaton Canyon bridge closed it again. At press time the Toll Road was open—if you're planning a night ride, forget it; the gate at the entrance is locked at dusk—but soil erosion continues to be a problem. Check with the Arroyo Seco Ranger District before riding in the area.

Getting There: The entrance to the Mt. Wilson Toll Road is off Pinecrest Drive in Altadena. The easiest way to get there from the 210 Freeway is to exit at Sierra Madre and turn left on Altadena Drive. Follow Altadena Drive to Crescent Drive. Turn right, then right again on Pinecrest Drive. There is an entrance on the right of the road at a gated chain-link fence that drops into Eaton Canyon and heads up the Toll Road. It is a little obscure, but chances are you will see other folks milling about the entrance.

Homeowners here have complained about the parking situation. You might consider leaving your vehicle at Eaton Canyon Park or one of several dirt lots lining the canyon along Altadena Drive, then riding to the Toll Road entrance. This would help ease tensions considerably. If you do park at the Toll Road gate, please be quiet—especially early on weekend mornings—and be careful not to block driveways.

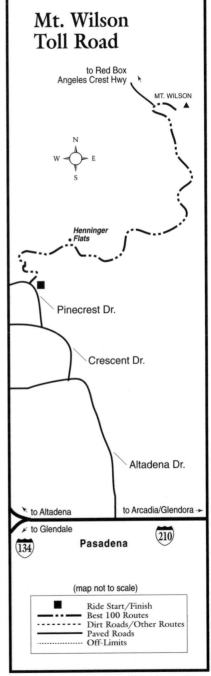

©1998 Fine Edge Productions

Route: Ride through the gate and drop down into Eaton Canyon, cross the bridge, and begin to climb the Toll Road. Steep, isn't it? Get used to it. Learn to love it. You have 9 miles to go. You will quickly gain elevation and, before long, Altadena will be far below. There are many turnouts where you can look around you. Let's stop at one and talk about some of Mt. Wilson's history.

Mt. Wilson is named after Benjamin Wilson, owner of a local vineyard. He considered Mt. Wilson as a source of lumber for fencing and wine barrels. Later, looking to exploit the mountain in a different way, a private enterprise built the first developed pathway to the top with the intent of charging for passage. In 1891 the Toll Road opened to the public as a trail with the toll being 25 cents for foot traffic and 50 cents for individuals on horseback. The Toll Road was a popular but rugged trip, and many hardy souls reached the summit by way of it.

As years went by, the trail was widened to accommodate vehicle traffic and the transport of a 60-inch telescope to the top of the mountain. Later, bigger and better observatories were designed and a bigger and better road was required to transport the equipment, resulting in the final width of 10 feet. All this road widening was done by hand! As you suffer along, think about that. Maybe it will make you feel better.

All through this time, the Toll Road drew scores of people to Wilson. This was a grand time in the history of the mountain. A hotel was built on top, meeting the needs of weary travelers who arrived on foot, horseback, or in more comfort by private car or bus.

The late 1920s saw a slow decline for the Toll Road. Angeles Crest Highway was pushing its way into the forest and, when it reached Red Box, soon gave the public an easy option to the top of Wilson. There was no way the Toll Road could compete with a modern, public highway, and it soon ceased operation and was turned over to the Forest Service. The hotel was torn down in 1966 to make way for the Skyline Park.

Back to our ride. At 2.7 miles you come to Henninger Flats Campground. Named for "Captain" William K. Henninger, an early rancher-farmer in the area around 1880, Henninger Flats is a lovely campground and the destination for many travelers on the Toll Road. There are restrooms and water here. Henninger Flats is operated by Los Angeles County, which allows camping by permit. There is also a restored log cabin and lookout tower here. If you are feeling a little the worse for wear, this is a good spot to turn back.

To continue, follow the Toll Road through the campground and to the right. Stay on the main road, avoiding the upper campground. Soon you ride around a right-hand switchback and begin climbing above the campground. At the road to the heliport, go right again and continue climbing.

Although the grade is still pretty tough, this part of the ride is cooler and shadier, and you encounter many fewer trail users. About a mile past Henninger Flats, you go by Idlehour Trail and begin to switchback your way to a small saddle near Upper Henninger Flats. The grade eases somewhat beyond here, but a rocky trail surface makes the going still difficult. At 7.5 miles you pass the Little

Tony Quiroz

The Angeles National Forest offers miles of challenging singletrack.

You pass a spur road to Mt. Harvard at about 8.0 miles. A little more grinding brings you to the pavement at 9.0 miles. To add a little salt to your wounds, this short bit of pavement is as steep as anything you've done thus far.

Ride around the gate at the top and head right through another gate to Skyline Park. Once a concession stand where you could eat, drink and use the bathroom, Skyline Park has been closed for several years. Now there are no facilities for riders. Don't count on finding water.

From the parking lot, you have great views into the valley and beyond. It's at this point that you can be impressed with yourself for making it all the way up here.

Santa Anita Trail and, just as you pass the trailhead, you can look up ahead to the communication towers on Wilson. Every TV station and many radio stations broadcast from here, and the mountain top fairly bristles with them.

Unfortunately, the towers look deceptively close. You still have 1.5 miles of grunting and groaning left. This last section can drive you nuts as you swear the top has to be around the next bend. It isn't.

The return trip down the Toll Road is potentially very fast and dangerous. (One local cyclist died when he overshot a corner and went over the side.) The grade is so consistent that it is possible to coast almost the entire way back to Eaton Canyon—you have to pedal in just one spot. Enjoy yourself—you earned it—but *use common sense and control your speed*, especially as you near Henninger Flats.

38 Mt. Lowe/Echo Mountain Loop

Distance: 12.5 miles
Difficulty: Very strenuous, not technical to very technical
Elevation: 2,800' gain
Ride Type: Loop on pavement, fire road and singletrack
Season: Year-round
Map: Fine Edge Productions' San Gabriel Mountains Recreation Topo Map

Overview: There is a lot of history in this highly recommended ride. The first 2.5 miles of steep pavement is by far the most difficult. Once you hit the dirt, the grade eases considerably. This ride can easily be broken up into shorter (and easier) rides, but no matter what, you need to make it past the brutal pavement section. For example, riding out to the ruins at Echo Mountain would be 3.5 miles one-way and would be doable, albeit a strenuous beginner ride. Bring plenty of water—there's none en route.

Getting There: From the 210 in Pasadena, take Lake Avenue north to its end. Go left and continue for a few miles until you see a yellow light. This marks Chaney Trail. Turn right and climb to the top of Chaney Trail (at Sunset Ridge) where the road splits to drop left into Millard Campground and right up to Mt. Lowe. The road to Mt. Lowe is gated at this intersection. Parking here is limited and fills up quickly on the weekends. If full, you can start from the Millard Campground parking lot, although

Henninger Flats (Ride 37), site of the annual Mt. Wilson Bicycling Association's pancake breakfast fundraiser.

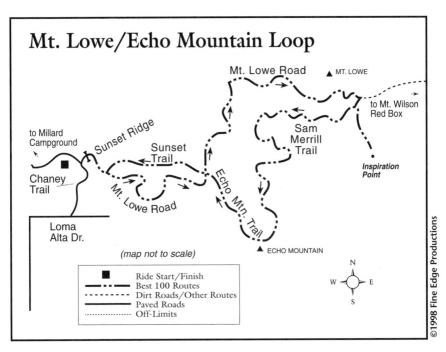

Mt. Lowe/Echo Mountain Loop

to Millard Campground

Sunset Ridge

Sunset Trail

Mt. Lowe Road

Mt. Lowe Road

▲ MT. LOWE

to Mt. Wilson Red Box

Sam Merrill Trail

Chaney Trail

Echo Mtn. Trail

Inspiration Point

Loma Alta Dr.

(map not to scale)

▲ ECHO MOUNTAIN

■ Ride Start/Finish
— · — Best 100 Routes
– – – – Dirt Roads/Other Routes
— Paved Roads
············ Off-Limits

N
W ⊕ E
S

©1998 Fine Edge Productions

this would add a tough climb up from Millard to the gate at the Mt. Lowe Road.

Route: Even though it is paved, the first section of the roadway up to the Cape of Good Hope is by far the most strenuous of the trip. Plug along, enjoying the view of the city below, and I'll tell you a story about a man and his vision.

In 1888, Professor Thaddeus Sobieski Coulincourt Lowe (Thad to his friends)—Civil War balloonist extraordinaire and self-made man—settled in Pasadena with retirement in mind. Professor Lowe was no couch potato, however, and he felt like a man without a mission. Looking up into the San Gabriels every day from his home, Lowe was inspired to do something. He just didn't know what. In 1890, he had a fateful meeting with another visionary, David MacPherson, an engineer by trade. Together they hatched a plan to build a railway to the summit of Mt. Wilson, carrying folks up into the heights of the front country for a modest fee.

Problems with easements dashed their hopes of ascending Mt. Wilson, so they turned their attention to a lesser peak, Echo Mountain. Mac-Pherson oversaw the construction of a cogwheel railway from Rubio Canyon up to Echo Mountain, a marvelous feat of engineering. The Great Rubio Incline exceeded a 60 percent grade in some places and rose some 1,300 feet in a little over half a mile—real pixie ring stuff. At the end of the incline, Professor Lowe built a hotel, a small observatory and a zoo. All this came to be known as the White City. In 1893, the first public trip was conducted on the railway. To much fanfare, honored guests were winched up the incline by a 3,000 pound cable attached to a great bullwheel, all located on the top of the mountain.

The Echo Mountain complex was a great success, and Professor Lowe set out to continue his railway up into the San Gabriels to the summit of Mt. Lowe. The railway never quite reached the top of Mt. Lowe, but it did follow a winding and scenic four-mile course up to Crystal Springs, a beautiful oak-shaded cove on the side of Mt. Lowe; there Lowe constructed Ye Alpine Tavern, a Swiss chalet-style resort. Scores of people rode the railway into the mountains and hiked, rode horses, played tennis or just lounged around the tavern, enjoying the remote beauty of the quiet forest.

Although seemingly very successful, the endeavor placed a great financial strain on Lowe and he lost his beloved railroad to mounting debts. Although operated by other parties into this century, an unsure economy and changed interests on the part of the public brought a gradual decline to the railway. Fire and other natural disasters spelled the end for Professor Lowe's dream, and by the late 1930s, the Mt. Lowe Railway had ceased operation.

Back to the ride! Still on the pavement, at 1.5 miles stay right. At 1.7 miles you swing left, pass an open gate and a sign that reads: *1.5 Miles - Echo Mountain; 3.5 Miles - Mt. Lowe Campground; 1.7 Miles - Mt. Wilson Road*. Just past here there's a roadside map showing the old railway route. A little more cranking brings you to the beginning of Sunset Ridge Trail (on the left). This nicely technical trail takes you back to the gate at Chaney Drive. Just past Sunset Trail on the right is the signed Echo Mountain Trail to—surprise, surprise—Echo Mountain. Both of these trails are ridden on the return trip, but anyone who is too pooped to pedal uphill anymore would be well

advised to ride out to Echo Mountain and explore the ruins of the White City before returning home.

A tad farther up the Mt. Lowe Road, the pavement ends at the Cape of Good Hope and you begin to ride on the route of the original railway. This is a nice railroad grade and is much easier than the pavement behind you. As the miles pass by, you ride through history, passing such noted locations as the Circular Bridge (3.3 miles), where the railway negotiated a sharp curve by means of a trestle over the canyon below, and the Granite Gate (4.4 miles), where the railway bed was blasted through solid rock. Some of the original electrical wires that supplied power to the railway cars are still visible here.

At 5.2 miles you reach the Mt. Lowe Campground, built on the site of the Alpine Tavern. This is a fine lunch spot since the climbing is mostly over and the ruins of the tavern are fun to sit on as you try to imagine the way it was in its heyday some 90 years ago. Unfortunately, as of the fall of 1996, the campground was closed because local rodent populations are infected with plague.

Back on the Mt. Lowe Road, ride a little bit farther uphill (0.3 mile) to a Y-intersection. The road to Inspiration Point and the trailhead for the Sam Merrill Trail are to the right. Straight ahead is the Idlehour trailhead. The Mt. Lowe Road continues to the left.

Take a right toward Inspiration Point fire road and ride the short distance out to some ruins, where sighting tubes point out distant landmarks like Venice, the Rose Bowl, and Los Angeles. Unfortunately, it is rare when a peek through the pipes provides anything other than haze. There's a new shelter, picnic table, and kiosk with historical information here as well. *Note:* The Castle Canyon Trail which takes off from here is *not recommended* as a bike trail.

Return to the trailhead for the Sam Merrill, on the left now at 6.0 miles, and then turn left onto the singletrack. This trail has many personalities in its 2.6 miles to Echo Mountain. It is lovely and shaded, then exposed and rocky, and almost always technical and challenging. (If your technical skills are dubious, you can take the Mt. Lowe Road back down.) On one of the many large rock outcroppings in the lower part of the trail, I suffered my first double-pinch flat of the year, a dubious accomplishment

Smooth and easy singletrack is rare in the Angeles National Forest.

indeed. There are also many sharp switchbacks to negotiate, and proper riding techniques are required to reduce the impact on the trail structures. Some are better walked than ridden. Don't brakeslide! As always, ride softly and watch for other trail users.

At 8.6 miles you reach the ruins at Echo Mountain. As you intersect with the Echo Mountain Trail (to the right), the Sam Merrill continues on down the mountainside. This section is very narrow, tight and exposed, and it is *not recommended* for bikes. If you like, take a left and ride out to the ruins of the White City, past the great bullwheel and the ruins of the power

house. There are still remnants of the railroad tracks heading toward the precipice into Rubio Canyon.

To continue the ride, follow the Echo Mountain Trail back to the short section of railroad bed that makes a fine trail. There is some exposure. *Use caution:* There are also a lot of hikers using this trail and the Sunset Ridge Trail.

Back on the pavement now (Cape of Good Hope) at 9.6 miles, turn left and ride 150 feet or so to the trailhead for the Sunset Ridge Trail. Turn right and proceed onto the trail. Still a technical trail (winding above Millard Canyon), it is more shaded and damp than the Sam Merrill. Watch for poison oak! It thrives here. As with the Sam Merrill, there are several tight switchbacks to negotiate. At 10.6 miles you come to a paved spur road from the Mt. Lowe Road. If this technical trail is over your head, you can bail out here. Continue straight ahead on the trail. At 11.6 miles stay left. This last section of trail is mellow and rolling. At 12.1 miles you are back at the pavement of the Mt. Lowe Road, and a right turn brings you down to the gate and your starting point after 12.5 miles.

39 Gabrieleno Trail from Red Box through the Arroyo Seco

Distance: 15 miles
Difficulty: Moderate, technical
Elevation: 3,500' loss
Ride Type: One-way on singletrack, shuttle required; several loop options possible
Season: Year-round
Map: Fine Edge Productions' San Gabriel Mountains Recreation Topo Map

Overview: One of the best, most scenic singletracks in all of Southern California, the section of the Gabrieleno Trail from Red Box to Switzer's and through the Arroyo Seco is a very popular shuttle ride. It has a little bit of everything: smooth sections of trail, boulder fields, switchbacks, stream crossings, exposure, technical climbing and technical descending. The scenery ranges from sycamore and oak-filled streamside habitat to waterfalls. And, oh yes, there's plenty of poison oak.

Although the ride is described here as a shuttle, I am not comfortable endorsing it as a downhill-only "bomb" run. Unfortunately, I have seen many inexperienced cyclists doing this. The Gabrieleno is a popular trail, and you need to ride courteously and in control, for your own safety and the safety of others. As an alternative, I would like to suggest several loop options for riders of different abilities.

The first 4 miles of trail from Red Box to Switzer's picnic area makes an excellent ride for those learning singletrack skills. For a 9-mile loop, advanced beginners can park in the pullout for Switzer's on Angeles Crest Highway, just past the intersection with Angeles Forest Highway. Ride the Crest Highway for just over 4 miles up to Red Box and take the singletrack down to Switzer's. Finish by climbing a steep 0.5 mile back up to the Crest. The trail from Switzer's through the Arroyo Seco is best left to advanced riders with strong technical skills.

I firmly believe in earning my downhills, so I recommend that experienced riders climb Mt. Lowe and drop down to Red Box to catch the Gabrieleno Trail. An even tougher option is to climb Mt. Wilson and descend its north side to access the trail. Both of these options are roughly 25 miles long and very strenuous.

Red Box may seem like a strange name to you; it's named for the red box that the fire department maintains here. Note that there are restrooms and water available. Those coming from Mt. Wilson or Mt. Lowe should

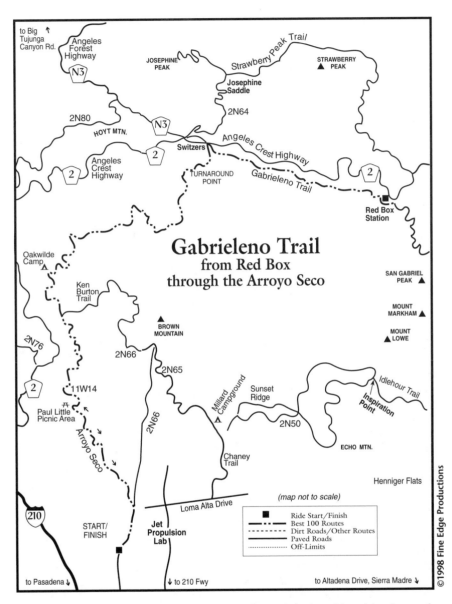

to Big Tujunga Canyon Rd.

Angeles Forest Highway

N3

JOSEPHINE PEAK

Strawberry Peak Trail

STRAWBERRY ▲ PEAK

Josephine Saddle

2N64

2N80

N3

HOYT MTN.

2

Switzers

Angeles Crest Highway

Angeles Crest Highway

2

TURNAROUND POINT

Gabrieleno Trail

2

Red Box Station

Gabrieleno Trail
from Red Box
through the Arroyo Seco

Oakwilde Camp ▲

SAN GABRIEL PEAK ▲

Ken Burton Trail

MOUNT MARKHAM ▲

2N76

▲ BROWN MOUNTAIN

MOUNT ▲ LOWE

2N66

2

2N65

11W14

Idlehour Trail

Paul Little Picnic Area

2N66

Millard Campground

Sunset Ridge

Inspiration Point

Arroyo Seco

2N50

ECHO MTN.

Chaney Trail

Henniger Flats

Loma Alta Drive

(map not to scale)

210

START/ FINISH

Jet Propulsion Lab

	Ride Start/Finish
■	Best 100 Routes
	Dirt Roads/Other Routes
	Paved Roads
	Off-Limits

©1998 Fine Edge Productions

to Pasadena ↓

↓ to 210 Fwy

to Altadena Drive, Sierra Madre ↓

definitely refill their water supplies.

Getting There: For the shuttle, leave a car near the Jet Propulsion Lab on Windsor Avenue. From the 210 Freeway, take the Arroyo Boulevard/ Windsor Avenue exit and go north (toward the mountains). Just before a sharp right-hand bend in the road, there's a parking area on the left. You almost certainly will see other cyclists parked here. (Beginners note that from here you can ride up the Arroyo as far as you please. It starts out easy and gets more difficult the farther you go.)

To get to the start, take Highway 2 (Angeles Crest Highway) north from Interstate 210 in La Canada to Red Box where the paved Mt. Wilson Road (not to be confused with the Mt. Wilson Toll Road) climbs the backside of Mt. Wilson. Red Box is about 5 miles past the Angeles Crest Highway and Angeles Forest Highway intersection.

For those riding up Mt. Lowe, leave a car at the parking lot on Windsor and either ride your bike (this would add a half-hour of pavement climbing to an already tough ride) or drive a second vehicle to the starting point of the previous ride. To do so, from the parking lot on Windsor, make the hard right onto Ventura. A few blocks later at the second pedestrian sign, go left on Casitas. At the T-intersection go right on Altadena Drive. At the next stop sign go left on Lincoln, then right on Loma Alta, and then left on Chaney Trail.

Expect shade—and plenty of poison oak—during canyon riding.

Tony Quiroz

Follow the Mt. Lowe route directions to the Y-intersection at 5.5 miles. Instead of going right to Inspiration Point, go left to stay on the Mt. Lowe Road. You have about 3 miles of climbing to go to reach Eaton Saddle. You know you're getting close when you ride through the Mueller Tunnel, constructed to replace the gnarly and appropriately named Cliff Trail. You can still see very sketchy traces of the trail on the outside of the tunnel. The road ends at a gate at the Mt. Wilson Road. Go left on the pavement and enjoy the swooping descent to Red Box. *Be careful of vehicle traffic on the road.*

For those riding up Mt. Wilson, follow the directions for Ride #37. From Skyline Park, at the top of Mt. Wilson, catch the paved Mt. Wilson Road and descend past the towers. Continue descending past Eaton Saddle and the end of the Mt. Lowe Road to Red Box.

Also, you can leave a vehicle on Windsor Drive and either ride your bike or drive a second vehicle to the bottom of the Toll Road. To get from Windsor to the Toll Road, go right on Ventura, left on Casitas and right on Altadena. Take Altadena to Allen (there's a stop sign) and then go left on Pinecrest to the Toll Road gate.

Route: Find the trailhead in the far northwest corner of the Red Box parking lot. There's a metal culvert and access to the trail is a little dicey. You may want to walk your bike onto the trail.

Tight at first, the trail opens up to more of a road width every so often. The wide trail descends at a moderate grade through the pine and oak wooded canyon then winds and twists its way to the canyon floor. Numerous rocks and stutter bumps in the corners will help keep you from daydreaming too much.

At the trail junction at 2.3 miles, go left. The trail quickly grows rockier and soon you are faced with your first real technical challenge—a rock-choked chute that my riding buddies refer to as The Waterfall. You'll recognize it when you see it. Believe it or not, it is rideable.

Past here the trail parallels the stream, and you catch glimpses of the creek with its numerous concrete waterfalls. At 2.9 miles, two switchbacks (the first one of which is better walked) bring you down to the water. Splish, splash, you cross in and out of the creek, up and down several more switchbacks.

The trail continues to roll along with a few rocky downhills and a couple of short, technical uphills. Starting at 3.7 miles, small plaques describe trailside vegetation. You are approaching Switzer's picnic area, so

control your speed. You reach it at 4.2 miles.

Switzer's used to be a very heavily-used area, but in recent years the road into the area has been closed because the local rodent population has bubonic plague.

Those doing the 9-mile loop should bail out here. Ride through the concrete water crossing, past a bathroom and into the parking lot. Make a sharp right turn and begin the steep climb up to the Crest and your car.

Those continuing through to the Arroyo have about a mile of portaging through Switzer's. Cross the bridge at the far end of the parking lot and ride through the picnic area. Soon the trail grows rockier and becomes an off-the-bike, on-the-bike kind of affair as you follow the stream. Occasionally it's unclear where the trail picks up on the other side of the stream. Persevere and it won't be long before you come to the streamside foundation ruins of Switzer's.

Credited with being the first tourist camp in the San Gabriels, Switzer's Camp was little more than a tent camp along the trail to Strawberry Peak, the Colby Ranch, and the Chilao backcountry. It wasn't until 1912, when Lloyd B. Austin and wife came to this spot in the canyon, that the resort took off in a big way. Renaming the resort Switzerland, they expanded the facilities and constructed sturdy rock buildings which offered all the comforts of home among the beauty of the mountains. Switzerland drew many people—some quite famous—to its tennis courts, library, and hiking trails, and it was a popular jumping-off point for travel into the backcountry.

In the 1930s foot travel into the San Gabriels declined and auto traffic increased with the encroachment of the

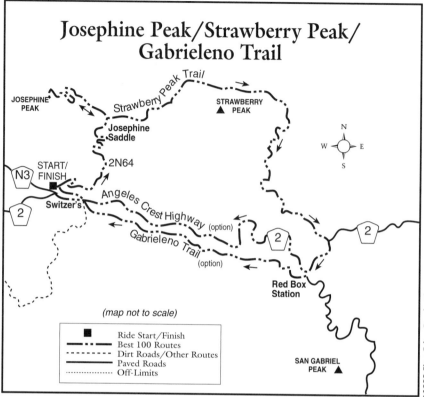

Josephine Peak/Strawberry Peak/ Gabrieleno Trail

©1998 Fine Edge Productions

Angeles Crest Highway. As with most other resorts in the mountains, Switzerland lingered, then fell gracefully away, a casualty of a more modern age.

From the ruins, the trail crosses the stream and heads very steeply up two very sharp switchbacks. Push through here, and ride and push the rocky climb that follows. The trail soon winds high above Switzer's Falls. A chain link fence protects you should you begin what would certainly be a deadly fall.

Less than 0.5 mile from Switzer's, go right and up at the trail junction with Bear Canyon Trail. Beyond here the trail continues to climb but the grade eases and the trail surface is much smoother. Watch your speed around corners as the trail is narrow.

You begin to descend gradually and then more steeply into the upper Arroyo Seco. Once you begin to follow the creek, the route is up and down, but mostly down, with a few rocky technical spots and a few steep, loose pitches to keep you honest. At one point you even cross over the top of a waterfall! Use common sense and walk here.

At just under 9.5 miles you ride over a log and into Oakwilde Camp (there's a trail sign here). You are now in the Arroyo Seco proper.

In 1911, J.R. Phillips built a resort at this spot. Improving an old road from the mouth of the canyon to his doorstep, he made the trip to Oakwilde a possible, though adventurous, trip by auto with lots of creek crossings. The road, subject to frequent washouts, had to be rebuilt nearly every year. The resort was a great success till the great flood of 1938 washed the road away for the last time. In the early forties Oakwilde Camp closed. Now it makes a good rest stop.

As you ride into the camp, look for a flight of concrete steps off to your left. Head down them and straight through the wide streambed. Sandy sections alternate with fields of baby heads and stream crossings. Count on some pushing and on getting wet.

A mile from Oakwilde you begin a 0.25-mile climb over the Brown Canyon debris dam—steep but short. This is followed by a loose and tricky descent complete with switchbacks

and exposure—and more protective chain link fence. You drop steeply into Paul Little Picnic Area at 11.3 miles.

From here it's more stream crossings, some of which you probably will have to portage. Be careful of the ones with big cement blocks that appear to stretch across the stream. They don't; they drop off at the far end—the perfect recipe for an endo. It seems inconceivable today that autos used to travel this canyon.

The trail grows gradually wider and less technical until you're finally back on pavement. Stay on the main road, passing some residences and other miscellaneous buildings. Soon the JPL complex appears on your right. At 15 miles you are back to your shuttle vehicle on Windsor Drive.

40 Josephine Peak/ Strawberry Peak

Distance: 21 miles; 8 miles if you just do Josephine Peak and 18 miles if you just do Strawberry Peak
Difficulty: Very strenuous, very technical
Elevation: 2,000' gain
Ride Type: Loop on fire roads, singletrack and pavement
Season: Year-round
Map: Fine Edge Productions' San Gabriel Mountains Recreation Topo Map

Overview: The tough 4-mile climb to Josephine Peak offers spectacular 360-degree views. The downhill return is fast and fun, while the singletrack loop around Strawberry Peak provides plenty of technical challenge. Either peak can be done as a discrete ride. Those without the necessary singletrack skills can simply climb and descend Josephine, while those who don't want to make the full climb can turn off onto the Strawberry singletrack. Please note

that the 9-mile trail around Strawberry is very narrow, technical, and exposed in places. It is not a trail for the inexperienced or the faint of heart. Once you're on it, there aren't any bail-out points. Also note that the only water available is at Red Box—late in the loop.

Getting There: From the 210 Freeway in La Canada, take Highway 2 (Angeles Crest Highway) north to the intersection with the Angeles For-

Winter ascent of Josephine Peak.

ahead to the north, you can see broad-shouldered Mt. Gleason. To the east sits Mill Creek Summit and Pacifico Mountain.

To continue toward Josephine Peak, turn left. The grade is a little bit easier but the trail surface is rockier so you're still working hard. The scenery is better and it's usually cooler and shadier.

Soon you begin to circle the mountain, kind of like you're riding up and around a giant Hershey's Kiss. When the road dead-ends at 4.0 miles, your reward is sweet. Follow the footpath to the summit proper and sign the trail register. It's hidden in a tin can under a rock pile. There used to be a fire lookout tower on the peak, but it was destroyed by fire and the foundations are all that remain.

Gobble some food and enjoy the view. To the north-northeast you can see Gleason, Roundtop, Granite, and Pacifico. To the west sits Mt. Lukens and its towers. To the south are Mt. Wilson, Mt. Lowe, Mt. Disappointment, Mt. Markham, and San Gabriel Peak.

When you're ready, descend to Josephine Saddle which you reach at 5.5 miles. Strawberry Peak Trail leads off to the east. Wide at first, the trail makes its way to the junction with the Colby Canyon Trail on the right at 6.0 miles. Go straight.

est Highway. Park in the dirt area on the northeast corner.

Route: Turn onto Angeles Forest Highway for about 200 feet. Turn right onto gated fire road 2N64. Ride around the gate and begin the grunt to Josephine Saddle. The first mile is among the steepest of the whole ride. Hang in there. The grade eases somewhat as the road swings to the left along a ridge.

Beyond, you begin a series of switchbacks up the south face of Josephine. At 2.5 miles you reach Josephine Saddle. Looking straight

Along here are some narrow, rock-slide sections that should be walked. Past them the trail wiggles around the backside of Strawberry Peak, passing through dry chaparral before heading into a lovely oak section. At 8.0 miles you drop into a piney, flat area beneath the dramatic sheer rock face of the peak. This is Strawberry Potrero.

Route finding through here can be a little tricky. Look for a large boulder with an arrow painted on it. You negotiate some sand and rocks on your way to the Colby Ranch trail intersection at 9.0 miles. There used to be a trail sign here, but the last time I was through here it was broken. There is, however, a trail register in a metal standard to the right of the trail.

Stay right and begin a very steep, switchbacked climb that requires some pushing. The grade soon eases but you continue to climb on narrow, winding singletrack. While there is some exposure, the trail is not too technical. You soon pass Strawberry Springs. Mossy and cool under large pines, it offers a welcome respite from the heat.

Continue the gradual climb to the saddle between Strawberry Peak and Mt. Lawlor. Go left. This section of trail is hotter, drier, rockier and narrower. Most disconcerting, however, is that the exposure is no longer to your left, but is now to your right. It takes a few minutes to get used to. You can see Angeles Crest Highway far below you.

You cross another small saddle and really begin to descend. Watch for waterbars and switchbacks! The trail soon widens and turns into an old road bed before dropping down to the Crest.

You can turn right and take the Crest back to your starting point to finish the loop. Or, if you're up for even more singletrack, cross the Crest to Red Box and take the Gabrieleno Trail (see Ride #39) to Switzer's.

41 Chilao Three Peaks Loop

Distance: 19.5 miles; shorter, easier options possible
Difficulty: Strenuous, technical
Elevation: 2,000' gain
Ride Type: Loop on pavement, dirt roads, and singletrack
Season: Year-round; can get snow in winter
Map: Fine Edge Productions' San Gabriel Mountains Recreation Topo Map (doesn't show trail over Mt. Hillyer)

Overview: When I quiz people about the best rides in the San Gabriels, invariably the first word out of their mouth is "Chilao." And with good reason. This area of the Angeles backcountry sees a lot less use than the front range.

The area is also crisscrossed by the 53-mile Silver Moccasin Trail, a National Recreation Trail that winds its way from Mt. Baden-Powell across the range and down into Chantry Flats in Santa Anita. Boy Scouts who finish the backpacking trip up to Mt. Baden-

Vetter Mountain Lookout

Tony Quiroz

Powell, named for the organization's founder, receive a special merit badge.

Where the trail passes into wilderness areas it is closed to bikes; however, it is open from Three Points through to Chantry Flats. This ride takes in some of the choicest sections of that trail, linking it to two other superlative singletracks: the Mt. Hillyer Trail and the Vetter Mountain Trail. The view from the Vetter Mountain lookout tower, one of the most beautiful spots in all of the San Gabriels, adds enormous scenic value to the ride.

The loop I present here gives you the maximum amount of fun singletrack for the least amount of work—not that the ride is effortless! There are lots of options and bail-out points for riders of various abilities. Beginners can enjoy the Mt. Mooney portion, while advanced beginners can tackle Mt. Vetter. Intermediate riders can do the first and last sections of the full loop, omitting the climb to Alder Saddle and the Mt. Hillyer/Horse Flats section. The full loop is the ultimate ride for fit riders who enjoy technical challenges. Water is available at the ride start.

Getting There: From the 210 Freeway in La Canada, take Highway 2 (Angeles Crest Highway) for 24 miles to the Charlton Flat Picnic Area. Turn left into the picnic area and take the main road past the bathrooms and to the first parking area on the right (ignore the road that branches off to the right).

Route: Head back out to Angeles Crest Highway and go left. Almost immediately, turn right onto a paved road. (There's a sign that reads *Overnight Camping.*) At the sign to the trailer dumping station, fork right. Then go straight to where the road turns to dirt and starts to climb.

This is a relatively moderate climb through shady pine trees across the eastern flank of Mt. Mooney. Soon, at

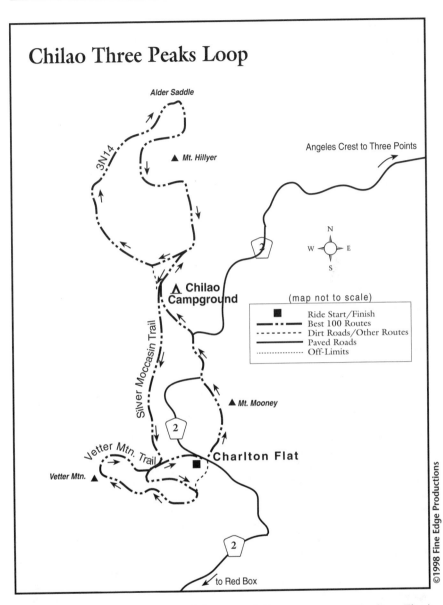

Chilao Three Peaks Loop

0.8 mile, it tops out and you go left. This is a fun, fast 1.5-mile descent back to the highway—more than a just reward for the minimal climbing involved. Watch for ruts at the bottom of the downhill.

When you reach the highway at 2.3 miles, go right. (Beginners can go left to return to Charlton Flat.) Pass the highway maintenance station on your right and, at 2.7 miles, turn left into Chilao Campground (water available).

At 2.8 miles, turn right onto the Silver Moccasin Trail. There's a sign here which indicates *Little Pines*

Campground. This fun section of trail descends a bit before it begins climbing. The trail surface is a little sandy, but nothing ugly. After just 0.4 mile of uphill you begin a swooping downhill that winds along a creekside. Nearly 0.5 mile later, the trail drops into and climbs steeply out of the stream. Downshift!

Just through the stream crossing, at 3.7 miles, you hit pavement. Although the trail continues on the other side, you go left on the pavement. (We'll be coming down that bit of trail later in the ride.) When the road forks at 4.1 miles, go right. (Intermediate riders can go left and catch the Silver Moccasin Trail to Vomit Hill—described later.) At 4.5 miles, roads go to the left and the right; you go straight. Continue straight on the main road past a visitor center, ranger houses, and other assorted buildings. The road, 3N14, soon turns to dirt.

At 5.4 miles you pass the gated road to Loomis Ranch on your left. You continue on 3N14 to the right. Settle in as you have a 2-mile climb ahead. By San Gabriel standards it's a relatively modest grade as you make your way around the west flank of Mt. Hillyer. To your left enjoy the unfolding views of Roundtop Mountain, Granite Mountain, and Mt. Pacifico.

You reach Alder Saddle and a paved road at 7.4 miles. Go right and continue climbing just a bit more until you top out at 7.7 miles. Pull right into a dirt turnout here. There are several wooden posts, two small rock walls, and a white *No Shooting* post. Several cars will probably be parked here. Pass between the posts to continue on a sandy trail.

Soon the sand gets deeper and you begin to climb in earnest. Some pitches are very steep and you may have to walk and push. You're almost to the top when you reach a hard right-hand switchback. After nearly a mile of climbing, you summit Mt. Hillyer.

Once you top out, the trail becomes quite pleasant, winding its way through rock formations and past Jeffrey pines. In the 1860s and 1870s Mexican bandit Tiburcio Vasquez, having stolen horses from the San Gabriel and San Fernando valleys, hid out in these rocks. Thus was born such local place names as Bandido Campground.

Don't let the pleasant trail fool you. The gentle sections alternate with nasty boulder fields full of intimidating drop-offs. At one point you ride up a pile of rocks, over a tree and down a pile of rocks on the other side. Immediately thereafter, take the scary but direct line over a large boulder. If you try to go left around the boulder, you're likely to have a close encounter of the mineral kind!

A couple of boulder fields later, the trail grows steep and loose. Hold on around those corners! At 9.9 miles, after a short, steep drop into and out of a dry streambed, the trail ends at Horse Flats Campground (water available). Go right on the pavement and follow it until it turns back into trail.

At 10.1 miles go right. This section of trail is quick and nice. Soon, little boulder sections begin to crop up; then they become more frequent. Before you know it, you're heading around the first of many rocky, gnarly switchbacks. Peeler-log waterbars and dropoffs choke the trail before, during, after, and in between the switchbacks. Great fun for those of you who like a technical challenge!

At 11.2 miles the trail ends at a paved road. The trail picks up across the road—this is the section of singletrack that you rode at the beginning of the ride. Don't take it unless you feel like hitting your max heart rate!

Instead, turn right on the pavement. At 11.6 miles, go left. (You went right earlier to make the climb to Alder Saddle.) Follow the pavement around until, at 12.4 miles, you reach a pullout on your right where a sign indicates *Little Pines Campground.* (This is directly opposite where you caught the ride's first piece of singletrack.)

Take the singletrack to your right and up a short, rocky climb. The trail can get a bit difficult to trace through here. Follow the signs for the Silver Moccasin Trail. At the top of the hill go right; at the bottom of the hill go left. There's a clear trail marker here.

The next section is fun as you roll over one railroad tie waterbar after another. Watch your speed as a rocky left-hand switchback comes up quickly. Continue winding and dropping until the trail ends at a dirt road at 13.2 miles.

Go left and start climbing. After the first steep pitch you get some relief in the form of a little descent. Soon you cross a wide streambed and really start to climb. (My riding buddies and I call this Vomit Hill; one of our gang pushed a little too hard and hurled at the top of it.) The climb gets progressively steeper—real granny gear stuff—before mellowing out.

At 14.4 miles, you reach a gate at the top of Vomit Hill. If you're beat, you can go left and head back to your car. If you have any energy at all, it's worth the work to turn right and head toward Vetter Mountain.

Vetter Mountain Lookout

Tony Quiroz

You climb gradually on the pavement for 1.5 miles until you reach a gate. A left will take you back to your car, and a right takes you to Vetter Mountain.

Go right and continue climbing for another mile. At 16.7 miles the pavement ends at a cul-de-sac. There are two dirt roads on your right. Take the second one, signed 3N16B.

Keep climbing. The grade will probably be steeper than you want at this point in the game, but you will be rewarded. Trust me. Stay on the main road until two switchbacks bring you to the top at 17.4 miles.

Climb the stone steps to the lookout tower and enjoy the panoramic views. On a clear day you can see as far as Catalina Island. Honest! Closer in, you get a 360-degree view of most of the San Gabriel's major peaks: Wilson, Harvard, Disappointment, Lowe, Markham, San Gabriel, Lukens, Lawlor, Strawberry, Josephine, Gleason, Roundtop, Granite, Pacifico, Waterman, Twin Peaks, Baldy, and Monrovia.

The view is great, but you should know by now that I wouldn't make you climb up here without rewarding you with even more singletrack. Backtrack for 0.1 mile. As you head around the second switchback (a right-hander) look to your left for a spur road. It leads to the clearly signed Mt. Vetter Trail dropping off to the right.

You almost immediately begin a series of 5 or 6 switchbacks. These are much easier than the ones coming down from Horse Flats and make good practice for advanced beginner and intermediate riders. Don't worry if you have trouble with them. Once past them, the trail becomes much easier, rolling along beside a creek.

At 18.2 miles the trail crosses a paved road. It crosses another paved road at 18.4 miles. (This is the road you climbed from the top of Vomit Hill to Mt. Vetter.) Follow the trail past a picnic table and continue descending. Half a mile later you drop steeply into and out of a streambed. Here, at 18.9 miles, the trail ends at a paved road. Go right for 0.6 mile back to your car.

42 Roundtop/Mt. Pacifico

Distance: 18.6 miles
Difficulty: Very strenuous; technical if you take the 4WD loop option
Elevation: 2,400' gain; 7,124' high point
Ride Type: Out-and-back on fire road
Season: Spring, summer, fall
Map: Fine Edge Productions' Recreation Topo Map of the San Gabriel Mountains

Overview: Rising out of the northern section of the Tujunga, Mt. Gleason's broad shoulders offer fine roads for exploring the pine forest. The 6,500-foot elevation brings relatively cool temperatures year-round. During most winters, the slopes of Mt. Gleason are covered with snow. The paved road (3N17) from Mill Creek Summit allows easy auto access to the top of Mt. Gleason and lends itself well to cycling, although it involves two good climbs to get there.

For families, driving the road to the summit of Mt. Gleason and ex-

ploring the area by bicycle would be a great adventure.

The area's greatest attraction is the 7,124-foot Mt. Pacifico. It is criss-crossed with jeep roads and hosts the desirable Pacifico Campground. You reach the summit by way of a long and very constant climb.

This ride also visits Roundtop and Granite mountains as optional side roads.

Getting There: The ride begins at Mill Creek Summit Rest Area, located on Angeles Forest Highway, 23 miles

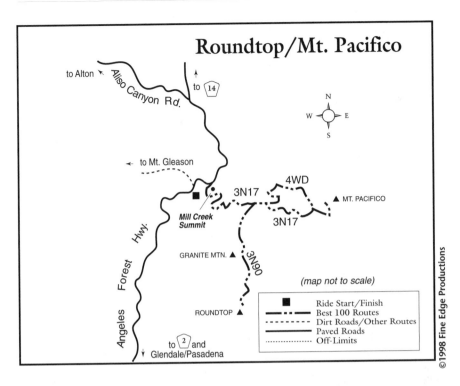

Roundtop/Mt. Pacifico

to Alton

Aliso Canyon Rd.

to (14)

N
W — E
S

to Mt. Gleason

4WD

3N17

▲ MT. PACIFICO

Mill Creek Summit

3N17

Forest Hwy.

GRANITE MTN. ▲

3N90

(map not to scale)

Angeles Forest

ROUNDTOP ▲

■   Ride Start/Finish
— · —   Best 100 Routes
- - - - -   Dirt Roads/Other Routes
———   Paved Roads
·········   Off-Limits

to (2) and
Glendale/Pasadena

©1998 Fine Edge Productions

above La Canada via Angeles Crest and Angeles Forest highways. Here, 3N17 descends from the east face of Mt. Gleason and crosses Angeles Forest Highway before heading up toward Pacifico. Mill Creek Rest Area has toilets in case you want to start in comfort. You may start from here or drive up 3N17 through Mill Creek Station and park at the end of the pavement at the parking lot. There are restroom facilities here and good water. Fill up at least 4 bottles! The parking lot is for day-use only, and the gate at Angeles Crest Highway may close at dusk. If you plan to take a long time on your trip, it would be best to check this out or park at Mill Creek Rest Area.

Route: Starting from the upper parking area, go up 3N17 past the gate and onto the dirt. This isn't a really difficult climb, but it is constant and gives

you little rest. One of the nicest things about riding the north side of the range at these higher elevations is the nifty view into the Antelope Valley and on rare, clear days, to the Tehachapis and beyond—the patchwork of the valley floor is quite a sight. At 3.2 miles you reach the intersection with the road to Roundtop Mountain. The trip out to Roundtop and back is a worthwhile diversion if you're not too tuckered out, and it offers a different perspective of the Pacifico area.

As you are standing there at the crossroads munching your Power Bar and deciding which way to go, you can see a time-worn and decrepit trail that takes off to the left of the sign that points the way to Mt. Pacifico. This "trail" skirts the north side of the mountain and is not rideable, but a short and careful scramble out a ways offers you an outstanding look down

*Silver Moccasin Trail (Ride 41)
—one of the San Gabriel's finest trails.*

road. (A return option that uses this road is discussed later.) At 10.3 miles turn left and up. At 11.4 miles you pop up on, or poop out on, the top of Pacifico.

There are numerous paths to explore, but if you keep left and continue climbing a little more, you reach Pacifico Campground at 11.9 miles. Situated amidst boulders large and small and well shaded by large pines, this is a lovely campground where you can have lunch and scramble around. There are tables and pit toilets here. Looking down toward the desert floor, Little Rock Reservoir is the small blue puddle 4,000 feet below. When you tire of clear, thin air and solitude (if you ever do), returning to your vehicle is a downhill joy as you retrace your path down the mountain.

If you're looking for a more adventurous and technically-challenging route off Pacifico, the 4WD road you passed on your way up at 9.1 miles will do nicely. Ride down the main road off the mountain until, at 13.1 miles (about 1 mile from the campground), you can take a branch road off to the right. You know you are on the right road if you see the Pacific Crest Trail crossing nearby. *(The Pacific Crest Trail is closed to bicycles.)* Follow the 4WD road for steep, challenging climbs and nasty downhills. At 13.7 miles turn left, then right again, and continue west along the ridge. At 14.2 miles you pop up on a small hill and can see down to Mill Creek Summit.

From here it gets somewhat con-

Tie Canyon toward Aliso Canyon Road.

Feeling up to the challenge of a little side trip? Good. Then Roundtop it is. Turn right on 3N90 where a sign reads *Granite Mtn. 1 mi., Roundtop Mtn. 3 mi.* (The campground on Roundtop no longer exists.) This is a roller coaster of a road and a good workout up to the road's end at 6.2 miles on the 6,300-foot Roundtop Mountain. From here, you have a clear view over Chilao Flats and Angeles Crest Highway into the San Gabriel Wilderness.

There is no place to go but back the way you came. A right turn on 3N17 toward Pacifico continues the ride. At 9.1 miles go past a steep 4WD

fusing as there are numerous paths to choose from. However, you can see 3N17 below you to your left and, with a little searching, the path down to it is obvious. It is also rough, rocky, and knee-deep in whoop-dees. When you drop onto 3N17, turn right and enjoy a rapid cruise back to your car at Mill Creek Summit. At 18.6 miles you are there!

Saugus District

43 Sierra Pelona Ridge/ Five Deer Trail

Distance: 11.8 miles
Difficulty: Strenuous, technical; not technical if you don't take Five Deer Trail
Elevation: 1,400' gain/loss
Ride Type: Lollipop loop on fire road and singletrack
Season: Spring, summer, fall
Map: Sleepy Valley

Overview: Road 6N08 accesses fine riding in the Sierra Pelona area of Bouquet Canyon. The Sierra Pelona is a pretty, windswept landscape dotted with oaks. This road takes you to Sierra Pelona Ridge, where you can connect many other roads and trails. The area's premier singletrack, Five Deer, provides a fun, technical return route. Watch for OHV traffic in the area, and plan on wind and cooler temperatures on the ridge than at your starting point.

Getting There: From I-5 take Valencia Boulevard and head east. At Bouquet Canyon Road turn left (north). Drive up Bouquet Canyon Road past the reservoir's dam site and find road 6N08.

From Highway 14 take Palmdale Boulevard west (N2), which becomes Elizabeth Lake Road. Continue to Bouquet Canyon Road, turn left, and follow over the hill to 6N08 on the left.

Road 6N08 takes off from Bouquet Canyon Road just a little to the east of the dam overlook at Bouquet Canyon Reservoir. It is not marked but it is easily found. A good parking spot is located 100 yards up 6N08 at a wide area where 6N06 comes in. Pack plenty of water as there is none on this ride.

Route: Start along 6N08 on a nice downhill grade that ends all too soon. At a sharp right turn, you begin climbing toward the backbone of the Sierra Pelona. This is a hot ride in summer, and the only shade you can find is at 2.0 miles when you roll past Artesian Springs. Not marked by any sign, Artesian Springs is located to the right of the road and is liberally sprinkled with oaks and crisscrossed with motorcycle paths. This spot is used as a base camp by many motorcyclists, and you can do the same if you wish.

Continuing on 6N08, the route steepens somewhat. At 3.8 miles, bear left. At 4.4 miles, you pop over onto a saddle on Sierra Pelona Ridge and the

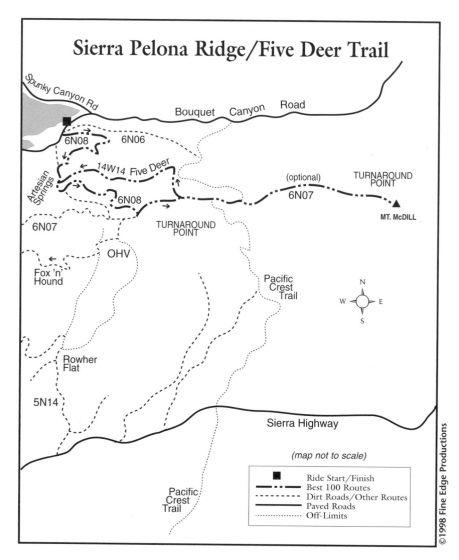

junction with 6N07. Looking south, you can see the northern slopes of the San Gabriel Mountains. To the east is tower-crowned Mt. McDill.

From this point, you can return the way you came, take 6N07 east (left) to its end at Mt. McDill, or return via the Five Deer singletrack.

To get to Five Deer (14W14), take 6N07 east (left) for 0.8 mile (about 5.2 miles total) to the un-

marked trailhead. Go left onto the trail. It drops down the slope onto an old motorcycle track. Ride down the rutted, rocky trail past grass-covered knolls on the mountain's north side. Many motorcycle trails crisscross your route, but stay on the main trail and descend rapidly. Half a mile later (5.7 miles total), take the second left (west). The trail has a series of motorcycle jumps and whoops before it drops steeply to the north. At the bottom of the drop, go hard left and ride down to the edge of the chaparral.

From this point you head west. First, though, you can take the trail to the right for 0.3 mile to view the remains of the Big Oak—the world's largest recorded canyon live oak before fire destroyed it years ago. The tree's remains are still quite impressive—nearly as thick as a mature redwood in girth. A small spring bubbles from the foot of the tree, almost as though life still flows from it. Return 0.3 mile up the trail to the Five Deer junction.

Go right (west) at the junction and climb a bit before rolling across the mountainside. Brushy, shaded and downhill, this is a very popular route, with tight chutes, turns and rutted descents. Watch for poison oak which is abundant here. At 9.6 miles you cross an OHV trail that climbs the mountain. Continue 0.2 mile to rejoin 6N08 at Artesian Springs Camp. Then turn right on 6N08 and head 2 miles back down the mountain to your vehicle.

44 Upper Shake and Sawmill Mountain Campgrounds with Alley-Oop Option

Distance: 6 to 9 miles
Difficulty: Easy to fairly strenuous; Alley-Oop option is technical
Elevation: 600' to 1,300' gain/loss
Ride Type: Fire road out-and-back with singletrack option
Season: Spring, summer, fall
Map: Burnt Peak

Overview: The variances in mileage and elevations indicate there is more than one way to skin this route—either as an easy or moderately strenuous ride. Upper Shake and Sawmill campgrounds are the loveliest in the Saugus District (lots of pines and great views), and spring and fall are particularly good times to visit. There is no water available at either campground.

Getting There: We get to this ride via I-5 to Castaic and then driving the 25 miles up Lake Hughes Road, but it is accessible from many directions (consult your map). From the intersection of Lake Hughes Road and Lake Elizabeth Road, turn left (northwest) and you immediately find yourself on Pine Canyon Road. Approximately 4.4 miles up Pine Canyon Road you can see an area on the left and a road leading into the mountains. A sign here reads *Upper Shake 3 mi., Sawmill Campground 5 mi., Burnt Peak 7 mi.* Park at this dirt area.

Route: Jump on your bikes and begin climbing immediately up 7N23 past the sign for Upper Shake. This section is a constant uphill, but for the average rider it is an entirely manageable grade. As you continue you come to an area that gives some views of the valley to the east toward Rosamond, and as you continue to climb, you can look ahead and up toward the Sawmill and Burnt Peak areas, with their stands of oak and pine trees.

At 2.0 miles, you reach the intersection of 7N23 and 7N23B. For a nice beginner ride or simply for the adventure of it, you can take 7N23B, the upper of the two gated roads on your left, and descend into Upper Shake Campground. Upper Shake is very pretty, and it is well shaded by large pines. In summer the area is cool, while winter may bring a good covering of snow. One winter day, two of us did this route under threatening skies and found out that snow and ice have an interesting effect on mountain bike brakes. At least falling didn't hurt much! To return to 7N23, simply retrace your steps back up the fire road.

To head up to Sawmill Campground, return to 7N23, turn left, and continue up the mountain on a steeper grade. The surroundings become less and less like the usual brushy hills of the Saugus District as you ride past large pines and oaks. Several viewpoints along the way give you the opportunity to see the west end of Antelope Valley and points north.

At 3.5 miles, you reach the saddle at Burnt Peak. Here you are at a junction of three fire roads. To your right is a sign for Sawmill Campground (a mile ahead), and you ride in that direction on 7N23. Ride uphill for

just a little longer, as you move along into a nice, grassy grove of black oaks that turn vivid colors in autumn—flaming reds, oranges, and browns from nature's palette.

At 4.9 miles, after a short downhill, you reach the turn-off to Sawmill Campground. Taking off to the right, the road descends into a cool and shady picnic area with tables. Here on the north side of Sawmill Mountain at 5,200 feet, the wind is nearly a constant companion, and the sound of the pines being gently stirred by these breezes is soothing. This campground sees some use, although it has never been occupied by more than three or four campers in the times that we have been there.

Return to your vehicle by retracing your route down 7N23. It is very nearly all downhill on the return leg. It's a great downhill, too, with challenging corners and reasonably good surfaces. There are some loose, rocky sections, so use caution. Watch for vehicle traffic, since this is an access road used by many visitors.

A technical one-mile singletrack

Prepping for a ride.

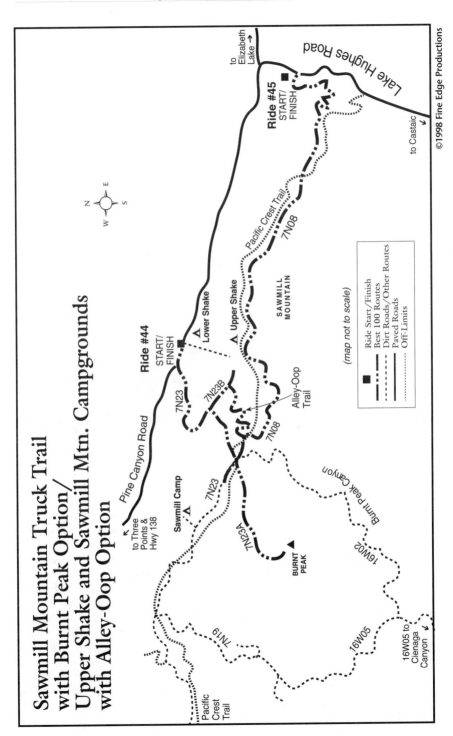

Sawmill Mountain Truck Trail
with Burnt Peak Option/
Upper Shake and Sawmill Mtn. Campgrounds
with Alley-Oop Option

©1998 Fine Edge Productions

(map not to scale)

Ride Start/Finish
Best 100 Routes
Dirt Roads/Other Routes
Paved Roads
Off-Limits

option to this ride is the Alley-Oop Trail. This trail earns a technical rating for its narrow upper half, which is somewhat exposed and follows steep switchbacks. The bottom half is much easier and fun to ride. No brush interferes, and the half-dozen or so jumps near the bottom earned this trail its name.

Follow the directions above to the intersection of 7N23, 7N23A and 7N08 between Upper Shake and Sawmill campgrounds. From the intersection, go east on 7N08 for half a mile. At the first right-hand sweeper, Alley-Oop Trail dives off from a wide spot on the left and heads due east. About 25 feet down you cross the Pacific Crest Trail. It is clearly marked and easy to distinguish from the trail you are on. *(Do not ride on the PCT; it is off limits to bicycle travel.)*

Continuing straight ahead and down, you pass a sign that reads *Upper Shake 1 mile, Lower Shake 2 miles.*

The Saugus District boasts lovely trees and great fall color.

Just past this sign is a sharp switchback to the right. Control your speed at all times, since the top section is full of these beauties, some rideable, some not. Use caution: They tend to sneak up on you. One of these is reached at 0.6 mile and is a sharp, sharp, switchback to the left. Walk your bike around. If you overshoot this one, you will run right over the edge for a very painful drop.

After the switchbacks, the trail narrows and follows along a hillside. There is a fair amount of exposure here, so watch your speed and choose your lines carefully. As you move

along, the grade eases a little and the trail opens up and becomes truly a joy to ride. There is little brush to contend with, and a series of bumps in the trail discourages vehicles and makes for a high grin factor. Some of the bumps are quite high, so be very careful lest you fly more than God intended you to. At 2.0 miles, you come to the road to Upper Shake Campground, 7N23B.

This trail could be worked into many loop trips. Starting from Upper Shake, riding up 7N23, and returning on the trail would be 3 to 4 miles.

45 Sawmill Mountain Truck Trail with Burnt Peak Option

Distance: 18 to 23.5 miles
Difficulty: Very strenuous, not technical
Elevation: 2,200' to 2,700' gain/loss
Ride Type: Fire road out-and-back with pavement loop option
Season: Spring, summer, fall
Map: Burnt Peak

Overview: This is a lovely ride and shows some very nice views off the east side of Sawmill Mountain. The climb is long but never very difficult, and the return half of the ride is mostly downhill. There are several options in this ride, including a choice of return route and whether or not you want to summit Burnt Peak, the highest point in the range.

Getting There: From Castaic on I-5, drive 25 miles up Lake Hughes Road. Just 0.3 mile before reaching Pine Canyon Road, 7N08 takes off to the west. Located among some houses, it would be difficult to recognize as an entrance to one of the most beautiful areas of the Saugus District if it weren't for the sign. Park your vehicle along the beginning of this road, being careful not to block access to any of the residences here. Bring all the water you need.

Route: The road is in excellent condition, and it is mostly a middle-chainring ride as you work your way up the shoulder of Sawmill Mountain.

After riding up 7N08 a little over 2 miles and 800 feet of elevation gain, you pass a television antenna site. Springtime brings a carpet of wildflowers among the small pines planted here.

At 3.9 miles you come to a fork. Take the left road and descend, enjoying great views of Elizabeth Lake and the surrounding communi-

ty. It is easy traveling for a while, and at 4.2 miles you pass by some beautiful black oaks. At 5.5 miles, you begin climbing again, passing some mature pines, and the view to the east is striking at times. At 7.8 miles, look left for a fantastic view of four consecutive mountain ridges all the way to the San Gabriels. Here you work a little harder, because the grade increases and the road is sandy in places.

After about 8 miles, all the uphill work is done as you roll over the shoulder of Sawmill Mountain. You have labored your way up 2,200 feet of elevation gain and can cruise downhill for a while until, at 9.8 miles and about two hours of riding, you reach an intersection with 7N23 and 7N23A (you are traveling on 7N08). To the west is Burnt Peak, with microwave towers perched atop its 5,700-foot crown. Straight ahead lies Sawmill Campground and the road to Atmore Meadows and Liebre Mountain. To the right is 7N23, one of the return options.

Rest here if you like and enjoy the beauty of an area that is very much out of character with the rest of the Saugus Range. Instead of scrub oak and buckthorn, deciduous oaks and pines surround you. Smog? Only what is below you obscuring the valleys from view. While summer is fine for riding here (it is usually cooler at this elevation), fall is our favorite time to visit. The air is clearer and the leaves are turning. Late in the winter though, expect snow.

If you wish to visit Burnt Peak, it is a challenging but short 2.7 miles on 7N23A with 588 feet of climbing that rewards you with fairly fantastic views of the surrounding countryside. (*Note:* Mileages to and from Burnt Peak are not combined with the ride mileages that follow.) A sign points the way at the crossroads of 7N23, 7N23A (gated) and 7N08. The electronic site crowning the mountaintop is easy to see from the starting point. Although you start by descending, the road soon climbs fairly steeply, winding around the north side of Burnt Peak before popping out on top. At 2.5 miles, take the right road. At 2.7 miles, you come to a gate. To the right, a road leads to more microwave facilities a little lower on the mountain.

It would be a shame to come this far and not go to the top, so walk the remaining 30 feet or so past the gate and up to the summit. The view speaks for itself. One clear and cold winter day, with the ground frozen beneath our feet, we could see the faint glimmer of the Pacific Ocean on the horizon.

There is nowhere to go but down, and the return trip to the saddle is a simple retrace of your path to the top.

Back at the crossroads, you have more choices. You may continue north on 7N23 and rest at Sawmill Campground (1.4 miles north from the crossroads, on the right of 7N23). Or you could turn right and head down 7N23 and enjoy a fine downhill run to Pine Canyon Road 3.1 miles farther. Turning right onto the paved Pine Canyon Road provides a fast, big-ring pavement return to Lake Hughes Road, where you turn right and ride the short distance to your starting point.

Our favorite option is to return on the route we came up, taking 7N08 back down to Lake Hughes Road. Remember the long climb to the saddle? Going back it becomes a long downhill, the last section being a real hoot as you plunge down to your starting point.

46 Liebre Mountain/ Golden Eagle Loop

Distance: 16.2 miles
Difficulty: The full loop is strenuous and fairly technical. The level of difficulty can be varied by shortening the loop into smaller loops or driving to the top of the mountain.
Elevation: 1,500' gain/loss
Ride Type: Fire road and trail loop with small pavement section
Map: Liebre Mountain

Overview: This fairly long climb on a good fire road up the west shoulder of Liebre Mountain offers excellent views. The return on Golden Eagle Trail is fun and not too difficult, with some of the finest legal singletrack in the entire range. Springtime wild-

flower displays can be spectacular. In fall, *be careful—the area is popular with hunters.* There is no water, so come prepared.

Getting There: Travel north on Interstate 5 from Castaic and exit at

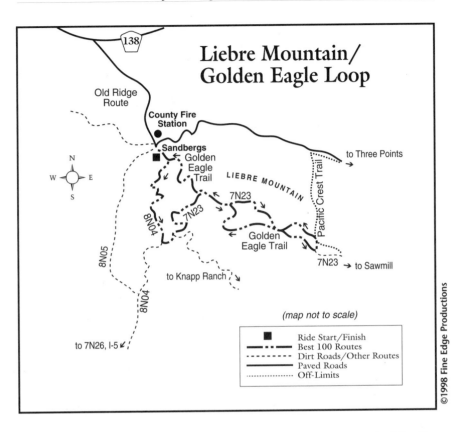

Liebre Mountain/ Golden Eagle Loop

Old Ridge Route

County Fire Station

Sandbergs

Golden Eagle Trail

LIEBRE MOUNTAIN

7N23

to Three Points →

Pacific Crest Trail

Golden Eagle Trail

7N23 → to Sawmill

to Knapp Ranch

8N05

8N04

8N04

7N23

to 7N26, I-5 ↙

(map not to scale)

- ■ Ride Start/Finish
- ▬▪▬▪▬ Best 100 Routes
- - - - - - Dirt Roads/Other Routes
- ▬▬▬ Paved Roads
- ·············· Off-Limits

©1998 Fine Edge Productions

the Highway 138/Quail Lake off-ramp. Drive 4.2 miles to the turnoff for the Old Ridge Route Road. Turn right. Drive uphill on 8N04, a paved road, for 2.6 miles to the ruins of Sandbergs Resort on the right. Park here. These foundations are all that's left of one of the greatest rest stops on the Old Ridge Route.

Route: Return to the pavement of 8N04 and continue south (right). Cruise along on the broken pavement until at 2.6 miles you intersect with 7N23. The sign on the left reads *Castaic 25 mi., Bear Campground 9 mi., Sawmill Campground 14 mi.* Turn hard left on 7N23. Except for a short section near the top, the first mile is the steepest of the entire ride. Don't

lose heart, it gets easier. At 3.2 miles keep left, bypassing 7N22. (7N22 to Knapp Ranch is not recommended since it leads to a ranch located on private property. The ranch is used for cattle and the area is fenced.)

Settle in and enjoy the climb, because the road improves considerably and the views start to come into their own. Beyond Pyramid Lake to the south are White Mountain, Black Mountain and Cobblestone Mountain. Looking more westerly, you see Hungry Valley, Frazier Mountain, and the rolling Gorman Hills.

At 6.5 miles you reach the first summit and begin to roll along more gradually. There are too many roads branching off of 7N23 to mention, but the main road is always clearly defined. The terrain becomes strikingly pretty as you move into lovely oak woodland. Keep an eye out for golden eagles soaring on the thermals above you, a reminder of the solitude the backcountry can offer.

At 7.8 miles a short rocky climb brings you over the top. Roll along to 9.8 miles, and just after a small rise in the road with a pull-out, a doubletrack takes off to the left. This path leads to Horse Camp Canyon, 17W01. Down this jeep road 0.1 mile is a fence and a sign that reads *Bear Camp 2 mi., Burnt Peak Junction 10 mi., Wilderness Camp 1 mi., Oakdale Canyon Road 5 mi. (The Pacific Crest Trail,* which incorporates 17W01 from here to Horse Camp Canyon, *is closed to bicycle traffic.)* To pick out Golden Eagle Trail, follow the fence line to the left. At first it seems only a game path through the trees, but it soon opens to a good trail winding through the oaks.

Tony Quiroz

The ride is easy now and runs slightly uphill. Except for some occasional brush and fallen limbs, beginners will have little trouble on this section. At 10.6 miles you cross 7N23 and pick up the trail on the other side to the southwest. The last time I was through here, the area had been bulldozed. Keep searching and you will pick up the trail. The route has some brushy areas but is still a good, clean trail. At 11.8 miles you cross a spur road from 7N23 and continue straight across this road on a doubletrack for 300 feet or so. On the right, with a massive old oak in the background, the trail picks up again. There should be a stake with a yellow ribbon marking the trail.

After a little more riding, you drop into a gorgeous oak forest as the trail roller coasters along a hillside. (Watch for little nubs of oak root sticking up out of the trail. They are hard to pick out of the shadows and could easily cause a flat.) After leaving the oak forest, the trail opens up as you roll toward a lovely grass knoll with a great view of Pyramid Lake.

At 13.7 miles you cross 7N23 again. From here the going becomes much more difficult with brush crowding over the trail. It seems to have been cleared somewhat in late 1996 and is now in pretty good shape—although narrow and sandy in spots. If you like, turn left on 7N23 and enjoy a fun fire road descent on 7N23 back to the Old Ridge Route. *Caution:* This is a long, fast descent, so control your speed at all times. To continue on the trail, cross 7N23 and follow the singletrack. At 16.2 miles the Ridge Route Road is visible to the left. Drop down to the road, turn right and ride the last 100 feet to your vehicle.

Valyermo District

47 Jackson Lake Loop with Pinyon Ridge Option

Distance: 16 miles
Difficulty: Moderately strenuous; strenuous with Pinyon Ridge; singletrack is mildly technical, but narrow and loose in spots
Elevation: 2,500' gain/loss
Ride Type: Lollipop loop on fire road and singletrack
Season: Spring and summer; fall can be cold, but there can be good autumn colors
Map: Tom Harrison's Trail Map of the Angeles High Country

Overview: Often overlooked by the hordes of people who frequent the front range of the San Gabriels, the Valyermo District offers some of the best, most scenic, and least crowded riding in all of the Angeles National Forest. It's easy to get to for residents of the Antelope Valley, but it also makes a good weekend escape for others in the southland. In fact, since the trail network is relatively small, you can easily sample the best rides in the district in a single weekend.

The Valyermo District is long and narrow and runs from its western border near Little Rock Reservoir to the eastern border at Wrightwood. To the north lie Valyermo and Pearblossom and the expanse of the Mojave. The San Gabriel and Sheep Mountain Wilderness Areas line its southern border.

The northeastern corner of the district houses the bulk of the riding, and this area is well known to snow bunnies since it contains several ski areas. The fun really begins when the snow melts, uncovering a network of roads and trails that pass through beautiful forest with thin, clean air. Trails that are not included here but that are worth trying include the Blue Ridge Trail and the Manzanita Trail.

This particular ride offers an easy climb if you leave out Pinyon Ridge, and a more challenging one if you don't. The carrot at the end of the Pinyon Ridge stick is a sweeping view of the tortured rock formations of Devils Punchbowl. The loop ends with a great 3-mile singletrack, which isn't particularly technical, except that it is quite narrow in spots. If you don't feel comfortable with this, you can turn around and go back the way you came.

Getting There: From Highway 138 in Pearblossom, turn right on Longview Road. About 0.4 mile later, turn left on Valyermo Road. Follow it through Valyermo and past the Valyermo Ranger Station. Just beyond

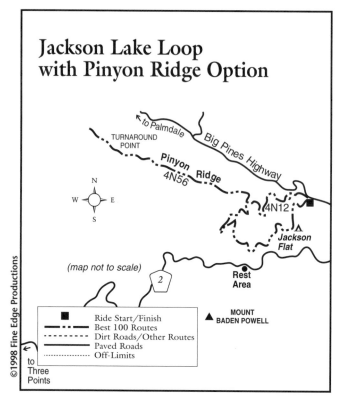

Jackson Lake Loop
with Pinyon Ridge Option

to Palmdale
TURNAROUND
POINT
Big Pines Highway
Pinyon Ridge
4N56
N
W   E
S
4N12
Jackson
Flat
(map not to scale)
2
Rest
Area

■   Ride Start/Finish
▬ ▬ ▪   Best 100 Routes
- - - - - -   Dirt Roads/Other Routes
▬▬▬   Paved Roads
. . . .   Off-Limits

▲ MOUNT
BADEN POWELL

to
Three
Points

©1998 Fine Edge Productions

by the truly lovely scenery. In the fall, the leaves on the big leaf maples turn auburn and red, awaiting the first cold snap to fall away and litter the ground, and the air is cold and clear.

At 2.7 miles, you reach a Y-intersection, the turnoff to Pinyon Ridge. This section, of a different character, rolls along a sometimes rocky and sometimes sandy road through stands of pinyon pine and ends with a nifty view of Devils Punchbowl.

If you're up for the challenge, turn right and climb up 4N56. The first pitch is the hardest section, and once you grunt your way over it, you're on a big rollercoaster to road's end. Short spurs and pullouts give you ample opportunity to stop and enjoy the desert views.

At 6.9 miles the road ends and you can see down into Devils Punchbowl County Park. The twisted rocks you see are the result of the San Andreas Rift Zone, which cuts through the desert on this northern side of the San Gabriels.

When you're done oohing and aahing, head back the way you came. A much harder ride in this direction, the road regains lost elevation in short, steep bursts until, at 11.1 miles, you're back to 4N12.

Go right on 4N12 and resume

here, after the intersection with Big Rock Creek Road, Valyermo Road turns into Big Pines Highway. Follow it for 3.5 miles to the Jackson Lake turnoff (a right turn) and park in the lot here. Bathrooms are available.

From Wrightwood, take Angeles Crest Highway west to Mountain High, and turn down Big Pines Highway for 3 miles to the Jackson Lake parking area.

Route: Follow the paved entrance back out toward Big Pines Highway. Just before the highway, there is a dirt cutoff to the left. Take this path under the oaks and you will come to fire road 4N12. Follow this dirt road straight ahead and up through the organization camp, rolling along an easy grade. The climb is made less stressful

climbing, but at a much easier grade. At 12.4 miles keep left at the intersection. It gets steeper for a mile or so till you get to another split in the road. The right fork takes you down to Angeles Crest Highway at Vincent Gulch Road. You go hard left onto 3N26 (which may be gated) to keep on climbing.

You reach a trail on your left (in the middle of a right-hand corner) at 13.2 miles. This is the 3-mile single-track return to Jackson Lake. A lovely trail, it sidehills around, at times covered with shale and at other times loose, never dropping too steeply.

Eventually it cuts into the trees and you lose the exposure. You can relax now and enjoy the swooping ride. Near its end, there's a distinct split in the trail. You can take either route as they both very quickly dump you onto a dirt road. Go left and follow it back around into the parking area.

A winter descent.

Tony Quiroz

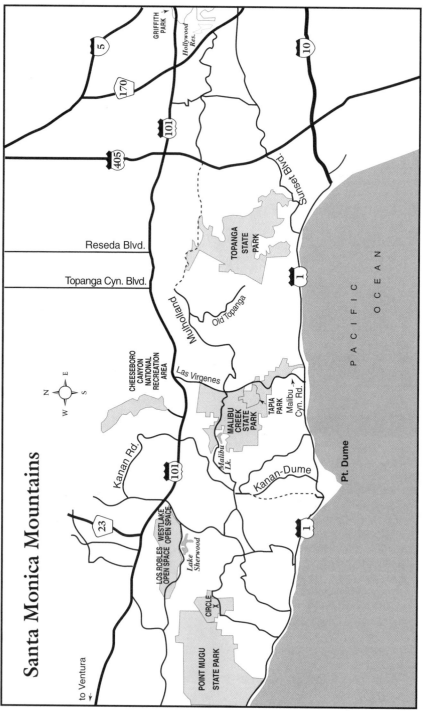

CHAPTER 6

Santa Monica Mountains

By Jim Hasenauer and Mark Langton

Within minutes of Los Angeles, one of the largest urban centers in the country, the mountain bicyclist enters a world more natural, more rugged and in striking contrast to the sprawling city and suburbs below. This is the Santa Monica Mountains National Recreation Area, with more miles of more varied mountain bike riding than any other urban park in the United States. Wildlife and natural vegetation abound; deer and bobcat are occasionally seen within yards of residential developments.

The Santa Monica Range is narrow—1 to 10 miles wide—and steep. Most canyons run in a north-south direction, carrying water either to the ocean or the inland valleys. Bicyclists usually find themselves climbing or descending; there is not much flat land or ridge riding. While this can be discouraging for beginners, some parks, such as Malibu Creek and Point Mugu, do offer great beginner rides. Once bicyclists are comfortable climbing long hills, they will be able to enjoy most of the rides in this chapter. No matter what your ability level, be sure to carry plenty of water. Water sources are few and far between.

Along with the miles of tremendous riding opportunities in the Santa Monicas come certain responsibilities and restrictions. Mountain bicyclists must be aware of current land management policies and honor all regulations; they must minimize impact on the land and be cognizant of the safety and enjoyment of other users. At press time, all the rides in this chapter are legally open to bicyclists, but regulations are in flux and changes occur regularly. For up-to-date information contact the appropriate land managers.

We hope you will join the rest of the responsible mountain bikers in the Santa Monica Mountains National Recreation Area to spread the message of conscientious, courteous mountain biking throughout the Santa Monica Mountains and continue to make mountain biking safe and fun for all users.

Topanga State Park

Trippet Ranch/East Topanga Loop

48

Distance: 19.5 miles
Difficulty: Very strenuous, not technical
Elevation: 3,500' gain/loss (approximate)
Ride Type: Loop on fire road
Season: Year-round
Map: Fine Edge Productions' Santa Monica Mountains Recreation Topo Map

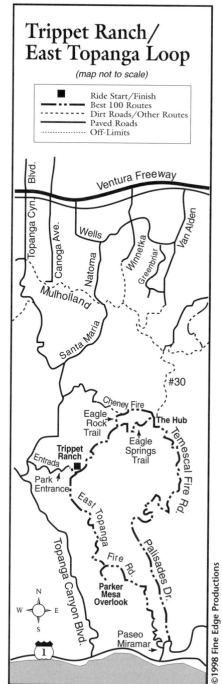

Trippet Ranch/
East Topanga Loop
(map not to scale)

■ Ride Start/Finish
— Best 100 Routes
- - - Dirt Roads/Other Routes
Paved Roads
Off-Limits

©1998 Fine Edge Productions

Overview: This 19.5-mile ride has plenty of climbing for intermediate to expert cyclists.

Getting There: The best access to this state park is from Trippet Ranch. From the San Fernando Valley, go south on Topanga Canyon Boulevard. From the top of Topanga, turn left on Entrada and proceed uphill to Topanga State Park. Stay on Entrada, passing two lower lots. At the junction, bear left on Entrada, left into the parking area, and pay a day-use fee. At the fire road entrance on the southeast end of the parking lot a sign reads: *2 miles to Eagle Rock, 2.2 to Waterfall Santa Inez Trail* (closed to bikes), *4.8 to Mulholland* (fire road #30), *8 miles to Temescal Conference Grounds, 8.7 miles to Will Rogers, 3 miles to Parker Mesa Overlook* (south), *4.8 Pacific Palisades* (Paseo Miramar).

Route: Leaving the parking lot at Trippet Ranch, ride uphill to a T and go left. At 1.3 miles there is a three-way fork. (No bikes allowed on the left fork, Musch Trail.) Trippet Ranch Trail on the middle fork climbs to Eagle Rock. For this ride, however, take the right fork, descending to Eagle Springs and climbing to the Hub at mile 3.3. Head right (south) on East Temescal fire road. If you want to do a shorter ride, turn left—a switchback actually—and uphill to the west, which will take you back toward your starting point, past Eagle Rock and back to Trippet Ranch for a 6.4-mile round trip.

On the longer route, at mile 6.3, go through the fire gate and on to the junction of Temescal and Trailer canyons (left is Temescal, and the trail is closed to bikes farther down). Turn right on Trailer Canyon, a long, steep, rutted downhill. *Control your speed.* At 7.9 miles go through a closed fire gate and continue descending to mile 8.7. Go through another closed fire gate

and leave the dirt. This is a short cul-de-sac at Michael Drive; the sign reads *Topanga State Park, Trailer Canyon Entrance.*

Turn right on Michael Drive and left at the T-intersection at Vereda de la Montura. Go half a block and turn right on Palisades Drive (deli with restrooms and water). Descend to mile 11.8; turn right on Sunset Boulevard. At mile 12.0, turn right on Paseo Miramar. Dig in, it's a climb! Follow the yellow lines in the road to the fire road entrance at 13.3 miles. Continue climbing. The junction with Parker Mesa Overlook fire road is at 15.5 miles. For a short out-and-back with nice views, turn left and go 0.5 mile to a dead-end overlook. At mile 16.5 you're back heading north on East Topanga fire road. It returns you to the Trippet Ranch parking lot at mile 19.5.

Malibu Creek State Park

49 Crags Road/Bulldog Loop/Lakeside Lateral Loop

Distance: 6.8 miles / 15 miles / 8.6 miles
Difficulty: Varies from easy to difficult, depending on options taken
Elevation: 300' gain/loss; 3,500' gain/loss; 1,000' gain/loss (all approximate)
Ride Type: Out-and-back; loop; out-and-back with loops; all on fire roads
Season: Year-round
Map: Fine Edge Productions' Santa Monica Mountains Recreation Topo Map

Overview: Malibu Creek State Park, one of the three large state parks in the Santa Monica Mountains, offers connecting trails from the coast to the south and west. The variety of terrain and natural features enables bicyclists to enjoy a diversity of riding experiences. There are suitable rides in this area for mountain bicyclists of all levels.

The Visitor's Center at Malibu

Creek State Park has fascinating exhibits that document past uses of the park land, an area rich in history. A year-round stream that cuts through Malibu Gorge has always supported a bountiful plant and wildlife population. Human habitation dates back at least 5,000 years. The Chumash Native Americans had their largest Santa Monica Mountains settlement near here. Later

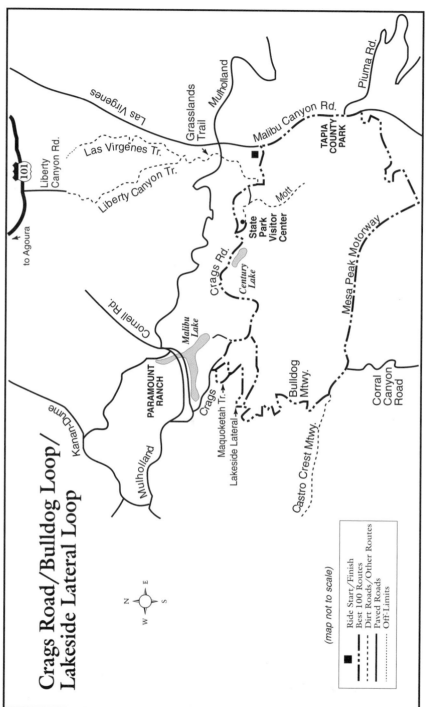

Crags Road/Bulldog Loop/
Lakeside Lateral Loop

©1998 Fine Edge Productions

(map not to scale)

Ride Start/Finish
Best 100 Routes
Dirt Roads/Other Routes
Paved Roads
Off-Limits

the valleys and grasslands were used for cattle grazing in the Mexican rancho days. An old adobe ranch house from this period is currently being restored just east of the park.

The property was later developed as the Crags Country Club, a private hunting and fishing club. Century Lake was built in 1901 for the members, some of whom built small houses here as weekend retreats. The ruins of one home, the John Mott adobe, can still be seen. The area was then acquired as the 20th Century Movie Ranch. Dozens of films were made here, since the variety of terrain and plant life allowed filmmakers to re-create settings from around the world. In addition to many westerns, the 20th Century Ranch simulated Africa in several Tarzan movies. Perhaps its most famous set was for the television series "M*A*S*H." Some of you may remember an episode in which the 4077th returned to the smoldering remains of their camp. The episode was filmed after a terrible brush fire swept the park in 1982. Now all that remains of the "M*A*S*H" site are a couple of burned-out jeeps.

Today, Malibu Creek State Park is used by bicyclists, hikers, equestrians, fishermen, picnickers and, most recently, campers who come to enjoy its rugged character. The Grotto and Century Lake are rich with bass. This much water is rare in the Santa Monicas, so unusual plant and animal life abound. The trails on the floor of the park are generally flat, inviting users of all levels, but the trails that climb to Castro Crest are steep and demanding. Because the park is so heavily used, bicyclists should always use extra caution.

Getting There: Park entrance is at Mulholland and Las Virgenes. Take Freeway 101 to Las Virgines-Malibu Canyon. Go south 3 miles, cross Mulholland, and continue 0.3 mile to the park entrance on the right (day-use fee). There is parking outside the entrance, too. You can also access Malibu Creek State Park via the Liberty Canyon and Grasslands trails. For the Liberty Canyon Trail, travel north on 101 past Las Virgenes Road/Malibu Canyon Road to Liberty Canyon Road, and then go south (left) approximately a mile to the intersection of Liberty Canyon and Park Vista. There is a black wrought iron fence with a walk-through that passes between some houses and horse stables. The Grasslands Trail crosses Mulholland Drive about a quarter-mile north of Las Virgenes Road. You can park along Mulholland and access the park from here—the trail starts with a horse walkover next to a private driveway. There is also access to Malibu Creek on Crags Drive: From Lake Vista Drive off Mulholland Highway, turn on Crags Drive to the park boundary. Within 0.8 mile you come to a parking area. A sign at the park gate reads *Bulldog Motorway*.

Route: At the last parking lot by the restrooms just off Malibu Canyon Road, set your odometer to 0.0. Take the road signed *Authorized Vehicles Only*, cross a little bridge, and begin Crags Road, which here in the park is dirt. At mile 1.7 cross another bridge and continue on the main trail. At mile 2.4, Lost Cabin Trail on the left is marked by a native mortar rock. (Lost Cabin goes 0.7 mile to a dead end.) Just past Lost Cabin Trail, you ride through a burned-out set of the television series "M*A*S*H." You'll recognize the mountains as those in helicopter scenes in the opening credits of the series.

At mile 2.7 go right at the fork (left is Bulldog Motorway, marked by a sign that reads *Park Boundary 4.3 Miles, Castro Peak Motorway 3.4 miles*). Within 0.4 mile you come to another fork. Go left here, and continue about 0.3 mile to Crags Drive at the park boundary, mile 3.4. (A right takes you 0.3 mile to a dead end at another park boundary and the waterfall end of Malibu Lake. The lake is private and not accessible.) Retrace your route to the parking lot for a 6.8-mile out-and-back.

For a tougher ride, try the brutal climb up Bulldog. From the fork at 2.7 miles, head up Bulldog to the ridge of Castro Crest and Mesa Peak. At 0.3 mile past the fork you come to a closed gate. Lift your bike over the railroad ties and reset your odometer to 0.0 mile. Continue straight at mile 0.8. The road to the right is a dead end. At mile 1.1 bear left. (To the right begins the Lakeside Lateral fire road/Lookout Loop, described at the end of this ride.)

Next there is a false summit—a cool, shady saddle with a little downhill. Enjoy it, that's all you get! Mile 3.3: Closed gate. Mile 3.4 marks the top of Bulldog and the junction with Castro Crest Motorway. Turn left. (Right goes to antenna towers on Castro Peak and descends via Newton or Brewster Motorways to Latigo Canyon.)

After the left turn, descend to mile 4.2 and the Corral Canyon parking lot, continuing through the parking lot and out onto the pavement. Watch for a fire road on the left at mile 4.6. There is a wooden fence where telephone wires cross the road. Turn left on the fire road (Mesa Peak Motorway), which has several good climbs and descends to

a fork at 7.2 miles with Puerco Canyon on the right. Go left at the fork.

In a short distance, Mesa Peak fire road comes in from the right. Bear left, descending. At mile 9.1 (you are now on Tapia Motorway) there is a hairpin right turn at a chain link fence, and the trail forks. Bear right up a little hill. At mile 9.8 the fire road ends at Malibu Canyon Road just south of Tapia County Park. A sign by the fire road reads *Tractors only*. Watch for cars, cross the street, and then turn left back to Malibu Creek State Park, passing the Hindu Temple on the right. Turn left into the state park, and at almost 12 miles you're back at the parking lot where you started.

For the Lakeside Lateral/Lookout Loop, take the Lakeside Lateral fire road at the junction 1.1 miles from the beginning of Bulldog Loop. Climb the short hill and turn right at the top. This takes you over to Lookout Road, which descends back to paved Crags Road and the park entrance. It is a good alternate route if you want to add a little distance to the Crags Road/Malibu Creek route or don't want to do the entire Bulldog Loop. Be careful as you descend after rolling for about 0.7 mile. The fire road gets very steep and, depending on the time of year, can either be extremely rutted, loose, rocky, or all of the above.

At mile 1.9 you come to the park boundary and the pavement. You can either make a right on Lookout and follow it all the way down to Crags Road, or continue down on Maquoketah Trail (paved), which winds over to Lookout where you turn left to Crags. Turn right on Crags to the park entrance. Total distance of Lakeside Lateral/Lookout Loop from Bulldog is 3.2 miles.

50 Solstice Canyon/Latigo Canyon/Backbone Trail

Distance: 6.5 miles one way
Difficulty: Very difficult
Elevation: 1500' gain (approximate); lots of ups and downs
Ride Type: Out-and-back on singletrack
Season: Year-round
Map: Fine Edge Productions' Santa Monica Mountains Recreation Topo Map

Overview: The Solstice Canyon/ Latigo Canyon/Backbone Trail, on National Park Service property, was opened up largely by the efforts of CORBA. It is virtually all single-track—very technical, with steep pitches, rocky outcroppings, deeply rutted sections, and several stream crossings. For the beginning rider it is not recommended; for the intermediate rider, it is a challenge; for the advanced rider, it is pure fun.

Getting There: From the Ventura Freeway 101, go south 7.8 miles on Kanan-Dume to the third tunnel. The parking lot is on the right just before the tunnel. From Pacific Coast Highway, go north on Kanan-Dume 4.3 miles to the first tunnel ("Tunnel One"); the parking lot is just on the other side of the tunnel on the left. To access the ride from Corral Canyon at Mesa Peak Motorway on Pacific Coast Highway, 2.4 miles west of Malibu Canyon Road, turn right on Corral Canyon Road and climb 5.3 miles to a gravel parking lot. (*Note:* Do not leave valuables in your car in the Corral Canyon parking lot; it has been the site of several thefts.)

Route: There are two ways to ride the Solstice Canyon/Latigo Canyon/ Backbone Trail: out-and-back from either the Kanan-Dume trailhead at Tunnel One or from Corral Canyon

parking lot at Mesa Peak Motorway. Both are equally challenging and offer excellent examples of the area's riparian oak habitat. Access is quite a bit easier from Kanan-Dume Road since there is less mountain road driving.

Even though it is only six miles one way, this route is an all-encompassing ride that will challenge even the best riders. For additional mileage you can ride over to Puerco Canyon via Mesa Peak Motorway.

It's best to do a good warm-up before you start the trail from Kanan-Dume Road, since it begins with a strenuous uphill section. The climb is only a quarter of a mile long, but it is very taxing for the beginning of the ride. If you want to add on about two miles of fun singletrack as a warm-up, you can go down to the right-away from Kanan-Dume Road onto the still uncompleted extension of the Backbone Trail as it heads west. At 0.3 mile you come to a footpath that leads along a stream down into Zuma Canyon. This is a bike portage at best—the trail is very steep and overgrown. Continue on the main single-track as it climbs back up toward Kanan-Dume Road. At 0.5 mile, the trail comes up to a connector that feeds a smaller turnout off Kanan-Dume Road (7.3 miles from Ventura Freeway). Continue straight along the trail until it ends. At the time of this printing, the trail extension was

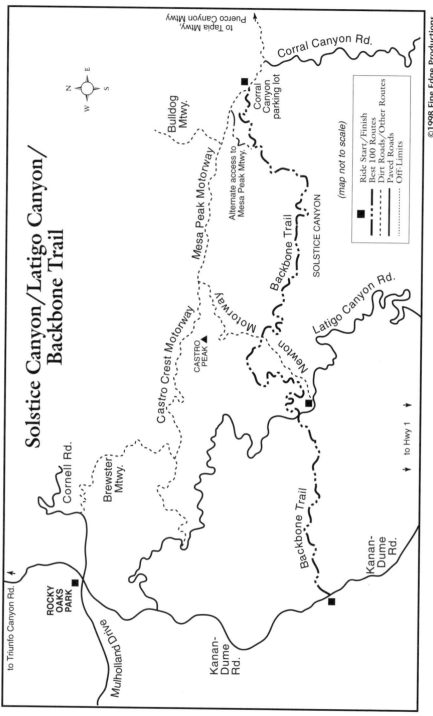

Solstice Canyon/Latigo Canyon/Backbone Trail

©1998 Fine Edge Productions

(map not to scale)

Ride Start/Finish
Best 100 Routes
Dirt Roads/Other Routes
Paved Roads
Off-Limits

just under a mile long. At the end, turn around and ride back to the Tunnel One parking lot to begin the section of the Backbone Trail described below.

Mileage from Kanan-Dume Road: 0.0 mile: From the parking lot at Tunnel One, the trail climbs steeply toward the coast, up to the top of the tunnel. After climbing the steep hill, turn left and cross over the tunnel. Continue a short way to a paved drive, cross straight over, and continue to Latigo Canyon Road at 2.3 miles. (You can either go straight across to the other side of Latigo Canyon Road and through the parking lot to the continuation of the Solstice Canyon/Latigo Backbone Trail, or turn right and continue to the Hellacious Acres trailhead where Newton Motorway meets Latigo Canyon Road.) Continuing across Latigo Canyon Road, you descend into a beautiful canyon full of ferns and oak trees. As you climb out of the canyon, the trail becomes very steep and rutted, most likely requiring dismounting. After the steep section, the trail becomes more rolling and then intersects Newton Motorway at 3.8 miles. Above you to the left is Castro Peak with its radio communication towers. Across Newton Motorway and slightly to the right is the continuation of the Backbone Trail into Solstice Canyon.

If you choose to turn right on Latigo Canyon Road instead of going across Latigo Canyon Road onto the Latigo section of the Backbone Trail, go to 2.6 miles (a wrought iron sign reads *Hellacious Acres)* and turn left, past a fire gate marked private, and continue climbing. This climb tops out and then descends quickly to a Y at mile 3.2. Take the left branch

(right goes to private property; please do not trespass). At mile 3.3, you come to the intersection of the Latigo portion of the Solstice Canyon/Latigo Backbone Trail from Latigo Canyon on the left, and the Solstice Canyon portion as it comes from Corral Canyon at Mesa Peak Motorway on the right.

After crossing Newton Motorway, continue back on the singletrack (turn right if you came from Hellacious Acres). *Be careful!* This trail is very narrow in some places, and it can be very rutted as well. There are also four tight switchbacks as you descend into the canyon, one of which is very eroded. Once you drop into the canyon bottom, the terrain becomes rocky with several stream crossings, depending on the time of year. At 4.8 miles, you begin climbing out of the canyon and up toward Mesa Peak Motorway. Here the trail becomes more rolling, with several little steep climbs and descents. At 5.5 miles, you come to a wire break dirt road. (You can go left for another short, steep climb that ascends to Mesa Peak Motorway approximately a quarter of the way to its intersection with Bulldog Motorway. Right leads to a wire tower.) Continue straight on the wide dirt road to go to the Corral Canyon parking lot. In just 0.1 mile (at 5.6 miles) the singletrack comes back in on the left and continues to Corral Canyon parking lot, 6.5 miles. (Mileage without the middle Latigo section of the Backbone singletrack is just over 6 miles.)

Mileage from Corral Canyon parking lot: Mile 0.0: Descend the switchbacks and turn right onto a wide dirt road that comes in at mile 0.5. When you come to another wide dirt road, continue straight onto a singletrack.

This trail is rolling, with several short climbs and descents. At 1.3 miles, you reach the canyon bottom. After several stream crossings you climb four sharp switchbacks then reach Newton Motorway at 2.7 miles. From here you can continue straight across to the middle Latigo single-track section of the Backbone Trail, or you can turn left and take Newton Motorway toward the coast to Latigo Canyon road 0.7 miles farther.

For the Newton Motorway option, you climb a bit before turning right just past the gate at a Y, away from private property. At 3.4 miles you come to Latigo Canyon Road. To get onto the remaining section of the Backbone Trail, turn right and go downhill to mile 3.7, where the trail comes in on the left. Take this trail back to the Kanan-Dume Tunnel One parking lot.

If you chose to stay on the Latigo section of the Backbone Trail rather than taking Newton Motorway, the trail rolls along for a mile or so before you reach a very steep, rutted des-cent that is quite dangerous. After the rutted section of the trail drops into a lush, fern-infested canyon, it climbs back up to Latigo Canyon Road and a parking lot at mile 4.2. Go across Latigo Canyon Road to hook up with the last section of the Backbone Trail (Newton Backbone) as it descends to Kanan-Dume Road. At mile 6 you come to a paved drive; go straight across to the trail with the railroad ties. You will probably be able to hear traffic on Kanan-Dume at this point. At 6.3 miles you are on top of Tunnel One and, unless you arranged a shuttle, you may want to turn around here rather than drop-ping down the quarter-mile into the Tunnel One parking lot. If you want to add about two miles of fun single-track, however, you can go down in-to the parking lot and veer left, con-tinuing down onto the still in-complete extension of the Backbone Trail as it continues west. This is the warm-up ride outlined at the begin-ning of Solstice Canyon/ Latigo Canyon/Backbone Trail description.

Pt. Mugu State Park

Point Mugu State Park is one of the most popular bicycling areas in the Santa Monicas. It has spectacular scenery and several loop options for bicyclists. The main trail—actually an old fire road—is relatively flat and connects Newbury Park with the beach, where there is camping at Sycamore Canyon Campground.

The park offers five miles of ocean shoreline, two long rides in canyon bottomland, and a long ridge ride overlooking both the canyon and ocean. La Jolla Valley (currently closed to bikes) has one of the finest displays of native grasslands left in California. Bluffs near the ocean are among the few places in the world with giant coreopsis, a small tree-like shrub with bright yellow spring flow-ers. Silvery sycamores, thriving on deep underground water, mark the canyon floor and put on a wild dis-play of color in the fall.

The park is inhabited by several large animals, including at least two mountain lions (one is called Big Tail). In winter, thousands of Mon-arch butterflies come through during their migration south from colder

Trail work ensures open trails for mountain bicyclists.

climes. Because Point Mugu is located on the northwest tip of Santa Monica Bay, it provides an excellent viewing point for the California gray whale migrations in winter and spring.

Four miles northwest of Sycamore Cove, an observation platform on the west side of Pacific Coast Highway overlooks the saltwater Mugu Lagoon. There is a picnic table here, and it's a good place to watch for birds. Point Mugu Rock, a popular bouldering area for climbers, is located one mile to the southeast. From the observation platform you can see several rare or endangered birds, including the brown pelican, clapper rail, Belding savannah sparrow, California least tern and marsh sandpiper. To the east of the lagoon grows the giant coreopsis. Do not disturb these birds or plants; they are protected species. *Note:* The property behind the fence belongs to the government.

Unauthorized persons must stay out.

Many archeological sites from the Chumash culture have been discovered at Point Mugu State Park. Ranching began during the Spanish period when the area was known as the Guadalasca Land Grant. Most recently it was the Danielson family ranch. The Danielsons sold the land to the state to be preserved as a park. This was a critical event in the development of the Santa Monica Mountains National Recreation Area, since there were plans to develop a hotel and golf course on the Point Mugu park land. Local environmentalists joined efforts, and eventually this western cornerstone to the Santa Monicas was acquired for public use.

Sycamore Canyon in Point Mugu State Park draws big crowds. Use extra caution if you ride here, especially on summer weekends. For a more pleasant ride, we suggest cycling during the week or in winter.

51 Sycamore Canyon/ Guadalasca Trail Loop with Wood Canyon View Trail Option

Distance: 13.2 miles
Difficulty: Moderate with some steep climbs and descents
Elevation: 2,700' gain/loss
Ride Type: Loop on mostly dirt roads and singletrack
Season: Year-round
Map: Fine Edge Productions' Santa Monica Mountains Recreation Topo Map

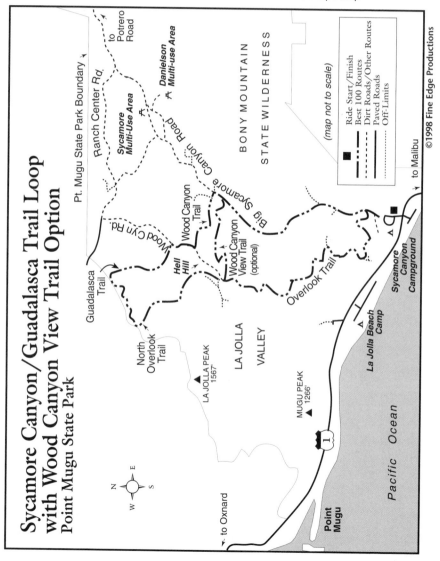

Overview: While there are several options available to both the recreational and hard-core mountain biker, this ride offers the best that Point Mugu has to offer. Riding this route in reverse would add fire road climbing and singletrack descending. Beginners can simply ride up Sycamore Canyon as far as they like before returning.

Getting There: The best access is from the beach at Sycamore Canyon Campground, 5 miles north of Leo Carrillo State Beach on Pacific Coast Highway. An entry fee is required for campground day use.

Route: Begin at the Big Sycamore Canyon fire road at the back of the Sycamore Canyon Campground. At 2.0 miles you pass a picnic table under a huge overhanging oak tree. At 3.9 miles on the left is the entrance to the Wood Canyon View Trail, a 1.8-mile singletrack that climbs up to Overlook Trail. It is moderate to difficult most of the way, a good challenge to experienced riders. You may choose to descend this trail back down into Sycamore Canyon after climbing Guadalasca Trail—mileage markers are described later in this section.

Continue past the entrance to Wood Canyon View Trail 0.1 mile to Wood Canyon Trail. Bear left and continue to Deer Camp Junction at mile 4.8. Turn right (to the left is the infamous Hell Hill climb) and go to mile 5.2 and the intersection of Guadalasca Trail on your left. The trail starts out fairly wide and groomed as it used to be an old ranch road that serviced the Spanish Guadalasca Rancho. Climb through a beautiful riparian oak forest and then gain elevation into scrub oak. At 6 miles a singletrack comes in from the left. Take the singletrack and begin climbing several perfectly radiused switchbacks. At mile 7.8 you come to the intersection of North Overlook fire road. Turn left up a short hill and then descend to the intersection of Hell Hill and Overlook Trail just past mile 9.

Option: Just a few yards past this intersection on Overlook Trail is the upper entrance to Wood Canyon View Trail to the left. Turn left here to descend the moderate-to-difficult singletrack back to Sycamore Canyon. Turn right at Sycamore Canyon to return to the campground.

For the main route, continue straight on Overlook Trail for about a mile of gentle climbing and then a great descent back into Sycamore Canyon with panoramic views of Sycamore Canyon and the Pacific Ocean. At mile 12.7 you meet up with Big Sycamore Canyon fire road. Turn right and ride 0.5 mile back to the campground for a total of 13.2 miles.

Cheeseboro Canyon National Recreation Area

Technically, Cheeseboro Canyon National Recreation Area is not part of the Santa Monica Mountains. It is, however, the major National Park Service (NPS) holding in the Santa Monica Mountains National Recreation Area, and it is the major wildlife corridor for animals traveling from the Angeles Forest and Santa Susanna Mountains to the Santa Monicas. It's one of the few parks with open singletracks. The NPS is very good about signing trails for approved travel. Please obey signs that indicate approved use.

Part of an old cattle ranch, the area resembles Marin County—rolling hills, coastal oaks, sea breezes on the ridges and enough horse and cow plop to remind you that this is the West. Wildlife includes golden eagles, deer, bobcat, hawks, coyotes, and the usual assortment of reptiles. *Caution: There are many rattlesnakes here.*

In 1994, the National Park Service purchased Palo Comado Canyon and China Flat to the west and north, effectively doubling the size of the Cheeseboro Canyon holding. This has expanded the riding opportunities significantly.

Currently the property to the east and north of Cheeseboro Canyon remains accessible via park roads, yet it is technically private and you are subject to any enforcement deemed appropriate by law.

52 Sulphur Springs Trail

Distance: 12.5 miles
Difficulty: Moderate, somewhat technical
Elevation: 500' gain/loss (approximate)
Ride Type: Out-and-back on dirt road and singletrack
Season: Year-round
Map: Fine Edge Productions' Santa Monica Mountains Recreation Topo Map

Overview: The main Sulphur Springs trail is a 6.25-mile dead-end route with four offshoots. Riders on the main trail can explore the canyon bottomland which rolls through grasslands and coastal oak groves into dense chaparral. The side trails that climb to the ridges above the park afford bird's-eye views of the canyon below.

Getting There: Take Freeway 101 to the Cheseboro exit (2.7 miles west of Las Virgenes Road or 2.4 miles east of Kanan-Dume Road). Head north and make a quick right on Chesebro Road. (No one seems to know why, but the road name and the canyon name are spelled differently.) Follow the narrow street 1 mile to a right turn just before the sign: *Agoura Hills City Limit.* You can park here or continue up the gravel road a quarter-mile to another parking lot.

Route: Begin at the outer gate off Cheseboro Road, and proceed 0.3 mile to the other parking lot and the Sulphur Springs trail entrance. There is a bulletin board information center where you can study maps and read about the Cheeseboro Recreation Area's natural history. There are port-a-potties here, but no water is available. At mile 0.8 go past the south entrance to Modello Trail on the left. Just short of mile 1.0, you pass the junction with Canyon Overlook Trail on the right. At 1.3 miles the area to the side of the trail is signed *Research Area.* (*Stay out; do not leave the main trail.* The Park Service is trying to restore native grasslands and to study the impact of fire and other phenomena on the oak and native flora.)

At 1.5 miles, bear left past the Y with Baleen Wall Trail on the right. At 1.6 miles, go straight at the junc-

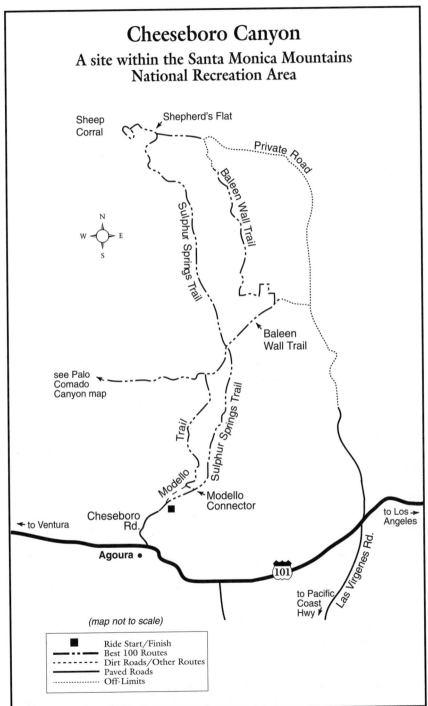

Cheeseboro Canyon
A site within the Santa Monica Mountains National Recreation Area

Sheep Corral

Shepherd's Flat

Private Road

Baleen Wall Trail

Sulphur Springs Trail

N
W   E
S

Baleen Wall Trail

see Palo Comado Canyon map

Trail

Modello

Sulphur Springs Trail

Modello Connector

Cheseboro Rd.

← to Ventura

to Los Angeles →

Agoura ●

101

to Pacific Coast Hwy ↓

Las Virgenes Rd.

(map not to scale)

■	Ride Start/Finish
▬ ▪ ▬ ▪	Best 100 Routes
- - - - -	Dirt Roads/Other Routes
▬▬▬	Paved Roads
....	Off-Limits

©1998 Fine Edge Productions

tion with Modello Trail (on the left), and at mile 4.1 you pass a hiking trail headed toward the Baleen Wall posted *No bikes.* (It is illegal to take your bike on this trail.) At mile 4.4 the road turns to singletrack and crosses a stream. On the left, just after you cross the stream, you can see a rock with some interesting fossils.

The singletrack follows the sometimes sandy streambed up the canyon. There are short, steep dips and climbs and plenty of rocks on the trail. At about mile 5.7 the trail comes to a T-junction. Right (east) is a dead-end. Left (west) connects to Palo Comado. In spring the area around these forks has plenty of wildflowers. Return to the trailhead from the T, watching for Modello Trail on the right. Take it (see Modello Trail below), or continue straight to the main parking lot at mile 12.5.

From the Sulphur Springs Trail, you have several optional trails to explore. **Canyon Overlook Trail** leaves Sulphur Springs Trail about one mile from the park entrance. Turn right for a non-technical 0.7-mile, 500-foot climb (east and then south) to a hill overlooking some of the canyons and ridges of Cheeseboro Park. When the mustard is blooming in the spring this area is carpeted in yellow. The road is quite rutted so *watch your steep downhill return* to the Sulphur Springs Trail.

Baleen Wall Trail offers 5.4 miles of moderate dirt road with a 2-mile service road option. You gain 2,000 feet in elevation on this out-and-back ride. At 1.5 miles on the Sulphur Springs Trail, turn right onto the Baleen Wall Trail. Reset your odometer to 0.0 mile. Bear left past the service road at mile 0.7 on the right. (It climbs for a mile up to electric towers and great views of the canyon.) The trail climbs steeply. At 1.3 miles you

pass a water tank on the left and head back to the north. At 2.5 miles the road forks again; follow the main road. The hiking trail to the left is just that: *illegal for bikes.* The road deadends at the last electric tower at mile 2.7 in high grass. From here, you can see the top of the Baleen Wall rock formations. Return down the long descent to Sulphur Springs Trail.

Modello Trail, an easy to moderate doubletrack and dirt road combination, is a good optional return route to the parking area. There is a 1,000-foot elevation gain and some exposure. At 0.8 mile on the Sulphur Springs Trail you pass the south entrance to the Modello Trail on the left. Farther up Sulphur Springs at 1.6 miles is the north entrance of Modello on the left. You will probably want to ride the rest of Sulphur Springs Trail and/or Balleen Wall Trail before returning to this point. When you are ready, reset your odometer to 0.0 at the north entrance to Modello Trail. Climb 0.3 mile (west) to a left turn onto doubletrack. Continue climbing to the junction at mile 1.0 and turn right to descend 0.3 mile to the parking lots. (The left descends to the south junction with Sulphur Springs Trail.)

You can also access the new **Palo Comado** holding from the Sulphur Springs Trail. Using the Sulphur Springs Trail/Modello Trail descriptions above, take Sulphur Springs Trail to the north Modello Trail connector at 1.6 miles on your left, but do not zero out your odometer. Climb the doubletrack to the intersection of Modello Trail at 1.9 miles. Across the small valley you can see a fence and open gate entrance along the ridge. Bearing right, drop down the short descent and then up to the ridge and through the gate. Then descend again into another deeper valley and climb up the opposite side. Stay on the main trail, a wide dirt road, as it crests yet another ridge and over a saddle. You descend once more into Palo Comado Canyon.

At 2.9 miles you come to the intersection of the lower Palo Comado Canyon main trail. To your left is the park boundary and private property. Please do not enter or exit here. Go right, up the canyon along the rolling fire road. At 3.6 miles you come to a fire road that comes in from the left. This is an old ranch road that takes you to Oak Park, but it is not a main access. It does, however, lead to a ridge road that takes you back down toward where you came into Palo Comado Canyon from Cheeseboro Canyon. Continue up Palo Comado Canyon to about mile 4.0 and a dirt road on your right. This is the middle connector between Palo Comado Canyon and Cheeseboro Canyon. (Ahead and to the left approximately 0.1 mile is the Oak Park connector dirt road that is the main access to Palo Comado from Oak Park. See Palo Comado Canyon/Cheeseboro Canyon Loop with China Flat Option description to con-

tinue up Palo Comado Canyon.)

To return to Cheeseboro Canyon, turn right uphill. The climb gets very steep here for about 0.5 mile. At 4.7 miles you cross over a ridge and begin descending steeply into Cheeseboro Canyon. At 5.2 miles you intersect with Cheeseboro Canyon at Sulphur Springs Trail. Turn right and begin a gentle descent back toward the parking lot.

Almost immediately you come to a Y, with the right branch taking you onto a short singletrack that connects with Sulphur Springs Trail. If you go left, there will be a wider connector on the right in just a few yards. If you go straight at this connector, the dirt road connects with Sulphur Springs Trail approximately 0.5 mile down canyon.

Using the singletrack connector (it's the most fun), continue down-canyon to 6.2 miles and the north entrance to the Modello Trail. You can either climb 0.3 mile to the intersection and take the Modello Trail ridge route and singletrack back to the parking lot, or stay low and take the main canyon trail. Total mileage is about 7.6 miles using the lower main canyon route.

53 Palo Comado Canyon/ Cheeseboro Canyon Loop with China Flats Option

Distance: 10 miles; China Flats out-and-back, 7.5 miles
Difficulty: Moderate-to-difficult with some technical singletrack
Elevation: 1400' gain/loss
Ride Type: Lollipop loop on dirt roads and singletrack
Season: Year-round
Map: Fine Edge Productions' Santa Monica Mountains Recreation Topo Map

Overview: Palo Comado Canyon and China Flats are wonderful examples of what can be accomplished by commu-

nity activism and political vision. At one point, it looked as though this beautiful oak-lined canyon and rugged

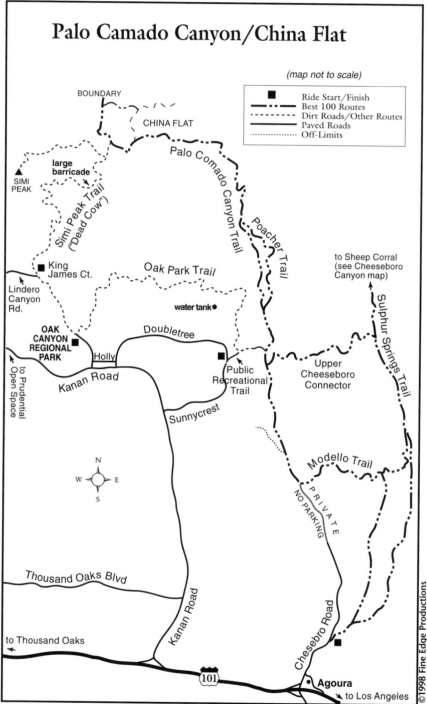

Palo Camado Canyon/China Flat

(map not to scale)

Legend:
- ■ Ride Start/Finish
- —·—·— Best 100 Routes
- - - - - Dirt Roads/Other Routes
- ——— Paved Roads
- ·········· Off-Limits

BOUNDARY

CHINA FLAT

Palo Comado Canyon Trail

SIMI PEAK ▲

large barricade

Simi Peak Trail ("Dead Cow")

Poacher Trail

to Sheep Corral (see Cheeseboro Canyon map)

King James Ct.

Oak Park Trail

Lindero Canyon Rd.

water tank ●

Sulphur Springs Trail

OAK CANYON REGIONAL PARK

Doubletree

Holly

Kanan Road

to Prudential Open Space

Public Recreational Trail

Upper Cheeseboro Connector

Sunnycrest

Modello Trail

N
W   E
S

PRIVATE NO PARKING

Thousand Oaks Blvd

Kanan Road

Chesebro Road

to Thousand Oaks

©1998 Fine Edge Productions

101

● Agoura

to Los Angeles

mountain meadow would be lost to developers. But tenacious environmentalists and creative politicians, along with the Santa Monica Mountains Conservancy and National Park Service, enabled the area to be saved in 1993, effectively doubling the area of Cheeseboro Canyon and making it the single largest NPS-held parcel in the Santa Monica Mountains National Recreation Area.

Getting There: There are several access points to Palo Comado Canyon and China Flats, as well as Oak Park Regional Park, which is part of the Rancho Simi Park and Recreation District. For purposes of simplicity, the Palo Comado Canyon/China Flats area is described as a loop beginning in Oak Park, using Palo Comado Canyon from Oak Park as the main entrance.

To access Palo Comado Canyon/China Flats from Oak Park: From Ventura Freeway 101, take Kanan Road east 2 miles past several traffic signals to a stop sign. The next street is Sunnycrest Drive. Turn right and follow up and around until you get to the second left-hand curve, 2.9 miles from the freeway. On your right is the Public Recreational Trail entrance with a cable barricade marked with an *Off-Road Vehicles Prohibited* sign. This curve is where Sunnycrest turns into Doubletree Drive. Parking is available all along the street. (For a longer ride, see the Palo Comado Access section of the previous Sulphur Springs Trail ride.)

Route: From Doubletree/Sunnycrest, take the Public Recreational Trail southeast down into Palo Comado Canyon. You come to a T at about 0.5 mile. Turn left up-canyon (or if you want to access Cheeseboro

Canyon, turn right and go a little over 0.1 mile to a dirt road on your left which takes you to the Sulphur Springs Trail.)

At 1.3 miles Palo Comado Canyon Trail begins climbing more steeply. At 1.4 miles, there is a trail that comes in on the right which is a moderately technical singletrack that climbs and parallels the Palo Comado Canyon Trail. It is locally known as the Parallel Trail or Poacher Trail because there are skeletal remains of cows along it. The area is known for its illegal poaching activities even to this day.

Mileage and directions are as follows for the Poacher Trail spur. Begin climbing. At about 0.6 mile from the beginning of the spur (almost 2 miles from your car), you can see the Baleen Wall to the south (right) in Cheeseboro Canyon. At 0.7 mile you come to a reverse Y. Bear left. Just a little farther ahead, approximately 100 yards, is a trail coming in from the right which switchbacks to the right. This is the connector over to the Sheep Corral and into Cheeseboro Canyon. A little farther (2.2 miles total) you come to a T. To the left leads you to a 4WD hill and down to Palo Comado Canyon Trail. To the right is the preferred route, which also will take you to the main trail but which is much more rideable. At 0.9 mile you meet the main Palo Comado Canyon Trail fire road. Total mileage from you car at this point is nearly 2.3 miles.

If you ride the main Palo Comado Canyon Trail instead of riding the Poacher Trail, at just past 2.1 miles, you come to where the Poacher Trail/Shepherd's Flat (Cheeseboro Canyon) connector trail comes back into the main trail. Mileage is as follows for this fun and moderately technical singletrack. At 2.3 miles you come to a Y. Take the left trail uphill for a short distance. You then round an uphill corner and promptly begin descending into a narrow canyon. The trail dips and rolls, and finally comes to an old sheep corral at mile 3.0 (0.8 from the Palo Comado fire road). Continue on this singletrack for about 0.1 mile to a singletrack that enters from the right. Going straight takes you, with very little technical riding, to Shepherd's Flat, while the right trail is more technical and more fun. Mileage to Shepherd's Flat taking the right trail is almost 1.2 miles from Palo Comado fire road, or a total of 3.3 miles from Oak Park.

At Shepherd's Flat a trail goes straight ahead while another leads to the right. The trail to the right is Sulphur Springs Trail which leads down into Cheeseboro Canyon. To continue the loop, descend the Sulphur Springs Trail through rolling single- and doubletrack until you come to Modello Trail on the right (4.2 miles from Shepherd's Flat, 7.5 miles total). Go right uphill 0.3 mile, past a trail intersection on the left (which leads to the Cheeseboro Canyon parking lot). Across the small valley you can see a fence and open gate entrance along the ridge. Bearing right, drop down the short descent and then up to the ridge and through the open gate. Then descend again into another deeper valley and climb on the opposite side. Stay on the main trail, a wide dirt road, as it crests yet another ridge and crosses a saddle. You descend once more into Palo Comado Canyon.

At 8.7 miles you come to the intersection of the lower Palo Comado Canyon main trail. To your left is the park boundary and private property. *Please do not enter or exit here.* Go right up-canyon along the rolling fire road. At 9.5 miles you come to a fire road that comes in from the left. This is an old ranch road that takes you over to Oak Park, but is not a main access. It does, however, lead to a ridge road that takes you back down to where you came into Palo Comado Canyon from Cheeseboro Canyon. Continue up Palo Comado Canyon to 9.8 miles and a dirt road on your right. This is the middle connector between Palo Comado Canyon and Cheeseboro Canyon. Ahead and to the left approximately 0.1 mile is the Oak Park Recreational Trail that goes back to Doubletree/Sunnycrest and your car.

You can opt to lengthen your ride by riding out to China Flats and back. This would add 7.5 miles. Reset your odometer and continue up Palo Comado Canyon Trail. There are active springs along this section, so even in summer the ground may be wet. You climb steeply to 3.1 miles, then descend a short hill to an old horse corral just past 3.1 miles. From here there are two ways to access China Flats. The best way is to turn right at the old corral. If you continue on the main dirt road, it loops around and comes up to China Flats from the opposite direction.

Turning right at the old corral, you climb a short hill and then cruise over to a scenic oak-filled meadow at 3.3 miles. Bear right at the Y to continue around the meadow's perimeter and the scrub oak-covered mound directly in front of you. At 3.5 miles you come to a narrow trail that comes in from the right. This little out-and-back singletrack is fun; it takes you 0.5 mile toward the Albertson Motorway for an additional mile of riding.

Continuing on the oak meadow perimeter trail, you come to an intersection at 3.7 miles. This is the termination of the Palo Comado Canyon Trail (had you gone straight, instead of right, at the old corral at 3.1 miles). The trail directly ahead of you makes a short loop to a scenic overlook. To the right is the park boundary and private property. You can either turn around at this point or turn left downhill to return to the main Palo Comado Canyon Trail fire road, past the old corral, and back down into Palo Comado Canyon, where you can either take the connector over to Cheeseboro Canyon, the Poacher Trail paralleling Palo Comado Canyon, or Palo Comado Canyon Trail back down to the Oak Park Public Recreation Trail that leads back to Doubletree/Sunnycrest and your car.

Westlake Open Space

54 Conejo Crest/White Horse/Triunfo Park

Distance: 6.82 miles, with shorter loops available
Difficulty: Moderate-to-difficult, with some advanced technical singletrack skills required
Elevation: 1,500' gain (approximate)
Ride Type: Loop on dirt roads and singletrack
Season: Year-round
Map: Fine Edge Productions' Santa Monica Mountains Recreation Topo Map

Overview: The technical single- and doubletrack trails in this area offer a variety of options and lots of fun. This particular loop provides great views of the Santa Monica Mountains and Westlake.

Getting There: There are several access points to the Westlake Open Space. From the east side you can enter at Fairview off the 101 at Hampshire or across the street from the equestrian center off Potrero Road in Westlake Village. From the west, you can access the upper plateau before the Los Robles Ridge Trail by taking Moorpark Road off 101, going south to Los Padres, left to Hillsborough, and right to the top of the hill. Access is on the right. However, the majority of the trail network is off Hampshire to the east.

For Hampshire trail access, go north on Freeway 101 to Thousand Oaks, exit Hampshire Road, go south toward Westlake to Willow Lane (the first street after you go under the freeway from San Fernando Valley/Agoura or after turning right off the freeway coming from Ventura). Turn right on Willow to Fairview Road, then left on Fairview. Fairview ends at Foothill Road. Straight ahead you see a dirt road going between some houses. You can drive up this road to a locked gate, but the road is not well suited to vehicular travel.

Route: At Foothill and Fairview, set your odometer to 0.0. Continue up the fire road to a pump house on the left and a locked gate at mile 0.3. Go over the gate and turn right on the fire road. At almost 1.0 mile you come to

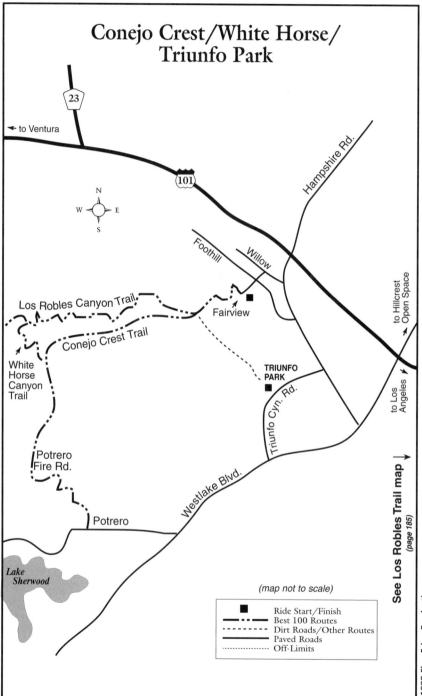

Conejo Crest/White Horse/
Triunfo Park

to Ventura

23

101

N
W — E
S

Foothill

Willow

Hampshire Rd.

to Hillcrest
Open Space

Los Robles Canyon Trail

Fairview

Conejo Crest Trail

White
Horse
Canyon
Trail

TRIUNFO
PARK

to Los
Angeles

Triunfo Cyn. Rd.

Potrero
Fire Rd.

Westlake Blvd.

Potrero

Lake
Sherwood

See Los Robles Trail map
(page 185)

(map not to scale)

■   Ride Start/Finish
▬ ·· ▬ ·· ▬   Best 100 Routes
- - - - -   Dirt Roads/Other Routes
▬▬▬   Paved Roads
············   Off-Limits

©1998 Fine Edge Productions

a three-way intersection. Straight ahead you can see the fire road as it dips down into a saddle and then reappears under a row of wire towers. Left takes you back toward Westlake and houses; to the right is a steep climb that leads to a very technical singletrack that ends up back down at Freeway 101 and Rancho Road.

Continue straight, descending quickly and then climbing steeply to another intersection at mile 1.2. To the right you can see a fire road descent, which is the Los Robles Canyon Trail over to the Los Robles Ridge Trail. Just behind you, back down the steep climb, is the entrance to Triunfo Park Trail. This is a very technical singletrack of 0.9 mile that goes down to Triunfo Park in Westlake. For the Conejo Crest and White Horse Canyon Trail, turn left uphill at this intersection onto the narrow, rocky doubletrack.

Continue climbing until the hill tops out at a T. Here you have a beautiful view of the Santa Monicas to the west. The road winding up behind the rocky knob hill across the valley is Decker Road. To the left you can see part of Westlake Lake, and above that and to the right is Westlake Reservoir. Go right from the T-intersection to continue on Conejo Crest (left drops quickly to houses).

You will be on a ridge trail that is known as The Cobbles because of the rocky surface of the trail. At mile 1.9 you come to a descent that is very steep and loose. *Please use caution*. At the bottom of the steep descent (mile 2.0) there is a trail to the right that takes you directly into White Horse Canyon. Continue straight on this fun, rolling doubletrack to mile 2.2 and a fire road T. Going right takes you into White Horse Canyon; left goes to the beginning of the White

Horse Canyon Trail.

Continue to the left downhill and then up and over another rise. At 2.4 miles there is a sign on the right for the White Horse Canyon Loop. The Equestrian Alternative Trail to the left is a route down to the houses below. Continuing on the fire road straight ahead will take you to Potrero Road and the equestrian center. Turn right onto the White Horse Canyon Trail for a short singletrack (lots of fun!) that takes you over to the main fire road at 2.7 miles into White Horse Canyon. Turn left downhill and follow to mile 3.4, and the main Los Robles Canyon fire road. Left takes you to the upper plateau and Hillsborough trailhead (and Los Robles Ridge Trail); right takes you back to your vehicle.

Continue right on the fire road for a fun-filled descent and then a series of moderate switchback climbs. To your left is the Conejo Valley and Freeway 101. At 4.6 miles you arrive back at the three-way intersection and the entrance to Triunfo Park Trail. From here you can go back to where you started or descend Triunfo Park Trail.

If you choose to take the Triunfo Park Trail, you come to the end of the trail at a locked gate. To the left is a trail that takes you around a sand volleyball court toward a steep walk-up. Continuing uphill, it flattens out a bit and then gets very steep again. At the top of this second steep section, you can turn left and follow the fire road up to the first three-way intersection you came to when you began your ride (just short of mile 1.0). From this point, turn right and continue back down to the locked gate and pump house on your left (Fairview).

For a less strenuous loop, instead of following the fire road up after climbing the two steep sections, go left downhill about 50 yards from the knoll you're on and turn right at the bottom onto a narrow doubletrack. Just a short way down is a motorcycle trail on the left going straight down into a small valley. On the other side you can see another fire road, which is what you want to access. Drop down the motorcycle trail and follow it up the other side of the valley to a trail that merges you into the fire road. Stay on the main fire road, bearing right past the first Y in about 50 yards, then left at another Y, mile 1.6. Continue to a locked gate and pump station (mile 1.9), then turn right to go back down to Fairview.

Los Robles Canyon Open Space

55 Los Robles Trail

Distance: 10 miles one way; 16-mile loop via Potrero Road
Difficulty: Moderate with some difficult, technical singletrack sections
Elevation: 2,500' gain (approximate)
Ride Type: One-way or loop on dirt roads and singletrack
Season: Year-round
Map: Fine Edge Productions' Santa Monica Mountains Recreation Topo Map

Overview: Administered by COSCA, Los Robles Canyon Open Space offers several miles of interconnected singletracks and fire roads with a variety of terrain and vegetation. Although surrounded by much development, you can quickly ride into narrow canyons rich with riparian vegetation, and onto ridges with spectacular views of the Conejo and Hidden valleys that make it seem like you are far away from the city. Yet you are never more than a few minutes from civilization. Still, the rides are challenging, and in season there are many wildflowers. *Caution: The area is heavily used by equestrians, especially on weekends.*

The main Los Robles Ridge Trail runs 10 miles west to east between Newbury Park and Westlake Village. (Hidden Valley and Rancho Sierra Vista are to the south.) There are several connectors coming in from the north and south along the way. At the east end, the main trail forks to three different trailheads: Fairview, Triunfo Park and Lake Sherwood (see Westlake Open Space). The trail described below goes from west to east, but you can ride it in either direction. If you do it as a one-way, you need to arrange a shuttle or pick up.

Getting There: From 101, exit at Wendy and go left toward the coast. When Wendy ends at Potrero, go left 0.5 mile to gravel parking lot on left. There's water and trail information at the trailhead. Other access: Moorpark Road/Fairview Road/Triunfo Park/Lake Sherwood.

Route: Starting at the trail heading out from the gravel parking lot, you climb a short way to a driveway

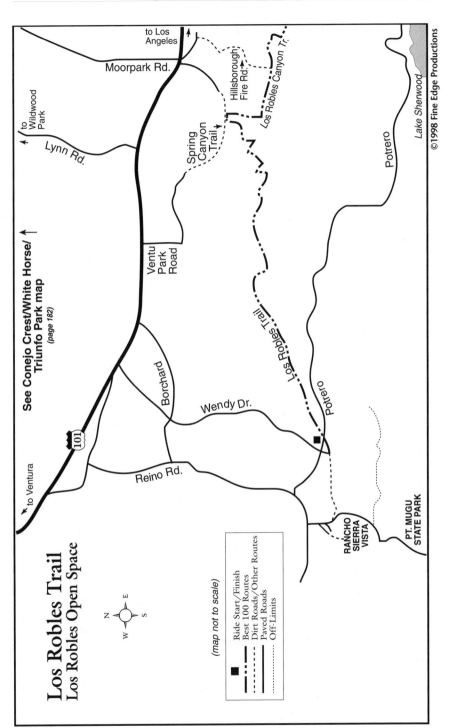

Los Robles Trail
Los Robles Open Space

N
W — E — S

(map not to scale)

See Conejo Crest/White Horse/ ←
Triunfo Park map
(page 182)

to Los Angeles

Moorpark Rd.

to Wildwood Park

Lynn Rd.

Hillsborough Fire Rd.

Los Robles Canyon Tr.

Lake Sherwood

©1998 Fine Edge Productions

Spring Canyon Trail

Ventu Park Road

Potrero

101

to Ventura

Borchard

Wendy Dr.

Reino Rd.

Los Robles Trail

Potrero

Potrero

RANCHO SIERRA VISTA

PT. MUGU STATE PARK

■ Ride Start/Finish
Best 100 Routes
Dirt Roads/Other Routes
Paved Roads
Off-Limits

(private). Go straight across and follow the trail to the right. Just a few yards up the hill (0.2 mile) the trail veers left downhill to a singletrack on the right. Follow the trail as it dips and rolls, with residential property below you. At 1.3 miles you come to the intersection with Felton Street Trail coming in from the left. This leads to Felton Street and Lynn Road.

Continue up and to the right for the Los Robles Trail. There will be a series of steep climbs and descents along a double rail horse fence. Just past mile 2.0, turn left at the Y. At 2.2 turn left at the fork heading uphill. *Do not go straight as it leads to private property.* The trail will switchback several times and come to another intersection at mile 2.6. (The left trail, called "4136" by locals—as of this printing it has no official name—leads to a great 1.8-mile descent that winds down to Lynn Road in Newbury Park, just west of Ventu Park Road.) Go right to continue on Los Robles Trail.

At almost 2.8 miles you come to another intersection just below private property. *Do not go onto private property.* Bear left at the intersection to continue. At 3.1 miles you come to a wide dirt road which is a private driveway extension of Ventu Park Road. *Do not go up or down this road.* Go straight across to the singletrack trail on the other side.

Climb the short steep hill and two switchbacks, and follow the contour of the mountain for approximately 1.5 miles. The trail then begins descending a mile-long section with a series of switchbacks. Be careful of other users coming uphill. *Use extreme caution through this entire section.* Control your speed and avoid skidding through the turns.

At mile 5.7 cross a metal bar, bear right and climb to a fork. Go right at the top of the hill, following signs to Lake Sherwood and Triunfo Park (left goes to Moorpark Road). Climb the steep hill. At 6.3 miles, you pass a picnic table in an oak grove where you go left at a junction just past the sign: *Los Padres Road .5 miles, Fairview Road 4 miles, Lake Sherwood Road 4 miles.* Climb the steep hill, cross a dirt road and then go through the center of Upper Meadow (upper plateau).

You come to an intersection with a gate on the right. To the left is Hillsborough Street which leads down to Moorpark Road. Climb past a metal gate at mile 7.7. The trail forks just short of 8.0 miles. To the right is the White Horse Canyon Trail. To ride the rest of the Los Robles Trail, continue straight on the main fire road.

There are several options once you get to the Westlake Open Space. You can turn around and go back the same way, which in itself is very different from the direction you just came. Many people take Potrero Road through Hidden Valley back to their cars in Newbury Park for a 16-mile loop. If you choose to do this, turn right back at the White Horse Canyon Trail. If you make no turns off the main trail, you eventually come to Potrero Road and the equestrian center. Once you are on Potrero Road, turn right and continue all the way through Hidden Valley. You pass by cattle and horse ranches, climb up out of the valley, and then descend a half-mile to the entrance to Los Robles Ridge Trail on Potrero and the Wendy Walk-In.

CHAPTER 7

Ventura County and the Sespe

By Mickey McTigue

Ventura County, located on the Southern California coast, adjacent to and directly west of Los Angeles County, is a small county by California standards. It's only 45 miles east to west, by 60 miles north to south. Almost all the population lives in the southern half on the coastal plains and river valleys. The Los Padres National Forest takes up most of the mountainous northern half. The many miles of trails and dirt roads in the forest, combined with a mild climate, make mountain bicycling an exciting year-round sport here.

Ojai Valley, a hub for mountain biking in the area, makes a great jumping-off spot for exploring farther afield. The valley gets much of its beauty from the surrounding mountains. Its many diverse trails along steep slopes enable mountain bicyclists to enjoy that beauty from many different angles and perspectives. The valley has retained its rural flavor by preserving the native oak and sycamore trees and by the cultivation of extensive orange groves. Farming was the first major activity here, but the mild climate and serene panorama soon attracted many winter visitors, creating a resort industry.

A great variety of places to stay are now available—from the usual motels and bed-and-breakfasts to full-service hotels that feature activities like diet and exercise regimens, tennis, swimming, golf, etc. Family and friends of hard-core mountain bicyclists can find many alternative activities here. The oldest tennis tournament in the country, started in 1899, attracts the nation's best interscholastic players. Held every year in late April, it uses every court in the valley for a week. The rest of the year there are enough courts for everyone.

A world-acclaimed music festival held every year since 1946 is staged outdoors in Ojai's Libby Bowl on the last weekend in May. A parade that involves most of the people of the valley is held every Fourth of July, and around mid-September the Mexican Fiesta does the same with plenty of special Mexican foods. There are also specialty shops, an unusual bookstore, plays, a Sunday sidewalk art display, camping, and fishing for state record bass at Lake Casitas.

To get to Ojai Valley from U.S. Highway 101 in Ventura take State Highway 33 north. In 11.2 miles State Highway 150 joins in from the west. Stay on 150 to the east when 33 branches northwest 2 miles farther. Another mile puts you in downtown Ojai with its famed arched arcade sidewalk cover. Highway 33 passes through the valley and continues north into the Los Padres National Forest where there's more excellent mountain bicycling; you may want to try those areas while staying in the Ojai Valley.

Winter rainstorms are often very heavy, causing flooded streams and muddy trails. The shale on the mountains drains fast and most trails are soon passable.

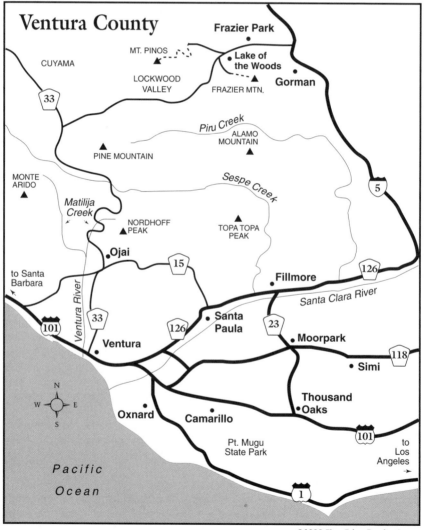

©1998 Fine Edge Productions

The valley floor, at 800 feet, seldom has snow although frost is common. Summer days can be very hot and dry, and riding early in the morning is advised. Unless you are used to extreme heat, don't ride in the noon sun. Always carry plenty of water.

Strong endurance riders will find bicycle transportation enough to get to and from the rides listed in this chapter. Most riders, however, will want a vehicle to get to the trailheads. On some routes where you come out at a second trailhead, another vehicle is needed to retrieve the first one. A simpler method is to have someone drop you off at the remote trailhead; you can ride back to town or wherever you are staying.

Alamo, Frazier, and Pinos mountains, in the northeastern part of the county, are accessible from Interstate 5. These 7,000- and 8,000-foot mountains have good roads near their summits. You ride through pine forests with amazing clear-day views of the San Joaquin and Antelope valleys as well as cross-county to the ocean. Visit during the summer and fall as there's heavy snow here in winter.

Mt. Pinos, the tallest peak in the small White Mountain Coastal Range, is quickly becoming one of the premiere mountain bike areas in Southern California. Located midway between Los Angeles, Lancaster, and Bakersfield, its pine-covered slopes, cool summer temperatures, and magnificent vistas beckon to the urban cyclist.

Streamside riding presents its own challenges.

Ojai Valley

56 Shelf Road

Distance: 1.75 miles one way
Difficulty: Easy, not technical
Elevation: 200' gain/loss
Ride Type: Out-and-back or loop on dirt road and pavement
Season: Spring, summer, fall
Map: Ojai

Overview: A short, easy dirt road that's 1.75 miles long, Shelf Road is a public route closed to motor traffic and gated at each end. It runs east and west at the north edge of Ojai between Signal Street and Gridley Road. Signal Street crosses Ojai Avenue at the main traffic light in downtown Ojai where the Post Office is located.

Getting There: Park along Signal Street, Grand Avenue, or near your favorite restaurant or ice cream shop. Take plenty of water since none is available en route. Riding in summer is best done in early morning or late afternoon.

Route: This delightful road climbs and descends less than 200 feet, staying most of the time around the 1,000-foot elevation contour. Take Signal Street north and uphill about 1.25 miles to its end, bearing slightly right past a white gate. Stay on the main dirt road and watch for walkers, runners, and horseback riders. You have views of the east end of Ojai, and the steep slopes put you right above some residences. An excellent way to start the day is a sunrise ride before breakfast or brunch. You can make this a loop ride by taking Gridley Road downhill from the east end of Shelf Road. Where Gridley crosses Grand Avenue, turn right and return to Signal Street. One way on Shelf Road takes about 30 minutes with enough time to look at the scenery. Meditative riders will take much longer, but it's time well spent.

57 Sulphur Mountain Road

Distance: 18 miles
Difficulty: Moderate, not technical
Elevation: 300' to 2,600'; 2,300' difference
Ride Type: Out-and-back or loop on dirt road, or loop on dirt road and pavement
Season: Spring, summer, fall
Maps: Matilija, Ojai, Santa Paula Peak

Overview: Sulphur Mountain Road is a county road, graded dirt and gravel. It is closed to motor vehicles, except property owners, the Edison Company, and Ventura County vehicles. It's open to walkers, bicycles,

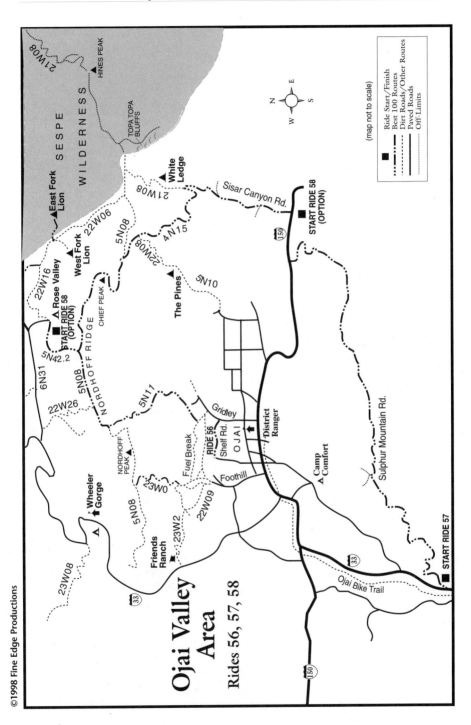

Ojai Valley Area
Rides 56, 57, 58

©1998 Fine Edge Productions

and horses. This ride is good all year except just after a rainstorm, when it usually is muddy. There is no drinking water available; bring plenty, it can be a hot ride. The views of the mountains to the north and Lake Casitas to the west are exceptional.

Getting There: Turn east off Highway 33, between Casitas Springs and San Antonio Creek Bridge, 6.5 miles south of Ojai and 7.4 miles north of Highway 101 in Ventura. Travel east on the paved road past the Girl Scout Camp on the left to a locked gate. Park at the turnout on Sulphur Mountain Road and Highway 33 (mile marker 7.40). Do not block the locked gate. Past the gate, all the land on both sides of the road is private and posted *No Trespassing*. You must stay on the road. The side roads are also private and posted. Only the main road is public property and open to bicyclists. This is a very popular bicycle route and you should be alert for other riders going the opposite way, and especially for hikers and equestrians.

Route: Past the gate you climb and turn to the north. About 100 yards up the dirt road you encounter heavy black oil on the right side of the road; a little farther up you will see the source—a natural oil spring that has been running for years, maybe centuries. Sometimes it runs out onto the road and the mess is hard to avoid.

The first mile is a steep but rideable climb through oak forest and the shade is welcome. After a short level section the climbing resumes at an easier grade; this is typical for most of this route. You climb to the east along the ridge of this mountain, first on the south side toward the ocean, and at other times on the north. There your view is of the whole Ojai Valley with the rugged mountains beyond that ring the valley.

The earth here is covered mainly with grasses, live oaks, and scattered sage. It's quite green in early spring with lots of flowers; later it becomes very dry and brown. Those who travel silently and watch carefully may see wildlife. I have seen several coyotes, some bobcats, deer, quail, hawks, snakes, and lots of small birds. Tarantulas, those large (6-inch diameter), black, hairy, scary-looking spiders, are sometimes common on the road in late afternoon in the fall. Just steer around them and you shouldn't have any trouble.

Often there are cattle on the road, including large bulls. Slow travel and patience are the best ways to get past them. Give them time and they usually get off the road. Don't run or chase them, just move slowly past. Close all gates you open.

As the road goes on and up to the top, you have views of Topa Topa Bluff, Sisar Canyon, and Santa Paula Peak. The southern view, after your initial climb out of Ventura River Canyon, looks across Cañada Larga to Ventura, Oxnard and the Pacific Ocean. On clear days, you can see several of the coastal islands: Anacapa, Santa Cruz, and Santa Rosa. There are occasional days of Santa Ana northeast winds when you can see all seven of the islands, including Catalina, Santa Barbara, San Nicolas and San Miguel.

You can turn around anywhere and return, or continue on to the top and beyond. After 9 miles, the road is paved and you may loop on through to Upper Ojai and Highway 150. Turn left (west) onto Highway 150 and it's 6 miles back to Ojai.

58 Upper Ojai to Ojai over Nordhoff Ridge with Rose Valley Option

Distance: 24 miles (33 miles if you ride from downtown Ojai)
Difficulty: Difficult, occasionally technical
Elevation: 1,600' to 5,200' to 800' (a 3,400' climb)
Ride Type: One-way on dirt roads and singletrack requires shuttle; the longer version is a loop
Season: Spring, summer, fall
Maps: Ojai, Lion Canyon, Topa Topa Mountains, Santa Paula Peak

Overview: This route along the Ojai Front Range is difficult due to the elevation gain, the long distance and the descent along the Gridley Trail singletrack. Start early and plan for an all-day ride. You should not attempt this ride if you dislike narrow trails or have little or no experience on singletrack. The route links Sisar Canyon Road in Upper Ojai to Gridley Trail, which leads toward downtown Ojai. You may ride in the reverse order if you prefer or just part way and return.

Getting There: First, you have to get to Sisar Road, 9 miles east of Ojai on Highway 150. Park along 150 next to Summit School. Very strong riders might just ride out from Ojai, but be aware of the 850-foot climb. If you have two cars, leave one in Ojai and one at Sisar Road to be picked up later; maybe someone can drop you off and take the car back to Ojai.

Route: From Highway 150 just east of Summit School, Sisar Road heads north, climbing 3,400 feet in about 8 miles. It has an almost continuous grade and is usually in good condition, although in winter snow occurs at upper elevations and in summer it can be very hot. Start at dawn and ride up in the shade on the southwest slopes to avoid the worst heat.

As you leave Highway 150, Sisar Road passes homes on both sides of the road. Past the last house, the road turns slightly right and you need to stay on the main road by keeping to the right, avoiding left forks until you reach the Forest Service locked gate. Beyond this gate there is one more right fork, a private road to a remote ranch—*Keep Out.*

The road soon switchbacks up Sisar Canyon and at 3 miles you are at the junction of Trail 21W08. (White Ledge Trail Camp, located about 1 mile up the trail, is a pleasant spot shaded by pungent bay trees. The spring there runs all year at considerable volume.) Past this junction, Sisar Road leaves the canyon and crosses a ridge out to the west of Sisar Canyon. Along the right side of the road at the 7-mile point, water is piped to a water trough from Wilsie Spring just above the road.

Near the top of Sisar Road, Horn Canyon Trail (22W08) crosses the road. This steep rough trail is not recommended for bicycle use. Just another 0.5 mile and Sisar Road ends at the top of the ridge and meets Road 5N08. From this ridge you get your first view to the north, looking out over the Sespe Canyon, past the Piedra Blanca Sandstone formation to the cliffs of Reyes, Haddock and

Thorn Point Peaks.

This marks the end of the 8-mile Sisar Road section of this ride. It's a good turnaround point if you just want a 16-mile out-and-back.

Continuing on to Nordhoff Ridge, the next section is more moderate riding with some steep downhills and a net elevation loss of 1,600 feet in about 7.8 miles. Turn left (west) onto Road 5N08 at its junction with Sisar Road. You quickly get a break, descending 250 feet in a mile on the north side of the ridge. At a low point on the ridge you start a long climb around the east and north sides of Chief Peak, regaining the altitude you just lost. It's not very steep and the scenery makes up for it. On

Sweet SoCal singletrack.

Tony Quiroz

the northwest side of Chief Peak, the road travels on Nordhoff Ridge and drops and climbs very steeply for about a half-mile. Some hills can be climbed with the momentum gained coming down the previous hill. This is also the highest elevation of the trip. There are places along the ridge where you look right down to Ojai Valley.

At 13 miles, Chief Peak Road descends to the right past a cattle-guard and gate. Continue on the ridge ahead to the west, easily descending 500 feet in 1.5 miles to the

junction with Howard Canyon Trail (22W26). When you look west over Nordhoff Ridge you can see Nord-hoff Peak, at the same elevation as you are. It once housed a lookout, and the steel tower is still standing. Now the road begins a much steeper descent of 900 feet in almost 1.3 miles to Gridley Saddle. At the saddle you will have ridden 16 miles from Upper Ojai. Gridley Trail, the third and last leg of this ride, is to your left (south) at the saddle.

Gridley Trail (5N11) hugs the side of the canyon and winds down into the valley with many switch-backs. Most of it isn't very steep (you go from 3,600 feet to 1,600 feet in 6 miles), but it is considered technical because of the huge drop-offs over the edge. (Go slowly or—if you're not sure of your skill—get off and walk, and live to ride another day.) About halfway down, the trail widens where it used to be a road. Water is available about a half-mile down at Gridley Spring, a former camp that washed out. A plastic pipe carries water to a horse water trough; your water (treat it!) is from the stream above the trail.

After a break you continue down on the west side of the canyon and soon pass avocado groves. Take the right (west) fork at the saddle and you are now on a road. Go down this road 0.3 mile and at the out-bend take the marked trail on your left steeply downhill. You need to walk the first part of this short connector trail, and might as well walk all of it due to rocks.

Now at 22 miles you are on paved Gridley Road, and it's a smooth ride back to town. Watch your speed down this steep twisty road until you get to the straight part. Turn right at Grand Avenue and ride to town. A left turn onto Montgomery Street will take you back to Ojai Avenue.

Rose Valley Option: An alternate way to access Nordhoff Ridge is via Rose Valley. You need to arrange a car shuttle. Leave one car in Ojai. Drive the second car west on Highway 150 to Highway 33 and head north past Wheeler Gorge. This is a scenic mountain highway and there are no services, so be sure to check your vehicle and have plenty of gas. As you drive up the mountain

you see vertical white signs along the roadside that mark the road edge and hazards like culverts. Many have the mileage from Ventura marked on them. At mile marker 25.84 take the signed Rose Valley Road east 3.5 miles. When you see a small lake on the left, take the signed road right to Rose Valley Falls and Campgrounds. Park beside the upper lake below the campground.

Begin riding through the camp-ground and take the gated road to the right (west). Although this road (5N42.2) is so steep in places it is hard to even walk, it is still the easiest way up to Nordhoff Ridge. This is because you climb only 1,600 feet to reach the high point of the ride instead of climbing 3,400 feet up Sisar Road.

When you get to the top of Nord-hoff Ridge you have two options. The first option takes you left (east) on Road 5N08 around Chief Peak to Sisar Road, down to Highway 150, and west 9 miles on pavement back to town for a total ride of 24.5 miles. (Just reverse the directions for the Upper Ojai to Ojai route starting at "At 13 miles . . .") Although longer, this route is easier because it is all on roads and the last 9 miles on the highway is almost all downhill. If you don't want to ride along the high-way, you can leave your car at Summit School near Sisar Road.

For the second, harder option, you turn right (west) on Road 5N08 and connect with Gridley Trail to Ojai for a total ride of 13.5 miles. This way is more difficult due to the steep descent to Gridley Saddle and the nar-row trail in Gridley Canyon. For this option, follow the directions for the Upper Ojai to Ojai route starting at "At 13 miles Chief Peak Road . . ."

Miles of Ventura County fire roads make for excellent bikepacking trips.

59 Monte Arido Road/ Murietta Canyon

Distance: 25 miles
Difficulty: Moderate to Potrero Seco; more difficult to Monte Arido; very difficult near Old Man Mountain; many steep hills, long distance
Elevation: 5,080' to 6,000' to 3,400'
Ride Type: One-way on dirt roads; requires shuttle
Season: Spring, summer, fall
Maps: Wheeler Springs, Old Man Mountain, White Ledge Peak, Matilija

Overview: This ridge-top road provides exceptional views of wilderness landscapes with few human alterations. Most of those are historic ranches at the northern end of the road between Highway 33 and Potrero Seco. In this area, the road runs near the border of the Dick Smith Wilderness, and from many high points you can look out over most of the wilderness to the northwest. The southern 15 miles of the ride take you along the border of the Matilija Wilderness to the east, with excellent views down into remote, steep, narrow canyons. Following the ridge, the road climbs and drops many times.

Excellent day-rides can be enjoyed by parking at the upper roadhead and traveling into Potrero Seco, returning the way you came in. Three miles one-way takes less than an hour with only a net descent of 150 feet. A more strenuous effort will take you farther out to the Three Sisters Rocks, 7 miles and 2 hours one-way. (These times include a lot of sightseeing. Fast riders can do it in half the time.) Bring a

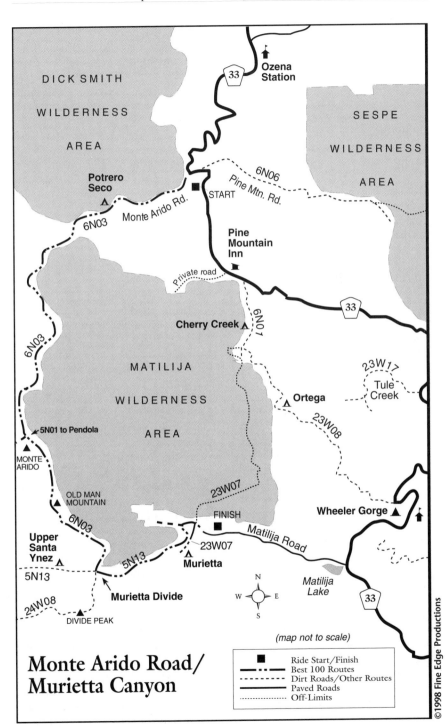

DICK SMITH

WILDERNESS

AREA

SESPE

WILDERNESS

AREA

Ozena
Station

33

6N06

Pine Mtn. Rd.

Potrero
Seco

Monte Arido Rd.

START

6N03

Pine
Mountain
Inn

Private road

33

Cherry Creek

6N01

MATILIJA

WILDERNESS

AREA

6N03

Ortega

23W17

Tule
Creek

23W08

5N01 to Pendola

MONTE
ARIDO

OLD MAN
MOUNTAIN

6N03

23W07

FINISH

Wheeler Gorge

Upper
Santa
Ynez

5N13

5N13

23W07

Murietta

Matilija Road

Murietta Divide

24W08

DIVIDE PEAK

N

W   E

S

Matilija
Lake

33

(map not to scale)

Monte Arido Road/
Murietta Canyon

■   Ride Start/Finish
━━━   Best 100 Routes
------   Dirt Roads/Other Routes
────   Paved Roads
⋯⋯⋯   Off-Limits

©1998 Fine Edge Productions

map, compass, and binoculars to locate distant landmarks; by remembering them you will be able to tell where you are. Riding past the Three Sisters puts you farther into the mountains on a ridge that gets tougher the farther you go. Somewhere about the 10-mile mark you need to decide to go back or continue past the point where turning back is not a good option.

Getting There: Park on Highway 33 at Pine Mountain Summit Pass (milepost 42.7). Leave a second vehicle at the parking area at the locked gate end of Matilija Road, just before Murietta Camp. *Note: Bring plenty of water since none is available.* Nearest services are in Ojai. *Caution:* Winter storms bring heavy snow, and the adobe mud is bad during spring thaw. Riding in on frozen roads in the morning can leave you stuck with a noon thaw miles from the highway.

Route: Starting from Pine Mountain Summit Pass, head west on Monte Arido Road (6N03) past the locked gate. Watch out for occasional motor vehicle traffic operated here under special permit from the Forest Service. Right away you have a steep descent and climb to a saddle at 0.3 mile, where a good road branches to the south, climbing slightly for 0.2 mile to a locked gate posted *No Trespassing*. Continuing west on Road 6N03 from the saddle, you climb a little more easily to the ridge.

Riding close to the ridge top you can see a deep canyon to the south; past that you cross a cattleguard (0.8 mile). A spur road branches southwest here to the Dent Ranch, and the main road passes between pine trees to the west. There is easier riding and you start passing the first large grass slopes; then at the top of a grade (1.6 miles) you can see down across the Potrero

Seco and the headwaters of the Sespe. Two ranches are located along the creek among the cottonwood trees. The descent to the ranches has two downhill runs separated by a slight climb over a saddle. As you approach the ranches keep right, cross a cattleguard (2.25 miles) and climb toward the west across a gently sloping field.

Just before a large green tank, take a road on the right 100 yards to Potrero Seco Trail Camp, 3 miles from the start. The camp is set in a hollow with hills on three sides, open to the east. There are three tables and fireplaces shaded by oak and pine trees, but no water. Just northeast is the abandoned site of the old Potrero Seco Guard Station.

Going farther south on Monte Arido Road (6N03), you first climb moderately for a mile, and then on the right pass the Loma Victor Road (7N05) that descends on a ridge along the Dick Smith Wilderness boundary to Mono Creek and Don Victor Valley. Past this junction you climb a little more and make a steep descent to a saddle, where there is a short side road south to a dam and pond. On this saddle at 6.2 miles the Three Sisters Rocks can be seen ahead. A short steep climb gets you to these surprisingly large, isolated sandstone boulders at 6.8 miles. Shade and wind protection is available here, making it a good rest stop.

Hildreth Jeepway (6N17) starts here past a locked gate on the north side of the rocks and can be seen along the ridge out to Hildreth Peak to the west. From Potrero Seco to these rocks, 6N03 has been gradually turning to the south and now the rest of the way is generally south.

A gate at 7.0 miles is the start of a very fast section, slightly downhill on good graded road. The climb ahead is typical with some short, steep, walk-

and-push hills mixed with rideable areas—you go over a peak, down a steep hill, and repeat it again. Another gate (locked) at 12.2 miles is next to a dam and pond on the west side of the road. Climb again to the northwest side of Monte Arido and at 12.45 miles pass the Pendola Jeepway (5N01), which heads down into an open saucer-shaped canyon before descending the ridge to Pendola Station at Agua Caliente Canyon. (Experienced mountain bicyclists seeking a tough, challenging ride can start at Juncal Camp—see the Santa Barbara chapter—and ride up past Murietta Divide, making the steep climb to Monte Arido and returning by the Pendola Jeepway.)

At 13.2 miles, Monte Arido, at 6,003 feet, is the highest point on Road 6N03. You can make the short walk to the summit, just west and a little above the road. The next 1.5 miles has the steepest descent, so use your brakes to keep control and lower your bicycle seat if possible. From another saddle on the north side of Old Man Mountain, the road climbs around on the west slopes of this double peak, giving you a good view looking down to Juncal Dam and Jameson Lake. Just when I am tired of climbing, there are two similar uphills where they shouldn't be on the south side of Old Man Mountain. Finally, you lose altitude steeply, with many switchbacks across a barren-looking landscape.

That scene changes suddenly while you make a short climb past pine trees growing among large sandstone boulders. There is another steep descent across a boulder garden until at 19 miles a road to your right leads to a small lake, too improbable to be overlooked. One more mile, and at 20 miles even, you are at Murietta Divide which is pleasantly level after so much downhill. Go left (east) on 5N13, and another 5 miles down Murietta Canyon to your shuttle vehicle.

Alamo Mountain

60 Alamo Mountain Loop Road

Distance: 8 miles
Difficulty: Easy, but the elevation is high
Elevation: 6,500' to 7,000'; 500' gain/loss
Ride Type: Loop
Season: Summer and fall are best
Map: Alamo Mountain

Overview: Alamo Mountain is a massive peak with a somewhat rounded top. Its highest point is 7,450 feet, but the road never gets higher than 7,000 feet. At this elevation snow occurs every year and sometimes remains for a long time. The best riding is in summer and fall. If you plan to camp during these warmer months, you still need to be prepared for cold nights on the mountain. Except for the noise and speed of motorcycles, this area has great riding. You get spectacular views of seldom-seen canyons from the higher elevations. Alamo Mountain is covered with huge trees, while Hungry Valley to the northeast is dry and desert-like.

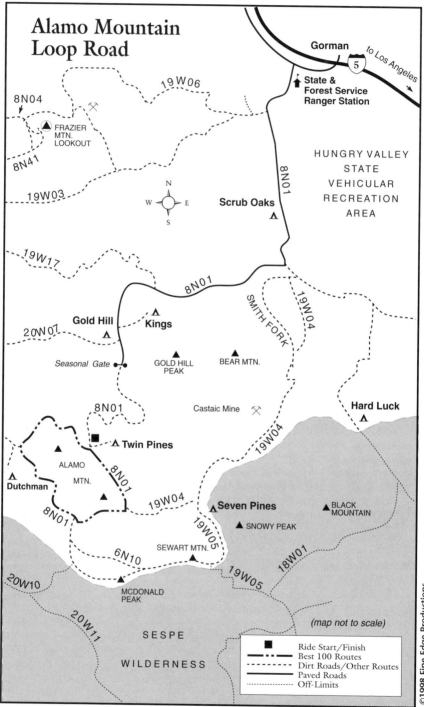

Alamo Mountain Loop Road

Gorman

to Los Angeles

5

State & Forest Service Ranger Station

19 W 06

8N04

FRAZIER MTN. LOOKOUT

8N41

19W03

8N01

HUNGRY VALLEY STATE VEHICULAR RECREATION AREA

Scrub Oaks

N
W   E
S

19W17

8N01

20W07

Gold Hill

Kings

SMITH FORK

19W04

GOLD HILL PEAK

BEAR MTN.

Seasonal Gate

8N01

Castaic Mine

Hard Luck

Twin Pines

ALAMO

8N01

MTN.

Dutchman

8N01

19W04

19W04

Seven Pines

BLACK MOUNTAIN

SNOWY PEAK

19W05

6N10

SEWART MTN.

18W01

19W05

20W10

McDONALD PEAK

20W11

19W05

(map not to scale)

SESPE

WILDERNESS

	Ride Start/Finish
	Best 100 Routes
	Dirt Roads/Other Routes
	Paved Roads
	Off-Limits

©1998 Fine Edge Productions

There is much evidence of gold mining in some areas of the region. Located on the north slope of the mountain above Piru Creek, the Castaic Mine was the most extensive and successful one, with two tunnels totaling over 2,200 feet in length. Mining continued here into the 1930s. Originally powered by a water wheel, the 5-stamp mill from this mine can now be seen in a historical museum in Santa Barbara. Gold panning is still a popular pastime along nearby streams.

Services and supplies are available only in Gorman on I-5. Most of the roads and trails in this area are open to motorcycles and ATVs. Car camping with limited facilities is available at Kings Camp, Gold Hill Camp, Twin Pines and Dutchman camps on Alamo Mountain, and at most sheltered spots in Hungry Valley (check with State Rangers).

Gold Hill Camp is located on a bluff above Piru Creek. The creek usually runs all year, although it's never very deep except during floods. Snow can occur here, but a lot of rain or snow is uncommon. Placer gold, washed downstream, is found along Piru Creek and in the bank under the bluff next to the camp. Panning and dredging are very popular.

Kings Camp, at the end of Road 8N01A, offers tables and fire pits in a grove of trees. To reach the camp, turn east from Gold Hill Road at mile 10.25 onto paved Road 8N01A and continue 0.5 mile. Water is not available at this camp.

You can ride your bike the 7 miles up Alamo Mountain Road on pavement, with a 2,500-foot elevation gain. Most riders, however, prefer to drive to the top and do the Alamo Mountain Loop Road which circles Alamo Mountain between 6,500 feet and 7,000 feet for 8 miles of easy riding in mature pine forest. The views from all sides of Alamo Mountain are splendid. Although you may drive a vehicle around the mountain on this road, riding a bicycle puts you more in touch with the surroundings. *Note: No water is available near Dutchman Camp.*

Getting There: Alamo Mountain is accessible by motor vehicle from Interstate 5 through the Hungry Valley State Vehicular Recreational Area (motorcycle and 4WD) on a generally paved road as far as the Gold Hill-Piru Creek crossing. Take Interstate 5 to Gorman (60 miles north from Los Angeles, 40 miles south from Bakersfield, and 70 miles from Ventura). Cross to the west side of I-5 opposite Gorman and go north on Peace Valley Road 1 mile. Turn left (west) at the SVRA Hungry Valley sign onto paved Gold Hill Road (8N01). A kiosk just ahead is run by the state to collect fees for SVRA use. Maps and current information are available from the State Ranger, and information is posted on large bulletin boards. Call ahead to check weather, closures, and special events scheduled here and in the National Forest.

On Gold Hill Road at mile 5 there is an abrupt right turn. A dirt fork to the left is Hungry Valley Road, which leads to Snowy Creek Trail and farther on to Hard Luck Road. Go right and continue west on paved Gold Hill Road to the 10-mile mark at Piru Creek. A gate near the creek crossing is locked during stormy winter weather and when ice and snow are hazardous at higher elevations. Here, from the base of Alamo Mountain, Road 8N01 twists and turns up the mountain's north side. Above Piru Creek, Gold Hill Road (formerly graded dirt) was paved in the fall of 1992.

As you come up the mountain, a

short spur road to the east leads steeply down to Twin Pines Camp, just a little before Alamo Mountain Loop Road begins. Dutchman Camp, 2.5 miles west on the loop road, is spread over a larger area with more level ground. Park at the turnout near Twin Pines Camp.

Route: The easiest way to do this loop is to ride counter-clockwise, starting toward the west. The 2.5-mile ride out to Dutchman Camp meanders along the slopes, passing through groves of pines. The 200-foot elevation gain isn't difficult, since it's done a little at a time. Where the road turns south, another lesser road heads farther east. This is the Miller Jeep Road (8N12) which connects with the many double-tracks to the campsites next to the loop. The sites are spread out in this open place among a few scattered pines of good size.

On the 3-mile stretch from the camp out to the south point of the loop road, you travel along fairly level terrain the first mile. The next 2 miles climb 250 feet, descend into a small canyon, climb again and end at the same elevation as the camp. Watch for rocks that fall onto the road from the steeper slopes around the small canyon.

At the south point, Road 6N10 to McDonald Peak and Sewart Mountain descends steeply south. It's worthwhile making the half-mile trip out to the ridge for the views down Alder Creek and out to the Sespe Narrows. Keep going south on A.M. Loop Road without turning to the east or west. By going out this half-mile you get most of the view afforded by doing a trip to Sewart Mountain. I highly recommend it if you have time.

Alamo Mountain Loop Road is cut through the ridge here and turns sharply to the northeast. The view is into the upper parts of Snowy Creek Canyon which starts from the south ridge of Alamo Mountain and curves around to the northeast. After riding northeast 0.7 mile from the south point on the Loop Road, you pass Snowy Creek Trail on the right. (Snowy Creek Trail is not recommended at this time; it may be rehabilitated in the near future, however.) Continue on 1.8 miles, descending 300 feet, to complete your turn around the mountain and return to the starting point. The trees along this last section are a mixed forest of maples, oaks, and pines.

Frazier Mountain

61 Frazier Mountain Road

Distance: 14.8 miles
Difficulty: Moderate, not technical
Elevation: 5,200' to 8,013', 2,913' difference
Ride Type: Out-and-back on pavement and dirt roads
Season: Summer and fall best
Map: Frazier Mountain

Overview: Good dirt roads and thick pine forests create a tranquil, relaxed mood while you ride on the wide ridges of this high mountain. The

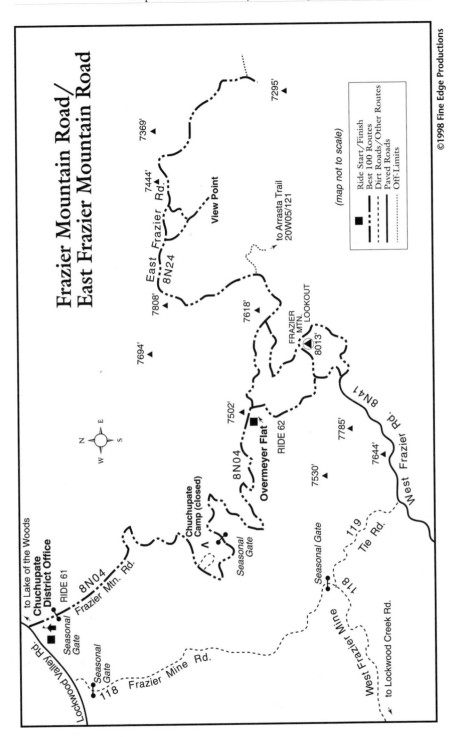

Frazier Mountain Road/ East Frazier Mountain Road

©1998 Fine Edge Productions

(map not to scale)

Ride Start/Finish
Best 100 Routes
Dirt Roads/Other Routes
Paved Roads
Off-Limits

trees muffle and block sound, so talking with hushed voices seems right here, like in a church or a library. Broken tops on the largest trees attest to the power of wind, lightning and heavy snow, but on a bright summer day when the heat is tempered by the 7,500-foot elevation, this is gentle backcountry. Most of the views through the trees are spectacular. The best view, of course, is from the fire lookout on the very top of the mountain at 8,013 feet—one of the few manned lookouts remaining in the southland forest. Visitors are welcome, but remember every day is a working day. Keep visits and distractions short.

Spring and summer thunderstorms are common with possible heavy rain and the danger of lightning on high places. During storms, keep away from tall trees and metal structures like the lookout and nearby radio towers. Heavy winter snow occurs, and strong winds cause whiteouts and severe wind chill. In the shade at this high elevation, snow and ice can last a long time. Check conditions at the ranger station on the way up or call ahead.

Getting There: From Interstate 5 exit at Frazier Park (also signed as Mt. Pinos Recreation Area), go west 6.5 miles to Lake of the Woods. Go left on Lockwood Valley Road 0.9 mile. Signs here direct you south (left) to Frazier Mountain Road and Chuchupate Ranger Station. Park off the road in this area. Mileages are from the ranger station.

Route: As you do this ride up the mountain, be sure to stop and survey the distant terrain. Use a map and compass to become familiar with the features of the area and it will help

you find your way.

For the first mile you climb steadily south on the road past chaparral and scattered pines. The road turns to the left a little and gets less steep at two houses—one stone, the other of logs. At 1.5 miles the first switchback turns to the right and cuts along the mountainside, which becomes much steeper. Camp buildings at 2.0 miles are on the left beyond a meadow of grasses and wildflowers where water flows out and across the road. Chuchupate Camp, at 2.5 miles, is closed due to ground squirrels infested with fleas that carry bubonic plague.

Switchback again and turn left to double back above the camp. At 3.0 miles the pavement ends at a seasonal closure gate. The dirt road past here is rocky but good. You keep heading southeast, and at 4.3 miles the road improves. Nearing the top, the trees are bigger and shade the road. At Overmeyer Flat, 5.8 miles, the road forks with East Frazier Road (8N24) branching left.

Keep to the right fork on Frazier Mountain Road for a nice ride to the lookout which loops back to Overmeyer Flat with many scenic surprises. From Overmeyer Flat, it's 1.1 miles to the lookout junction. The left fork leads up 0.5 mile to the lookout situated amid an amazing array of antennas on the mountain top. You can return to Overmeyer Flat by continuing past the lookout, heading south on a road that behaves itself, and traveling in a half-circle to the west for 0.6 mile to West Frazier Road (8N41). Turn right, travel 0.3 mile and you come back to the fork where you turned up to the lookout. Keep straight ahead, and 1.1 miles of riding will put you back at Overmeyer Flat. Descend Frazier Mountain Road the way you came up.

62 East Frazier Mountain Road

Distance: 10.4 miles
Difficulty: Moderate, not technical
Elevation: 7,500' start; 7,800' high point; 7,350' end; 450' gain/loss
Ride Type: Out-and-back on dirt roads
Season: Summer and fall are best
Map: Frazier Mountain

Overview: This is a good ride for a hot summer day. It is usually cooler at this altitude and there is plenty of shade on the road which travels along a broad ridge covered with pine forest. There are some less-traveled side roads and many clearings where you can get off the main road and enjoy the solitude. Bring a lunch, your camera, binoculars, a book, a harmonica, or even a hammock. This is such a peaceful place that you should plan time for quiet, relaxing activities to experience the mood of the mountain. Most of the ride is easy, but there are a few short steep hills where you can expend some energy.

Getting There: Park along Frazier Mountain Road at Overmeyer Flat. See the previous ride's **Getting There** and **Route** sections.

Route: Ride up to the signed road fork and go left on East Frazier Road (8N24). You continue to climb moderately for 0.5 mile around the north side of the mountain. The upper end of a canyon is below to the east, and the road descends slightly toward the ridge at the head of this canyon. Near the bottom of this hill, at 0.9 mile, a rough, steep road heads up the northeast side of the mountain to the lookout. You descend to about 1.1 miles and then climb until you reach the Arrasta Trail (20W05/OHV 121) on the right (mile 1.5).

The road continues east on the ridge, dropping and climbing through thick forest. At 3.2 miles, a doubletrack to the right crosses the ridge for 0.45 mile to dead-end at a viewpoint. From this promontory you can look west and see the microwave towers near the lookout. (On the way back, at 0.2 mile from the main road, another doubletrack heads east; at 3.5 miles a doubletrack on the right seems to head back up toward the road to the viewpoint. These two may connect, but I haven't tried it.) The main road crosses to the north side of the ridge where you can see out toward Bakersfield and down to Frazier Park. Just past that at 3.6 miles the road divides while climbing a short hill.

Turning southeast and staying on the ridge top, you pass East Frazier Trail (19W06/OHV 120) at 5.1 miles. In this area there are many viewing places between the trees where you can see out across the Antelope Valley to Lancaster. The road descends more to the south and ends at a turn-around circle, 5.2 miles from Overmeyer Flat. For an easier trip, skip the last steep rocky descents and turn around at 5.0 miles.

If you want a more strenuous ride, go up to the lookout first on Road 8N04 rather than turning onto

East Frazier Road. From the lookout, take the trail to the northwest, which heads down the mountain to the north, turns east, and then joins East Frazier Road 0.9 mile from its start at Frazier Mountain Road.

Mt. Pinos

63 Mt. Pinos/McGill Trail

Distance: 16 miles
Difficulty: Moderately strenuous and somewhat technical
Elevation: Begin/end 6,200'; high point 8,831'; gain/loss 2,625'
Ride Type: Out-and-back on singletrack and dirt roads; many options possible
Season: Spring, summer, fall
Maps: Cuddy Valley, Sawmill Mountain

Overview: This ride has it all: great views, good climbing, wonderful spring colors (and odors!) and outrageously fun singletrack. The route described here links the mountain's best singletracks and cross-country ski trails (McGill, South Ridge and Harvest) with a touch of fire road to take you up and down Mt. Pinos.

Intermediate and advanced riders will find this a fun and challenging ride. Beginners shouldn't be put off, however. It's possible to shorten the route or to create lesser loops by starting at one of the area's three major campgrounds: McGill, Mt. Pinos and Chula Vista. Some riders like to arrange a shuttle for a downhill-only ride; still others choose to climb the paved Mt. Pinos Road (roughly a 9-mile climb) before returning on singletrack.

No matter what your skill level is, the climb to Mt. Pinos is worth the effort. The summit is surrounded by the Chumash Wilderness, created in 1992. California condors have been reintroduced in the Sespe Wilderness, visible to the south, and you may catch a glimpse of these amazing birds.

Getting There: Exit I-5 at Frazier Park (also signed *Mt. Pinos Recreation Area*) and go left. At 6.5 miles go straight past Lockwood Valley Road. Continue to 11.5 miles where Mt. Pinos Road curves left. Park in the dirt lot on the right. The lower McGill trailhead (clearly signed) is about a mile farther up Mt. Pinos Road. Route mileages are from the trailhead.

Route: Begin by climbing McGill Trail. It's steep, but not brutally so. The trail is usually in good condition, so put it in a low gear and spin through the pines. At 1.1 miles you reach the first of five switchbacks. After the third switchback, you begin to get fabulous views to the north and then into Lockwood Valley to the east as you traverse a more open slope. You should be able to see where you parked and be impressed with yourself for gaining so much elevation already. The grade lessens

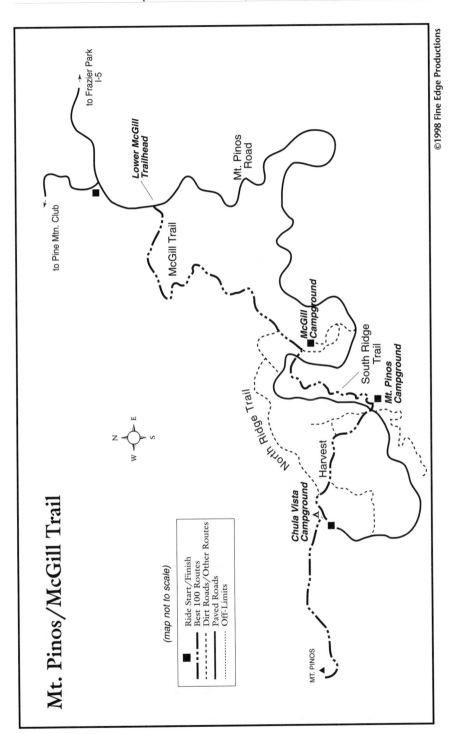

Mt. Pinos/McGill Trail

(map not to scale)

■ Ride Start/Finish
▬ ▪ ▬ ▪ ▬ Best 100 Routes
▬ ▬ ▬ Dirt Roads/Other Routes
▬▬▬▬ Paved Roads
········· Off-Limits

to Frazier Park I-5

Lower McGill Trailhead

Mt. Pinos Road

McGill Trail

to Pine Mtn. Club

McGill Campground

South Ridge Trail

Mt. Pinos Campground

North Ridge Trail

Harvest

Chula Vista Campground

MT. PINOS

©1998 Fine Edge Productions

somewhat here, too, so you can take in the view without any accompanying respiratory distress.

After you swing through switchbacks three and four, the trail flattens considerably and gets downright rolly and bermy. An occasional steep rocky pitch breaks up the fun as you head onto a south slope. Most of the work is over by the 2.5-mile mark.

At 3.3 miles you pass a bench on your right—a nice place for a break. Immediately past it is a trail junction. Go straight. Just past here is a second bench at a 4-way intersection. The two left trails drop down to McGill Campground if you need a bathroom break. (A shorter, easier loop can be fashioned by riding up the pavement to McGill camp and down McGill Trail.) A doubletrack makes a sharp right. You want to continue straight on a relatively smooth, flat track.

You hit paved Mt. Pinos Road at 3.6 miles. Go right. Almost immediately cross the road to where a blue cross-country ski trail sign marks the South Ridge Trail. Take this whoop-filled trail to Mt. Pinos Campground, 4.8 miles.

When you come into the campground, go right up the pavement to Mt. Pinos Road. Hang a left for 0.2 mile. Look for a big dirt turnout on the right. A dirt road starts from here, the entrance to which is covered by orange netting. Pass around the netting—there's a well-worn path.

Just over 5 miles you come to a trail junction. A blue cross-country ski trail sign indicates Mt. Pinos Loop, easiest, to the left and Harvest Trail, more difficult, straight. Take Harvest Trail straight and begin climbing a series of short, steep pitches. I always find this climb the most difficult and annoying part of the ride. Thankfully it's over in a little less than a mile. You emerge at Chula Vista Campground at 6.0 miles. Stay on the main trail, ignoring spurs. (Some riders choose to shuttle to this point and ride downhill from here.)

At 6.1 miles you enter a large, paved parking lot. Head diagonally across it. Look for the large brown road sign *Mt. Pinos, 2 miles.* Turn right and pass through an open gate to begin the climb to the summit. You pass a trail, North Ridge Trail, on the right (an alternate return route).

A handful of short, steep rocky climbs brings you to 7.0 miles. The grade lessens briefly as you approach a Y-intersection. Take the left fork. Continue on the main road past a few spurs (which lead to vista points). At 7.8 miles, stay left at another Y-intersection to begin the final push to the top. At 8.0 miles you reach the broad, usually windy, 8,831-foot summit. No matter how warm the weather when you start your ride, bring a windbreaker as there's often a cool breeze here.

A display announces this as *Iwihinmu (Mt. Pinos): A World in Balance.* Two benches beckon you to sit, have a snack, and enjoy the view. Note that the trail which takes off from here leads into a wilderness area —closed to bikes. At the far end of the parking lot a footpath leads to two port-a-potties.

To the north you can see the San Joaquin Valley and the city of Bakersfield. To the northeast, if the air is clear, you can make out the southern ramparts of the Sierra Nevada. Toward the east, Antelope Valley and the high desert stretch to the horizon. In springtime the desert explodes with color as the California poppies bloom. The rugged Dick Smith and Sespe Wilderness Areas span from west to south. These areas

Tony Quiroz

are home to the reintroduced California condor. These rare and majestic birds are sometimes spotted soaring over Mt. Pinos in search of food.

When you, too, feel in balance, head back the way you came. The fire road is fast, so watch yourself—it is open to vehicle traffic. You can opt to take the steep, loose North Ridge Trail back to McGill camp, or cross the parking lot and descend Harvest Trail. As much fun to descend as it was painful to climb, Harvest rails and rolls its way back to Mt. Pinos Road. Through Mt. Pinos Campground again, you catch South Ridge Trail, where if you're not careful you can catch dangerous air on the whoop-de-dos. The fun factor reaches crescendo point as you swing, swoop, and berm your way down McGill Trail (don't forget about those switchbacks!) back to your car. It truly doesn't get any better than this.

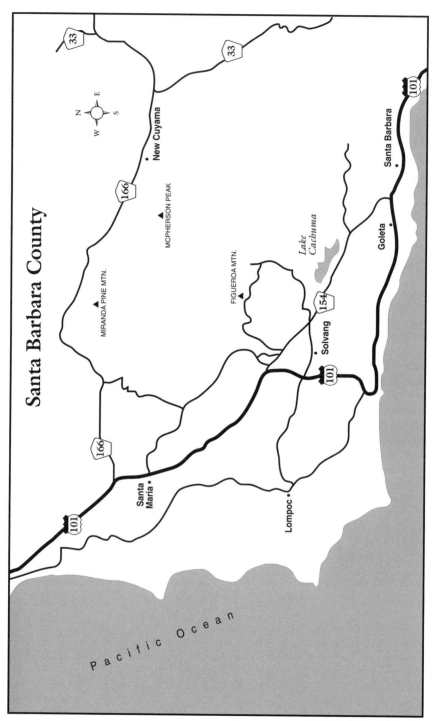

Santa Barbara County

©1998 Fine Edge Productions

CHAPTER 8

Santa Barbara County

By Mickey McTigue and Don Douglass

Santa Barbara County, west of Los Angeles and Ventura counties, is the epitome of Southern California. Mountains tumble to a strip of palm-lined sand under almost perpetual sunshine. Ocean breezes keep temperatures down so you can enjoy a variety of recreational activities year-round.

The Pacific Ocean borders on the south and west sides of this roughly rectangular county. Most of the population lives on a narrow strip between the mountains and the ocean on the south coast. The Los Padres National Forest takes up about one-third of the county, primarily in the east and northeast sections. Much of the west county is rural cattle- and horse-grazing land interspersed with vineyards. The center of the county's forested area is taken up by large wilderness areas (off-limits to bikes), and the mountain bicycle routes are located around their edges.

In southern Santa Barbara County the major land features are aligned in an east-west direction. Parallel to the beach, and only 4 to 6 miles inland, a formidable, steep-sided continuous ridge separates the south coast from the rest of the county. This mountain wall with peaks above 4,000 feet runs from the Ventura River to Point Conception and is broken only at Gaviota Creek where Highway 101 engineers used a tunnel to get the highway through the narrow canyon.

The abrupt turn of the coastline at Point Conception, the mountain barrier, and the Channel Islands just offshore, block the wind and smooth out the waves, creating a micro-climate considered the best in California. No wonder most of the county population lives on this narrow coastal strip, 5 miles long and 25 miles wide.

The south side of the barrier ridge is known as front country; everything to the north in the eastern half of the county is known as backcountry. This high ridge has made access to the backcountry difficult, first for the Native Americans and later for the settlers who improved the early trails. By the 1930s roads were built and now, during dry weather it is possible to drive into parts of the backcountry. This ability to drive over the range reduced travel on some trails and they were abandoned. The remaining trails are now more heavily-used as recreation increases.

This chapter begins with a look at the fire roads and trails of southeastern

Santa Barbara County —the front country access trail up Romero Canyon and the roads and trails along the upper Santa Ynez River. Four auto-accessible camps, two hot springs, fishing and swimming in the river, and isolated trail camps make this a popular area. Take your mountain bicycle and enjoy all this plus rides from easy to very difficult.

On the north side of the front range on State Highway 154 you can access Lower Santa Ynez River Canyon via Paradise Road. This paved road leads upstream past several campgrounds and many forest trails and dirt roads open to bicycles. My favorite trail is an 11.6-mile (one-way) ride on good fire roads to Happy Hollow near the top of Little Pine Mountain.

Figueroa Mountain, 25 miles northwest of Santa Barbara, overlooks the Santa Ynez Valley on the south and the San Rafael Wilderness to the north. The Zaca Ridge Road travels on a ridge 8.2 miles from Figueroa Mountain to Wildhorse Peak, surrounded by spectacular scenery. Campgrounds on the mountain or on the east and north sides are available. The nearby town of Solvang can provide plenty of distractions if you're tired of riding. Ride here in the spring, summer and fall. In winter, snow and mud are sometimes a problem.

The La Brea Canyon/Pine Canyon area is in the remote north central part of the county about 27 miles from Santa Maria over narrow paved and dirt roads. You should plan to day-ride here or stay at one of the campgrounds. This is a very good spot for those looking for less strenuous routes. Miles of nearly level road wind through canyons with meadows and oak and sycamore trees that beckon you around the next bend. Although best in spring, the area is nice in fall. Summer, however, can be very hot. The road is closed to car traffic in wet weather, but if the road isn't muddy and the streams are not high, winter can be a fine time to ride here, too. *Note:* Many of the rides in this chapter are in remote areas with no available water. We recommend a Camelbak-type system *and* water bottles.

64 Romero Trail

Distance: 13.2 miles
Difficulty: Moderate, somewhat technical
Elevation: 850' to 3,100'; 2,250' gain
Ride Type: Out-and-back on dirt road and singletrack
Season: Year-round; winter rain may force closure
Map: Carpinteria

Overview: Romero Trail has become a popular bicycle route. One of the few front range trails which is rideable uphill, it provides a good route to the Santa Barbara backcountry with connections to the major roads and trails. Since most of this trail is within 3 miles of the beach, the view south over the coast to the ocean and the Channel Islands is especially good. The south-facing slopes provide little shade, but ocean breezes moderate the high summer temperatures.

Formerly a vehicle route for access

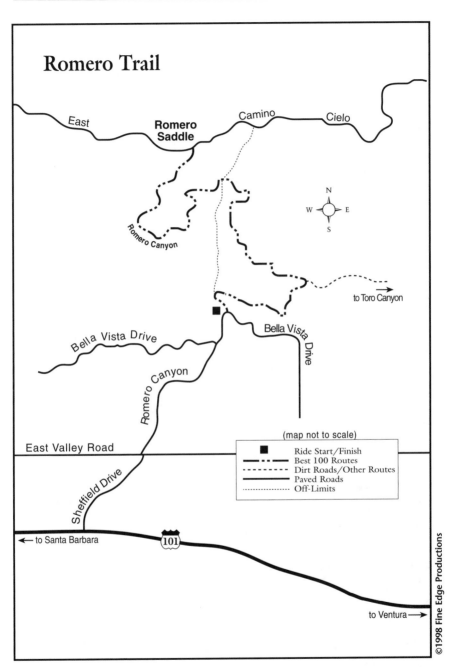

Romero Trail

East   **Romero Saddle**   Camino   Cielo

Romero Canyon

N
W—E
S

to Toro Canyon

Bella Vista Drive

Bella Vista Drive

Romero Canyon

East Valley Road

(map not to scale)

■ Ride Start/Finish
—··— Best 100 Routes
······ Dirt Roads/Other Routes
——— Paved Roads
············ Off-Limits

Sheffield Drive

← to Santa Barbara   (101)

to Ventura →

©1998 Fine Edge Productions

to water projects in the backcountry, the road has eroded so much that it is essentially just a trail now. Heavy rains in early 1995 caused many rockfalls and washouts that left boulders the size of small cars in the trail and showed just how dangerous these mountains are during storms. A volunteer effort reopened the trail and later regrading restored the doubletrack from the gate to the first saddle.

Getting There: Exit Highway 101 at Sheffield Drive and head north toward the mountains through Montecito. Where Sheffield Drive ends at East Valley Road, Route 192, turn left and then almost immediately take the next right onto Romero Canyon Road. Follow this paved road as it winds up into the foothills and joins Bella Vista Drive. Turn right and, 0.3 mile farther as you cross the canyon, look to the left to the locked gate at Romero Trail. Park alongside Bella Vista Drive, but be sure your wheels are off the pavement and you are not blocking the fire road.

Route: From the gate at Bella Vista Drive, Romero Trail (5N15) climbs somewhat steeply in the canyon, crosses a creek over a concrete bridge, turns east and crosses a second creek without a bridge. Here a hiking trail starts north along the creek, keeping to the canyon bottom until it crosses Romero Trail high up in the canyon.

Caution: This hiking trail is not suitable for bicycles and should not be ridden.

Past here, the trail (more like a doubletrack) climbs more moderately to the east out of Romero Canyon, circling around a foothill. You reenter Romero Canyon at a saddle where a road to the right leads down to private homes in Toro Canyon. Keep left here and continue climbing on the east side of the canyon, where regrading stops and the road turns into a singletrack for the rest of the route.

A small stream flows from the east and crosses the trail 3.3 miles from the gate. After circling to the west and crossing the upper part of the canyon, the hiking trail crosses at 3.9 miles and can be seen climbing with switchbacks above. Romero Trail continues climbing west around two south-facing ridges before heading north and crossing back into Romero Canyon again. Past this divide it is almost level and an easy ride to Romero Saddle on the Santa Ynez Ridge. The trail ends at a prominent concrete cistern next to paved Camino Cielo Road (also numbered 5N15).

65 East Camuesa Road/Juncal Camp to Mono Camp

Distance: 15.4 miles
Difficulty: Easy for 5 miles, moderate hills beyond
Elevation: 300' gain/loss
Ride Type: Out-and-back on dirt road
Season: Year-round; winter rain may force closure
Maps: Carpinteria, Hildreth Peak, Little Pine Mountain,

Overview: An easy ride, this riverside road is the best way to experience nature here. The quiet travel and unrestricted view will allow you to hear and see things others miss. Early morning and late afternoon are the best times to ride. An extra treat is the trip to the Little Caliente Hot Springs.

Getting There: Auto access to the Upper Santa Ynez River is by paved Camino Cielo Road. You can take

East Camuesa Road/
Juncal Camp to Mono Camp

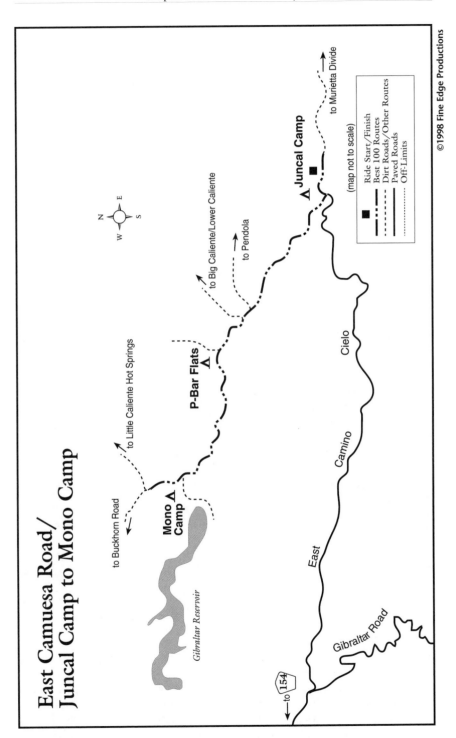

©1998 Fine Edge Productions

Santa Barbara's backcountry can be surprisingly wild and rugged.

State Highway 154 to San Marcos Pass and at the summit turn east onto Camino Cielo Road, or go up Gibraltar Road from Santa Barbara and meet Camino Cielo at the ridge top. Go east on Camino Cielo and pass Romero Saddle and the top of that trail where the pavement ends. It is 5.3 miles to Juncal Camp next to the Santa Ynez River on this good graded dirt road. You can park in turnouts along the road and at various camps. Be sure not to block access. *Cautions:* the road is closed during wet weather; beware of fast motor vehicles and their dust when you're riding.

Route: The road (5N15) heads west on the north side of the river and is fairly level past oak and sycamore trees for 0.75 mile. In the next mile you climb over two hills with a canyon in between. These are short hills, but the elevation will give you an overview of the area. After descending the second hill, you have more level cycling to the junction with Agua Caliente Road, 3.2 miles from Juncal Camp. The USFS Pendola Station is visible on the right about 200 yards up that road. It is an easy ride 2.5 miles up Agua Caliente road to the hot spring that is piped into a rectangular concrete tub set in the ground.

From Pendola Station, take Camuesa Road west, crossing Agua Caliente Creek just past the junction. The large Mid Santa Ynez Camp is on the left at 3.4 miles, and the smaller P-Bar Flats Camp is on the right at 4.3 miles. The P-Bar Jeepway comes down a ridge and joins Camuesa Road just east of the camp. Camuesa Road continues west over rather flat terrain past the camps along the north side of the river.

At 4.9 miles the Blue Canyon Trail starts out as a doubletrack on the left and crosses the river. Here Camuesa Road leaves the riverbank and climbs over a series of ridges, dipping into side canyons in between.

You pass over the first saddle at 5.4 miles, the second at 6.3 miles, and the last at 6.9 miles and an elevation of 1,875 feet. Now it's all downhill to Mono Camp at 7.7 miles.

Mono Camp is the last camp you can drive to and it's a good base camp or parking spot for riding in the area or deeper into the backcountry. A short trail from the northwest side of the camp leads to the Mono Debris Dam with its vertical waterfall. Just 0.2 mile past the camp on Camuesa Road, a right fork leads east and north 1.0 mile to Little Caliente Hot Springs. From the turn-around loop, take a footpath 50 yards to the right to a nice cement hot tub with deck. Beyond the loop Mono Road leads north along Mono Creek.

If you want to continue west on Camuesa Road past Mono Camp, go past the hot springs turn-off. Where Indian and Mono creeks come together there are several concrete fords through the water. There is a locked gate just past the Indian Canyon trailhead, 1.3 miles from Mono Camp.

When you've finished exploring, head back the way you came for a pleasant out-and-back ride.

66 Gibraltar Dam and Mine

Distance: 13 miles
Difficulty: Moderate; stream crossings can be technical
Elevation: 750' gain/loss
Ride Type: Lollipop loop on dirt road and trail
Season: Best in spring and summer
Map: Little Pine Mountain

Overview: This enjoyable spring and summer loop has water crossings and opportunities for swimming, including the gorgeous Red Rock hole. The Gibraltar Trail crisscrosses the Santa Ynez River, the longest stretch of free-flowing river with public access in Southern California, before depositing you at Gibraltar Dam. From there you can continue along the south side of Gibraltar Reservoir (source of Santa Barbara's drinking water) to Gibraltar Mine, an old quicksilver mine.

Note: The trail changes each year, especially after a hard winter. Some years, particularly in spring, it can be more of a portage than a ride. If that sounds like too much work, you can ride out-and-back on the upper road.

Getting There: From Santa Barbara, take Highway 154 north for 11 miles to Paradise Road. Follow Paradise Road to its end and park in the picnic area there.

Route: From the metal gate at the picnic area, head north up the canyon following an old wagon road. The first 0.25 mile of trail is pebbly and difficult to ride. The trail fords the river and climbs the western bank before turning east and crossing to the south side of the river. The river crossings are rocky and, while some are rideable, you'll get soaked—perfect for a hot summer day!

The trail continues up the canyon with intermittent, fast riding on the oak-shaded bluffs along the river, and slow torturous river crossings where it's sometimes easier to carry your bike than to ride it. You pass a number of rock outcroppings, examples of the faulting and folding processes which created this terrain.

About 1.5 miles up the canyon, after passing through a small oak forest and making a long river traverse, you come to one of the finest and most inviting pools anywhere. The sandstone cliffs on the north bank plunge steeply down into the river and there are long deep pools here. The best swimming hole is nearly 100 yards long! Reeds and willows along the ponds draw waterfowl and small animals. If you're alert you may spot wildlife in the quiet pools.

As you approach the dam, 3.5 miles, keep clear of it and its equipment. Trespassing and loitering are prohibited. From the dam you can loop back to your starting point, or you can continue to the mine. The high road which returns to the picnic area takes off from the east side of the dam, crosses a small creek bed and heads uphill in a westerly direction on the red rock road. (If you come to the green house where the damkeeper lives, you went the wrong way.) The road climbs several hundred feet in a westerly direction to a high point above the long swimming hole before making a fast descent to the parking area at the end of Paradise Road. Along the way oak trees provide shade, and you have views of the Santa Ynez River. *Caution:* A USFS locked gate blocks the road at the bottom of the hill on the east side of the parking lot.

To visit the mine, continue 0.5 mile past Gibraltar Dam to a closed gate. Head left and down to the reservoir. Begin a short steep climb around Gidney Creek. Follow the road to the east to the mine, 6.5 miles. There's much to explore here, including tracks and mine carts leading to a mine shaft. When you're done poking around, head back the way you came. Follow the directions above to find the high road back to your car.

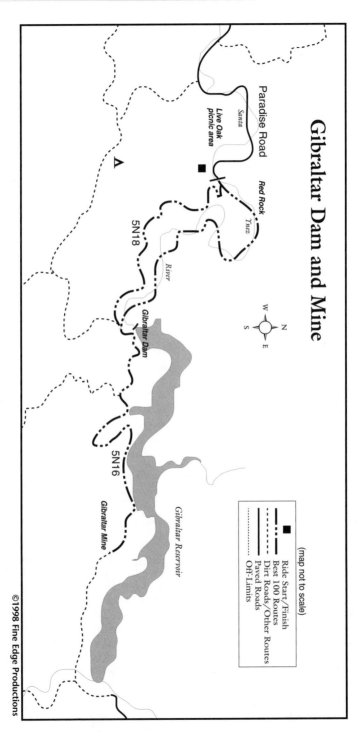

Gibraltar Dam and Mine

Paradise Road

Live Oak
picnic area

Santa

Red Rock

Trib.

5N18

River

Gibraltar Dam

5N16

Gibraltar Mine

Gibraltar Reservoir

N
W   E
S

(map not to scale)
Ride Start/Finish
Best 100 Routes
Dirt Roads/Other Routes
Paved Roads
Off-Limits

©1998 Fine Edge Productions

67 Little Pine Mountain: East Camuesa Road/Buckhorn Road

Distance: 23.2 miles
Difficulty: Moderate; good road but long climb
Elevation: 1,200' to 4,400'; 3,200' gain/loss
Ride Type: Out-and-back on dirt roads
Season: Year-round; winter rain may force closure
Maps: San Marcos Pass, Little Pine Mountain

Overview: This is a very popular route due to the good roads and spectacular views. It is a fairly strenuous ride because of the elevation gain, but the variations in grade and terrain keep it interesting. Frequent rest stops also provide opportunities for photography, map reading, and viewing the changing perspective of the backcountry.

Watch for motor vehicles on this ride. This is a designated motorcycle route and a major backcountry access road for official vehicles. These mountains can be treacherous during the winter. Heavy rain in early 1995 caused a massive landslide that took out the road in five places above the second switchback where the road zigzags up the mountain.

Getting There: From Highway 154 (San Marcos Pass Road) drive east on Paradise Road past the ranger station and cross the Santa Ynez River (one-way concrete ford) to Lower Oso Picnic Area. Here take the narrow paved road on the left (north) uphill into Oso Canyon. When you come to the campground, keep right to the Camuesa Road locked gate. Park in the Upper Oso Parking Area, not in the campsites.

Route: The first part of this ride is 4.8 miles up West Camuesa Road (5N15) to Buckhorn Road. Camuesa, pronounced ka-moose-ah, is derived from

"gamusa," which means buckskin or deer hide. This normally well-graded dirt road heads east from Upper Oso Camp, climbing and descending the canyon north of the Santa Ynez River to get around Gibraltar Reservoir. Camuesa Road is the area's main access road with connections to many other roads and trails.

From the northeast side of Upper Oso Camp, go around the east side of the locked gate. From this point you head east to enter a narrow canyon hemmed in by rock ledges where there is barely enough room for the creek and a road. After an easy 0.7-mile ride you come to the first switchback. Santa Cruz Trail (27W09) starts here and there is a sign listing mileages and a sign-in log for trail users. It is an extremely steep trail, heavily used by hikers and equestrians, and *we recommend that bicyclists not use it.*

From this junction, Camuesa Road climbs the mountainside with five more switchbacks beneath oak trees before traversing the south side of Oso Canyon heading east. Although the climbing is not very steep, the mountain is almost a vertical cliff and the road must have been blasted out of solid rock. This is around the 2-mile mark and here you must be very careful of the edge.

You level out some at 2.9 miles where the Camuesa Connector Trail starts down on the right across a

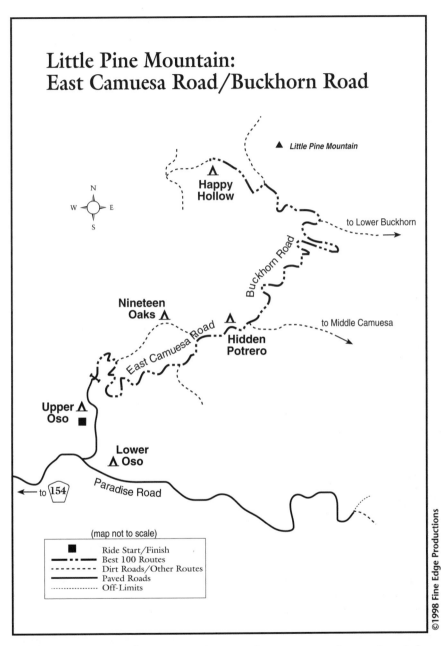

Little Pine Mountain:
East Camuesa Road/Buckhorn Road

▲ Little Pine Mountain

N
W ⬥ E
S

**Happy
Hollow** ▲

to Lower Buckhorn →

Buckhorn Road

**Nineteen
Oaks** ▲   ▲

to Middle Camuesa →

East Camuesa Road

**Hidden
Potrero**

Upper ▲
Oso ■

Lower
▲ **Oso**

Paradise Road

← to ⬡154⬡

(map not to scale)

■	Ride Start/Finish
—·■·—	Best 100 Routes
- - - -	Dirt Roads/Other Routes
———	Paved Roads
··········	Off-Limits

©1998 Fine Edge Productions

meadow. Here you have crossed to the south side of the ridge and the climbing is easier between the north side of the meadow and the ridge-top. After about a mile the ridge gets much steeper so the road switch-backs and turns to the north to cross back over to the north side of the ridge.

Where you cross this small saddle

there is a remarkable peaked rock on the left that glistens in the sunlight. Just ahead at 4.5 miles a trail on the left goes down at first and then levels past a fenced bog and on to Hidden Potrero Camp on the east side of the bog. This site has one table and fireplace next to the road at 4.6 miles from Upper Oso. Only 0.2 mile more and you are at the junction with Buckhorn Road (6N13) and the high point of East Camuesa Road, 2,797 feet.

Take Buckhorn Road north. Although not level, the first 1.6 miles is fast, with up-and-down grades that deposit you 150 feet lower than the junction. Next you have a steep 1-mile climb up a south-facing bluff, where on a hot day the sun is cruel. On the north side past this bluff the road is not as steep as it passes through the shade of oak trees. Out around another ridge you pass Buckhorn Trail (27W12) below on the right. That trail starts a little farther up the road, marked by a sign,

9.1 miles from Upper Oso Camp.

The road keeps climbing along the ridge heading west and you soon encounter the first pine trees after a short switchback. You come to the Little Pine Mountain Junction next to a concrete rainwater tank. Take the signed road left (southwest) which soon levels out and descends through oak and pine forest to Happy Hollow Trail Camp. This campsite with tables and fireplaces is located in a natural hollow filled with large trees. There is no water here, however; the nearest source is at Little Pine Spring Trail Camp about a mile north on the Santa Cruz Trail.

A short distance west, on a trail that connects to the Santa Cruz Trail, you come out of the trees and can look over the south side of Little Pine Mountain. Far below you can see Camuesa Road with the steep Santa Cruz Trail visible closer. Return the way you came up and enjoy the descent! Use safe speeds and watch for other travelers.

Figueroa Mountain

68 Zaca Ridge Road

Distance: 16.4 miles out-and-back; turn around anywhere for a shorter ride
Difficulty: Starts out easy and gradually becomes more difficult
Elevation: Start 3,440', climb to 4,200', descend to 3,400'
Ride Type: Out-and-back on dirt roads
Season: Spring, summer, fall
Maps: Los Olivos, Figueroa Mountain, Zaca Lake

Overview: Figueroa Mountain, 25 miles northwest of Santa Barbara, sits on the north side of Santa Ynez Valley. This wide pastoral valley with rolling, grass-covered hills and scattered oak trees is in sharp contrast to

the steep, rugged mountains to the north. Several small communities provide services in the valley, and the Danish town of Solvang is a tourist favorite. The streets are crowded with visitors walking through this quaint

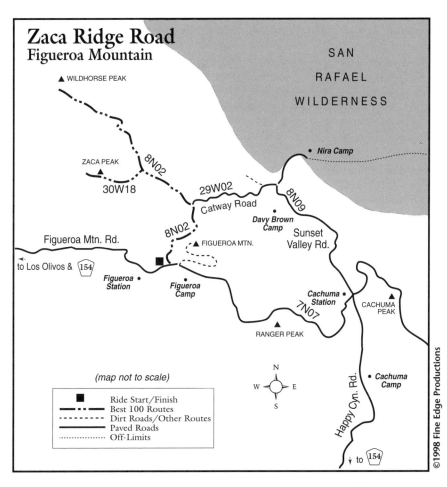

Zaca Ridge Road
Figueroa Mountain

WILDHORSE PEAK

SAN
RAFAEL
WILDERNESS

ZACA PEAK

8N02

30W18

Nira Camp

29W02

Catway Road

8N09

8N02

Davy Brown
Camp

Figueroa Mtn. Rd.

FIGUEROA MTN.

Sunset
Valley Rd.

to Los Olivos & 154

Figueroa
Station

Figueroa
Camp

Cachuma
Station

CACHUMA
PEAK

7N07

RANGER PEAK

Happy Cyn. Rd.

Cachuma
Camp

(map not to scale)

N
W   E
S

to 154

©1998 Fine Edge Productions

Ride Start/Finish
Best 100 Routes
Dirt Roads/Other Routes
Paved Roads
Off-Limits

village, visiting shops, and sampling unusual foods in the many restaurants. An open-air theater features plays in the evenings. To stay here make reservations in advance as it is usually booked up. If you are planning to camp, there are several campgrounds in the National Forest on and near Figueroa Mountain.

Figueroa Mountain, elevation 4,528 feet—a large mountain with several adjoining peaks—forms an east-west ridge from Cachuma Saddle, 7 miles west to the forest boundary. With its steep meadows, scattered trees, and chaparral contrasting

with large dark outcroppings of rock, the mountain presents a striking image from the south.

This route atop Zaca Ridge is one of the most scenic in the Los Padres National Forest and, except for a few short hills, is not very difficult. The views out over the surrounding countryside are spectacular all along the way, so even a short ride out-and-back is rewarding. Pine groves and scattered oaks throughout the ride provide secluded shady spots for picnics, sketching, photography or just taking time to enjoy the natural beauty. Connecting trails make this road your access to much of the country on both sides of the ridge.

Watch for motor vehicles on your ride as the road is closed only during wet weather. Also note that a wildfire in 1993 left many standing dead trees. Keep clear of them as they eventually fall, especially during windy weather.

Getting There: From the village of Los Olivos, on Highway 154, 3 miles east of Highway 101, take paved Figueroa Mountain Road north for 12.7 miles to the signed roadhead on the left. Park at the wide turn-around by the seasonal gate—don't block the road.

Route: Zaca Ridge Road (Catway Road) heads west from paved Figueroa Mountain Road at the 12.7-mile point and is marked by signs. A large white pipe gate about 100 feet up the road is used for motor vehicle closure during wet weather. Past this gate the road (8N02) turns north and with an easy and fairly steady climb traverses the steep western slope of Figueroa Mountain, most of this through thick forest of pine, fir, and oaks that shade the way. After 2.2 miles you arrive at a saddle on the ridge north of Figueroa Mountain. From here the view is out over Sunset Valley with Cachuma and McKinley mountains beyond. At this saddle a little-used doubletrack road is an easy climb to the south for a half-mile to a heli-pad on the hilltop.

The main road turns west and is level around the south side of the next hill on the ridge. At the west side of that hill you descend to a saddle at about 2.7 miles where a signed road comes in on the right. This is the Catway OHV route to Davy Brown Camp below. As you continue

west along Zaca Ridge there is another seasonal gate. Here the road starts to climb the first of two short steep hills, topping out at 3.0 miles. You have a good view of Santa Ynez Valley on the south to the ocean on the western horizon, and north across the San Rafael Wilderness.

The next 1.5 miles along the ridge you drop down to saddles and climb the hills that follow. At 4.5 miles you come to a high point on the southwest side of a peak where you can see ahead to Zaca Peak with a road traversing its south side. Surprisingly the ridge splits right where you are with the left fork going out to Zaca Peak west of you and the right fork (the main road) heading northwest and passing Zaca Lake on the north side. As you continue, the road descends into heavy forest and at 4.7 miles there is a fork with a small tree in the middle. The road to the left is the road you saw at Zaca Peak. It is an easy trip out to the south side of Zaca Peak. A rougher trail beyond that connects to Zaca Lake.

Beyond here the main road on the right is tougher going, climbing and descending longer and steeper hills on the ridge. A turnout on the right at 5.4 miles has a cliff on the north side and a great view below of Manzana Schoolhouse Trail Camp.

It is 0.8 mile to Cedros Saddle and all moderately steep downhill. Part way down you can see Zaca Lake on the left. Cedros Saddle is a shady, tree-filled hollow. The Sulphur Springs Trail crosses the road at the saddle and is marked by a sign on the north side of the road. It drops steeply down to Zaca Lake on the south and to Manzana Creek on the north. At Cedros Saddle you have come almost 6.3 miles.

Beyond the saddle the ridge is

narrow and less mountainous so the road remains on the ridge more often. You are able to travel faster in both directions here due to more level terrain. All along here, you have very good views of Zaca Lake below. You climb a little and pass south of Wildhorse Peak, go through a dip, and come to the road end at a large turn-around at 8.2 miles. A very rough road goes on from the bottom of the dip but dies out after turning around the hill below. Head back the way you came in.

69 La Brea and Pine Canyons

Distance: 15.7 miles (one-way) described; you can do any number of variations on the theme
Difficulty: Easy and not technical, to moderate with some steep areas
Elevation: 980' to 2,500' to 1,230' to 1,400'
Ride Type: One-way or out-and-back on dirt road
Season: Spring, summer, fall
Maps: Chimney Canyon, Miranda Pine Mountain, Manzanita Mountain, Tepusquet Canyon

Overview: Just 27 miles from Santa Maria, this pastoral canyon region, with five drive-in camps and good dirt roads, is an under-utilized area. Most of the year—except during the rainy season—the roads here are open and passable by passenger cars with reasonable ground clearance and careful drivers. *Remember—conditions can change quickly on remote mountain roads!* This beautiful area, with the wide, 7-mile La Brea Canyon Road, is one of the best for beginning riders. Oak and sycamore groves beside open grass fields and chaparral provide a varied landscape where it's a delight to ride. The nearly level road is easy to ride and fun to explore!

Pine Canyon is remote, but the two campgrounds and 3 miles of good dirt roads make the long drive over mountain dirt roads worth it.

Getting There: At Santa Maria take Betteravia Road east from Highway 101. Continue 8.4 miles to Santa Maria Mesa Road on your left. It crosses the Sisquoc River, and at 15.3 miles from Highway 101 connects with Tepusquet (Tip-es-kay) Road. Turn left, away from the river, and go up this beautiful canyon 4.5 miles where you turn right (east) onto Colson Canyon Road.

Colson Canyon Road is the main access route to the La Brea-Pine Canyon areas for mining, ranching, grazing and recreational activities. For 2.7 miles it passes private property before entering the federal forest at a large sign marked *Los Padres—Land of Many Uses.* The road follows the canyon bottom, crossing the usually dry streambed many times. For most of its length, Colson Canyon is quite narrow with sheer sides. The road climbs steadily but there are some steep sections. Near Colson Camp the canyon widens with clusters of oaks growing here and there. Colson Camp, 4.1 miles from Tepusquet Road on the north side of Colson Canyon Road, has eight sites with shade oaks, piped water, tables, fire

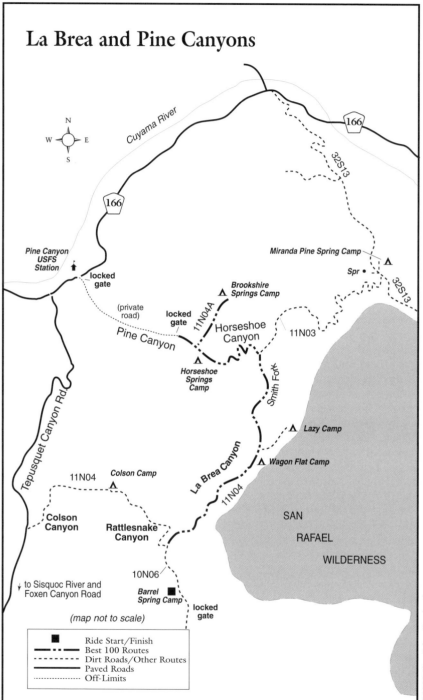

La Brea and Pine Canyons

Cuyama River

166

N
W—E
S

166

Pine Canyon
USFS
Station

locked
gate

Miranda Pine Spring Camp

Spr •

32S13

Brookshire
Springs Camp

(private
road)

locked
gate

11N04A

Horseshoe
Canyon

11N03

Pine Canyon

Horseshoe
Springs
Camp

Smith Fork

Lazy Camp

Wagon Flat Camp

La Brea Canyon

Tepusquet Canyon Rd

11N04

Colson Camp

11N04

SAN

Colson
Canyon

Rattlesnake
Canyon

RAFAEL

WILDERNESS

10N06

to Sisquoc River and
Foxen Canyon Road

Barrel
Spring Camp

locked
gate

(map not to scale)

■   Ride Start/Finish
━ ━ ━ Best 100 Routes
- - - - Dirt Roads/Other Routes
━━━━ Paved Roads
········· Off-Limits

© 1998 Fine Edge Productions

pits and pit toilets. *Please remember to pack out your own trash!*

Two-tenths of a mile farther up Colson Canyon Road, you pass the site of the former Colson USFS Station. All that remains are roads, building pads, pipes and telephone lines. Colson Saddle is located 0.5 mile above Colson Camp. Here you have the first view down into La Brea Canyon and over to the mountains and ridges beyond—an impressive sight. At the saddle a road north leads to some home sites and a very ugly strip-mining operation. To the south Alejandro Trail (31W15) takes off at a steel sign and switchbacks up the mountain. At the saddle there is a cattleguard and a gate for winter storm closure. Rattlesnake Canyon Road (11N04) continues down to La Brea Canyon east of here.

Rattlesnake Canyon Road is open to motor vehicle traffic, except during wet winter weather when the gate at Colson Saddle is closed to all vehicles—except ranchers—in La Brea Canyon. When the seasonal gate is closed, you can cycle down Rattlesnake Canyon to La Brea Canyon and return. (The grade is fairly constant and all rideable uphill coming back.) From the top down, the road stays high up on the north side of the canyon for 1.5 miles and then starts into a series of switchbacks that descend the north ridge of Rattlesnake Canyon into La Brea Canyon. Rattlesnake Road crosses the usually dry La Brea Creek and ends at La Brea Road at a large sign with directions and distances.

Turning right and going downstream (south), it's 1.4 miles to Barrel Springs Camp. This is one of the best camps in the forest with piped-in water, pit toilets, 5 sites with tables and fire pits. Park here or along La Brea Road. A large white locked gate with no trespassing signs 0.6 mile farther marks the boundary of private ranch lands and the end of the road for mountain bikes.

ROUTE:
La Brea Canyon

Begin at the junction of Rattlesnake Canyon and La Brea Canyon Road. Traveling north (upstream) 5 miles from Rattlesnake Canyon Junction to Wagon Flat Camp, La Brea Road meanders across meadows and in and out of oak groves, crossing La Brea Creek several times as the canyon gradually narrows. Wagon Flat Camp is located on the east side of the road and overlooks the creek, which flows more here than farther downstream. The stream is the only water source. *Treat all water because of the cattle and up-canyon road crossings.* There are five sites with oak trees, tables, fire pits and pit toilets. (Just past Wagon Flat Camp a rough spur road branches east 0.75 mile to Lazy Camp and the start of Kerry Canyon Trail #30W02. Lazy Camp has two sites with tables and fire pits. This road is in very rough condition and is not suitable for cars.)

La Brea Canyon ends at the junction of Kerry and Smith canyons, mile 7.0. The next section of La Brea Road takes off from the fork at Kerry Canyon Trail and goes to a ridge where it joins Horseshoe Canyon Road (11N04) and Miranda Pine Mountain Road (11N03).

Smith Canyon

When you enter Smith Canyon, its narrow profile is apparent. The road passes a cattleguard and gate and climbs up the west side of the canyon for a short distance. The canyon opens up a little, the road levels out and then repeats its narrow, westside climb. At about 8.8 miles, the road crosses Smith Creek and passes a water trough fed by a pipe from the hillside. (As the sign warns, *this water is unsafe to drink!*)

Just past the water trough, the brush on the mountainsides changes suddenly, and you can see shrubs whose loose red bark hangs like shreds. *[Editor's Note: Red bark chamiso, the dominant shrub in this one area of the Los Padres National Forest, is uncommon in California. A native of northern Baja California, it grows in only one other area of California—the Santa Monica Mountains.]*

At mile 9 the road crosses back to the west side of Smith Canyon. It then makes a serious climb out of the canyon onto the ridge. Buckhorn Ridge Road (32W01—a 4WD OHV route) starts south from La Brea Road just as it reaches the ridge top. La Brea Road follows this wide savannah-like ridge as it slopes up and north for one mile to join, at mile 10.7, Horseshoe Canyon Road (11N04) and Miranda Pine Mountain Road (11N03). From this point you look down into Pine Canyon toward Cuyama Gorge.

Horseshoe Canyon

The road down Horseshoe Canyon twists steeply down the mountain in a westerly direction to Horseshoe Springs Camp. (The 2.5 miles of steep switchbacks seem much farther!) Horseshoe Springs Camp is located at 13.9 miles in a beautiful meadow with large shade oaks. An old stone wall with built-in stairs echoes tales of the past. Three sites with tables, fire pits, and pit toilets are available. Water is piped to the camp.

Upper Pine Canyon

One-half mile west (downhill) from Horseshoe Springs Camp the road forks at an old oak tree. (The left fork is Pine Canyon Trail, #31W02, which continues up Pine Canyon.) Take the right fork (north), Road 11N04, into Upper Pine Canyon. This is a lesser-traveled road, open to all vehicles. This part of the canyon appears to have a narrow dead-end. The canyon sides are steep and end in white cliffs with many small caves. The first mile follows the east side of the canyon. At 14.6 miles you come to a USFS gate. (Close this gate!) The road crosses the creek and passes a wire-fence corral, then crosses to the east side of the canyon again.

The road ends at Brookshire Springs Camp, 1.8 miles from Horseshoe Springs Camp and 15.7 miles from the beginning of La Brea Canyon Road. There are two sites—one next to the creek, the other under a large oak. Tables, fire pits, and pit toilets are available. The water in the creek has been fouled by cattle, so *do not drink it.*

CHAPTER 9

Central Coast: San Luis Obispo to Monterey

By Delaine Fragnoli and Mickey McTigue

Tucked between Santa Barbara to the south and Santa Cruz to the north, California's storied Central Coast offers excellent road and mountain biking opportunities. Best known for its lovely beaches, San Luis Obispo County contains Pismo Beach and Morro Bay with the striking Morro Rock. Farther north is San Simeon and Hearst Castle, the fantasy estate of newspaper magnate William Randolph Hearst. Even farther north, in Monterey County, rise the dramatic cliffs of the Big Sur coastline.

Predictably, the best riding here is at the beach. Two state parks, Montaña de Oro and Andrew Molera, contain perhaps the most scenic coastal mountain biking in all of the state. West of San Luis Obispo and just south of Morro Bay (you can see Morro Rock from spots in the park), Montaña de Oro has eight trails, mostly singletrack, open to bikes. The rides in this chapter take you on all but one of those trails.

The park gets its name not for the precious metal, but for the brilliant gold color the landscape assumes in spring when it is covered by California poppies and other wildflowers. At over 8,000 acres and with half a million visitors each year, this is one of California's largest and most popular state parks—and for good reason. Seven miles of shoreline offer spectacular views and cooling sea breezes. Tide pools and miles of sandy beaches add to the dramatic meeting of land and sea. Facilities include a visitor center, picnic areas, and campgrounds.

Bisected by Highway 1, Andrew Molera State Park occupies a narrow strip of land between the Big Sur River and the Big Sur coast on its west side. The majority of its 4,800 acres sit across the highway; most of the park's trails and all of its facilities (including a walk-in campground) are on the beach side. Ridgeline and

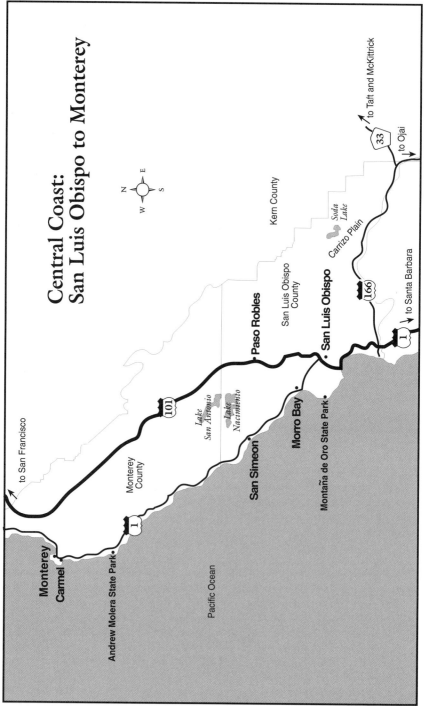

Central Coast:
San Luis Obispo to Monterey

©1998 Fine Edge Productions

View of Hazard Canyon from Manzanita Trail, Montaña de Oro State Park.

cliffside beach trails afford spectacular coastal views, while other trails circle meadows and meander along the river. Giant coastal redwoods, madrone, coast live oak, and ponderosa pine all grace the park.

Just inland, Los Padres National Forest continues into San Luis Obispo County from Santa Barbara County, while another chunk of the forest stretches from San Simeon almost to Carmel. Unfortunately much of it is designated wilderness and is thus closed to bikes. The areas that are open for mountain biking provide very steep climbing as the Santa Lucia range rises from sea level to over 5,000 feet in a few miles.

Farther inland the Monterey County Parks Department has done an excellent job of developing and signing mountain biking trails in the oak and chaparral landscape along the south shore of Lake San Antonio. Just north of Paso Robles, the lake is the county's premier freshwater recreation area. Fishing, swimming and boating opportunities abound. In May the 3,000-acre park hosts the famous Wildflower Triathlon. The riding here is generally easy, making the lake a great weekend destination for the whole family.

For something entirely different, try the little-known and remote Carrizo Plain Natural Area in the far southeast corner of San Luis Obispo Country. Midway between Bakersfield and Santa Maria, this arid flat valley boasts 85 miles of low-traffic dirt roads and 15 miles of paved roads ideal for the bicycle traveler.

A yearly average of 8 to 10 inches of rainfall drains from the surrounding mountains out onto the valley floor and makes its way to Soda Lake. The Carrizo Plain is a large depressed area with no outlet, so the water that drains into the lake leaves only by evaporation. The salts remain and the surface is a brilliant white. But in winter this 3,000-acre lake bed receives enough water to attract large numbers of migratory birds. Great numbers of hawks, eagles, owls and meadow songbirds spend the winter on the plains and thousands of lesser sandhill cranes and other waterfowl flock to the lake.

The San Andreas Fault is visible along the east side of the plain where stream channels are offset hundreds of yards to the north. Working with wildlife and conservation agencies, the Bureau of Land Management has reintroduced tule elk and up to 300 pronghorn antelope which can sometimes be seen on the west side. Also on the west side at Painted Rock are Native American pictographs, the most elaborate Native American rock art site in North America.

70 Carrizo Plain Loop

Distance: 72.6 miles
Difficulty: Moderate in good weather; long distance, but good roads and no long, steep hills; not technical
Elevation: 3,000' to 1,917'; 1,083' difference
Ride Type: Two-day ride on dirt roads and pavement
Season: Spring and fall best; spring wildflowers can be spectacular
Maps: Reward, McKittrick Summit, Simmler, Panorama Hills, Painted Rock, Chimineas Ranch, Fellows, Ballinger Canyon, Cuyama, Maricopa, Elkhorn Hills, Wells Ranch, Caliente Mountain

Overview: The Carrizo Plain is a long narrow valley with Soda Lake Road running the length of it. To the east is the Elkhorn Plain at the base of the Temblor Range, separated from the Carrizo Plain by the low Panorama Hills and farther south by the Elkhorn Hills. The Elkhorn Road runs the length of this very narrow and parallel plain. Elkhorn Plain is higher than the Carrizo Plain and from several places along the road you can see out across the Carrizo Plain, especially on the northern half. These roads are not connected by cross roads except near each end, making for a long ride.

With a start/finish at Reyes Station the whole loop is 72.6 miles. If you ride the 5 miles up to the primitive camping area at the Selby-Arco pad and back to Soda Lake Road you have a total of 82.6 miles. Carrying all your camping gear and the necessary 3 or 4 gallons of water is more than most people are willing to do.

An alternative is to leave the sec-ond day's water and camping equipment in a vehicle parked at the Painted Rock Visitor Center. Park the second vehicle at Reyes Station, ride northwest through the Elkhorn Plain, south across the Carrizo Plain on Simmler Road to Soda Lake Road and the Visitor Center. First day mileage would be 42.6. Drive 5.8 miles to the camping area and the next morning drive back to the Visitor Center. Park the car and ride 30 miles southeast on Soda Lake Road through the Carrizo Plain back to Reyes Station. For a one-day ride, just ride the part that interests you.

Caution: This is a very remote area with little traffic. The weather can change fast in the winter, and rain could leave you stranded in mud. The summers are very hot and on these treeless plains there is almost no shade. There are no stores, no gas stations and no water available in the reserve. Bring all the water you need; it is far better to overestimate your needs than to underestimate them.

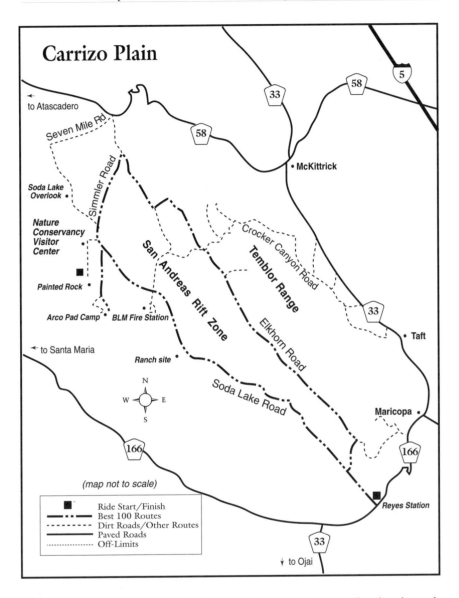

Carrizo Plain

to Atascadero

Seven Mile Rd

Simmler Road

Soda Lake Overlook •

Nature Conservancy Visitor Center

Painted Rock •

Arco Pad Camp • • BLM Fire Station

to Santa Maria

Ranch site •

San Andreas Rift Zone

Crocker Canyon Road

Temblor Range

Elkhorn Road

Soda Lake Road

• McKittrick

33

58

5

58

33

• Taft

Maricopa •

166

166

Reyes Station

33

to Ojai

(map not to scale)

N
W — E
S

■	Ride Start/Finish
—··—··—	Best 100 Routes
---------	Dirt Roads/Other Routes
————	Paved Roads
············	Off-Limits

Nearest Services are at the BLM Fire Station, Washburn Road; in an emergency, call 911 or 805-861-4119; for business, call 805-861-4110 or 861-4236. Other services are found in Maricopa or Taft.

Getting There: From Highway 101, just north of Santa Maria, take State Highway 166 east 65 miles through the Cuyama Valley to the junction with State Highway 33. Continue east 4.7 miles to the signed Soda Lake Road on the left (north) at Reyes Station. This 76 gas station is the last one on your way to the reserve.

From Interstate 5 south of

Bakersfield, take State Highway 166 24 miles west to Maricopa and then 9.3 miles southwest to Reyes Station and Soda Lake Road.

Park along Soda Lake Road near Reyes Station at Highway 166 or at Painted Rock Visitors Center on Soda Lake Road 30 miles northwest of Reyes Station. When you park at these places check with someone there to make sure your car is not in the way and let them know where you are going and when you will return. A good time to bring up parking arrangements is while making a purchase of gas or souvenirs or making a donation. It's a small price to pay to have someone watching out for you.

DAY 1—
Reyes Station to Painted Rock Visitor Center

This is a 42.6-mile ride, based on parking a camping vehicle at the Visitor Center. Start from Reyes Station and ride northwest on paved Soda Lake Road passing treeless, grass-covered, rolling hills. You descend and pass a salt-rimmed sag pond formed where the land sinks into the San Andreas Fault. The road is built right next to the fault as you can see while you climb up from the sag pond, cross the county line and drop down to another sag pond. On the north end of this pond, at 3.5 miles, you turn right (east) onto the signed Elkhorn Road.

This graded dirt road climbs very steeply in places but only gains 250 feet in 1.1 miles to the high point of the ride at 3,000 feet. The descent east starts out steep but moderates when the road switchbacks twice and levels out where you circle around the south side of a large corral at 5.9 miles from Reyes Station. There is a

good view northwest along this part of the Elkhorn Plain while you ride northeast 0.8 mile to the junction with Elkhorn Grade Road. Turn left.

The elevation at the junction is 2,406 feet. In the next 24 miles you go from 2,300 feet to 2,452 feet, and at the end of the plain you drop back to 2,354 feet. The scene is not a long, seemingly endless plain, but is broken up by low hills and washes that cross at right angles, breaking the ride into interesting segments. In each section the terrain changes slightly as do the plants. You pass many fences, cattle guards, water tanks and corrals; after a while you may notice a pattern as about one set of each occurs every mile. There are many side tracks remaining from ranching operations, but you should keep to the main road that heads mostly northeast.

At 25.6 miles from Reyes Station you come to the signed Crocker Grade Road on the right that climbs about 700 feet in 1.9 miles to Crocker Summit at 3,213 feet. Keep to the left and continue on Elkhorn Road across a deep gulch. On the other side is another junction. The road to the left (west) follows the water course you just crossed through the Panorama Hills down to the Carrizo Plain. There it joins with the San Diego Creek Road, which heads straight south to Soda Lake Road just opposite Washburn Road.

Take Elkhorn Road on the right for another 5.1 miles, crossing more gulches and climbing over low hills before coming to the end of the Elkhorn Plain. Here at 31 miles from Reyes Station and at an elevation of 2,354 feet, you turn west and descend a narrow canyon to Carrizo Plain. At 32 miles the road turns north, where a lesser traveled road joins in from the

Bluff Trail at Montaña de Oro State Park (Ride 71).

Jim MacIntyre

and at an elevation of 1,917 feet. Go south on Soda Lake Road 0.8 mile to the dirt road on the right; this leads to the Nature Conservancy's Painted Rock Visitor Center.

To get to the Selby Camping area, go southeast on Soda Lake Road, 0.7 mile from the Painted Rock Visitor Center drive. Take the dirt road right (south) 4 miles to a fork and take the left fork 1 mile to the Arco oil exploration pad where you may camp.

DAY 2—
Painted Rock Visitor Center to Reyes Station

At 30 miles, this segment is shorter; about a third of it is paved, making this day an easier ride except for the net elevation gain of 917 feet. About 300 feet of downhill that you have to make up again gives a total climb of around 1,200 feet. Almost all of it is gradual and not very difficult. The Carrizo Plain is much wider and flatter than the Elkhorn Plain.

Heading south on Soda Lake Road, at 5.8 miles from Painted Rock Road you cross a cattle guard at the intersection of Soda Lake Road and San Diego Creek Road on the north and Washburn Road to the south. The BLM fire station is 2.5 miles south on Washburn Road. The KCL ranch site, 5 miles farther southeast on Soda Lake Road, was to be a developed campground until it was found to be a significant archeological site.

The road stays on the west side of

south. You climb gradually, crossing several washes where debris has been strewn across the plain by flash floods. Go 0.4 mile past the power lines to the junction with Simmler Road at 36 miles. Highway 58 is 3 miles ahead to the north.

Turn sharp left and descend on Simmler Road back to the south, crossing under the power lines again. Simmler Road is less traveled and has some closed gates that you must reclose behind you. This road crosses the plain on a ridge that separates Soda Lake on the north from some smaller lakes to the south. The top of this ridge is fairly flat, but the sides have steep slopes down to the lakes on both side. This is a surprise, since from a distance, the area around the lake appears to be almost flat.

After 5.8 miles you come down off the ridge and Simmler Road ends at paved Soda Lake Road, 41.8 miles

the plain where most of the farming and ranching activities took place. Over time I expect almost all of the buildings, water tanks, and fences will be removed to restore the area to pre-settlement conditions.

After about 20 miles on the west side the road crosses the plain and starts climbing on the east side next to the Elkhorn hills. When you come to the paved part of the road there is one more short steep uphill and then a long steep downhill to where Elkhorn Road forks east. You pass the sag ponds and the county line, and climb the last hill to Reyes Station.

Montaña De Oro State Park

71 Bluff Trail

Distance: 3.5-mile loop; 4.4 miles out-and-back
Difficulty: Easy, not technical
Elevation: 60' to 100'
Ride Type: Out-and-back on dirt road or loop on dirt road and pavement
Season: Year-round
Map: Montaña De Oro State Park map, available at visitor center

Overview: This ride may have the best scenery for the least amount of effort of any ride in California. As the name implies, it follows bluffs (actually uplifted marine terraces). For drama it's hard to beat the sight of ocean waves crashing over these jutting rock formations. Beach access and views of wave-formed sea arches add to the scene. In April and May abundant California poppies, lavender, and mustard improve on the already eye-gasmic picture. Pack a lunch or snack—you'll want to dawdle on this ride.

Getting There: The park is about 12 miles west of San Luis Obispo and 7 miles south of Los Osos. From Highway 101 in San Luis Obispo, take the Los Osos/Bayward Park exit and go northwest on Los Osos Valley Road. After 12 miles it turns into Pecho Valley Road and leads into the park.

From Highway 1 near Morro Bay, take the Los Osos/Bayward Park exit.

Go right on South Bay Boulevard. At 5 miles you come to a T at Los Osos Valley Road. Go right and follow Los Osos Valley Road into Pecho Valley Road and the park.

Park headquarters are 2.5 miles past the park entrance sign. Park at park headquarters or at the trailhead, 0.1 mile farther on Pecho Valley Road in a dirt turnout on the right. There are restrooms and a pay phone at headquarters. *Note:* While the water here is not potable, you can buy bottled water at the visitor center (in the same building as headquarters).

Route: Begin by dropping to cross over a wooden footbridge. After the bridge you pass several trail junctions. Keep forking to the right, heading toward the ocean. It's pretty obvious which is the main trail. As you continue along the bluffs there are several spurs to your right which go to coastline vista points. You may want

to bypass the first few as the ones closest to the trailhead tend to be more crowded.

At 0.5 mile a spur leads to a lookout and a trail if you want to walk to the beach *(don't ride it)*. Just beyond this spur, at 0.6 mile you intersect a second wooden bridge that spans a creek. Go right, crossing the bridge. (If you go straight you end up back at Pecho Valley Road.) At 1.0 mile, overlooking Quarry Cove, there are restrooms and picnic tables—a nice rest stop.

At 1.3 miles fork right to stay on Bluff Trail (signed). About 0.2 mile later you have views of a large free-standing rock near the shore. At 1.7 miles turn left up the singletrack leading to Pecho Valley Road. You could go straight here; doing so would lead you to a turnaround at a fence marking the park boundary. Near this junction you have great views of Grotto Rock, its arches formed by the eroding power of wind and water.

Heading left up the singletrack you encounter the only technical part of the ride as the trail drops into and climbs steeply out of a small ravine. This portion of trail climbs gradually toward Pecho Valley Road and can be rutted.

After 2.2 miles of pedaling you reach a parking area and Coon Creek trailhead (closed to bikes). There are restrooms and picnic tables here. You can return to your car, 1.1 miles away, via paved Pecho Valley Road, or you can go back the way you came. I personally don't know why anyone would choose the road when you can ride along the bluffs. Riding the trail in the opposite direction, you will have a new perspective and will probably notice things you missed on the way out.

Trailside tools at Montaña de Oro State Park, East Boundary Trail.

72 Islay Creek and East Boundary Trail Loop

Distance: 9.0 miles
Difficulty: Moderate with some strenuous sections, some technical sections
Elevation: 1,000' gain/loss
Ride Type: Loop on dirt road and singletrack
Season: Year-round
Map: Montaña De Oro State Park map, available at visitor center

Overview: This ride combines a gradual climb up a pretty canyon with some steep and challenging singletrack. Beginners can ride up the fire road and turn around, eliminating the technical singletrack. The return on the Ridge Trail gives you panoramic ocean views.

Getting There: Park at park headquarters. See previous ride for driving instructions.

Route: Backtrack to Pecho Valley Road and go right 0.3 mile to the gated and signed Islay Creek Road on your right. This dirt road rolls

along, gaining eleva-
tion at an easy grade as
it heads inland. As you
spin along, you have
views into lush Islay
Creek with its willow,
sage, purple night-
shade, blackberry—and
poison oak.

At 2.4 miles you
pass a trail on your right
(closed to bikes). A
half-mile later you pass
another singletrack, this
one on your left. This is
the Barranca Trail, a
possible alternative re-
turn route which drops
from the East Boundary
Trail. Continue climb-
ing on the road past an
old barn on the right.

At 3.3 miles East
Boundary Trail (signed)
branches to the left.
Ahead of you on the
road you can see a
closed gate which
marks the park bound-
ary. (Beginners should
turn around here.) Go

Montaña de Oro State Park

Jim McIntyre

left onto East Boundary Trail. It
starts climbing almost immediately—
and gets steeper with each pedal
stroke. If the incline and the rocky,
loose trail weren't bad enough, you
soon have to maneuver around and
over waterbars as well. The longer
you go, the worse it gets. I mashed,
bashed, moaned, groaned, and swore
with a vengeance and I still couldn't
clean it. Thankfully this misery ends
when you top out at 4.0 miles.

From here the trail rolls rather
than pitches upward. At 4.2 miles you
pass a trail marker with trail tools,
donated by the Central Coast
Concerned Mountain Bikers. A sign

encourages you to pick up a tool and
spend a few minutes on trail work.
Good work to the CCCMB.

Temporarily level and then descending, the trail crosses a wooden
bridge at 4.4 miles. An equestrian trail
joins East Boundary here. This creek
crossing is followed by a short switchbacked climb across an open slope—
much easier than the earlier climb.

The trail then levels and you have
great views of the steep ridges and
canyons of these coastal mountains.
Don't take your eyes off the trail for
too long as you soon hit a technical
downhill section. Curvy with loose
soil, this bit of trail was filled with

braking bumps when I rode it.

At 4.9 miles you come to a short hike-a-bike pitch (at least it was for me) past a lovely oak tree on your left. Follow the trail along the fenceline marking the park boundary (thus, the trail's name). At 5.2 miles there's an unsigned singletrack on your left. You have a decision to make here. This is the Barranca Trail. You can take it back down to Islay Creek Road for a lollipop-shaped 9.5-mile loop or you can continue 0.2 mile farther to the Ridge Trail.

If you choose the Barranca Trail you climb 0.3 mile more, including a couple of switchbacks, to a T-intersection. The left branch goes to a picnic table with an ocean view (makes a nice rest stop even if you decide to take the Ridge Trail). The right branch drops steeply through a series of sometimes tight (but rideable) switchbacks and over some rocky

pitches (real butt off the saddle stuff) before depositing you at Islay Creek Road. I thought the trail was a blast, but its technicality might not be to everyone's liking. At Islay Creek Road a right takes you back to Pecho Valley Road.

If you opt for the Ridge Trail, continue straight for 0.2 mile to the trail intersection, also on the left. It rolls west along the ridgeline above Hazard Canyon (to your right) with a few short, steep uphills. (I had to push my bike up one of them.) You climb to Hazard Peak, at 1,076 feet, where you have fantastic ocean and shoreline views. From here it's a sometimes steep, sometimes rutted, sometimes rocky descent toward the beach. There are a couple of trail junctions, but you just keep heading toward the ocean. At the bottom, a left turn on Pecho Valley takes you 0.4 mile back to park headquarters.

73 Hazard Canyon, Manzanita Trail and Bloody Nose Trail Loop

Distance: 6.0 miles
Difficulty: Moderate, very technical in spots
Elevation: 650' gain/loss
Ride Type: Loop on dirt road, singletrack and pavement
Season: Year-round
Map: Montaña De Oro State Park map, available at Visitor Center

Overview: Like the previous ride, this one includes a scenic trip up a canyon, ocean views, fun singletrack and a gnarly descent. Conditions on the Manzanita and Bloody Nose singletracks have gotten decidedly more difficult since the first edition of this book. Beginners should turn around before heading down Bloody Nose. Advanced riders may want to connect these trails with the previous ride for a longer loop. The easiest way to access

the Ridge and Barranca trails would be via Hazard Canyon and Manzanita, described here.

Getting There: Hazard Canyon Road takes off to the left (east) just inside (about 0.1 mile) the state park boundary. A small brown post here says *Group Horse Camp*. Park in the dirt turnout across the road.

Route: Head down dirt Hazard

Canyon Road past the horse camp. Beyond here the road rises and falls, generally gaining altitude. Continue past a second gate. Soon the road curves to the right, and at 0.8 mile you come to a junction with the Manzanita Trail off to the right. Climb this singletrack out of the canyon.

Manzanita Trail rises from the wet, wooded (willow and eucalyptus) creek bed to manzanita and sage. This ascent constitutes the ride's major elevation gain. Although steep, it is rideable with a good line around most of the waterbars. Indeed, it is much easier than the previous ride's climb up East Boundary Trail.

At 1.4 miles you come to a T-intersection with East Boundary Trail. Go right. Almost immediately there's another trail joining on the left. You continue straight for this loop. (Going left would take you to the Ridge Trail or, a bit farther, the Barranca Trail. See the previous ride description for details.) There's a picnic table here with a view down Hazard Canyon and to the ocean. Photo op!

Continue along the now more level Manzanita Trail. At 1.9 miles you pass a closed trail climbing steeply on the left. Continue straight. You have more views toward the ocean and into steep-walled Hazard Canyon. Just beyond here there's a Y-intersection. The right fork climbs steeply for 0.1 mile to a small ridgetop and viewpoint where it dead-ends. The ride continues to the left.

Now you begin what can only be described as a very gnarly and bizarre piece of trail. (Beginners attempting this ride should turn around at this point unless they don't mind walking.) You are basically riding in a giant rut filled with deep sand with stands of the trail's namesake manzanita bushes lining the lip of the crevice. Black plastic erosion netting here seems to serve no purpose but to knock you off your bike.

I found it quite frustrating to be pedaling so hard through the bottomless sand to go *downhill*. But it's not all sand. You get rock, hard-packed soil with ruts, waterbars,

Harris Creek at Lake San Antonio (Ride 74).

drop-offs, all variety of hazards and obstacles. I believe I said a swear word or two along here.

At 3.1 miles go left at the Y. At this point you are on Bloody Nose Trail, although it is not signed as such. You go in and out of two streams, steeply of course. One water-bar-choked ascent will be a hike-a-bike for most riders. Throw in some ragged, jagged shale as well as more railroad ties and you've got yourself a challenge. Hmm, wonder how the trail got that name . . .

At 3.7 miles you reach a picnic spot. Stop if you like or continue on the trail into Camp Keep. Keep bearing right past the campsites and park residences. You are soon on pavement as you head out to Pecho Valley Road. Once there, go right for 1.5 miles to finish the loop. It's down, then up, then rolling back to your car.

74 Lake San Antonio: Long Valley Loop

Distance: 7.1 miles
Difficulty: Moderate, mildly technical
Elevation: Lots of ups and downs, but no major climbs
Ride Type: Loop on dirt roads, fire breaks and singletrack
Season: Year-round; can be extremely hot in summer
Map: Monterey County Parks Department produces a very good map, available at park entrance

Overview: This loop takes you through oak and chaparral along the Harris Creek arm of the lake, away from the boat launches and more developed shoreline of the main reservoir. In addition to 26 miles of hiking and mountain bike trails, the south shore of the lake has a full service resort with grocery store, restaurant, gas station, marina, and cabin rentals. One of the largest bald eagle winter habitats in central California, the park runs Eagle Watch boat tours Friday through Sunday in January and February.

The trail system here is a land access success story for mountain bicyclists. Trail development started 20 years ago when rangers realized that many of the park's fire breaks would make great hiking trails. Too much motorized recreation during the 1970s led to trail damage, and the park began roughing up the fire breaks so that they were impossible to ride. During the 1980s, the Wildflower Triathlon brought more hikers, runners, and bicyclists to the area, and a local mountain bike club began using the park as a race course. Although the trail system was temporarily closed to mountain biking because of concerns over liability and resource preservation, those issues have been resolved. Now the parks department is committed to building, rating, and signing trails for all levels of riders.

Getting There: From Paso Robles take G-14 north/northwest. (In town the G-14 is 24th Street. Outside of town it is signed Nacimiento Lake Drive. As you exit Highway 101 or 46 in Paso Robles, signs direct you to the

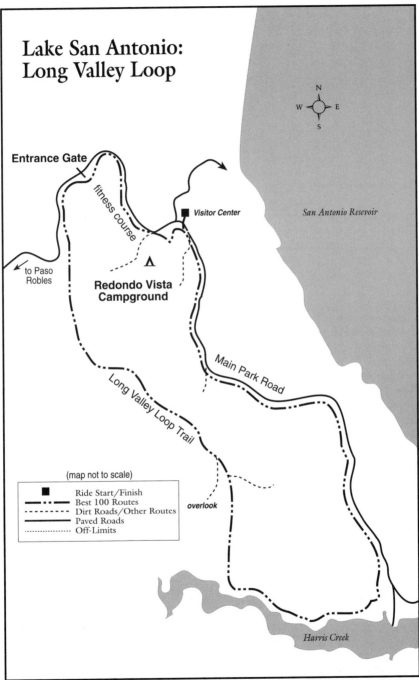

Lake San Antonio: Long Valley Loop

Entrance Gate

fitness course

Visitor Center

San Antonio Resevoir

to Paso Robles

Redondo Vista Campground

Main Park Road

Long Valley Loop Trail

(map not to scale)

■ Ride Start/Finish
—·—·— Best 100 Routes
- - - - Dirt Roads/Other Routes
——— Paved Roads
············· Off-Limits

overlook

Harris Creek

G-14.) Follow the signs for Lake Nacimiento and Lake San Antonio. At 8.5 miles G-14 makes a right. At 16.3 it curves right and crosses a dam (Lake Nacimiento). At 17.9 miles go left on G-14/Interlake Road just past the sign indicating North Shore, straight and South Shore, left. At 24.8 miles cross the Monterey County line. At 25.7 miles go right on San Antonio Road (signed South Shore) to the park entrance. There is a day-use fee. Take the main entrance road and follow signs to the visitor's center. Park here.

Singletrack near Harris Creek.

Route: Backtrack to the entrance road and go left. Immediately on your right is a bunch of big white boulders. Ride between them and you can see the backside of a trail sign. Pick up the Long Valley Trail here. Go right to begin the loop. We did the loop in a counterclockwise direction, but it could just as easily be done in the opposite direction. Neither way appears much harder or easier than the other. In both cases you have a few short, steep climbs.

At 0.1 mile cross a paved road. Trail continues on the other side. It is clearly marked here and throughout the loop. Continue following signs for the Long Valley Loop, alongside the fitness course. You parallel the entrance road here. Although the surroundings are not pristine wilderness, we did see deer here.

At 0.4 mile start the first of two short hills. At 1.0 mile you come to a fence. *Be sure to close it behind you as there are cattle in the area.* Just under 2.0 miles the doubletrack you're on swings left and begins a short pain-in-the-butt climb. It tops out and immediately, at 2.1 miles, passes through another fence. You can walk through the gate on the side, albeit awkwardly. Watch the barbed wire.

Down a steep, loose section, keep left at the fork at 2.3 miles. Not the least bit tempting, the right fork is a very steep uphill doubletrack. This junction, like the others, is clearly signed. On the left fork, you begin a fun singletrack section along a creek.

At 2.5 miles merge with a fire road and continue straight. (Once again, well signed.) Just beyond you fork right and roll up and down for awhile.

Be on the watch for a singletrack on your left at 2.9 miles. If you're not paying attention, you can blast right past it. Going straight takes you 0.2 mile up a steep rocky climb to Harris Valley Overlook. We rode up to it and concurred that it was not worth the trouble. So head left down the singletrack through braking bumps and a short rocky section.

At 3.0 miles go straight where Badger Trail branches left. A half-mile later the singletrack begins skirting the Harris Creek arm of the lake. This is the prettiest part of the ride. You are away from campgrounds and the entrance road, surrounded by oak-graced hills, the cool blue waters of the lake, and possibly a few fishermen. Adding a spooky, surreal touch, dead tree limbs poke out of the water, marking trees that were drowned when the reservoir was created.

Follow the fun-filled singletrack as it rolls beside and above the lake for a mile. At 4.5 miles go straight up the steep, rocky climb. You may have to dismount and push up this short section. At 4.6 miles go straight where a doubletrack merges from the right.

Begin a rolling dirt road climb—steep and loose in spots. It can be hot and exposed here, but when we did it we were blessed with a breeze. Soon enough, 5.6 miles, you begin a rolling downhill. At 5.8 miles cross another dirt road (Oak Hill Loop) and continue straight. Things get more park-like and less wilderness-like as you once again closely parallel the main park road.

At 6.2 miles veer right, cross the paved road and catch the trail to the right on the other side of the road (clearly signed). After this you cross a variety of other dirt trails and roads. Stay on the clearly-signed Long Valley Loop, following the main paved park road.

You're back at the boulders at 7.1 miles—at least that's what my computer said. The park map says this loop is 8.1 miles. Go figure. From the boulders, take a right and head back to the Visitor's Center (water and bathrooms available).

75 Andrew Molera State Park

Distance: 10 miles
Difficulty: Easy, mildly technical; ridge climb is strenuous and more technical
Elevation: Minimal; the Ridge Trail climbs 1,200'
Ride Type: Loop on dirt roads and trails with two out-and-back spur options
Season: Year-round. Spring brings great wildflowers. Seasonal footbridges for crossing the Big Sur River go up in early spring. In the fall and winter expect a cold, wet portage. Be careful—water levels can change considerably.
Map: Trail map and pamphlet available at the park or any of the nearby Big Sur parks. Note that the park trail map is not particularly accurate, nor is the information about which trails are open to bikes very clear. The following trails are legal to ride: River Trail north of the Beach Trail, Beach Trail, Ridge Trail, Bluffs Trail for 1.2 miles between the Ridge Trail and Spring Trail, the Trail Camp Trail, and East Molera Trail.
Comments: The park charges a day-use fee. If you've stopped at any of the other Big Sur state parks, you can enter for free.

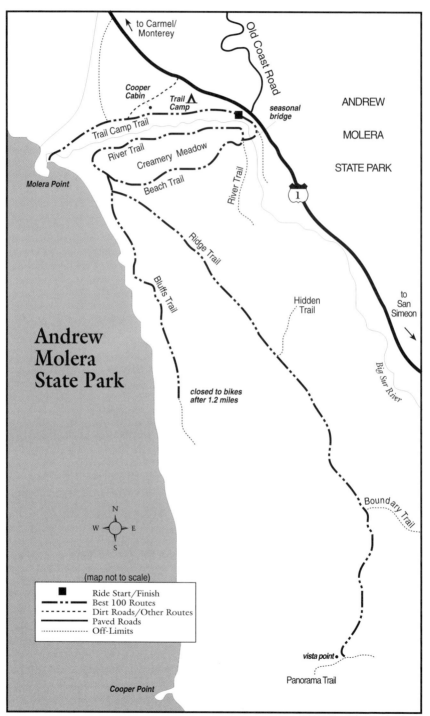

to Carmel/
Monterey

Old Coast Road

Cooper
Cabin

Trail
Camp

seasonal
bridge

ANDREW

MOLERA

STATE PARK

Trail Camp Trail

River Trail

Creamery Meadow

Beach Trail

Molera Point

River Trail

1

to
San
Simeon

Ridge Trail

Bluffs Trail

Hidden
Trail

Andrew
Molera
State Park

Big Sur River

closed to bikes
after 1.2 miles

Boundary Trail

N
W   E
S

(map not to scale)

■   Ride Start/Finish
── Best 100 Routes
---- Dirt Roads/Other Routes
── Paved Roads
...... Off-Limits

vista point •

Panorama Trail

Cooper Point

©1998 Fine Edge Productions

Ridge-top forest, Andrew Molera State Park.

Point are popular spots for viewing the gray whale migrations. Other animals you may see include deer, boar, sea otters, seals, sea lions, and a variety of shore birds. Banana slugs, too! Add to that the heavily-forested banks of the Big Sur River and you've got a spectacular slice of landscape.

The park has water and port-a-potties, primitive camping, and a small picnic area. Most of the park's 4,800 acres sit across the Pacific Coast Highway. Largely undeveloped, these lands contain several trails open to mountain bikes which looked largely unrideable to me. The Old Coast Road (see the following ride) takes off from this part of the park.

Overview: Although Andrew Molera State Park is small and offers limited riding, the scenery more than makes up for these deficits. An easy loop around Creamery Meadow via the Beach and River trails makes a good choice for beginners, who may want to venture along the Bluffs Trail as well. More advanced riders can add a vigorous climb up the Ridge Trail.

You have views of the beach, cliffs, and the spectacular Big Sur coastline from the Ridge Trail and the Bluffs Trail. Ferns, redwoods, and oaks add to the Ridge Trail's scenic appeal. In January, the Bluffs Trail and Molera

Getting There: AMSP is 22 miles south of Carmel on Highway 1. It's a short 10-minute drive north from Pfeiffer Big Sur State Park, an excellent choice for camping. The parking lot is on the west side of the highway. Or you can park at one of the walk-in gates along PCH north of the main park entrance.

Route: From the main parking area, backtrack past the ranger kiosk and go right under the *Molera Horseback Tours* sign. Follow this level dirt road for 0.1 mile to a gate with a fire road sign on your right. Take the path around the gate and drop down to the Big Sur River.

In the fall and winter you will have to portage across the river, but in summer simply cross on the plank bridge. I had to walk up the sandy embankment on the other side.

Just as the sand becomes rideable, there's an intersection and a trail sign. The sign indicates you are on Beach Trail (legal) while the trail to your left is the River Trail (closed to bikes). Immediately past here, a singletrack on the right is signed *Parking Lot*. This singletrack is also the River Trail and is open to bikes. At the end of the loop you will return to this intersection via this legal portion of the River Trail.

For now, continue on the Beach Trail toward the signed Creamery Meadow. At 0.8 mile you reach the turnoff to the Ridge Trail on your left. Intimidating in its steepness, it is rideable. Beginners should go ahead and push up this 0.1-mile climb as it is the only way to get to the Bluffs Trail. At the top, the Bluffs Trail takes off to the right and the Ridge Trail climbs at an even steeper grade off to the left.

If you're up to the challenge, go for the Ridge Trail. If you're not, skip ahead to the description of the Bluffs Trail. This first pitch is the worst. Honest. You make your way up the ridge in five or six anaerobic bursts like this. Surrounded by grasslands, you are rewarded with great views toward the ocean. At least that's what I'm told by people who have been there on a clear day. The March day I was there it was too misty to see anything.

At 1.9 miles you reach an intersection with Hidden Trail (closed to bikes). This intersection is at the bottom of a downhill and is obvious from some distance. Don't bother to slow down for it! Keep your momentum up for the next climb.

About a mile later, 2.8 miles, you come to another intersection (South Boundary Trail), also closed to bikes. The worst climbing is definitely over at this point, although you continue to gain elevation.

Cooper Cabin, Andrew Molera State Park

Big Sur River, Andrew Molera State Park

the point does indeed provide quite a vista. Here the Ridge Trail turns into Panorama Trail, which is closed to bikes. You have no choice but to return the way you came.

The trip down is a lot faster and a lot more fun. But watch out for the drainage ditches! You probably noticed them on the way up, and they have "endo" written all over them on the descent. Practice that front-wheel lift!

At 6.2 miles you're back at the intersection of the Ridge Trail and the Bluffs Trail. If you're up for more riding, go left onto Bluffs Trail. Very shortly you come to a Y-intersection. Go left. (The right fork, although not signed as closed to bikes on this end, soon drops to the beach where it is signed as closed to bikes. Uh huh.)

Stay on the main trail as it parallels the bluffs with views of the beach and ocean. There are a few mildly technical ups and downs, but in general the trail rolls along for 1.2 miles. At that point, 7.4 miles total, a sign declares that bikes are not allowed beyond here. Once again, retrace your tire tracks. Yes, it seems silly to keep backtracking, but the point here is to take in the dramatic Big Sur coast.

Back at the Ridge/Bluffs intersection, 8.6 miles, turn left and drop back down 0.1 mile to the Beach Trail (the trail you began on). Go left. Just 0.1

The vegetation gets thicker and denser along here and soon you enter a world of big trees and ferns. An incredible forest of coast live oaks arch overhead. Madrone, ponderosa pine, and coast redwoods poke through thickets of Douglas iris, thimbleberry, blackberry, redwood sorrel, wake-robin, ferns and, of course, poison oak. Ample reward for your climbing efforts. You have a little bit more climbing to do, but by now you won't care.

You reach a vista point at 3.6 miles. I couldn't see anything but fog; however, I've heard from others that

mile later (8.8 miles total) take a sharp, unmarked right turn. You could continue straight about 0.2 mile to the beach if you're ready for a break. I would recommend carrying your bike when the trail starts to get real sandy. Wet sand isn't exactly a great lubricant for your bike's bearings.

Back to that unsigned right-hand turn. This trail takes you through Creamery Meadow, the site of a habitat restoration program. Past agricultural use has left the meadow open to colonization by non-native plants. The park service along with volunteers are trying to rehabilitate the area and plant the meadow with native grasses.

At 9.5 miles the trail ends at a T. Go right. At 9.7 miles at the Y, go right. There's a short rocky section, but the trail soon smoothes out. Here you pass a trail sign and map indicating that you are on the River Trail and are heading toward the Beach Trail.

At 9.8 miles you reach a T-intersection. Go left onto the Beach Trail. (This is the trail you started on.) Cross the plank bridge over the river. Go around the gate and left onto the dirt road. You're back at your car at 10 miles.

If you still have any energy, there's an additional quick 2.2-mile jaunt you can make. Reset your computer. Head toward the far end of the parking lot from the ranger kiosk. Follow the Trail Camp signs. The trail climbs steeply at first, then drops even more steeply around a tight switchback. Signs here ask cyclists to walk their bikes—a prudent suggestion.

Just beyond, you can resume riding the singletrack which soon runs into a fire road. A right turn here would take you up to PCH. Continue straight through the trail camp. This is flat and easy cycling. You pass Cooper Cabin, on your right, where another spur climbs up to PCH. Cooper Cabin belonged to sea captain John Cooper who acquired this land in 1840. His descendants sold the land to the Nature Conservancy in 1968, and it became a state park in 1972.

At 1.0 mile, go right. (The very short left fork goes to the water and stops.) You pass Headlands Trail (closed to bikes) on your right. Here you are on singletrack, curving through criss-crossing trees. Just as you're thinking "this is cool," the trail ends at the beach, 1.1. miles.

Retrace your route for a 2.2-mile trip.

76 Big Sur: The Old Coast Road

Distance: 10.5 miles one-way; 18.5 miles as a loop; 21 miles out-and-back
Difficulty: One-way or loop, strenuous and mildly technical; as an out-and-back, very strenuous and mildly technical
Elevation: Over 1,800' one way or as a loop; more than 3,700' out-and-back
Ride Type: One-way shuttle on dirt road; loop on dirt road and pavement; out-and-back ride on dirt road
Season: Year-round. Spring, with wildflowers and without a lot of tourists, is best.
Map: AAA Monterey Bay Region
Comments: Nearest facilities are at the road's southern end in Andrew Molera State Park. The road is open to vehicle traffic. After the first mile, be sure to stay on the road as all land beyond that point is private (and is emphatically signed as such).

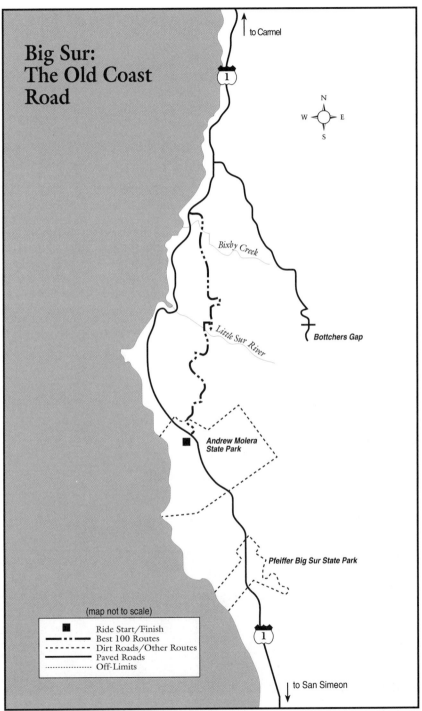

Big Sur: The Old Coast Road

to Carmel

N
W — E
S

Bixby Creek

Little Sur River

Bottchers Gap

Andrew Molera State Park

Pfeiffer Big Sur State Park

(map not to scale)

■ Ride Start/Finish
━·━·━ Best 100 Routes
------- Dirt Roads/Other Routes
━━━ Paved Roads
············· Off-Limits

to San Simeon

©1998 Fine Edge Productions

Overview: Before the Bixby Bridge was completed in 1932, the Old Coastal Road was the main route from Big Sur into Carmel. Today the graceful bridge is not only a lovely concrete structure, but it lets cars zoom through on Highway 1, leaving the Old Coast Road to you and me and our two-wheeled friends.

The Old Road can be ridden from Andrew Molera State Park in the south to Bixby Bridge in the north or vice versa. I prefer to start at AMSP. The parking situation is better there, there are facilities available in nearby Big Sur, the view as you descend to Bixby Bridge is spectacular, and on your return route down Highway 1, the ocean is on your right and the wind is at your back.

Either way, you do plenty of steep climbing as you make your way up and through the ranch land of the Big Sur Valley, in and out of the old-growth redwoods of the Little Sur drainage, and in and out of the Bixby drainage on your way to the ocean at Bixby Landing.

I prefer the loop option, but you can arrange to have a friend pick you up at Bixby Landing if the vehicle traffic on Highway 1 makes you nervous. As an out-and-back, the Old Road is a burly undertaking—although I have heard of people doing it.

Getting There: Start at Andrew Molera State

Park. See directions for the previous ride.

Route: From the parking lot, climb 0.1 mile back out to and cross Highway 1. The Old Coast Road takes off from the dirt pull-out directly across the highway. You can't miss it. There's a street sign which reads *Coast Highway/Cabrillo Highway* and several yellow signs declaring *Entering State Park Property* and *Impassable When Wet.*

The road climbs immediately. About 0.1 mile up, a trail takes off to the right. It's signed as being open to bikes, but a quick hike up it convinced me it's not particularly rideable—at least uphill. At 0.3 mile you begin to get views of the coast. A

Andrew Molera State Park, Bluffs Trail (Ride 75).

Bluffs at Montaña de Oro State Park (Ride 71).

turnout at 0.6 mile offers a nice vista of the beach and ocean. The hard-packed gravel road turns inland just beyond here.

At 0.8 mile, you cross a cattle-guard and gate with signs indicating private property on both sides of the road for the next 6 miles. In other words: stay on the road. Route-finding for the rest of the ride is easy as there are no other roads or trails you can take.

At 1.5 miles the grade lessens a bit before pitching upward again. One more mile and you top out and begin a 2-mile downhill. It's over at 4.5 miles as you begin the ride's toughest climb. You grunt through several steep, tight switchbacks with loose gravel and rocks. You will loath these. To add to the misery factor, this por-

tion of the climb lacks any shade.

Fortunately the agony lasts "only" 2 miles. When you top out at 6.5 miles, you are greeted by an awesome 3-mile descent through a cool, old-growth redwood forest. These are the best trees on the ride. Although the coastal views are long gone, this is my favorite part of the route. This is the main reason, in my mind, for doing the ride.

At 9.5 miles you have one final climb. Thankfully it is short. Just under 10 miles, you can see Bixby Bridge and the ocean—a great photo op.

At 10.1 miles, start your descent to Highway 1. A left turn onto the highway and an 8-mile spin back to your car completes the loop. Or, if you've arranged a shuttle pick-up, your ride ends here.

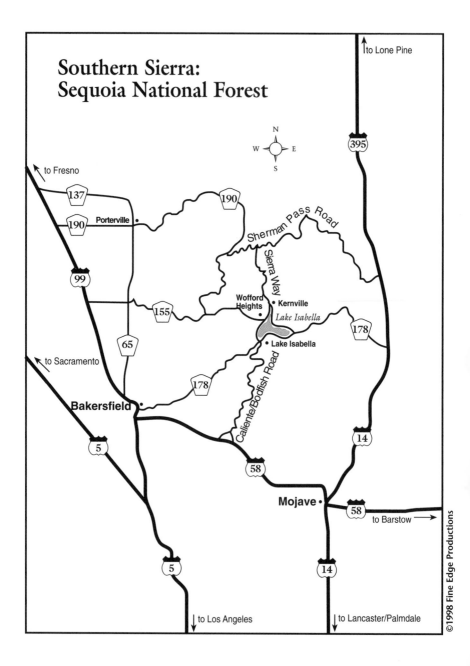

Southern Sierra:
Sequoia National Forest

©1998 Fine Edge Productions

CHAPTER 10

Southern Sierra: Sequoia National Forest

By Delaine Fragnoli

Rising from the San Joaquin Valley to 12,000 feet near the Sierra Nevada Summit, the Sequoia National Forest contains some of the Golden State's most dramatic landscape. Bordered by the wild and scenic Kings River to the north and the Kern River and Piute Mountain Range to the south, the forest boasts over one million acres. Over 850,000 of those acres are non-wilderness areas, featuring some 1,500 miles of maintained roads, 1,000 miles of abandoned roads and 850 miles of trails. In short, it has enough riding area to keep you busy for years, and the scenery to inspire you to do so.

The riding here can be tough, thanks to the steep slopes rising precipitously from the banks of the Kern River. High elevations add to the challenge. Many of the most popular mountain bike trails are, or were, motorcycle trails. Motorcycles have pounded many of the trails to dust and dug deep ruts in others— rideable but challenging conditions. Because of the steep elevation changes, many of the best rides are largely downhill and require car shuttles. But the paybacks are great scenery and miles of uncrowded singletrack. (One Fourth of July weekend, while riding most of the trails in this chapter, I encountered just one other trail user!)

The best times to ride are in the spring—when trails are not as dusty and alpine meadows are filled with wildflowers—and in the fall. Summer riding is fine at higher elevations, but it can get very hot down below. Fall brings great color and cooler weather, although early snow can reduce your riding options.

The Sequoia National Forest is an easy hour's drive from the central California town of Bakersfield, and many Southern Californians flock to the area's waterways to raft or fish the Kern River, or to fish, jet ski or boat at manmade Lake

Isabella. The towns of Lake Isabella and Kernville are the recreation centers for exploring the area. You can find all services in both towns.

Kernville is the site of an annual (usually Halloween weekend) mountain bike festival, organized by outdoor outfitter Mountain and River Adventures (MRA). I discovered three of the rides featured in this chapter (Cannell Trail, Shirley Meadows to Wofford Heights and Kern Canyon Trail) through the festival. If you don't have the necessary time or vehicles to do these on your own, the festival is by far the easiest way to handle the logistics of these rides, particularly the epic drive to the start of the Cannell Trail. Your entry fee covers ride shuttles (worth the cost by itself), raffle, pancake breakfast, pizza dinner, Halloween party, T-shirt and fun events. MRA also organizes mountain bike tours and shuttles throughout the summer. Even if you don't sign up for a tour, they're a good source for information, and they offer bike supplies and services.

Another popular local event is the Keyesville Classic Stage Race, held every spring. A NORBA classic race, the event uses BLM land near Lake Isabella's main dam. Participants race in uphill, downhill, and cross-country events to determine an overall winner. Most of the courses are singletrack and a lot of fun. Keyesville is an old mining site, and the area is laced with trails and roads, which make for great exploring any time of the year.

77 Big Meadow Loop

Distance: 10 miles
Difficulty: Moderate, not technical
Elevation: 7,800'; 200' gain/loss
Ride Type: Loop on dirt roads
Season: Spring, summer, fall
Maps: Sirretta Peak, Cannell Peak

Overview: This is the easiest ride in this chapter and one of the few that doesn't require a shuttle, although it's a long drive (one and a half hours from Kernville) to the starting point. I recommend camping in the area at Horse Meadow Campground. You could ride from the campground to the start of the ride; that would add a couple of pretty easy miles.

The ride loops around a high-alpine meadow through pine forest on gently rolling fire-roads. Other than one 0.3-mile climb, the route is easy—a good choice for beginners or families.

Getting There: From Kernville, take Sierra Way (SM99) north 17.6 miles to Sherman Pass Road (22S05). Proceed up this steep, winding road for 5.6 miles and make a right onto clearly signed Cherry Hill Road (22S12). Follow the signs to Big Meadow, forking left 4.2 miles later. A mile later the road turns to dirt. Continue to follow signs to Big Meadow, bypassing other roads and spurs. Pass Poison Meadow on your left and, a bit later, bypass the turnoff to Horse Meadow on the right. Continue to stay on 22S12 and follow the signs to Big Meadow. Finally, just

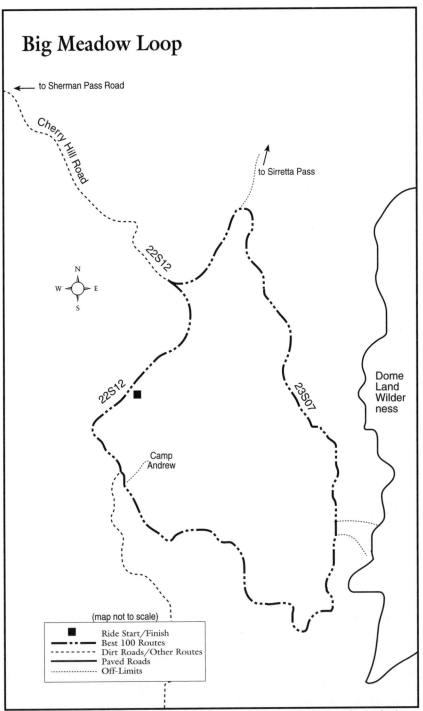

Big Meadow Loop

to Sherman Pass Road

Cherry Hill Road

to Sirretta Pass

22S12

N
W   E
S

22S12

23S07

Dome
Land
Wilder
ness

Camp
Andrew

(map not to scale)

■   Ride Start/Finish
━··━··━ Best 100 Routes
━ ━ ━ Dirt Roads/Other Routes
━━━━ Paved Roads
············ Off-Limits

©1998 Fine Edge Productions

over 11 miles after turning onto Cherry Hill Road, you come to Big Meadow on your left. Continue 0.4 mile farther and park at the Big Meadow West/ Horse Camp on the left.

Route: Go back out to Road 22S12 and turn left. At first the grade is flat, then gradually uphill. At the Y at 0.8 mile, go left. You are now on 23S07. Pass Camp Andrew (private) on your left. The road here is generally flat with some gentle ups and downs on a slightly sandy surface.

At 2.0 miles you pass through a clearcut area—the only scenic blight on an otherwise lovely route. Soon you pass into a nice pine forest and lose your views of Big Meadow.

At 2.8 miles at the top of a small rise, 23S07A comes in on the right. You continue straight. You climb a little at 3.2 miles, then roll, then descend. Half a mile later, Trail 34E15 crosses the road you're on. It leads to Dome Land Wilderness and is off limits to bikes. Next you pass some stock pens on the right and then the Manter Meadow trailhead. There's an information sign, map, and parking area here. The Manter Meadow Trail also leads to the Wilderness and is

thus closed to bikes.

At 5.4 miles you pass Trail 34E14, yet another singletrack into Manter Meadow which is closed to bikes. Beyond, you pass a dirt road on the right, continuing straight on 23S07 and passing stock pens on your left. Along here you have glimpses of Big Meadow. At 5.6 miles you ride over a cattleguard and through a gate.

Half a mile later you come to a major intersection. The Main Summit Trail 33E32—the upper part of the Cannell Trail (see next ride)—goes hard right; you continue straight on 23S07. You immediately pass a sign regarding public pastures. Now you begin the ride's "big" climb. It gets steep and a little rocky, but it's short, topping out at 6.5 miles.

Next you begin an equally steep, if not steeper, descent. Don't get carried away. A mere 0.3 mile later you make a hard left back onto 22S12. (You should recognize this intersection; you drove by it on your way in.) As you make your way along 22S12 back to your car, note the interesting granite ridge on the right through the trees. At 7.5 miles you're back to your car.

78 Cannell Trail

Distance: 18.5 miles
Difficulty: Strenuous, technical
Elevation: Start 7,800'; high point 8,200'; end 2,800'
Ride Type: One-way on singletrack and dirt roads; requires car shuttle
Season: Spring, summer, fall
Maps: Sirretta Peak, Cannell Peak, Kernville

Overview: For the experienced rider, the Cannell Trail is the premier singletrack in the Lake Isabella area. Originally a motorcycle route, it is

now closed to motorized vehicles, although some motorcyclists seem to be ignoring that fact.

The route begins with a brief fire-

Big Meadow

road climb along the ramparts of Cannell Peak before climbing steeply on singletrack. After the first 3.5 miles, the route rolls alongside Cannell Meadow to Pine Flats, where the Cannell "Plunge"—a final 9-mile stretch of steep, technical descending—begins.

The actual trail begins even higher up the mountain near Sherman Pass. Starting there would mean a 25-mile ride with much more climbing at even higher elevations (over 9,000 feet). Forest Service personnel recommend this ride as a two-day venture. If you're interested, check with Mountain and River Adventures in Kernville. They offer one- and two-day Cannell Trail trips.

Getting There: Follow the directions for the previous ride and park at the Big Meadow West/Horse Camp. Or, if you're camping at Horse Meadow you can start from there.

For the shuttle you need to leave one car in Kernville. Or, you can park at the lower trailhead, 1.1 mile out-side of Kernville on Sierra Way where there are corrals and a turn-out.

Route: Backtrack to Cherry Hill Road (22S12) and go left. The graded dirt road is flattish until about 0.8 mile. At the Y-intersection here, go right (signs indicate Cannell Meadow and Cannell Trail) and begin climbing steadily to 2.0 miles. You top out at a small saddle. On your left is a trail sign nailed to a pine tree. This is the Cannell Trail. Although you could catch it here, it is quite sandy. I recommend staying on the fire-road which descends for another half-mile. At 2.6 miles Cannell Trail crosses the dirt road. Take it on your right and begin a steep singletrack climb.

This climb is just steep enough and has just enough rocks and just enough elevation (8,200 feet) to make not dabbing a challenge. At 3.3 miles the grade levels, rolls briefly, and drops into a rocky, rough downhill. Watch for stone waterbars! There are a couple of rock gardens just before the trail hits a dirt road, 4.5 miles.

The trail resumes on the other side of the road. For now, however, go right on the road and bypass the trail. Pass a 4WD road on the left (sign indicates Horse Camp) and continue on the dirt road. At 4.7 miles, fork left to follow the sign to Cannell Meadow (7,500 feet). Descend to a Forest Service cabin at the edge of the meadow. The cabin, with benches and an impromptu fire pit, makes a good rest stop and photo op.

When you're ready, backtrack up the fire-road to where the Cannell Trail crosses. Take the trail, now on your right. A sign says *Cannell Trail 33E32, Big Meadow 5 miles, Pine Flat 3 miles.* As you head toward Pine Flat, the trail roughly parallels the eastern edge of the meadow on your right and dirt road 24S12 to the east (on your left). The terrain is rolling. Occasionally the trail may be hard to follow—there are cattle trails running through the area—but frequent trail signs help keep you on track. Stay on the main route, heading south.

At 7.1 miles, go right through the trees. At 7.2 miles, don't go onto the road (there's a culvert and water trough here); stay on the trail, where you soon bounce through several rocky sections alongside Cannell Creek. At 8.6 miles the trail hits a dirt road. Go left and cross the stream between a culvert on the left and a big pine tree on the right. A trail sign on the pine tree directs you immediately back onto the trail.

At 8.7 miles at another big culvert, go left and then immediately right onto the doubletrack road. Not even a tenth of a mile down the road, a big pine tree on your right has a blaze and a trail sign pointing you back onto the trail.

Begin a loose climb and pass a sign indicating Pine Flats, 7,200 feet—the beginning of The Plunge. Soon you pass another trail sign on the left where the trail curves right. At 9.2 miles you pass through a cattle gate and begin a fun, loose downhill. Beyond Pine Flat you leave the creek and meadow and enter a drier, sandier, more open world of oak scrub, manzanita and yucca.

At 9.6 miles you have a view of Lake Isabella to your left. Those

Cannell Trail

Jim MacIntyre

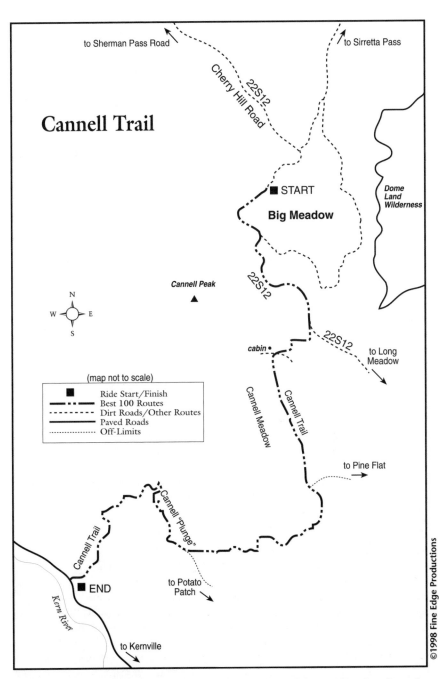

Cannell Trail

to Sherman Pass Road

to Sirretta Pass

Cherry Hill Road

22S12

■ START

Big Meadow

Dome
Land
Wilderness

Cannell Peak ▲

22S12

cabin •

22S12

to Long
Meadow

Cannell Meadow

Cannell Trail

to Pine Flat

N
W ─○─ E
S

(map not to scale)

■   Ride Start/Finish
▬▬▬   Best 100 Routes
▪ ▪ ▪ ▪   Dirt Roads/Other Routes
▬▬▬   Paved Roads
· · · · · · ·   Off-Limits

Cannell "Plunge"

Cannell Trail

■ END

to Potato
Patch

Kern River

to Kernville

©1998 Fine Edge Productions

familiar with Lake Tahoe's Flume Trail will immediately feel that they are riding a drier Southern California equivalent: a scenic, occasionally technical trail with a lake view that can easily draw your eyes off the narrow ribbon of singletrack.

You pass through some interesting rocks, cross a ridge and then cross back to the south-facing slope, where you have a second panoramic view of the lake at 10.7 miles. After this photo op, you head into pro-gressively gnarlier rock gardens and drop-offs.

At 11.5 miles you pass the Potato Patch Trail (signed) on your left and hit a steep uphill. Most riders will probably have to push their bikes up at least part of this. As you be-gin the climb, a sign on a pine tree on your left tells you that Kernville is 4 miles away. (You actu-ally have another 7 miles to go.)

After the climb, surf through several loose

View of Lake Isabella from Cannell Trail.

Jim MacIntyre

downhills to a small saddle and a Y-intersection at 12.5 miles. Go right. (To be honest, the left fork doesn't even look inviting.) You contour along the east and then the north sides of a mountain on a narrow trail. At 13.0 miles you reach a couple of switchbacks.

Things get progressively more technical and, at 13.6 miles, you start a series of a dozen or more gnarly switchbacks. Motorcycles have chewed up the inside and outside lines on many of these, yet the expert rider can still clean the whole lot. But remember: discretion is the better part of valor!

After a mile of full-fisted braking, you pass through a cattle gate at 14.6 miles. This part of the trail is relative-

ly mellow. It ends at a T-intersection with a road at 15.3 miles. Go left and climb 0.2 mile to a metal gate. Pass through it and pick up the trail imme-diately on the right.

At 15.6 miles the trail rejoins the dirt road. Go right downhill. Stay on the road until 16.1 miles, where the trail veers to the right (trail sign). About 0.2 mile later go through a gate. Watch your speed as two switch-backs come up quickly. At the first one, a right-hander, motorcyclists have cut two alternative routes. Stay on the trail.

You traverse an open slope and soon you can see a corral and gate below you. Veer right and drop to the gate and trailhead. A left on the high-way (Sierra Way) takes you 1.1 miles to Kernville.

79 Shirley Meadows to Wofford Heights

Distance: 16.1 miles
Difficulty: Moderate, somewhat technical
Elevation: Begin 6,600'; end 2,650'
Ride Type: One-way on singletrack and dirt roads; requires car shuttle
Season: Spring, summer, fall
Maps: Alta Sierra, Lake Isabella North

Overview: For pure fun and cool scenery, this ride is hard to beat. It has a little bit of everything. Whoop-de-do-filled singletrack, more technical singletrack, a "Miniature Forest," views of Lake Isabella, a little bit of fire-road climbing, some rough fire-road descending, and some hellaciously fast, wide-open fire-road descending. At one point, you even ride through a tunnel of huge manzanita trees. Intermediate and better riders will have a blast. While advanced beginners might find some of the singletrack challenging, they are sure to enjoy many other parts of the ride. Unlike some of the other shuttles described in this chapter, this one is not an expedition in itself to set up. If you don't mind over 9 miles of steep pavement climbing, you can turn this into a loop by riding to Shirley Meadows.

Getting There: From the town of Wofford Heights (on Highway 155 between Kernville and the town Lake Isabella on the west shore of Lake

Cabin at Cannell Meadow, Cannell Trail (Ride 78).

Jim MacIntyre

Isabella) take Highway 155 west toward Alta Sierra. Seven miles up the steep, winding road at Greenhorn Summit, go left on Rancheria Road toward Shirley Meadows. Pass the Greenhorn Summit Station and proceed another 2.2 miles to the Shirley Meadows ski area. Park in the wide pullout on your right.

Leave your second pick-up vehicle anywhere in the town of Wofford Heights. The ride finishes just south of town, coming down Old State Road past Live Oak Campground. You could park across Highway 155 at the Tillie Creek picnic area.

Cannell Trail (Ride 78)

Jim MacIntyre

Route: Continue on Rancheria Road (Forest Service Road 25S15) which turns to dirt just past the parking area. This road is flat and gradually downhill. You soon come to a Y-intersection; continue to the right. Pass through a gate. A sign here (hidden by brush) indicates that the road you're on is 25S15.

At 0.4 mile an unsigned trail rises steeply to your right. Take it. It is a little uphill at first but soon stops climbing. At 0.7 mile, veer left to stay on the trail. Begin a fun downhill filled with whoop-de-dos. Bet you can't resist yelling "Wheee!"

At 1.1 mile the trail crosses a dirt road and resumes on the other side. At 1.4 mile it Ts into a road. Go right very briefly and the trail picks up again on your left. A short uphill squirt takes you into the "Little Forest." I don't know what the story is behind this area, but you are riding a tight, twisty singletrack through a group of closely clustered, midget pine trees—real bar-end grabbers!

At 2.2 miles the trail ends at a third road. Go right on the road (signed 26S09A). Don't get up too much speed on the downhill here because at 2.3 miles you make a hard left onto road 26S09 (signed). Begin a rutted descent. At 2.9 miles a trail veers off the road to the right; there's a big downed tree here with red ribbon in it.

This section of trail goes from "yikes" to "wow" as you first maneuver around, in and through a very deep Death Rut and then pass into a tunnel of manzanita bushes, their limbs arching overhead. I defy you not to take a picture. One autumn I rode through here with some friends

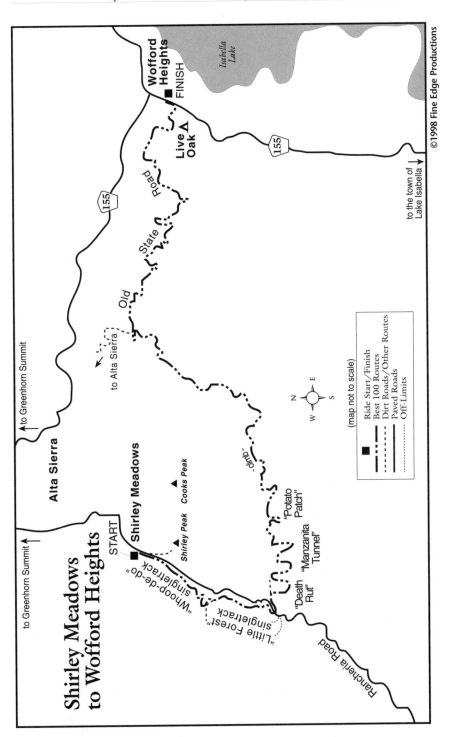

Shirley Meadows
to Wofford Heights

©1998 Fine Edge Productions

(map not to scale)

■ Ride Start/Finish
Best 100 Routes
Dirt Roads/Other Routes
Paved Roads
Off-Limits

and it had just snowed. The snow dusting the red manzanita limbs created an incredible scene.

You cross a stream and make a steep climb at 3.7 miles. You pass more manzanita. These specimens have to be called trees—they're the largest I've ever seen. In the next half-mile you begin to ride beside oak trees. At 4.2 miles, there's a particularly impressive oak near an interesting rock.

At 4.3 miles you cross a stream, gnarlier than the first, and proceed into a meadow (actually Potato Patch) at 4.7 miles. Soon you begin a tough single-track climb. It's a challenge not to dab. You top out at 5.2 miles in an open area. There's a Y-intersection here.

Shirley Meadows to Wofford Heights.

Jim MacIntyre

Go left and begin a fire-road climb. It's very gradual at first and grows steeper toward the end. At 6.6 miles you cross a cattleguard and gate. At 7.2 miles you can see Lake Isabella to your right. At 7.4 miles you top out.

The road bends to the left and heads downhill. Got suspension? This is a rough descent—rocky and full of ruts, and it's easy to get going too fast. Don't! These ruts have "separated shoulder" written all over them. After 2.5 miles of this abuse—hope you have V-brakes as well—you reach a Y. Go right.

You are now on *graded* Old State Road. This is blissfully smooth in comparison to what you've just come down. You can get going very fast as the road sweeps around switchback after switchback, each revealing a new vista of Lake Isabella. Once again, watch your speed—the road is open to vehicle traffic.

At 14.7 miles, the road turns to pavement. Continue downhill to the left on the main road. Soon you begin to pass houses and the likelihood of running into motor vehicles increases. At 16.1 miles Old State Road ends at Highway 155. Go left to return to Wofford Heights.

80 Kern Canyon Trail/ Kern River Trail

Distance: 17.5 miles
Difficulty: Strenuous, somewhat technical
Elevation: Between 2,000' and 3,400'; lots of up and down
Ride Type: One-way on singletrack and dirt roads; car shuttle required
Season: Spring, summer, fall
Map: Miracle Hot Springs (Note that the trails are not shown on any maps, including the USFS and USGS maps.)

Overview: Almost all singletrack, this ride contours along oak-studded hillsides, in and out of several drainages, and up and down several ridges, paralleling the Kern River and Highway 178 for much of the route. Although it requires a shuttle, this ride—unlike most of the others in this chapter—is not a downhill ride. It is definitely more of a cross-country workout. Although there are no sustained climbs, there is a lot of short climbing involved. Because much of the route is exposed and is at lower elevations, it is best done in spring and fall. Summer can be very hot.

Getting There: The logistics for this ride are a bit vexing. Here we have a great 20-mile route, yet it is virtually impossible to access the western trailhead. The two trails run along the north side of the Kern River on the north side of Highway 178 for most of the route. The highway crosses the river at several points. Once the highway crosses to the south side of the river just south of Delonegha Hot Springs, you cannot access the trails from the highway without crossing the river—a difficult and dangerous, if not impossible, task at most times of the year.

This means that the best way to do the ride is to start at the eastern end and ride west. *Caution:* You must, however, bail out before the

highway crosses to the south side of the river or you won't be able to get across. Or you will have to backtrack. Now, to make things more difficult, Highway 178 is technically a freeway from Lake Isabella to Delonegha Hot Springs. That means you cannot park along it, nor can you ride your bike on it. So, how do you fashion a ride, taking into consideration all these constraints?

You could do the ride as an out-and-back venture. That would be pretty brutal and beyond the physical abilities of most riders. The following is the best shuttle alternative I could conceive.

Leave one vehicle just south of the bridge where "Freeway" 178 turns into "Highway" 178. From Lake Isabella take Highway 178 for 11.5 miles. At this point the "freeway" bridges across the river and turns into a highway. Park in the broad turnout on the left immediately after the bridge.

To get to the start with the second vehicle, from Lake Isabella take Highway 155 toward Kernville. Look for the turnoff to Keyesville, 1.5 miles later; it is on the left across from the Main Dam Campground. Take Keyesville Road 1.9 miles until it turns to dirt. Bear right here. You pass the Old Keyesville site on the right (there's a stone marker). Continue uphill. Stay on the main road

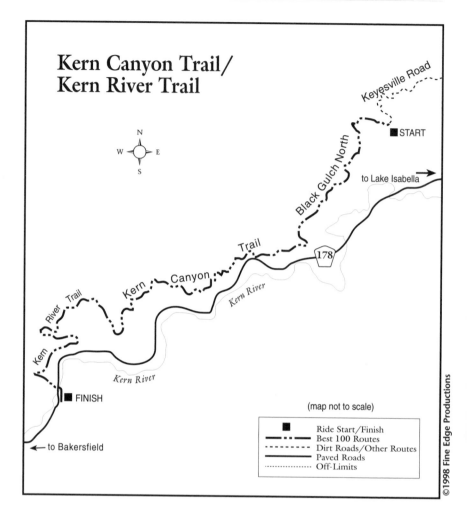

Kern Canyon Trail/
Kern River Trail

START

to Lake Isabella

178

to Bakersfield

FINISH

(map not to scale)

■ Ride Start/Finish
▬▬▬ Best 100 Routes
– – – Dirt Roads/Other Routes
▬▬▬ Paved Roads
⋯⋯⋯ Off-Limits

©1998 Fine Edge Productions

and keep climbing for 1.5 miles to a small saddle. Park off the road here. Parking is limited. If you can't park here, you can park in other turnouts in the Keyesville area. Depending on where you park, this could add 2-3 miles of climbing to the route.

Route: Descend the dirt road, opposite the direction you drove in from. At 0.9 miles turn left. A sign here says *Black Gulch North*. Another sign indicates this is the way to the Kern Canyon Trail. A third sign reads *4WD*

Vehicles Recommended, Next Turnaround 1.9 miles.

Proceed downhill and continue to roll and descend, always staying on the main route. Trail signs continue to direct you to Kern Canyon Trail (31E75). At 2.0 miles go right (signed). At 2.2 miles the trail veers left (signed). At 2.3 miles after a steep, loose downhill pitch, the trail veers right across a small stream. At 2.4 miles it crosses a second creek, signed on the other side as *Black Gulch Creek*.

On the other side of the creek, go left and join a dirt road briefly. Continue straight. At 2.7 miles the trail veers right (signed). The trail crosses several dirt roads in quick succession. It always resumes on the other side and is always signed. At 3.1 miles you stay on the road for awhile.

At 3.3 miles a very steep road and trail rise up before you. Yes, you go up this. Downshift! Continue straight up the road, which soon bends to the left and turns to trail. This is very steep—portage time for most of us. To add to the misery, if it's warm out you might hear the seemingly mocking sounds of people laughing and splashing in the Kern River below you.

This climb is less than 0.5 mile, but it feels longer. You top out at 3.7 miles. The trail rolls after this, and you can see the river and highway below you. You pass onto an exposed slope with scattered oak trees and rocks. Soon you begin to see evidence of fire—a wildfire burned through here in the summer of 1996.

At 5.5 miles you reach an intersection with the Freeway Ridge 4WD trail (signed). The Kern Canyon Trail resumes on the other side (signed). You could drop to the highway here, but there is no legal parking at this point for your pick-up vehicle.

Continue on the trail. You begin a fun downhill with 2 or 3 loose switchbacks, the last one of which deposits you at a stream crossing. At 6.0 miles you pass through a cattle gate. You

Kern Canyon Trail/Kern River Trail

are very close to the highway at this point. There are stock pens here. You could bail out here, too, but once again there is no legal parking for a pickup vehicle.

The trail beyond begins climbing again and, as you make your way through several switchbacks, the evidence of fire is greater. At 6.9 miles you top out briefly. A short descent follows, and then more climbing with more switchbacks. The trail gets harder to follow because of loose soil from the burn. Follow the little red trail flags stuck in the ground. You may have to push your bike some as the ground is very loose and soft.

At 7.6 miles you come to a confusing intersection. The trail goes left

Kern Canyon Trail/Kern River Trail

Jim MacIntyre

through some cool rocks.

At 10.5 miles you reach a small, flat saddle. Three trails radiate from here. Avoid the two left ones; curve right to stay on the main trail. Fork left soon thereafter. There are several more criss-crossing trails, most of which are blocked by tree branches. Stay on the main, most traveled route. Although you can see several trails that drop toward the highway, you stay higher, contouring along the hillside and heading inland. Soon you find yourself on a fun, rolling descent.

At 11.8 miles you pass through a cattle gate and fence. Immediately you encounter a rock garden. At 11.9 miles you reach a major trail junction in a shady oak and sycamore grove with a stream—a pleasant rest stop. Several signs indicate that this is Delonegha Creek and that the doubletrack here is the Delonegha 4WD Trail.

To continue on the Kern Canyon Trail, cross the creek and turn left onto 31E75 (signed). Don't climb the doubletrack. Follow the rolling trail and climb just a bit more before beginning a BIG, Yee-Hah downhill. This descending fun lasts until 15.5 miles, where there's a major trail intersection. Go right onto the Kern River Trail (32E49). Left would take you to the highway where, need I say it again, there is no legal parking for a pickup vehicle.

After a final climb and descent, you reach a trail junction at 17.1

across a very rough doubletrack, then between a burned oak on the left and a big rock on the right. The following 2 miles are an up-and-down affair. At 9.3 miles at the Y, go left on the lower route. The upper route has largely been washed out. At 9.4 miles, cross a stream, signed *Greenhorn Creek, Kern Canyon Trail 31E75*.

Half a mile later you reach a brief hike-a-bike section. At 10.3 miles, go right and up the doubletrack. Although the first 10 miles has had a lot of ups and downs, you will probably feel like you've done enough climbing for the day at this point. Persevere, for at the top the trail forks left and begins a fun downhill

miles. To end the ride, go left and follow the trail to the highway, where a right turn takes you to your waiting vehicle, about 0.3 mile away.

The Kern River Trail does continue to the right from this junction. It is 4 miles to Democrat Springs and the end of the trail. I once did these 4 miles. In a word, they stunk. The trail is much rougher, barely more than a cattle trail in spots, and there is lots more climbing. And, of course, once you get to Democrat Springs there's no way to get across the river. As a form of self-flagellation, you could do these final miles for an 8-mile out-and-back addition. But I'm heading back to my truck.

81 Breckenridge Lookout

Distance: 6.6 miles
Difficulty: Moderately strenuous, not technical
Elevation: 948' gain/loss; 7,548'/high point
Ride Type: Out-and-back on dirt road
Season: Spring, summer, fall
Map: Breckenridge Mtn.

Overview: A moderate climb, this ride takes you to Breckenridge Lookout, where 360-degree views are your reward.

Getting There: Start at Breckenridge Campground. From the town of Lake Isabella, take Lake Isabella Road south through Bodfish to Havilah. About 12.5 miles from Lake Isabella, paved Breckenridge Road (28S06) heads west. Go right onto Breckenridge Road (clearly signed). Climb this steep, winding road. At 6.2 miles you pass the turnoff to Remington Ridge Trail. Stay on the main road past the Penny Pine Plantation and to the Breckenridge Lookout junction. Here dirt road 28S07 goes left (sign says *Campground 0.5 mile; Lookout 5 miles*). Take this dirt road. About 0.1 mile later you pass through a gate. Half a mile past that, the campground is on your left.

The campground makes a good base for doing this ride and the following two rides. The campsites are free, but a permit is required. The sites have picnic tables and toilets but no water. Bring all the water you need with you.

Route: From the campground, backtrack to 28S07 and go left. At first the road is rolly, easy and not too technical. After a mile 28S10 goes to the left; you continue straight on 28S07. Begin a steady climb through a forest of big pines. Overall the grade is not too steep, but there are some steeper, dusty pitches.

At 2.7 miles you come to a Y-junction. A sign here says *KABC and Breckenridge Lookout to the left; KERO TV, right on 28S62; Deer Springs Camp, 3 miles to the right.* You head left toward the lookout. Just 0.1 mile later a left leads to TV towers and a right goes to Breckenridge Lookout (signed). Continue toward the lookout.

At 3.2 miles you pass 28S07C on

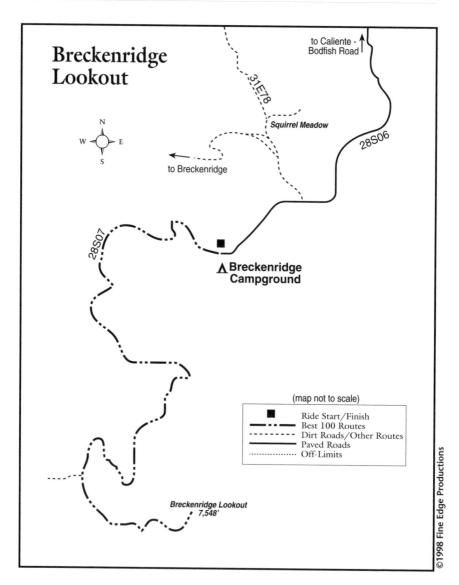

Breckenridge Lookout

to Caliente -
Bodfish Road

31E78

Squirrel Meadow

28S06

to Breckenridge

28S07

■ Breckenridge
▲ Campground

(map not to scale)

■ Ride Start/Finish
Best 100 Routes
Dirt Roads/Other Routes
Paved Roads
Off-Limits

Breckenridge Lookout
7,548'

©1998 Fine Edge Productions

the left (it goes 0.1 mile to a locked gate). You continue straight through a gate, up a final steep 0.1-mile pitch to Breckenridge Lookout, 3.3 miles total.

The lookout is manned 11 a.m. to 6 p.m. during fire season. You can climb a flight of very steep stairs to the tower. From the top you have 360-degree views. To the north is Lake Isabella. Northeast is a ridgeline of mountains, including Bald Eagle Peak, Bodfish Peak, Liebel Peak, Brown Peak and Piute Peak. To the southeast is Walker Basin.

When you're done admiring the view and your own fortitude, return the way you came. Be careful on the descent as the road is open to vehicles.

82 Mill Creek Trail

Distance: 7.5 miles
Difficulty: Moderate, technical
Elevation: Begin/6,680'; end/2,400'
Ride Type: One-way descent on singletrack; requires long car shuttle; shuttle could be shortened by adding 12 miles of pavement riding
Season: Spring, summer, fall
Maps: Breckenridge Mtn., Miracle Hot Springs

Overview: Virtually all downhill, this trail drops from thick pine forest through oak woodlands to open chaparral. Although the name suggests lots of stream crossings and wet boulder riding, the trail stays above the creek for most of its course until the end—when getting wet sounds like a good idea.

The drawback to this fun-fest is the long car shuttle involved. It's best done as part of a weekend of riding and camping near Breckenridge.

Getting There: Follow the directions for the previous ride to the turnoff to Breckenridge Campground. Instead of turning onto dirt 28S07 toward the campground, continue on paved 28S06. You pass Squirrel Meadow (6,600 feet) on your right and a sign indicating you are on 28S06. About 0.2 mile past the campground junction a sign indicates Mill Creek Trail, 31E78, 0.25 mile to the right. Turn right here and go another 0.2 mile. Turn left (signed) for 0.1 mile to the trailhead. If you're

staying at the campground you can ride to the trailhead which would add 1.1 miles to the ride.

To arrange the shuttle, you need to leave a second vehicle at the bottom of the trail, along Old Canyon Highway. From the town of Lake

Kern Canyon Trail/Kern River Trail (Ride 80)

Jim MacIntyre

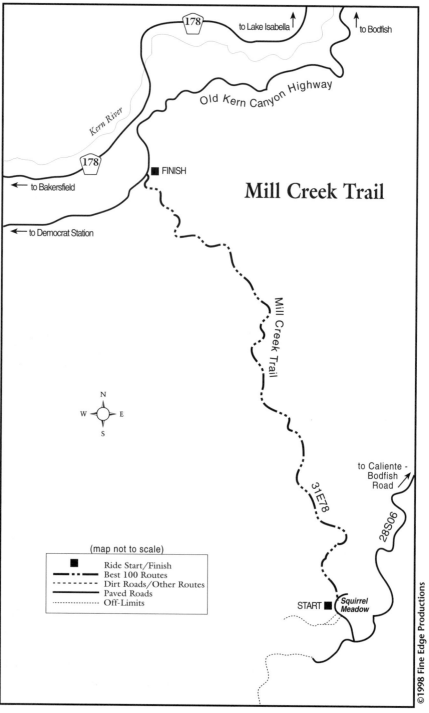

178

to Lake Isabella

to Bodfish

Old Kern Canyon Highway

Kern River

178

to Bakersfield

■ FINISH

Mill Creek Trail

to Democrat Station

N
W   E
S

Mill Creek Trail

to Caliente - Bodfish Road

31E78

28S06

(map not to scale)

■   Ride Start/Finish
■-■-■ Best 100 Routes
- - - - Dirt Roads/Other Routes
———   Paved Roads
·········   Off-Limits

START ■ *Squirrel Meadow*

©1998 Fine Edge Productions

Isabella, take Highway 178 toward Bakersfield for 13.2 miles. Take the turnoff for the old highway (signed *Kern Canyon Road*), a left turn. Immediately pass Democrat Station on your right. Cross a creek at 14.6 miles and continue another 0.5 mile to the trailhead (clearly signed). Leave your car in a turnout along here.

To shorten the shuttle, you could arrange to be picked up in Bodfish. This would entail riding 12 miles on the paved Old Canyon Highway from the end of Mill Creek Trail to Bodfish. The old highway is a pleasant ride with some climbing and some descending, but it has little traffic.

Mill Creek Trail, view to the north.

Route: A sign at the trailhead says *Mill Creek Trail 31E78, Old Kern Canyon Road, 7 miles.* My odometer clocked 7.5 miles by ride's end.

Head down the trail alongside a dry creekbed. When I rode the trail, it was a little overgrown through here, but the main challenge was staying out of the motorcycle-induced ruts. After a short rise out of the streambed, you have a brief view through the trees. But mostly you are surrounded by good-sized pines. (At 0.3 mile you pass a nice specimen.)

At 0.4 mile, you pass through the first of several downed trees. Immediately after, you hit two loose switchbacks. A little later, you make two stream crossings, one right after the other. You ride through a second downed tree and pass a trail sign on your left at 0.6 mile.

After a couple of rock drop-offs you pass through a third downed tree. At 1.0 mile you swerve through two broad switchbacks and start following a ravine. More oaks begin popping up amid the pines. At 1.2 miles you cross an open slope with a view. The trail is narrower here. Watch for loose patches.

You come out onto a ridge with great views to the north around the 2-mile mark (photo op). In the next half-mile, the trail becomes more technical with loose ruts, rocks, and a sandpit of a switchback at 2.5 miles.

You're losing elevation quickly and you begin to see yucca. At 3.5 miles you hit a huge motorcycle rut. (When I rode it, the motorcycle damage had made the trail unrideable in parts. Hopefully some trail work will have been done by the time you ride it.)

At 4.0 miles the trail goes right at a big pine tree. A faint track goes straight. Don't miss this turn. At 4.4 miles you cross, and then parallel, a dry creek bed shaded by oaks. You head into the last few steep downhill pitches, and then the trail levels off among big, arching oaks.

At 5.0 miles you start to parallel a fenceline and pass a trail sign. There are more cactus here and the trail is sandy. Soon you head into a series of fun and rideable switchbacks. At 5.7 miles you cross a stream—the first one with running water. Surrounded by boulders and sycamores, it's a pretty, cool spot. This is followed by another stream crossing full of sand and rocks.

You hit a Y-intersection at 5.9 miles. Go left on the main trail. About 0.2 mile later you make a short, steep, rocky climb. At the crest of the hill, go straight and downhill. You have two more wet stream crossings at 6.3 and 6.5 miles. The trail begins to climb away from the creek, but at 6.7 miles you have a final dry, yet technical, stream crossing. You will probably have to carry your bike up the other side.

Beyond this, the trail begins to climb and then to roll, paralleling the old highway which you can see below you. There are several spurs in the final miles, but the main route is obvious. At 7.2 miles, cross a cattleguard and gate. At 7.4 miles several spurs drop down to the old highway, where your car is waiting for you.

If you decide to ride the old highway back to Bodfish, go right (northeast).

83 Remington "Hobo" Ridge Trail

Distance: 7 miles
Difficulty: Strenuous, technical
Elevation: Begin 5,560'; 6,200'/high point; end 2,480'
Ride Type: One-way on singletrack; requires car shuttle
Season: Spring, summer, fall
Map: Miracle Hot Springs

Overview: Like the previous ride, this trail—mostly downhill on single-track—requires a car shuttle. The shuttle can be shortened by riding 5.4 miles along the Old Canyon Highway back to Bodfish. The trail begins with a strenuous climb, followed by a steep, loose, ridgeline descent on what is mostly a motorcycle trail. Note that the trail (32E51) is signed as the Remington Ridge Trail,

but Forest Service maps label the ridge Hobo Ridge.

Getting There: To get to the ride start from the town of Lake Isabella, take Lake Isabella Road (turns into Caliente-Bodfish Road) south through Bodfish to Havilah. About 12.5 miles from Lake Isabella, paved Breckenridge Road (28S06) heads west. Go right onto Breckenridge

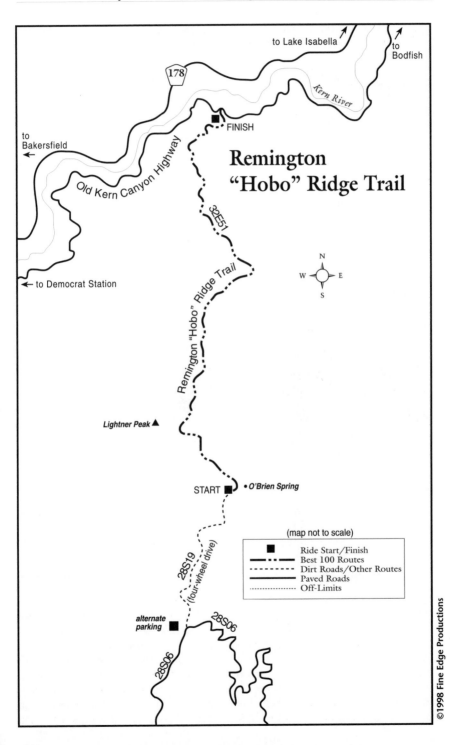

to Lake Isabella

to Bodfish

178

Kern River

to Bakersfield

FINISH

Remington "Hobo" Ridge Trail

Old Kern Canyon Highway

32E51

Remington "Hobo" Ridge Trail

to Democrat Station

N

W   E

S

Lightner Peak ▲

START   • O'Brien Spring

(map not to scale)

28S19

(four-wheel drive)

■   Ride Start/Finish
▬▪▬▪▬   Best 100 Routes
- - - - Dirt Roads/Other Routes
▬▬▬   Paved Roads
⋯⋯⋯ Off-Limits

alternate parking

28S06

28S06

©1998 Fine Edge Productions

View of Lake Isabella from Remington Ridge.

not up to it, go left at the Y to a turnaround and vista point. Park here. Most people will probably need to park here.

Leave the second vehicle at the Remington Ridge trailhead along the Old Kern Canyon Highway. From Bodfish drive 5.4 miles on the old highway. The trailhead is on the left.

Route: The following mileages are from the upper trailhead, not the vista point parking spot. If you parked at the vista point, you will have to climb and then descend the 1.2 miles to the trailhead. A few other faint doubletracks cross the area, but the main route is always clear. Reset your computer at the trailhead. A sign here says *Remington Ridge Trail 32E51, Old Kern Canyon Road.*

Road (clearly signed). Climb this steep, winding road for 6.2 miles to the clearly signed turnoff for Remington Ridge Trail (32E51). Go right on this dirt road. You immediately pass another sign indicating that O'Brien Spring is 2 miles away and that you are on 28S19. Continue straight for 0.6 mile to a Y-intersection. A sign directs you to the right for Remington Ridge Trail and also indicates 4WD only beyond this point. If you and your vehicle are up to it, proceed right for another 1.2 miles to the trailhead on the left side of the doubletrack. If your vehicle is

From the trailhead, the route begins on a sandy, overgrown patch of doubletrack. Another faint 4WD track cuts through the area, but the main route is obvious. You begin a very steep climb. At 0.2 mile you reach a steep, rocky climb on your right. A cairn marks this junction. Although the doubletrack route you're on looks much easier, you go right then push your bike up this pitch. At the top, pass through a barbed-wire gate. There's red flagging in a tree here and blazes in an oak tree. You are now on singletrack.

Viewpoint on Remington Ridge.

The singletrack follows a fence-line and parallels the 4WD track, almost re-connecting with it in one spot. You stay on the singletrack and follow the trail blazes carved in the trees. After this brief, flatter section, you begin a brutal climb, switchbacking up the east side of Lightner Peak. Motorcycle use has reduced the trail to dust; this and an off-camber slope to the trail make it hard to hold a line. These conditions continue on and off for the whole ride.

Fortunately, at 0.8 mile the worst is over. The trail rolls along for awhile and you get views of Bodfish on your right. While the overall grade is easier, some pitches will probably have you pushing as you make your way near the summit of a small bump of a mountain north of Lightner Peak. At 1.6 miles, as you come around from the east to the north side of this unnamed peak, you have a good vista. You can see Lake Isabella from here, and a little later you can see Highway 178 below and to your left.

From this ridge, the trail drops. Steeply! Hang on and surf through the loose stuff. You lose 600 feet quickly before beginning a short climb up to and over another unnamed bump on Hobo Ridge. From here you drop steeply again toward the northeast. Ignore the 4WD tracks that drop to the southeast.

Instead of continuing north off the ridge, the trail makes a left and drops even more steeply toward the Kern River and Highway 178. At first, the trail is high above a stream and a ravine. Eventually it drops to the stream (usually dry) and crosses a spring (usually wet).

The grade eases somewhat beyond here and gets as close to flat as it ever gets before crossing the creekbed again. A brief climb out of the streambed and over the nose of a ridge follows. Then you begin the final switchbacking plummet to the old highway where your car awaits you.

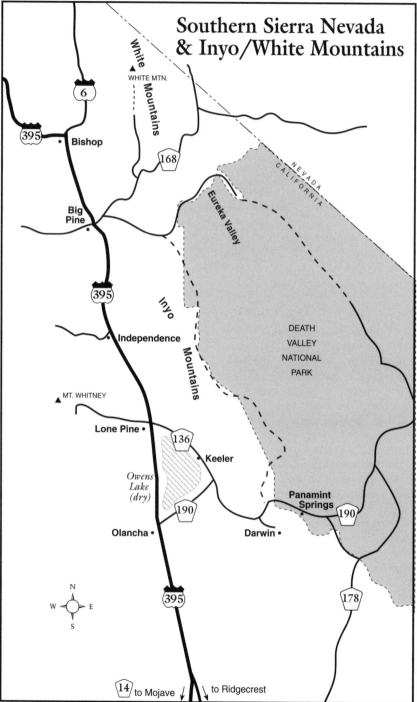

CHAPTER 11

Southern Sierra Nevada & Inyo/White Mountains

WHITE MTN. ▲

White Mountains

6

395

Bishop •

168

Big Pine •

Eureka Valley

N E V A D A
C A L I F O R N I A

395

Inyo

• Independence

Mountains

DEATH
VALLEY
NATIONAL
PARK

MT. WHITNEY ▲

Lone Pine •

136

• Keeler

Owens
Lake
(dry)

190

Panamint
Springs

190

Olancha •

Darwin •

178

N
W   E
S

395

14 / to Mojave ↓   ↓ to Ridgecrest

©1998 Fine Edge Productions

Southern Sierra Nevada & Inyo/White Mountains

By Réanne Douglass, Mark Davis and Don Douglass

The eastern slope of the Sierra Nevada is one of the most scenic and least populated areas in the entire United States. Here you will find a flat, high desert corridor that runs from the Mojave Desert on the south to the Nevada border on the north. The western wall of this corridor is formed by the magnificent peaks

View of Sierra from valley floor, Independence.

and slopes of the Sierra Nevada; the eastern wall by the rugged Inyo-White Mountains. Highway 395 runs up this corridor and offers you easy access to old mining roads, logging roads, and yes, even a singletrack here and there.

The Eastern Sierra encompasses natural wonders found nowhere else: bristlecone pines—the oldest living trees on earth, volcanic craters, hot springs, earthquake faults, and the southernmost glacier of the fifty states.

Imagine riding under sunny skies in the high desert while the rest of the country is overcast, frigid and raw. Imagine pedaling along secluded dirt roads at the foot of Mt. Whitney, the highest peak in the continental United States, or on a remote doubletrack in the White Mountains at 14,000 feet, with golden eagles soaring in an azure sky. Take an expedition ride up Mazourka Canyon into the mining past of the Inyos or simply enjoy fantastic alpine landscapes.

If solitude, natural beauty, pure air, and unique biking terrain appeal to you, try some, or all, of these rides for unforgettable cycling experiences.

84 Hogback Loop

Distance: 22.2 miles
Difficulty: Strenuous, minimally technical
Elevation: Lowest point: 3,700'; highest point: 6,450'
Ride Type: Loop ride on pavement and gravel roads
Season: Year-round
Maps: Lone Pine, Mt. Langley, Union Wash, Manzanar

Overview: The route takes you through the Alabama Hills, a fantastic, rocky landscape, where many movies have been filmed. There are lots of side roads to explore.

Getting There: Take Highway 395 to the center of Lone Pine and the junction with Whitney Portal Road.

Route: Go west on Whitney Portal Road, crossing the Los Angeles Aqueduct before entering a small canyon into the Alabama Hills. The road follows the creek where fantastic weathered granite surrounds you. As the canyon opens up, there is a natural amphitheater to the right.

Continue up the road toward the Sierra, past Movie Road and Tuttle Creek Road. You can soon see switch-backs winding uphill toward Whitney Portal.

A long, steep climb up the alluvial plain leads past the Cuffe Ranch and around granite knolls. Stay on the paved road to Lone Pine Creek Campground at 7.0 miles. Cross the wash of Lone Pine Creek and begin the brutal climb toward the canyon.

Just before you reach the switch-backs there is a wide gravel road to the right (north)—Hogback Road—marked by a sign that reads *Not recommended for Trailers.* Turn right onto Hogback and drop down into the trees where you have magnificent views of Owens Valley. The road descends the crest of a lateral moraine, "the Hogback." Enjoy this long, beautiful downhill across wide-open high desert.

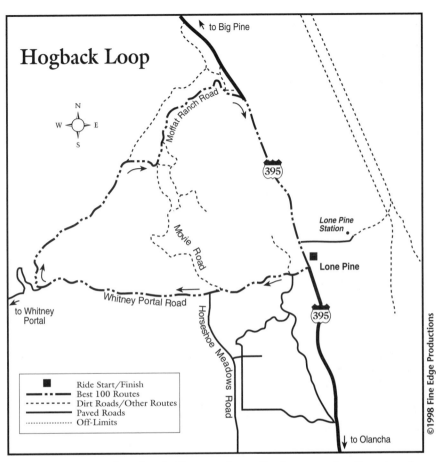

Hogback Loop

©1998 Fine Edge Productions

You parallel willow-lined Hogback Creek for miles, passing several camps along the creek. At a small depression, you pass a dirt road to the left, curve right on the graded road and head for the Alabama Hills.

At the intersection of Movie Road and Hogback Road (13.7 miles), go left downhill along the creek. When you reach Moffat Ranch Road, veer left again. The road runs between the Alabama Hills and the meadows of the creek bottom—a green strip in stark contrast to the vast high desert.

At 17.1 miles, the road ends at a junction with a broken pavement road. Go right onto this road and immediately cross the Los Angeles Aqueduct. The road parallels the aqueduct and Highway 395 for 0.75 mile where you then make a quick left to the highway.

Go right on Highway 395. The Alabama Hills are on your right; to the left is a large marsh, a reserve for tule elk. Ride on the wide shoulder for 3.3 miles to the edge of Lone Pine and the historical marker for the victims of the 1872 earthquake. The 15-foot-high ridge at the site is the fault scarp; a short trail leads to the mass grave.

Continue south on Highway 395 into Lone Pine, past the City Park to your starting point.

85 Mazourka Canyon

Distance: 36 miles round trip
Difficulty: A strenuous ride into the remote Inyo Mountains
Elevation: Lowest point: 3,900'; highest point: 9,000'
Ride Type: Out-and-back on good dirt roads and jeep roads, with many optional side trips
Season: Spring, summer, and fall; lower elevations are possible in winter
Map: Independence, Bee Springs Canyon, Mazourka Peak

Overview: Ride from the desert floor of the Owens Valley to the alpine meadows at the crest of the Inyos. There are many mines located in this area which provide opportunities for side trips if you want to see them. Please stay off posted property. Some amenities are available in Independence, the Inyo County seat for 125 years. A permit is needed for overnight camping. Check with the BLM or USFS.

Getting There: Start at the south end of Independence at the junction of Highway 395 and Mazourka Canyon Road (Citrus Road on some maps). Park well off the highway. Remain on existing roads at all times.

Route: Head due east on Mazourka Canyon Road. Just beyond the Los Angeles Aqueduct at 1.9 miles, the road drops down a 15-foot fault scarp formed by the 1872 earthquake. Cross the Owens River at 3.8 miles. At 4.4. miles, the pavement changes to gravel. Cross the old Carson & Colorado railroad right-of-way where Kearsarge Station once stood. Climb an alluvial fan eastward, then head north on a well-graded gravel road and begin your climb.

[**Side trips:** At 5.8 miles, the Snow Cap Mine Road goes off to the left. The mine is about 7 miles away. At 7.2 miles, the Copper Queen Mine is to the west. At 8.3 miles, Lead Gulch Road (with gate) leads east for several miles to the Betty Jumbo Mine at 7,500 feet.]

Short of 9 miles, you enter Inyo National Forest. At 9.3 miles, pass Squares Tunnel and two cabins east of the road. Paiute Monument (also called Winnedumah), an 8,369-foot granite monolith, lies 3 miles due east along the Inyo Ridge.

At 11.7 miles, you pass some houses, mining equipment, water tank, and wrecked cars. *This is private property; do not enter.* At 12.1 miles, cross a cattle guard and go 0.2 mile to a sign: *Santa Rita Flat to the left. Badger Flat straight ahead.*

[**Side trip:** At this point you can add a loop west to Santa Rita Flat, rejoin your ride, then continue to Badger Flat. About 14 miles long, this loop is not included in total mileage.]

As you continue on your ride, Sunday Canyon enters from the west at 12.8 miles. You pass a seldom-used jeep road on the right, staying left on the main road that enters Rose Canyon.

At Pop's Gulch, 14.3 miles, a gravel road offers an additional route to Santa Rita Flat. At 18 miles, you reach Badger Flat, a large, bowl-shaped area surrounded by tree-covered ridges where mining and hunting trails lead off in many directions. In the spring, this area is bright with wildflowers.

[**Side trips:** Tamarack Canyon trail

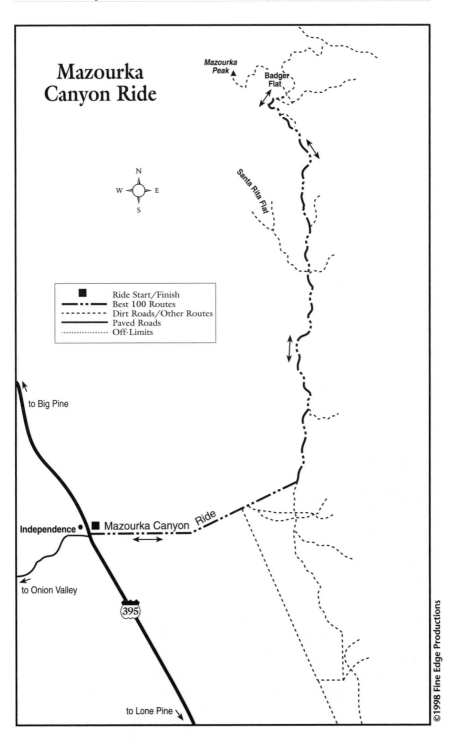

Mazourka Canyon Ride

Mazourka Peak ▲

Badger Flat

Santa Rita Flat

N
W ◆ E
S

■ Ride Start/Finish
▬▬▬ Best 100 Routes
---- Dirt Roads/Other Routes
▬▬▬ Paved Roads
········· Off-Limits

to Big Pine

Independence ● ■ Mazourka Canyon Ride

to Onion Valley

395

to Lone Pine

©1998 Fine Edge Productions

leads 3 miles east to the north side of an unnamed peak, elevation 10,724 feet. From the east side of Badger Flat, you can head northwest to the Blue Bell Mine complex, 1.5 miles.]

For your return, retrace the route, controlling your speed and guarding against heat buildup on your brakes and rims. The trail descends nearly 5,000 feet in one swoop!

Taboose Creek near Aberdeen.

86 Taboose Creek Loop

Distance: 12.5 miles
Difficulty: Difficult, strenuous, and technical
Elevation: Lowest point: 3,800'; highest point: 5,861'
Ride Type: Loop ride on pavement, dirt road, and jeep road
Season: Spring, summer, and fall
Maps: Aberdeen, Fish Springs

Overview: This challenging ride leads through lava flows and cinder cones with views of the Sierra, Inyo Mountains, and Owens Valley. Parking, phone, store, water and a cafe are available at Aberdeen which was once a stop on the Owens Valley stage route.

Getting There: From Independence, take Highway 395 north about 15 miles. Turn left on Goodale Creek Road and continue one mile to the junction with Tinemaha Road. Turn left (west) and go 100 yards. Park near the Aberdeen store/restaurant, being careful not to block access.

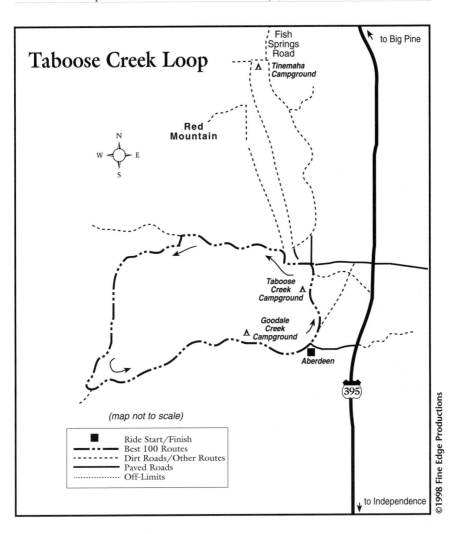

Taboose Creek Loop

Fish Springs Road

to Big Pine

Tinemaha Campground

Red Mountain

N
W   E
S

Taboose Creek Campground

Goodale Creek Campground

Aberdeen

395

(map not to scale)

■ Ride Start/Finish
—·—·— Best 100 Routes
- - - - - Dirt Roads/Other Routes
———— Paved Roads
················ Off-Limits

©1998 Fine Edge Productions

to Independence

Route: From the four-way stop at Aberdeen, go north on Tinemaha Road toward the Poverty Hills along old highway 395. Cross under two big power lines and continue north toward a line of trees.

At 1.4 miles you cross a bridge in Taboose Creek Campground. Continue north 0.75 mile to Taboose Creek Road, then turn left and head uphill toward the Sierra, paralleling Taboose Creek. Stay on the graded road.

As you climb, there are expanding views of the eerie volcanic landscape. Red Mountain, to the north, has extensive lava flows. To the south are several cinder cones and a massive lava field. Taboose Creek crosses a big alluvial fan between the two lava flows.

At 2.7 miles you cross a gate and enter BLM land. Take a left at the next junction and follow the jeep road close to Taboose Creek which is lined with willows and tall grasses.

At 4.5 miles there is a junction by the creek. Go left across Taboose Creek, up its opposite side, then along the edge of the black lava field. At the next junction, go left and ride along the base of the Sierra.

You cross a gate near three volcanic cones. Continue along the edge of the lava flow to a saddle—a long climb in coarse sand. The crest of the saddle at 6.9 miles is close to a red cinder cone. Descend toward Goodale Creek, cross it, and climb. At a junction, go left on 11S02 and climb to a crest on the alluvial fan, the apex of the ride.

Now you begin a 3-mile-long, rugged and technical downhill on a "road" that is nothing but rock. When you can risk a look, there are outstanding views of Owens Valley. Stay on the road heading east toward Aberdeen. The last part, which is quite sandy, ends at Tinemaha Road. Go left to Aberdeen and your starting point, 12.4 miles.

87 McMurry Meadows Loop

Distance: 13 miles
Difficulty: A challenging loop ride on jeep roads
Elevation: 3,900' at Big Pine to 6,500' at McMurry Meadow
Ride Type: Loop ride on dirt road and jeep road
Season: Spring, summer, and fall
Maps: Big Pine, Coyote Flat, Fish Springs, Split Mtn.

Overview: This ride includes stunning volcanic landscape: a vaulted volcanic field, nearly 80 feet high, extending from the east side of Crater Mountain to Red Mountain, and the extensive lava flows along the foothills of the Sierra and the Inyos. Crater Mountain, 3 miles due south of Big Pine, is the highest of several volcanic cones and is an Area of Critical Environmental Concern and a Wilderness Study Area. The Poverty Hills are not of volcanic nature but are built upon an uplifted block of granite and marble. Amenities are available in Big Pine. Be sure to carry a minimum of 3–4 pints of water.

Getting There: From the flashing light at Highway 395 in Big Pine, take Glacier Lodge Road west for 2.5 miles. Just past the bridge over Big Pine Creek, turn left and park on the McMurry Meadows Road.

Route: Start this ride just above Big Pine Creek on the left side of Glacier Road. Go downhill on McMurry Meadows Road, around a curve, and under a power line. Go right at the first junction and head uphill toward Crater Mountain, crossing Little Pine Creek. The road runs along the black lava flow and at one point you can see an island of granite surrounded by rough black lava.

At 1.5 miles, as the road goes along the base of the granite ridge, you pass a sand pit. Cross the dry drainage and ascend toward the saddle. The road leads across a wide basin up to a second saddle.

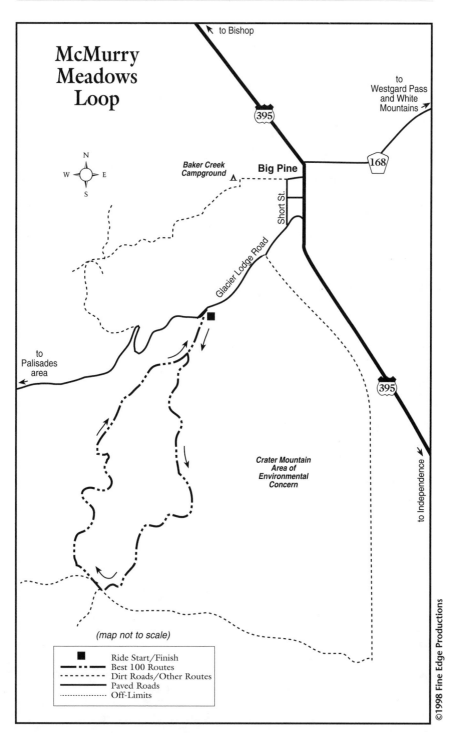

McMurry Meadows Loop

to Bishop

to Westgard Pass and White Mountains

395

168

N
W   E
S

Baker Creek Campground

Big Pine

Short St.

Glacier Lodge Road

to Palisades area

Crater Mountain Area of Environmental Concern

395

to Independence

(map not to scale)

■ Ride Start/Finish
—··—··— Best 100 Routes
---------- Dirt Roads/Other Routes
———— Paved Roads
················ Off-Limits

©1998 Fine Edge Productions

McMurry Meadows Loop

At 3.1 miles, the top of the second saddle is close to Crater Mountain. Stay right on the road around the base of the granite ridge and climb over the shoulder of the ridge. In a second bowl, there is an amazing view of the Owens Valley. Climb to a crest by a granite point. McMurry Meadows sit at the base of the sheer granite mountains.

Drop across a bowl and climb uphill toward McMurry Meadows. At 5.6 miles there is an intersection above Birch Creek. Go right at this intersection onto the jeep road, ascending toward McMurry Meadows.

[**Side trip:** At a junction at 6.2 miles, a road to the left heads uphill to McMurry Meadows, a fantastic alpine meadow with a spectacular wall of granite above. This vast meadow fills with flowers shortly after the snow melts. The road climbs through the meadow up to the mountain, pro-

viding spectacular views across Owens Valley. Distance for visiting the meadows is not included in this loop.]

To continue the loop, go right at the junction. Head north across the edge of a big bowl and along the base of a bare granite ridge. Stay right as you ride to the far side of the bowl. Take the third possible left and ride over a low saddle, cross into a new drainage, and begin a traverse.

At 8.1 miles, take the road to the right that leads down the gully to a narrow canyon where the road deteriorates into a primitive singletrack. Follow the wash to the creek and climb the bank where the road begins again.

The road exits the canyon and descends northeastward across the alluvial plain toward Big Pine. Parallel Little Pine Creek and cross it twice. Descend toward the lava flows and your starting point, with Crater Mountain to your right.

88 Andrews Mountain Loop

Distance: 25 miles
Difficulty: A strenuous expedition across the crest of the Inyo Mountains
Elevation: Starting point: 6,600'; crest: 9,126'
Ride Type: Loop ride on primitive roads
Season: Late spring, summer, and early fall. (Check with local authorities before setting out.)
Maps: Uhlmeyer Spring, Cowhorn Valley, Waucoba Mtn., and Waucoba Spring

Overview: This area offers high elevation, alpine meadows, incredible vistas, and old mines and cabins. There are no facilities. Carry extra clothing, food, first aid, and a minimum of two quarts of water. Treat all water from local sources. *Note:* Some of the roads are access corridors to wilderness areas where bicycles are not allowed. Please respect these areas. If you wish to camp in this area, you must obtain a campfire permit in advance. Amenities are available in Big Pine.

Getting There: Just north of Big Pine, turn off Highway 395 onto Highway 168. Go 2.3 miles and turn right onto the Saline Valley/Eureka Valley Road (9S18), formerly called Waucoba Road. Continue past Devils Gate to a dirt road (9S15) on the right at 13.6 miles. Park off the road.

Route: Begin this ride only in the morning. Take the dirt road that parallels the main road for several hundred yards, then turns south. At 0.2 mile there is a fork and a sign reading *Papoose-Squaw Flat 4 x 4 advised.* Go right and south onto a sandy gravel road, passing through a wide flat valley of sagebrush.

At 1.5 miles, the road makes a U-turn and drops into a wash. Pinyon and juniper appear. At 3.0 miles, the canyon narrows and the road becomes deeply rutted. Ignore a road

to the left, and continue up a draw to a fork at 4.1 miles.

Go left up the switchbacks to the summit at 5.1 miles and 9,126 feet. Take a short walk northwest along the crest to examine some unusual vertical

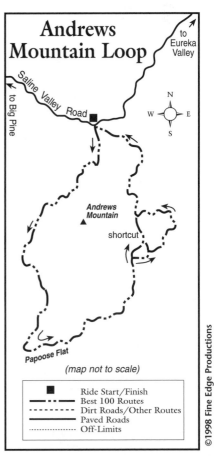

Andrews
Mountain Loop

to Eureka Valley

to Big Pine

Saline Valley Road

N
W   E
S

Andrews Mountain ▲

shortcut

Papoose Flat

(map not to scale)

■	Ride Start/Finish
-----	Best 100 Routes
------	Dirt Roads/Other Routes
----	Paved Roads
······	Off-Limits

©1998 Fine Edge Productions

shale formations and enjoy the view directly across to Crater Mountain, and the full southern Sierra Crest.

From the summit, the descent into Papoose Flat passes through juniper and sage. At 6.8 miles, take the left fork. At 8.0 miles, you cross a major drainage—the wash to the east flows into Squaw Flat—and climb a shallow pass to a Y-junction at 9.0 miles. Go left and begin the steep descent east to Papoose Flat.

In the flat, at 10.3 miles, there are some primitive campsites. Did you remember to get a campfire permit? Yes? Then it's okay to camp but please keep this area clean by packing out all your trash.

A short walk to the west gives you an outstanding view of the Owens Valley and Sierra Crest. *Warning:* If you are low on water, find the trip too taxing, or are running out of daylight, retrace your route now; it's much easier and faster to return from this point.

To continue your loop ride, go 200 yards south to a major junction at 10.4 miles. Go east toward Squaw Flat on an easy downhill. Ignore a jeep road at 11.5 miles and another that comes in from the south which leads to Mazourka Canyon.

At 12.1 miles, there is a granite monolith on the left. As the wash widens, you leave the granite formations behind. Stay in the middle of the wash, heading toward Squaw Peak (10,358 feet), and contour across upper Squaw Flat. Waucoba Mountain (11,123 feet) comes into view to the right of Squaw Peak.

Follow the wash to mile 14.1, where it narrows before opening up again at the 8,000-foot contour. Cross a wash at 15.3 miles where a road joins from the south.

[**Option:** There is a three-way intersection at 16.4 miles. The route dead ahead climbs steeply to the north, passing close to an unnamed red peak. This is a shortcut if you wish to avoid the narrows.]

To continue the longer loop, go east (right) through the narrowing canyon. At 17.0 miles, you drop into a sandy wash due south of Peak 8173. The road narrows slowly and the ramparts of Squaw Peak close in on you. There are interesting red lava flows along the way.

At 17.8 miles, you leave the wash temporarily and climb a short ridge. At 18.6 miles you reach the narrows of Marble Canyon where there are two old mining cabins. Leave your bike and walk into the narrows of Marble Canyon for a look, proceeding carefully on foot. The descent into the canyon is steep, and there are mines all around. Since this canyon is so rarely visited, no one would find you if you fell or had an accident.

Back on your bike, continue up the canyon to the left on a steep, rocky road composed of shale with poor traction. With perseverance, you reach a small flat area at 20.5 miles. Head north, ignoring a faint track to the west, and at 20.7 miles you intersect the main road from the southwest (the short cut).

At 21.2 miles, you reach the ridge where there are primitive campsites on the right. From here, you can see White Mountain directly to the north.

At 21.4 miles, you pass three tunnels on the left. If you wish to explore on foot, *use caution.* At 22.7 miles, the canyon again narrows and becomes rockier. At 23.0 miles, the trail splits; you can take either fork as they rejoin around the bend.

Continue down the broad wash to the Papoose Flat sign (mile 24.8) and then back to your starting point.

View of Hammil Valley, Casa Diablo Mountain from White Mountain Peak.

89 White Mountain Ride

Distance: 14 miles
Difficulty: Extremely difficult ride due to its high elevation and remoteness; for well-prepared expert riders only
Elevation: From 12,000' to the summit of White Mountain at 14,280'
Ride Type: Out-and-back on difficult jeep road
Season: Summer and early fall. Keep an eye on weather patterns!
Maps: Blanco Mtn., Mt. Barcroft, White Mtn. Peak, Juniper Mtn.

Overview: White Mountain Ride is the highest mountain bike ride in California, an epic ride through a remote alpine zone with panoramic vistas. Be aware that this is a fragile area. Deep snow, extreme cold, and hurricane-force winds define the life of the small plants that survive here, and crushing them causes irreparable damage. Remain on the road at all times, be courteous to any hikers you encounter, and do your part to preserve this area in its natural state. There are no facilities in the area. You must be fully self-sufficient. Barcroft Laboratory has an emergency phone only. Carry a minimum of two quarts drinking water.

Getting there: From the junction of Highway 395 and Highway 168, take 168 (Westgard Pass Road) east to the summit 13 miles; turn left on White Mountain Road and continue until 4.6 miles past Patriarch Grove to a locked gate. Park here.

Route: Start at the closure gate in the saddle. Go around the gate and up a steep graded road. Fragile alpine flowers and grasses grow in the poor soil alongside the road.

At 1 mile, the grade slackens. Patriarch Grove lies across the huge basin to the south, and Barcroft Laboratory is ahead. The laboratory—a huge Quonset hut that stands at 12,500 feet—is a high-altitude research area, property of the University of California. Do not disturb anything.

Follow the primitive jeep road uphill. The road is steep and rocky, leading through alpine tundra to the crest where there is an observatory and a tremendous view of White Mountain. From this point, you can see the road leading to the summit.

You drop down to a sandy bowl covered with sparse alpine grasses and flowers, cross a small rise, then drop into a second bowl, before starting up the technical rocky road that leads to the crest of a small peak within 1.5 miles. (You can see the road ahead across the saddle.)

Drop down the loose, technical road to the saddle, cross a sparse green meadow, and start up the final approach to White Mountain, where the terrain is steep and loose. Even if you are acclimated to the high elevation, you may find cycling slow going. Take one switchback at a time,

breathe deeply, and drink plenty of fluids, no matter whether you feel thirsty or not! The air is dry and thin and your system needs those fluids to keep you going.

At the top of the third switchback, you leave the band of beige rock and enter black rock. Continue up the switchbacks across the east face of White Mountain. At the top of the seventh switchback, you crest the south ridge, then climb to a higher terrace. After you cross the top of a black ridge, you ascend several last switchbacks to the crest.

From the gate where you began, it is 7.0 miles to the summit of White Mountain where you'll find a small cement building, some solar panels, and a radio tower. Stay out of the building, but you may climb onto the roof which makes a great sun deck and offers a 360-degree view that includes the crest of the White Mountains, Owens Valley, and the Sierra all the way from Independence to Bishop. To the north you can see Glass Mountain ridge, Mono Basin, and the Bodie Hills beyond. Nevada

The upper "lip" of Silver Canyon, looking toward the Sierra (Ride 90).

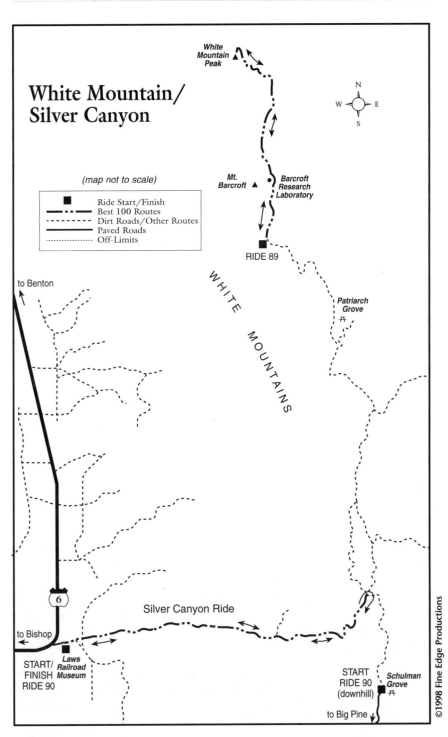

White Mountain/ Silver Canyon

(map not to scale)

■ Ride Start/Finish
▬▪▬▪ Best 100 Routes
---- Dirt Roads/Other Routes
▬▬ Paved Roads
······ Off-Limits

White Mountain Peak ▲

N
W   E
S

Mt. Barcroft ▲   ● Barcroft Research Laboratory

■ RIDE 89

to Benton

WHITE MOUNTAINS

Patriarch Grove ⛺

6

Silver Canyon Ride

to Bishop

START/ FINISH RIDE 90   Laws Railroad Museum

START RIDE 90 (downhill)   Schulman Grove ⛺

to Big Pine

©1998 Fine Edge Productions

stretches east with lines of mountains and basins fading forever into the distance.

When you are ready, return down the road. Ride slowly on the steep and technical sections, yielding to hikers. Take some rest breaks—this is no place to risk injury. At 8.6 miles you are back at the low saddle. Most cyclists walk the next section to the top of the smaller peak; the ride down the other side is also challenging.

Cross the double bowl and climb to the observatory, then continue to Barcroft at 11.9 miles. The last part of the ride is good road and a fast downhill to the closure gate.

Note: To date, entry to this area has been open to foot-traffic and mountain bikes, but closure could occur at any time if adverse impact is found on the fragile slopes. For information phone White Mountain Ranger Station 760-873-2500.

90 Silver Canyon Ride ("The Ultimate Kamikaze")

Distance: 23.2 miles round trip; 11.6 miles downhill with shuttle
Difficulty: Extreme ride for advanced, self-sufficient riders only
Elevation: Valley floor: 4,000'; highest point: 10,800'
Ride Type: Out-and-back on steep jeep road or long descent only with optional shuttle
Season: Late spring, summer, and early fall
Maps: Blanco Mtn., Laws

Overview: Silver Canyon, known for one of mountain biking's most insane rides, was the route of the Plumline Outback Ultimate Kamikaze Race held during the 1980s. During the race, unusual safety precautions were taken with full communication and rescue teams in place. In the late 1980s the Kamikaze was moved to Mammoth Mountain. Laws Railroad Museum, at the foot of Silver Canyon, features the history of Owens Valley, with emphasis on the railroad. Be sure to schedule time to visit it. There are restrooms and water at Laws Railroad Museum. For out-and-back trips, carry snacks, first aid, and at least two quarts of water; there is none on your route.

Getting There: For the round trip: from the Y-junction of Highways 395 and 6 in Bishop, take Highway 6 north for 4 miles. Just past the Owens

River Bridge, go right on Silver Canyon Road to Laws Railroad Museum. Park across the road from the museum.

For the shuttle, leave one car at Laws Railroad Museum. Drive a second car south on Highway 395 to the junction of Highways 395 and 168. Take 168 (Westgard Pass Road) east to the summit 13 miles; turn left on White Mountain and continue 9.8 miles to Schulman Grove. Park there. Ride your bike north for 3 miles to the turnoff for Silver Canyon. Turn west for several hundred yards to the crest proper where you begin the downhill into Silver Canyon. Please remain on existing roads at all times.

Route: For the round-trip ride (up and down), head east from Laws Museum on the wide road past fields and across two irrigation ditches. At the end of the pavement, follow the gravel road toward Silver Canyon. At 2.0 miles, you make your first creek crossing and enter the canyon where the road narrows and steepens. Ride up deep Silver Canyon, crossing willow-lined Silver Creek several times. Aspen appear as you climb higher up the canyon. Ride through a narrows, cross the creek for the fifth time, and see the switchbacks ahead. This is your future! Continue up the road past a couple of mines.

After the eighth creek crossing (about 7.0 miles), there is a closure gate at the bottom of the first steep switchback. The impossible slope becomes merely difficult after the first switchback. After the road enters pinyon forest, the route is still steep, and rocks, ruts, and off-camber turns give it additional spice.

At a junction with a power line road, go right on the better road. Portions of the road are bare rock and it becomes extremely steep, rutted and technical, climbing 800 feet in the last mile to the top—a ride to the sky.

At the crest, 11.6 miles, there is a level pad from which you can enjoy the quintessential view of the Sierra—from the Palisades to Yosemite. Take time to rest and eat, because the ride down is difficult and dangerous.

On the way back down, the steep and technical road is a constant workout. *Rims can heat up enough to melt tubes, so stop and rest your braking hands and let your rims cool.* Slow down before each sharp curve. The road, rough and uneven, is often solid rock or strewn with rocks, and its upper section requires skill and judgment. Walk, if you're in doubt or if fatigue sets in—remember, this is the Ultimate Kamikaze! From the top of the last switchback, stop to enjoy the view down Silver Canyon.

At the bottom of the last switchback the character of the ride changes. The road no longer has sharp turns and is much less steep and technical. This is the fastest part of your return and each of the many creek crossings is a refreshing splash. For over 5 miles the exhilarating downhill continues through Silver Canyon.

Once you reach the flats, follow the road to Laws Railroad Museum

White Mountain Peak from Patriarch Grove area.

for a glimpse into the early history of Owens Valley.

To do the downhill ride only, head north from Schulman Grove for 3 miles along the White Mountain Road. Go left (west) at the saddle onto Silver Canyon Road, climbing several hundred yards over the Inyo crest proper, passing a radio relay station located on Peak 10,842 to the north.

From this point, follow the round-trip ride directions above—from the 11.6 mile point—in *reverse* order.

91 Coyote High Sierra Traverse

Distance: 21.7 miles with shuttle
Difficulty: Expedition-level ride due to high elevation and remoteness; route-finding skills required
Elevation: Average elevation about 10,000', with some elevations over 11,000'; 4,370' gain, 5,000' loss
Ride Type: Expedition-level trip; 5 miles of technical singletrack. Riders must be self-sufficient, fully prepared with topo maps, compass, clothing, first aid; start with at least 2 quarts of water
Season: June through fall, depending on snow. Keep an eye on the weather!
Maps: Coyote Flat for route-finding on the singletrack section, Big Pine, Mt. Thompson

Overview: This high traverse of the Coyote Flat area through high alpine meadows and stunted forests offers outstanding vistas of northern Owens Valley, the White Mountains, and the Sierra Crest. This is an excellent overnight adventure. Food, water, and toilets at Bishop Creek Lodge. Treat all water from local sources. All amenities can be found in Bishop.

Getting There: Leave a shuttle vehicle in downtown Big Pine and return to Bishop. Go west on West Line Street (Highway 168) for 13 miles, turn left onto South Lake Road, and drive about 6 miles. Park your second vehicle in the turnout to the right just beyond Bishop Creek Lodge.

Route: From the parking area off the paved road, ride about 500 feet uphill to a dirt road on your left. Take this road and cross a bridge over Bishop Creek. The road quickly becomes a doubletrack, curves north through an aspen grove, and climbs through loose sandy soil to a lateral moraine. At the top of the moraine, you round a corner and enter a hanging valley (elevation 8,800 feet). Ignore the faint road to the right.

After many switchbacks and sandy spots, you reach a T-intersection at 3.0 miles where you go left and climb to a minor ridge at 10,000 feet. You have now climbed 1,600 feet with another 1,100 feet to go to the top of Coyote Ridge. Don't give up!

A short descent and a gentle climb bring you to the remains of an old log cabin at 3.5 miles. From this point, the road averages a 14 percent grade to the top of 11,070-foot Coyote Ridge at 5.0 miles. Catch your breath here and take time to enjoy the spectacular views.

You now begin a 1,500-foot descent through an alpine meadow where there are wonderful fields of lupine in springtime. At 7.0 miles, at an intersection, continue straight ahead. [**Side trip:** The right-hand trail leads to a pleasant camping area at the usually dry Coyote Lake.]

Another mile brings you to the first crossing of Coyote Creek at elevation 9,950 feet. The road improves

as you continue to descend. At 9.2 miles you reach a road junction. It's decision time now: the described route to Big Pine Creek goes right (south) downhill and heads into Coyote Flat. If you've had enough at this point take the option. [**Option:** If you continue straight, the main

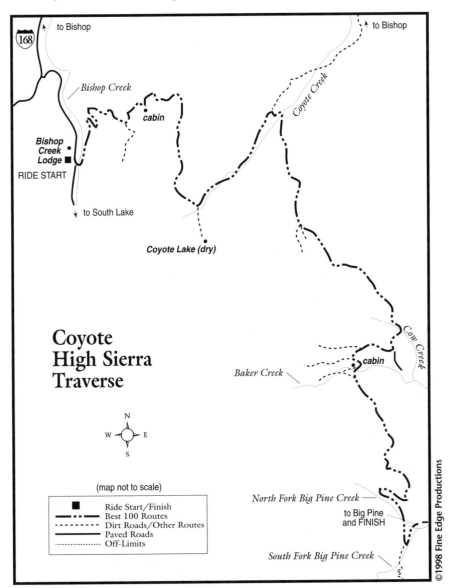

to Bishop

168

to Bishop

Bishop Creek

cabin

Coyote Creek

Bishop Creek Lodge

RIDE START

to South Lake

Coyote Lake (dry)

Cow Creek

Coyote High Sierra Traverse

cabin

Baker Creek

N

W ← → E

S

(map not to scale)

■	Ride Start/Finish
▬ ▬	Best 100 Routes
- - -	Dirt Roads/Other Routes
▬▬▬	Paved Roads
....	Off-Limits

North Fork Big Pine Creek —

to Big Pine and FINISH

South Fork Big Pine Creek

jeep road takes you down to Reata Road west of Bishop. This route is easier, shorter, and less technical; a definite short way back.]

To follow the full route, go right and downhill, crossing Coyote Creek again. After 5.2 miles of easy riding, you reach the southern end of Coyote Flat, a plateau running north-south. At mile 14.4, cross Cow Creek, pass a cattle guard, and go to a junction and a ridge forming the edge of the Baker Creek drainage.

Go right (west) and climb to 10,290 feet and another junction at 15.5 miles. Go left (southwest) and downhill to another junction, then left again. This brings you to Baker Creek and the Baker Creek Cabin at 16.0 miles. From here, elevation 10,070 feet, you find the last water until Big Pine Creek. *Treat any water.*

The next section, the start of the technically demanding singletrack, requires route-finding skills. Go upstream from the cabin about 500 feet and cross the stream; you should be in the trees and just upstream from a swampy meadow area. Avoid any trails that lead away from the north side of the stream.

Look for a trail that either parallels the creek on its south side or goes up the hillside to the south. If the trail parallels the creek, go left and downstream. If the trail goes up the hill, follow it south. If you have trouble at this spot, you may not have gone far enough upstream from the cabin. (The Coyote Flat topo map helps at this point.)

In 0.3 mile, go left at a junction and to the top of the ridge at 16.4 miles. From here, the singletrack goes 0.6 mile downhill to High Meadow (10,020 feet), then climbs steeply to a rounded ridge at the edge of Big Pine Canyon. Views of 14,000-foot peaks and two of the largest glaciers in the Sierra unfold as you ride toward some rocks at the southern end of the ridge at 17.7 miles.

Ahead is the South Fork of Big Pine Creek; to the right is the North Fork, into which you descend along a steep, technical route to Grouse Spring. Walk your bike if necessary.

Past Grouse Spring (there is little or no water here) the trail becomes easy to the end of Logging Flat. You then descend steeply through sand and several switchbacks before contouring around a draw and climbing to a minor ridge.

The trail now drops into Big Pine Canyon to a four-way junction at 20.0 miles (8,600 feet). Go straight downhill. Watch for hikers! You are now on a heavily-used hiking trail. In 0.5 mile you reach an abandoned road which you take across the creek. Within a few hundred yards a sign indicates that the hiking trail goes left. Your route continues straight down the abandoned road.

Caution: Due to the sand, the next few hundred yards are the worst of the loop. As you approach Big Pine Creek South Fork, watch for a trail at 21.3 miles that is not visible ahead of time. Turn left for 0.5 mile to the trailhead and paved Glacier Lodge Road, where you go downhill for a 9-mile descent into Big Pine.

Note: This ride follows the route of the Sierra 7500 mountain bike competition held in the mid-1980s. Billed as the most difficult mountain bike race course in the United States, the original route covered 50 miles. Cindy Whitehead achieved legendary status when she completed it after breaking her saddle and seatpost in the first mile. (See her foreword for more on this feat.)

92 Buttermilk Country Loop

Distance: 17.4 miles
Difficulty: Difficult and sometimes technical, strenuous climb
Elevation: Lowest point: 5,100'; highest point: 8,250'
Ride Type: Loop ride on good dirt road and jeep roads
Season: Spring, summer, and fall
Maps: Tungsten Hills, Mt. Tom, Mt. Thompson, Mt. Darwin, Bishop

Overview: This loop takes you high into the foothills of the Sierra for views of the Bishop area. Wildflowers abound in spring and early summer. The name Buttermilk Country comes from the fact that a dairy, known among miners for its buttermilk, was once located along this route. Carry a minimum of 3-4 pints of water. Treat all water from local sources. All amenities are available in Bishop.

Getting There: From the junction of Highways 395 and 168 in Bishop, go west on Highway 168 (West Line Street) for 7.2 miles to the intersection of Buttermilk Road and park off the road.

If you're interested in camping opportunities, contact BLM or USFS for information.

Route: Ride west on dirt Buttermilk Road directly toward Mt. Tom, passing the Peabody Boulders ("Grandpa" and "Grandma" are the pair of boulders to the north). At 3.6 miles there is a cattle guard and the Horton Roubaix cutoff to your right. Keep going about 300 yards to where a short singletrack loop heads left and rejoins Buttermilk Road in 0.25 mile.

Looking up toward Coyote Flat from Buttermilk Country.

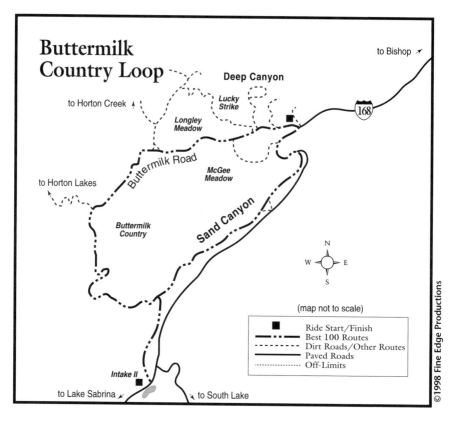

Listen for the sound of a waterfall. [**Side trip:** A 50-yard walk takes you to a deep-carved overlook above McGee Creek. Work your way carefully along this gorge to find a waterfall where birch, willows, and ferns grow along stream.]

Back on the singletrack, ride west to rejoin Buttermilk Road which becomes narrow and rocky. [**Side trips:** Pass several turnoffs; the second jeep trail is the approach to Mt. Tom and a short road on the left heads to McGee Creek (4.9 miles) at the base of Grouse Mountain.]

Ride to the first stands of aspen at 5.7 miles, where your road levels off and heads south. Crossing the 7,600-foot contour, you can see Table Mountain to the south, Coyote Ridge to the southeast, and Grouse Mountain, a large granite outcropping, to the east.

At 6.1 miles, you pass a cattle crossing, and go through an area that is sometimes marshy. [**Side trip:** A small trail to the right of the road leads to a spring. *Treat all water.*]

Your road closes in on the ramparts of the Sierra at 6.9 miles where another trail leads up to another spring. Pass springs and marshes until you reach pines at 7.4 miles.

Climb a short ridge to the left, double back and head west, and climb to 8,240 feet (8.8 miles), the high point of this ride. Head easterly into aspen and pine, passing a jeep road on the right and the Birch Creek culvert.

From here, the road is sometimes

bladed and you have a fast downhill. There are primitive campsites at 9.0 miles. Continue due east to 10.4 miles where a road goes sharp right and up the ridge, south to Highway 168 (Intake #2). You could use this spur as a bailout point if you want to avoid the last few miles of the loop.

To complete the loop, turn left downhill along a narrow ridge, following the Aqueduct pipe and, at 12.7 miles, cross the left side of the ridge. You can see the upper end of Owens Valley and all the way to Montgomery Pass in Nevada.

[Option: There is a locked gate where an SCE service road heads west, paralleling the pipeline back to Highway 168. This short cut allows you to avoid the rocky, steep ascent ahead.]

Continue east out of the sandy wash and climb to a small ridge at 13.9 miles. You can see the USFS parking area below.

At 14.5 miles you reach the USFS parking lot where there is room for about 15 cars. Take Highway 168 back to Buttermilk Road on your left at 17.1 miles. The highway descends steeply; watch for cars and guard against excessive speed.

93 Pleasant Valley Loop

Distance: 14 miles
Difficulty: Moderate, not technical
Elevation: Starting point: 4,100'; highest point: 4,600'
Ride Type: Loop ride on paved road, dirt road, and jeep road
Season: Year-round
Maps: Rovana, Fish Slough

Overview: You travel through cool, pleasant riparian habitat rich with bird life, and view the Owens River Gorge with its dramatic, sheer rock faces that rise to the blue desert sky. Water and toilets at Pleasant Valley Campground; gas and store at Mill Creek Station. All amenities are available in Bishop.

Getting There: Drive seven miles north of Bishop on Highway 395, turn right (east) onto Pleasant Valley Road and park off the road.

Route: Ride northeast on Pleasant Valley Road across a big meadow. The white bluff ahead is Chalk Bluff, the edge of the Volcanic Tableland. Cross Mill Creek and climb to a low saddle. Below you can see Pleasant Valley with the Owens River running through it. Lush marshlands occupy the bottom and cottonwoods and willows line the river. Hawks and eagles are common here. In summer, it is cooler here near the river, and the tall green grasses and trees contrast with the surrounding high desert.

Follow the road as it dips down and then continues up the canyon past Pleasant Valley Campground and across Owens River. You come to a gate across the road with a sign that warns of falling rock and rising water. This is Los Angeles Department of

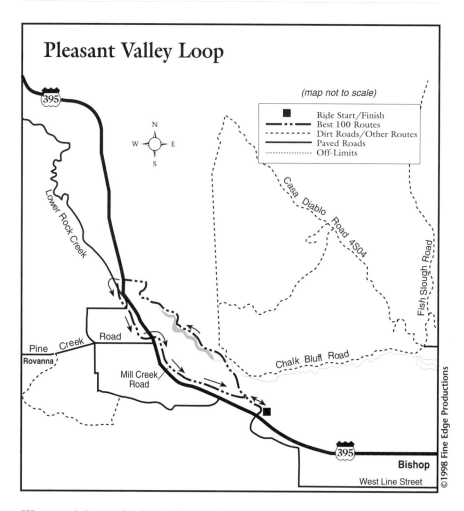

Pleasant Valley Loop

(map not to scale)

■ Ride Start/Finish
——·—— Best 100 Routes
- - - - - Dirt Roads/Other Routes
——— Paved Roads
········· Off-Limits

N
W — E
S

Lower Rock Creek

Casa Diablo Road 4S04

Fish Slough Road

Pine Creek Road

Rovanna

Mill Creek Road

Chalk Bluff Road

395

Bishop

West Line Street

©1998 Fine Edge Productions

Water and Power land. Cyclists and pedestrians are welcome to use DWP roads and trails for day-use recreation. But enter at your own risk. No camping or fires are permitted.

Go around the gate and up to the crest of the dam. Stay on the trail along the reservoir. About halfway up the reservoir there is a single tree and a boat ramp. This is an excellent rest spot—a Pleasant Valley!

As the reservoir continues, it gradually narrows to a river. Cottonwood, willow, and aspen trees grow along its bank and grasses, cattails, and brush create a dense jungle appreciated by the numerous birds that visit the area.

At 5.4 miles you cross a small bridge by a DWP power plant—one of four along the Owens River Gorge. From here most of the river flows into the huge penstock, or conduit. Bear left around the building and then right, uphill along the tuff.

As you ascend to the crest, the Sierra comes into full view. Mount Tom is the magnificent triangular peak across Round Valley with Pine Creek Canyon cutting along its

Pleasant Valley Reservoir

northern base. Wheeler Crest is the long granite crown to the north of Mount Tom; the low desert hills to the south of Mount Tom are the Tungsten Hills.

Follow the paved road to an intersection by the giant water pipe, take a left, and go downhill. Cross Highway 395 and continue a short distance to the road's end at paved Lower Rock Creek Road.

Turn left onto Lower Rock Creek Road, paralleling 395 and head south. Large cottonwoods line the irrigation ditches and creeks and there are ruins of old ranches amid the trees. Low stone fences, visible in several places, are remains of the historic Sherwin Toll Road. Follow Lower Rock Creek Road for 2 miles to its end at Pine Creek Road (9.4 miles). Take a left and cross Highway 395 to Mill Creek Road, once the historic stage route; follow it south to Mill Creek Station Store. Just north of the store, you can see a couple of

old stone buildings that once served as the stage station.

Past the store, continue south on the paved road paralleling the main highway, then continue straight on the old road which first becomes broken pavement, then dirt. Follow the base of the bluff, parallel to Mill Creek, still on the historic stage route to Mammoth Lakes.

Along the way you can find petroglyphs if you look carefully. *Admire, but do not touch.* This rock art is fragile and irreplaceable.

Continue along Mill Creek below the cliffs, cross under some power lines and pass through a gate. The road, now almost a trail, passes through dense willows. Cross under three more power lines and keep heading straight along the base of the cliff.

At 13.5 miles, the dirt road ends at Pleasant Valley Road. Go right, cross a broad meadow, and head toward Highway 395 and your vehicle.

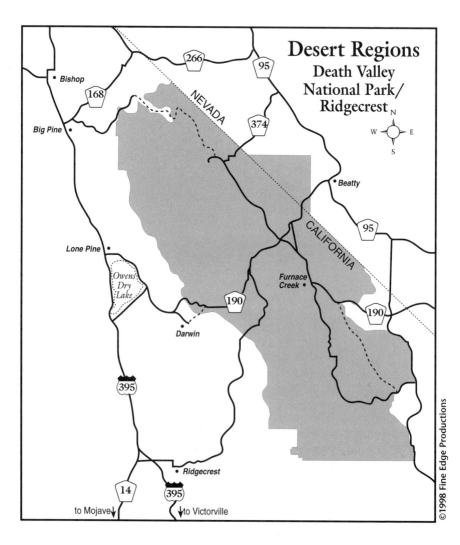

Desert Regions
Death Valley
National Park/
Ridgecrest

CHAPTER 12

Desert Regions: Ridgecrest and Death Valley

By Delaine Fragnoli

Talk to people who have spent some time in the desert and certain words get repeated—vast, quiet, still, reflective—all qualities sorely lacking in modern life. Perhaps that's why more and more Californians are discovering their desert.

What they are discovering is an intricate environment that is both tenacious and fragile. The California desert, located in the eastern portion of the state, covers a full one quarter of state lands. It contains 1,836 species of plants, 420 birds, 94 mammals, 63 reptiles, 43 fishes and 16 amphibians in 46 distinct ecological communities ranging from riparian marsh to desert forest. Over 100,000 archeological sites, including some of the most concentrated collections of rock art in the world, dot the desert's ninety mountain ranges. As if that weren't enough, the oldest living known organism, a 11,700-year-old creosote ring, lives in the desert. Nowhere else can geology buffs see so clearly the work of wind and water on the land. Yet 38 varieties of plant, animal and insect life are threatened or endangered, including the desert tortoise, California's official state reptile.

As Southern California's population surges past the 16-million mark, more and more people are moving to the desert, and more and more people are seeking recreation and a respite from urban blight in these seemingly empty spaces. Fortunately much of the desert has already been preserved. Its crown jewel, Death Valley, was adopted by the National Park Service in 1933 as a national monument. Three years later, 560,000 acres were protected in Joshua Tree National Monument. With the passage of the California Desert Protection Act in 1994, both areas became national parks.

Death Valley and Joshua Tree are among the best areas to explore in the desert. Both feature unique plants and animals as well as mind-boggling geologic

View of the Funeral Mountains from Aguereberry Point, Death Valley National Monument.

formations. They are accessible and have facilities for camping and day use. Many other areas of the desert are remote, accessible only with 4WD vehicles, and lacking any facilities. Death Valley and Joshua Tree also have the distinction of being part of a UNESCO (United Nations Educational, Scientific, and Cultural Organization) International Biosphere Reserve as part of the Colorado and Mojave Desert Biosphere Reserve, along with Anza-Borrego State Park (see Chapter 1) and the Santa Rosa Mountains Deep Canyon Research Center (see Chapter 3).

Despite the influx of visitors to the California desert, a frontier spirit still persists. Curmudgeonly old miners still eke out an existence. Off-road motorcyclists tell stories of finding hidden landing strips, pentagrams and satanic paraphernalia, and men living in caves.

Near the junction of Highways 14 and 395, the town of Ridgecrest makes a great jumping-off spot for exploring the California desert, particularly Death Valley, and there is some good riding immediately around Ridgecrest. Much of the land to the north is part of the China Lake Naval Weapons Center; to the east are China Lake and Fort Irwin. The Bureau of Land Management oversees 2.3 million acres of public land around Ridgecrest and Inyokern.

The BLM prints a mountain bike pamphlet with suggested routes in the area. *Be forewarned:* the directions are not very detailed. I have 4-wheeled here and there are no signs or facilities. It is very easy to get off-route and end up in extremely deep sand or in a canyon with no outlet that deposits you miles from where you want to be. Even if you do manage to find some of the designated routes, I consider several of the BLM's recommendations, particularly in the El Paso Mountains, completely unsuitable for mountain biking—fun on a motorcycle, misery on a bicycle. If you do decide to explore the area, arm yourself with good maps and plenty of food, water and sunscreen. Better yet, hook up with a local rider. The area is very popular with motorcyclists and 4WD enthusiasts, so watch out for motorized vehicles when you ride.

94 Ridgecrest: College Loop

Distance: 7 miles
Difficulty: Moderate, somewhat technical
Elevation: 500' gain/loss; 3,300' high point
Ride Type: Loop on singletrack and dirt/sand roads
Season: Fall, winter, spring
Map: BLM

Overview: Ridgecrest hosts the Ridgecrest Desert Classic mountain bike race, one of the most popular and longest-running events in Southern California. The race begins very near the town's community college. This loop starts there and takes in part of the race course. The route is marked by short, steep climbs and equally short and steep descents. Trail surface varies from hard-packed to rocky to sandy. It's a fast fun loop with no sustained climbs. Numerous other trails, motorcycle tracks and doubletracks lace the area, and you can easily spend several hours exploring these. It's a popular spot and you will more than likely see other cyclists.

Getting There: From North China Lake Boulevard, turn onto College Heights Boulevard. (You can only go one direction on College Heights as the other way leads directly into a shopping area parking lot.) Follow College Heights up past the new housing tracts (Ridgecrest's version of suburbia) and to the college. The paved road runs into a dirt road just south of the college. Park in the dirt area on the southwest corner.

Solitude is one of the greatest resources in the California desert.

Route: Head west from the parking area on a dirt road. Stay on the dirt road until you come to a Y-intersection marked by a brown trail sign with a bike and an arrow on it. Go left here to begin the signed race loop. From here trail finding is easy—just follow the signs and arrows.

You make a sandy climb up into the hills and soon top out on a ridge. Once up there you drop into a kind of big bowl with numerous smaller

hills. You have views to the south, where you can see a paved road in the distance, and to the north, where you can see the college and the town of Ridgecrest. Keep your bearings using these landmarks and you can find enough trails to entertain you for several hours. Or, play it safe and continue to follow the race loop.

The loop throws several short steep climbs and short rocky descents your way, interspersed with flatter,

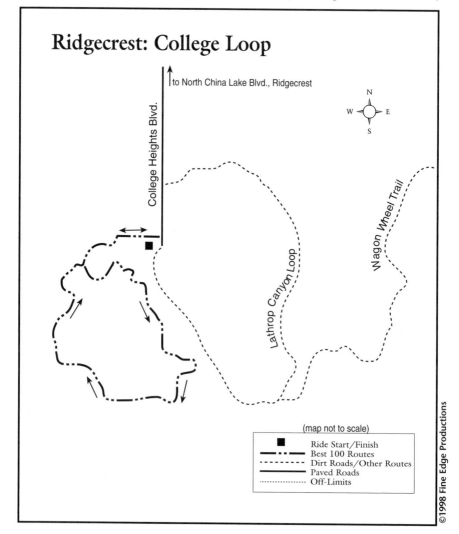

Ridgecrest: College Loop

to North China Lake Blvd., Ridgecrest

College Heights Blvd.

Wagon Wheel Trail

Lathrop Canyon Loop

(map not to scale)

■   Ride Start/Finish
━ ･ ━   Best 100 Routes
╌ ╌ ╌   Dirt Roads/Other Routes
━━━   Paved Roads
‥‥‥   Off-Limits

© 1998 Fine Edge Productions

rolling, sandy sections, and ending with the descent back to the Y. It can get windy on top. When I was up here in the evening I nearly got blown off the trail.

Once back at the parking area, you can call it a day, or you can climb up the dirt road heading south for more exploration. About 1.5 miles up there's a turnoff to your left which leads to a steep, rocky climb to a vista point. From there I could see a singletrack heading back down toward the college. It looked interesting but I did not have time to explore it.

Farther up the dirt road, about 4 miles from the college, is another left-hand (north) turn that takes you into Lathrop Canyon, a very sandy, technical route back to the college. Unlike the race loop, these routes are not signed.

Death Valley National Park

The ominous-sounding Death Valley is a narrow trench, 4 to 16 miles wide and 120 miles long. The Panamint Range runs along its western flank and the Amargosa Range along the eastern flank. Among the many startling contrasts here is the juxtaposition of low elevations and high elevations. Telescope Peak, at 11,049 feet, towers over the valley, while Badwater marks the lowest spot in the United States at 282 feet below sea level.

The valley was formed millions of years ago when folding and faulting uplifted the surrounding mountains. During the last ice age large lakes intermittently formed in the basin, depositing layers of clay and silt. Their evaporation left salt deposits that are still visible today.

The valley got its name when a group of gold seekers tried a shortcut across the desert in 1849. Before long a lack of food and water split the panicked band apart. At least one of the travelers died. This image of death is reinforced by other names in the valley like Devil's Golf Course, Hells Gate and Funeral Mountains.

Other human visitors have had better experiences than the ill-fated gold seekers. Native Americans occupied the area for some 9,000 years. Borax was a veritable gold mine for prospectors who built roads to transport it, and twenty-mule teams drew loads of the mineral that were as heavy as 36 tons. Abandoned mine sites and several ghost towns can be found in the park today.

Contrary to the image its name paints, the valley contains 900 species of plants and trees, 21 of which are unique to the valley, including the Panamint daisy, the Death Valley sage and the Death Valley sandpaper plant. Staggering geological formations distinguish the park: sand dune formations, sculpted rocks, isolated valleys and volcanic craters.

Dirt roads and more rugged jeep roads crisscross the area. Bicycling is encouraged in the park, but stay on roads that are open to automobile traffic. Bikes are not allowed on trails or service roads. It's a good idea to check with rangers to find out current road conditions before attempting any rides.

If you don't get enough of a workout exploring the area's dirt roads, you could participate in the Death Valley to Mt. Whitney road race. The two-day event climbs from

Sunrise on Mt. Whitney.

Badwater to Mt. Whitney, the highest point in the contiguous U.S. (Technically the race ends at Whitney Portal, a good 6,000 feet short of the peak.) A foot-race follows a similar course. Although it too officially ends at the portal, tradition dictates that runners continue up a trail to the summit at 14,494 feet.

Getting There: From Los Angeles, take Interstate 5 or Interstate 210 to Highway 14 (north). Stay on Highway 14 until it joins and becomes northbound Highway 395. (From eastern Los Angeles County, take the 15 to Highway 395.) From 395 take Highway 190 to Death Valley. It's about a five-hour drive from Los Angeles.

Stovepipe Wells or Furnace Creek make good bases for exploring the park. There are hotels and other facilities in both spots, including the luxurious Furnace Creek Inn. A Visitor Center is located in Furnace Creek, open year-round. You can pick up a handout there listing suggested mountain bike routes in the park. Stovepipe Wells has its own ranger station. The ranger station across the state line in Beatty, Nevada is open seven days a week from 8 a.m. to 4 p.m.

There are nine camping areas in the monument as well. Reserve through MISTIX. You must bring your own firewood. Some campgrounds are closed at various times of the year, usually because of very hot or very cold weather. You can request a folder, "Camping in Death Valley," from the Visitor Center. The best time to visit is November through April. Winter can be cold, and summer temperatures can reach over 130 degrees. Bring *lots* of water, at least 2 gallons per person per day.

The American Automobile Association (AAA) puts out an excellent map of the area with very good information on the back. It's a good idea to pick up a copy before you go.

95 Titus Canyon

Distance: 26 miles
Difficulty: Strenuous due to length and climbing, mildly technical due to trail surface
Elevation: Begin 3,400', climb to 5,250', descend to 200'
Ride Type: One-way on dirt road; requires car shuttle
Season: November through April
Map: Trails Illustrated Death Valley National Park

Overview: Titus Canyon is the premier off-road ride in Death Valley. This is a one-way road, so you must ride in the direction described (east to west). After crossing desert terrain, the road climbs via steep switchbacks to a crest, then begins a long, gradual descent. Parts of the road are covered

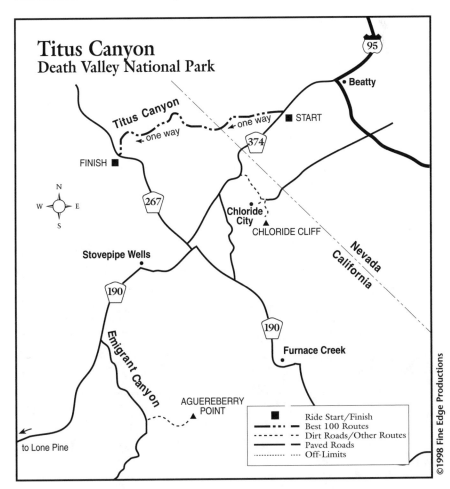

Titus Canyon
Death Valley National Park

Titus Canyon

one way

one way

FINISH ■

• Beatty

■ START

374

267

N
W ← ⊕ → E
S

Chloride
City
CHLORIDE CLIFF ▲

Nevada
California

Stovepipe Wells •

190

190

• Furnace Creek

Emigrant Canyon

AGUEREBERRY
POINT ▲

to Lone Pine

■   Ride Start/Finish
—·—■ Best 100 Routes
------ Dirt Roads/Other Routes
——   Paved Roads
.... Off-Limits

©1998 Fine Edge Productions

with deep gravel—tough and slow going. West of the crest you find the rusting remains of Leadfield. You can pick up a road guide to Titus Canyon at the Visitor Center. The guide describes and explains the remarkable geology of the canyon. Although intended for automobile use, the guide gives mileages and information that are useful to bicyclists as well. *Note: Titus Canyon is closed in summer.*

Getting There: Begin 7 miles east of the Nevada line on the north side of Highway 374. Leave a pick-up vehicle or have someone pick you up at the canyon's terminus 14.3 miles northwest of the junction of Highways 190 and 374 on Highway 267.

Route: Head gradually up the well-graded dirt road. I hope you brought a lot of water with you. You don't want to emulate Morris Titus, a young mining engineer who entered the canyon in search of water and never came back. That's the hard way to get a landform named after you!

At 0.9 mile you pass the road to Rhyolite on your right. One of the more successful mining towns in Death Valley, Rhyolite prospered on gold in the early 1900s. At one time nearly 6,000 people lived in the town, but like many mining communities, it eventually went bust, leaving little but concrete foundations and a gloomy cemetery behind.

As you pedal these first few miles you traverse the Amargosa Valley. The Bullfrog Hills are on your right and the Grapevine Mountains are in front of you. During miles 6-8 you pass many other signs of volcanic activity, including ancient basalt and ash flows.

In the ensuing miles the climbing gets steeper as you pass more fascinating geologic history. The rocks on your left are older rocks, those on your right younger. About 11 miles out you pass Titanothere Canyon and you summit a couple of miles later. Give your legs a rest, the climbing is over! It's a gradual downhill the rest of the way.

At 16 miles you come to the ghost town of Leadfield, one of the shortest-lived towns around—one year during the 1920s. Investors were

Desert vegetation along the Darwin Loop.

fooled by an unscrupulous promoter who tricked them into believing the area was rich in lead ore. The Titus Canyon Road was originally built to bring supplies to the town.

As you descend from Leadfield the canyon steepens and narrows. Twisted rock layers of reddish gray dominate. The last 3 miles are a highlight of the trip as the canyon walls soar to over 500 feet above the canyon floor. These narrows are why only one-way traffic is allowed.

In the final section (two-way) you cross a wide alluvial fan. At 26 miles you're at the junction with the paved highway. Hopefully your car or a friend is here to pick you up.

Be sure to ride in the morning when the sun is at your back!

96 Darwin Loop

Distance: 35.5 miles
Difficulty: A strenuous, technical expedition
Elevation: Starting point: 4,000'; Darwin: 4,746'; highest point: 4,975'
Ride Type: Loop ride on paved road, graded road, and jeep roads
Season: Spring, fall and winter; due to elevated temperatures, riding in summer is not recommended. Occasional flash floods thunder down Darwin Wash, so avoid this ride in unsettled weather.
Maps: Talc City Hills, Darwin

Overview: Pass by the historic Darwin silver mine where dozens of buildings still stand. Huge piles of tailing stand as a testament to the trainloads of silver ore, zinc, lead, and other minerals that were shipped from this once-busy mine. Darwin Canyon contains fantastic rock formations and several mines. An optional side trip to China Springs features goldfish, shady cottonwoods, ruins and mines. Darwin Falls is a

Santa Rosa Flat, north of Darwin Loop (Ride 96).

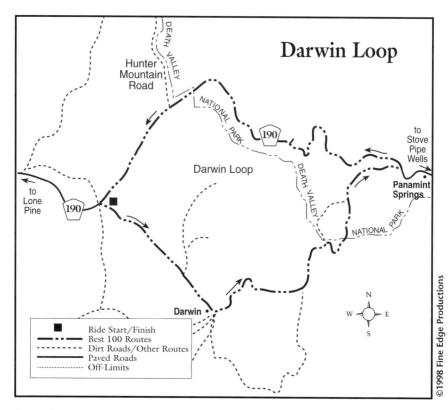

beautiful oasis with diverse plant and bird life, gorgeous rock slabs, and a swimming hole at the base of the falls. Museum (not always open) and water available in Darwin. Carry minimum of 3-4 quarts of water with you.

Getting There: From the Interagency Visitor Center at the south end of Lone Pine, go east on Highway 136. Continue 7 miles to its junction with Highway 190. Go east on Highway 190 for 26 miles to Darwin Road on the right. Park off the road by the historic marker. Please cycle on existing roads.

Route: Start your ride at the junction of Darwin Road and Highway 190. Ride south on the paved Darwin Road up a long, straight incline to an

obvious saddle. Look carefully and you will see an old railroad grade and the ruins of several mines.

At the crest (4,975 feet), you can see down into Darwin Basin with the Coso Range behind it. Drop into the desert basin and enjoy a mild climb. At 5.0 miles you come to the main entrance to Darwin mine. This is *private property.* Please keep out.

The road continues into "downtown" Darwin. The museum is quite interesting when you can gain access. Darwin is home to a number of people, so please remain on the roads and keep off private property.

Your route goes left at the T-intersection. Take a broken pavement road steeply up to a gap in the ridge. At the crest you can see Darwin Canyon and the Coso Mountains. You then

View north of Hunter Mountain, north of Darwin Loop (Ride 96).

continue downhill for three miles, passing mines, ruins, a water pipe, and wrecked cars.

At 9.8 miles the road joins a sandy route in the wash. Go left down the Darwin wash where the rock is fantastic. You pass some mines and a ranch with several water tanks; scraps of wood and metal are scattered everywhere. Continue past two small side canyons as you ride down Darwin Wash. At 12.3 miles, the road climbs a side canyon.

[**Side trip:** A road left leads down the canyon to China Springs from where a stream flows to Darwin Falls. Mileage for this side trip is not included.]

Continue up and out of Darwin Canyon, climbing steeply onto a ridge where, at the crest, you have a great view of Darwin Canyon, the Darwin Hills, and old mines.

The road is steep, stony, and rutted on the downhill section—a technical descent that you may want to walk. There are occasional overlooks

into Darwin Canyon along this section, and the mill and mine near the road are interesting ruins. An old wagon road with handmade stone walls parallels the route.

At the bottom of the downhill, back in Darwin Canyon, a spur road on the left leads to a parking area from where a difficult but fascinating hike of 1.5 miles takes you to Darwin Falls. Although this area seems too remote to worry, lock up your bike before hiking to the falls.

For the main bicycle route, continue on the dirt road 1.5 miles to Highway 190, where you turn left onto the pavement. This fantastic road climbs for several steep miles around endless curves, circling higher and higher and rewarding you with ever-expanding views of Panamint Valley. The colorful rock is strangely shaped, and Joshua trees and cactus dot the landscape. The brutal ascent is offset by the beauty of the mountains, valleys, and canyons. Near the crest of the hard climb, stop at Father

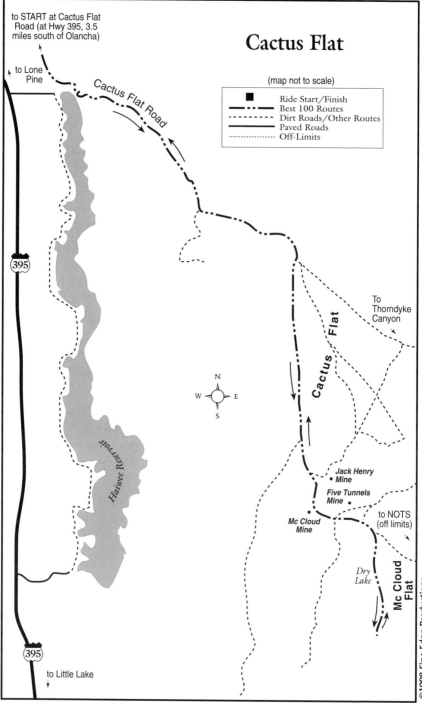

to START at Cactus Flat
Road (at Hwy 395, 3.5
miles south of Olancha)

to Lone
Pine

Cactus Flat Road

Cactus Flat

(map not to scale)

■ Ride Start/Finish
▬ ▪ ▬ ▪ Best 100 Routes
- - - - - Dirt Roads/Other Routes
───── Paved Roads
········· Off-Limits

395

To
Thorndyke
Canyon

Cactus Flat

N
W · E
S

Haiwee Reservoir

Jack Henry
• Mine

Five Tunnels
Mine •

Mc Cloud
Mine

to NOTS
(off limits)

*Dry
Lake*

Mc Cloud
Flat

395

to Little Lake

©1998 Fine Edge Productions

Crowley Overlook to look out over brilliant Rainbow Canyon and Panamint Valley. The overlook honors Father J. J. Crowley, a Jesuit, known in the 1930s and 1940s as the Eastern Sierra's traveling priest.

Past the overlook the road is less steep. The curving road traverses the Darwin Hills and climbs across a high desert basin. You pass Saline Valley Road junction on your right, climb to a crest on Highway 190, and continue downhill to Darwin Junction—a total of 35.5 miles.

Haiwee Reservoir looking south.

97 Upper Mojave Desert: Cactus Flat Ride

Distance: 27.2 miles round trip
Difficulty: Easy to moderate
Elevation: Owens Valley floor 3,700'; Jack Henry Mine 4,800'; McCloud Flat 5,200'
Ride Type: Out-and-back on dirt roads
Season: Year-round, depending on snow conditions or flash floods
Map: Haiwee Reservoirs

Overview: This scenic high desert is surrounded by mountains and beautiful stands of Joshua trees and cactus. Water is not available. Carry several gallons in your vehicle to refill your water bottles. You can find primitive camping at Jack Henry Mine or along the route. *Note:* The area north of Cactus Flat lies within the Coso Wilderness. Please remain on existing roads and do not enter the wilderness.

Getting There: Go 3.5 miles south of Olancha on Highway 395 to Cactus Flat Road (sign on the west side of the highway reads *Butterworth Ranch Rd)*. Turn east onto Cactus Flat Road at the Olancha Highway Maintenance Yard and park at the side of the road.

Route: Begin your ride from the parking spot and head east on the paved road. The pavement ends at 1.4 miles and the road turns to dirt. At 2.6 miles, you pass Haiwee Reservoir and start uphill, heading southeast. At 6.6 miles you reach the top of the hill where you have a view of Cactus Flat. Continue south on the level road among Joshua trees and cholla cactus, ignoring any trails that lead to Thorndike Canyon.

At 9.0 miles, there are roads to the west that lead to a mine on the ridge. A mile later, a side road leads 3.5 miles up a large box canyon to the southwest. (If you feel like adding some mileage, this is an interesting side trip.)

At 10.3 miles, take the fork that heads due east to Jack Henry Mine and a primitive campsite where you can see the foundation and fireplace of an old cabin. This is a good base camp for exploring on foot or by bicycle. [**Option:** From the cabin foundation at Jack Henry Mine you can make a beautiful loop trip leading directly northeast toward Thorndike Canyon on any of three jeep trails that lead down through Joshua trees and eventually rejoin the main road.]

The main road continues southeast toward the McCloud Flat turnoff and, although it is sometimes subject to wash-outs, preventing vehicle passage, you shouldn't have trouble negotiating it. There are excellent views of the high desert and Cactus Flat. At about 11.0 miles, a half-mile walk south up the canyon takes you to the McCloud mine where a rock cabin still stands. (Be cautious of the deep hole here.) Just past the McCloud mine, you can head northeast to the Five Tunnel Mine, then easterly up a beautiful draw. The main road continues east to a dry lake bed and the turnoff to McCloud Flat at 11.6 miles. Go south for about 2 miles to a large area of boulders.

McCloud Flat, one of the most scenic high desert areas you will find, is worth hours of exploration. The valley is entirely surrounded by desert mountains and, although extensive mining was once carried on at its north end, it is now unusually serene.

Note: The Naval Ordinance Training Station (NOTS) lies to the east; entry is prohibited. This is strictly enforced.

Joshua Tree National Park

Two large deserts, the Colorado Desert and the Mojave Desert, meet in Joshua Tree National Park, where they offer a vivid illustration of the differences between the low and high desert.

The Colorado Desert, at elevations under 3,000 feet, occupies the eastern half of the park. The area is dominated by abundant creosote with small stands of spidery ocotillo and jumping cholla cactus (yes, it does jump when in bloom). The western half of the park, the Mojave Desert, is higher and slightly cooler and wetter. This is where you find extensive stands of the park's namesake. In addition, five oases, graced with stately palms,

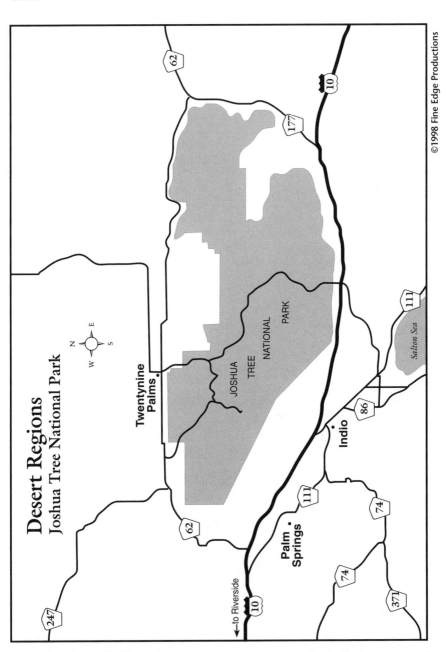

Desert Regions
Joshua Tree National Park

JOSHUA TREE NATIONAL PARK

Twentynine Palms

Salton Sea

Indio

Palm Springs

to Riverside

draw abundant wildlife to their natu-
rally-occurring surface water. In
spring visitors throughout the area are
treated to a brilliant wildflower show.
    Joshua Tree also contains very

interesting geologic displays—rugged
mountains of twisted rock and exposed granite monoliths show the
tremendous earth forces that shaped
the land. In the summer of 1992, a

7.5 earthquake dislodged boulders and sent rocks tumbling throughout the area.

Early morning and evening are the best times to see wildlife because they normally wait out the daytime heat. Coyotes, lizards, jackrabbits, rats, owls and bobcats all inhabit the desert. Keep an eye out for golden eagles and roadrunners as well. Less pleasant creatures—stinkbugs, tarantulas and sidewinders (a kind of rattlesnake)—keep you from getting too careless.

Although the most common human visitor to Joshua Tree these days is of the rock climbing genus, the earliest inhabitant—indeed, one of the earliest inhabitants of the whole Southwest—was Pinto Man, who hunted and gathered here during wetter times. Later, other Native Americans traveled through, following the harvests of pinyon nuts, mesquite beans, acorns and cactus fruit, leaving behind rock paintings and pottery ollas. Some of the rock paintings can still be seen today.

During the 1800s, explorers, cattlemen and miners changed the face of the land, leaving behind Lost Horse and Desert Queen mines among others, and the Desert Queen Ranch. The area is still full of old mine sites. Stay clear of abandoned mine shafts —don't let your curiosity get the best of you. Some of the shafts are hundreds of yards deep. The cattlemen left tanks, small dams constructed to catch rain water.

Today a half-million acres constitute the park, 467,000 of which are wilderness (bikes prohibited). In the remaining areas bikes are limited to paved roads, dirt roads and 4WD roads. All trails, service roads and any roads closed to vehicles are closed to bikes. Off-road bike travel is prohibited—probably a good thing since cactus is not friendly to tires or human flesh.

Getting There: Joshua Tree National Park is 140 miles east of Los Angeles, about a two-and-a-half-hour drive. From the west, take Interstate 10 to Highway 62 (29 Palms Highway) to the park's north

Joshua tree

entrances, one in the town of Joshua Tree, the other in Twentynine Palms. The south entrance is 25 miles east of Indio and can be reached from the east or west by Interstate 10. The north entrances give you access to the western part of the park, while the south entrance accesses the eastern half.

There is a campground, visitor center and picnic area at the south entrance. Mountain biking possibilities here are limited to three dirt roads—Pinkham Canyon Road, Black Eagle Road and Old Dale Road (which turns into Gold Crown Road). These are best done as out-and-back rides. Fashioning a loop would require long rides with much pavement. Paved roads in the park are narrow and offer no shoulder—not the most pleasant riding environment.

Rock formation, Joshua Tree National Park.

I recommend the western half of the park. There is an information station at the west entrance in the town of Joshua Tree, but the main entrance in Twentynine Palms has the Oasis Visitor Center—a good place for maps and brochures.

Once inside the park, head for Hidden Valley Campground, Ryan Campground, Sheep Pass Campground or Jumbo Rocks Campground. These are the most centrally located and provide access to the best riding in the area. Most of the campgrounds have toilets, fire rings and picnic tables, but no showers or water. Bring all the water you will need, and do not underestimate—this is the desert! Rangers recommend at least one gallon per person per day, two gallons per person per day if you're involved in strenuous exercise. Some water is available at Oasis Visitor Center, Indian Cove Ranger Station, Black Rock Canyon and Cottonwood Campgrounds. Also bring firewood and kindling—all of the park's vegetation is protected. Services are available at Joshua Tree or Twentynine Palms. There are several day-use picnic areas, too.

Spring and fall are the best times to visit. Winter can be cold and windy. I was hailed and snowed on one weekend in February. Summer is scorching. Avoid canyons and washes during rainstorms, since flash floods do occur.

98 Barker Dam/Hidden Valley

Distance: 12 miles
Elevation: Route is virtually flat
Difficulty: Easy, not technical
Ride Type: Loop on dirt road and pavement with recommended short hikes
Season: Spring and fall best
Map: Trails Illustrated Joshua Tree National Park

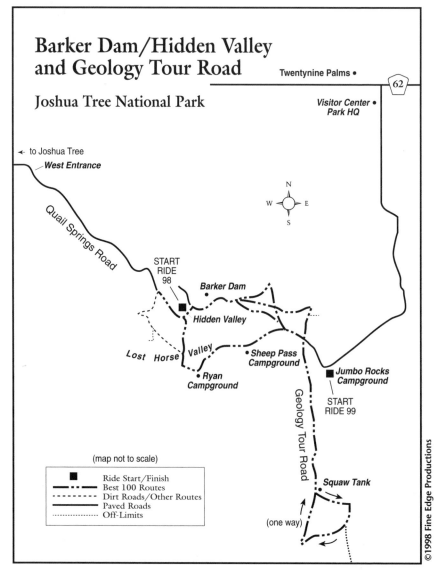

Barker Dam/Hidden Valley
and Geology Tour Road

Joshua Tree National Park

Joshua Tree National Park

Overview: A 13.4-mile network of roads crisscrosses this valley of boulder piles and Joshua trees. Several bike racks have been placed in this area so you can lock your bike and go hiking. What I recommend is a biking/hiking tour that takes you to the area's best sights.

Getting There: From either the western entrance or the main entrance, take Quail Springs Road to Hidden Valley Campground.

Route: Beginning at Hidden Valley Campground, take the dirt road that heads east, following signs to Barker Dam. Continue straight and stay on the main road. At 1.5 miles take the spur on your left and go a quarter mile to the parking area and trailhead.

Lock up your bikes (there's a rack) and hike the 1.1-mile loop trail to Barker Dam. It was built to collect water for the cattle of early ranchers. On the way back to the parking lot, the trail takes you past Native American petroglyphs. These authentic carvings were unfortunately painted over by a film crew in an attempt to make them more visible. Do not touch or disturb any carvings or artifacts in the monument!

Backtrack to the main dirt road and make a left, away from the direction you originally came. At a four-way intersection at just under 3.0 miles you can take your pick of the two open routes. Both eventually lead to paved Quail Springs Road. The right fork is the most direct route. This is typical desert riding—hard pack alternating with washboard sections and sand traps.

When you intersect the paved

road at 5.3 miles, turn right. You are now heading west on bumpy pavement that's mostly downhill.

Stop at Sheep Pass Campground if you like and lock up your bikes. From here you can hike up to Ryan Mountain. The 1.5-mile trail is moderately strenuous as it climbs to 5,461 feet. The trail offers several lookout points with fine views of Queen, Lost Horse, Hidden and Pleasant valleys.

Back on the paved road, you pass Ryan Campground, also on your left, at 9.5 miles. Stay on the main road. Do not take the turnoff to Keys View. Continue back to Hidden Valley Campground. If you have an aversion to pavement, you can return to Hidden Valley on the same dirt road you took out.

Note: You can start this loop from any of the three campgrounds named in the description.

99 Geology Tour Road

Distance: 20.8 miles
Difficulty: Easy-to-moderate, mildly technical
Elevation: Approximately 1,000' loss/gain
Ride Type: Pavement and dirt road loop
Season: Spring and fall best
Map: Trails Illustrated Joshua Tree National Park

Overview: This tour gives you the opportunity to explore some of the California desert's most impressive geologic features. Two highlights are prehistoric Native American rock carvings and a panoramic view at road's end.

Getting There: From either the western entrance or the main entrance, take paved Quail Springs Road to Jumbo Rocks Campground.

Route: Starting at Jumbo Rocks Campground, head west on the paved road. After 2 miles of pedaling, turn south (left) onto a dirt road. This is the 4WD Geology Tour Road. Pick up a road guide at the turnoff.

Traveling through a fascinating landscape, you head into a bumpy, sandy, mostly downhill section. At 7.4 miles you hit Squaw Tank. From here, veer left to take a 6-mile one-way circuit through Pleasant Valley.

Back at Squaw Tank after completing the loop, follow your tread marks back to Jumbo Rocks.

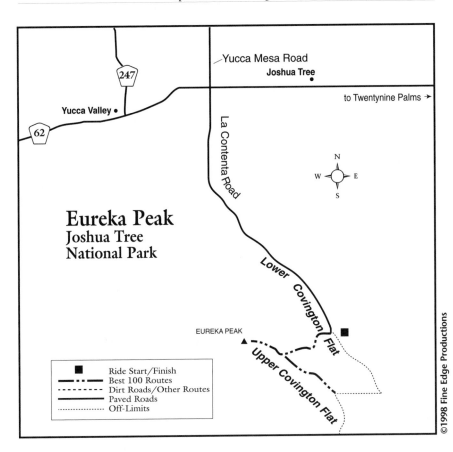

Eureka Peak
Joshua Tree
National Park

EUREKA PEAK

Yucca Mesa Road
Joshua Tree

to Twentynine Palms →

Yucca Valley •

247

62

La Contenta Road

Lower Covington Flat

Upper Covington Flat

N
W   E
S

■   Ride Start/Finish
▬ ▪ ▬ ▪   Best 100 Routes
- - - - -   Dirt Roads/Other Routes
▬▬▬▬   Paved Roads
··········   Off-Limits

©1998 Fine Edge Productions

100 Eureka Peak

Distance: 7.6 miles; 14.1 if you ride to the backcountry board
Difficulty: Moderate, mildly technical
Elevation: High point 5,516'
Ride Type: Out-and-back on dirt roads
Season: Spring and fall best
Map: Trails Illustrated Joshua Tree National Park

Overview: The climb to Eureka Peak (5,516 feet) takes you past some of the lushest vegetation in the monument and to a great view of Palm Springs and the Morongo Basin.

Getting There: From Highway 62, 2.8 miles east of the junction with Highway 247, head south on paved La Contenta Road. After it crosses Yucca Trail/Alta Loma Drive at 3.9

miles, the road turns to dirt. It can get sandy, so call for road conditions, especially after a rain. At 5.8 miles go left at the sign to Covington Flats. Two miles later you pass into the Joshua Tree National Park.

At 9 miles go right at the fork, and at 12 miles go left at a fork toward the picnic area. Park here. The picnic area is undeveloped—there's a picnic table and a port-a-potty, but no water.

Route: Begin the ride by backtracking to the fork and going left. The road climbs gradually through sand, washboard and rock. At 2.1 miles you come to a T. Go right. You get a brief downhill respite here before climbing again. You're close to the end when the road gently switchbacks before coming up on a ridge. From here you have great views in both directions. To your right you

can make out Yucca Valley. At 3.8 miles you reach a parking area with a vista. Take the time to hike up the short trail to the actual peak—it's worth it for the panoramic views.

This area features the largest Joshua trees in the park as well as junipers and pinyon pines. No one knows how the Joshua tree got its name. Some say it was named by Mormons who thought the giant yucca looked like it was raising its branches in prayer. You may be moved to pray or meditate yourself as you take in the surrounding desert.

On the way back, if you want to add mileage you can go straight at the T-intersection and continue to Upper Covington Flats and over to the backcountry board, where there's some good hiking. Going there and back would add 6.5 miles. Otherwise, you can just head back the same way you came.

APPENDIX

About the Authors

Delaine Fragnoli, former editor of *Mountain Biking* magazine, is the author of *Mountain Biking North America's Best 100 Ski Resorts* and co-author of *Mountain Biking Northern California's Best 100 Trails.* She is past editor of *Southwest Cycling* and frequently rides with the Pasadena Mountain Bike Club and the Los Angeles F.O.R.C.E. (Female Off-Road Cycling Enthusiasts). Her free-lance work regularly appears in *Bicycling, Women's Sports & Fitness,* and *VeloNews.*

Don Douglass, one of the founders and the first president of the International Mountain Bicycling Association (IMBA), has written extensively on the need for environmentally-sound and responsible riding habits. He has been inducted into the Mountain Biking Hall of Fame.

Réanne Hemingway-Douglass, editor and free-lance writer, published her first book, *Cape Horn: One Man's Dream, One Woman's Nightmare,* in 1994. She led the first women's cycling team to cross Tierra del Fuego. With her husband Don, she has pioneered many cycling routes in the Eastern Sierra.

Mark Davis is a Mammoth Lakes resident active in the local Mammoth Area Mountain Bike Organization (MAMBO) and in local public land access issues. He is an expert on Eastern Sierra bicycle trails. Mark has hiked the entire Pacific Crest Trail twice and has ridden his bike in all 48 contiguous state.

Jim Hasenauer, a founding member and past president of IMBA, has written and lectured widely on land access matters. Also a founding member and director of CORBA (Concerned Off-Road Bicyclists Association), he sits on a number of trail advisory groups. He is a tenured professor of Communications at Cal State, Northridge, and an active member of the Sierra Club. He currently serves as IMBA's Director of Education.

Mark Langton, an editor of *Mountain Biking* magazine, has been a long-time advocate of sound cycling principles and open trails. His writings document much of mountain biking's present and past history. He is a founding member of CORBA and has been nominated to the Mountain Biking Hall of Fame.

Paul Maag has been a spokesman for the biking community in the Coachella Valley for several years. He has served on numerous task force committees with the BLM and USFS regarding access concerns in the Santa Rosa Mountains. Paul has published a guide book in partnership with the BLM, with profits going to land access.

Mickey McTigue has been a backcountry cyclist since 1958. Active in trail building and maintenance, he leads cycling expeditions in Los Padres National Forest.

Robert Rasmussen, Orange County businessman and avid mountain biker, researched the trails of Cleveland National Forest and presently assists the Orange Country Trails Coalition.

Robert Shipley has cycled extensively for almost 40 years (including in China). He owned and operated a well-known bicycle shop near UC Riverside for a number of years. Currently he consults with USFS and other agencies on bicycle access and safety matters.

Allen Thibault, commercial artist and environmentally-aware cyclist, has been exploring ways to present computer-generated cycling maps.

Mike Troy is a co-founder of the Grapevine Mountain Bike Association, and he regularly performs trail building and maintenance in the Angeles National Forest.

Kevin Woten pioneered many popular routes in the Saugus District of the Los Padres National Forest. He was also a co-founder of the Grapevine Mountain Bike Association and a member of IMBA's south region board of directors.

Agencies, Visitor Centers & Mountain Bike Clubs

Aliso/Wood Canyons
Regional Park
714/831-2174

Andrew Molera State Park
c/o Pfeiffer Big Sur State Park
Big Sur, CA 93920
408/667-2315

Angeles National Forest
Arcadia, CA 91006
626/574-5200

Angeles National Forest
Arroyo Seco Ranger District
Oak Grove Park
Flintridge, CA 91011
818/790-1151

Angeles National Forest
Tujunga District
12371 N. Little Tujunga Canyon Rd.
San Fernando, CA 91342
818/899-1900

Angeles National Forest
Mt. Baldy Ranger District
110 N. Wabash Ave.
Glendora, CA 91740
626/335-1251

Angeles National Forest
Saugus District
30800 Bouquet Canyon Rd.
Saugus, CA 91350
805/296-9710

Angeles National Forest
Valyermo District
34146 Longview Rd.
Pearblossom, CA 93553
805/944-2187

Anza Borrego Desert State Park
760/767-5311
760/767-4684 (wildflower report)

Bishop Chamber of Commerce
& Visitors Center
City Park
690 N. Main
Bishop, CA 93514
760/873-8405

Bureau of Land Management
(BLM)*
Bishop Resource Area
785 N. Main St., Suite E
Bishop, CA 93514
760/872-4881
760/872-2894 (fax)

BLM/Caliente Resource Area
(for Carrizo Plain Natural Area)
4301 Rosedale Highway
Bakersfield, CA 93308
805/861-4236

BLM/Lone Pine-Ridgecrest
Resource Area
760/384-5400

BLM/Palm Springs South Coast
Resource Area
63500 Garnet Ave.
North Palm Springs, CA 92264
760/251-0812

BLM/Ridgecrest
300 South Richmond Rd.
Ridgecrest, CA 93555
760/375-7125

California State Parks
916/653-6995 Touch-Tone Information

Chino Hills State Park
1879 Jackson Street
Riverside, CA 92504
909/780-6222

Cleveland National Forest
10845 Rancho Bernardo Rd.,
Suite 200
San Diego, CA 92127-2107
619/673-6180

Cleveland National Forest
Descanso Ranger District
3348 Alpine Blvd.
Alpine, CA 91901
619/445-6235

Cleveland National Forest
Trabuco Ranger District
1147 E. 6th St.
Corona, CA 91720
909/736-1811

Coachella Valley Cycling
Association
P.O. Box 2355
Rancho Mirage, CA 92270
760/320-7135
760/360-0761

Concerned Central Coast
Mountain Bikers (CCCMB)
Box 16003
San Luis Obispo, CA 93406
805/528-0430
805/756-1284

Concerned Off Road Bicyclists
Association (CORBA)
818/773-3555

Crystal Cove State Park
949/494-3539

Cuyamaca Rancho State Park
12551 Highway 79
Descanso, CA 92016
619/765-0755

Death Valley National Park
Visitor Center
Furnace Creek
760/786-2331

Desert Map Shop
73612 Highway 111
Palm Desert, CA 92260

Eastern Sierra Museum
155 N. Grant
Independence, CA 93526
760-878-0364

Elfin Forest Recreational Reserve
Olivenhain Municipal Water District
1966 Olivenhain Road
Encinitas, CA 92024
619/753-6466

Grapevine Mountain Bike Associa-
tion
42762 Deerwalk Dr.
Lake Elizabeth, CA 93532
805/724-9066

Interagency Visitor Center
Highways 395 and 136
Lone Pine, CA 93545
760/876-6222

International Mountain
Bicycling Association
P.O. Box 7578
Boulder, CO 80306
303/545-9011

Inyo County Parks Information
224 N. Edwards
Independence, CA 93526
760-878-0272

Inyo National Forest
873 N. Main St.
Bishop, CA 93514
760/873-2400

Inyo National Forest
Mt. Whitney Ranger Station
P.O. Box 8
631 S. Main St.
Lone Pine, CA 93545
760/876-6200

Inyo National Forest
White Mountain Ranger Station
& Visitor Center
798 N. Main St.
Bishop, CA 93514
760/873-2500

Joshua Tree National Park
74485 National Park Drive
Twentynine Palms, CA 92277
760/367-7511

Julian Information Center
760/765-0707

Lone Pine Chamber of Commerce
126 S. Main
Lone Pine, CA 93545
760/876-4444

Los Padres National Forest
6144 Calle Real
Goleta, CA 93117
805/683-6711

Los Padres National Forest
Mt. Pinos Ranger District
HCl Box 400
34580 Lockwood Valley Rd.
Frazier Park, CA 93225
805/245-3731

Los Padres National Forest
Ojai Ranger District
1190 E. Ojai Avenue
Ojai, CA 93023
805/646-4348

Los Padres National Forest
Santa Barbara Ranger District
Star Route
Santa Barbara, CA 93105
805/967-3481

Los Padres National Forest
Santa Lucia Ranger District
1616 Carlotti Dr.
Santa Maria, CA 93454
805/925-9538

Los Peñasquitos Canyon Preserve
5201 Ruffin Rd., Suite P
San Diego, CA 92123
619/533-4067

Mission Trails Regional Park
1 Father Junipero Serra Trail
San Diego, CA 92119
619/668-3275
mtrp@tns.net

MISTIX
(Camping Reservations)
800/444-7275
800/365-2267
619/452-1950 (outside CA)

Montaña de Oro State Park
805/528-0513

Monterey County Parks
(for Lake San Antonio)
888/588-CAMP (2267)

Mountain and River Adventures
P.O. Box 858
Kernville, CA 93238
760/376-6553
800/861-6553

Mt. Wilson Bicycling Association
Box 8697
San Marino, CA 91118-8697
626/795-3836

The Nature Conservancy
Carrizo Plain Natural Area
P.O. Box 3098
California Valley, CA 93453

Orange Country Trails Coalition
(OCTC)
6552 Bolsa Ave. #D
Huntington Beach, CA 92647
714/890-3925

Pasadena Mountain Bike Club
347 Sierra Madre Villa Ave.
Pasadena, CA 91107-3141
626/799-8785

San Bernardino National Forest
1824 S. Commercenter Circle
San Bernardino, CA 92408-3430
909/383-5588

San Bernardino National Forest
Arrowhead Ranger District
P.O. Box 7
Rimforest, CA 92378
909/337-2444

San Bernardino National Forest
Big Bear Ranger District
P.O. Box 290
Fawnskin, CA 92333
909/866-3437

San Bernardino National Forest
San Jacinto Ranger District
P.O. Box 518
Idyllwild, CA 92349
909/659-2117

San Diego Mountain Biking Associ-
ation (SDMBA)
Box 881491
San Diego, CA 92168

San Luis Obispo County Visitors
& Conference Bureau
1037 Mill Street
San Luis Obispo, CA 93401
805/541-8000
800/634-1414

Santa Barbara Mountain Bike
Trail Volunteers
225 Valdez Ave.
Goleta, CA 93117
805/683-0371

Santa Monica Mountains National
Recreation Area
(Pt. Mugu State Park, Malibu Creek
State Park, Topanga State Park)
818/597-9192

Sequoia National Forest
900 W. Grand Ave.
Porterville, CA 93257
209/784-1500

Sequoia National Forest
Cannell Meadow Ranger District
P.O. Box 6
Kernville, CA 93238
760/376-3781

Sequoia National Forest
Greenhorn Ranger District
800 Truxton Ave., Room 322
P.O. Box 6129
Bakersfield, CA 93386-6129
805/871-2223

Sequoia National Forest
Hot Springs Ranger District
Route 4, Box 548
California Hot Springs, CA 93207
805/548-6503

Silverwood Lake State
Recreation Area
760/389-2303

Southern Sierra
Fat Tire Association
517 Walnut Dr.
Bakersfield, CA 93305
805/327-0875
805/861-0777

---

*The Bureau of Land Management (BLM) office in Bishop, California, conducts a unique environmental education program in the Eastern Sierra for interested individuals and groups. The program originated about five years ago when the BLM received donated mountain bikes from Dr. Al Farrell, a noted mountain bike philanthropist. Dr. Farrell's support motivated bike industry representatives such as Specialized, GT Bicycles, Bike Nashbar, Rock Shox, Yakima Products, and Fine Edge Productions to support the program. Since then, the BLM has coordinated dozens of educational bike trips for organizations, academic institutions, and interested parties. With this approach, the BLM has successfully used mountain bikes as a way to connect others to our environment. For further information on this program, contact the BLM at 760-872-4881.

Basic Skills for Mountain Biking

by R. W. Miskimins

Everybody knows how to ride a bike—at least almost everybody can ride around the neighborhood. If you learned to ride as a youngster, balancing comes very naturally. You can keep the bike upright without even thinking about it. In reality, riding any distance in a straight line requires a relatively complex series of "corrections," most of which are almost imperceptible; corrections that for most people are a subconscious interaction of little cues from the bike and little muscle movements in response. Once you learned how to move straight ahead on a bike, most likely you learned next how to stop. Finally, you had to learn how to turn. At very slow speeds on a kid's bicycle, you could just turn the handle bars to point the front wheel in the direction you wanted to go. With age, bigger bikes, and increased speed, bicycle riders discover that they can change direction simply by leaning right or left. Very aggressive, high-speed cornering requires both turning the handlebars and leaning.

With the advent of the mountain bike, riding a two-wheel, pedal-powered machine has gotten more complicated. Watch a pro-level race and the need for "technical skills" will become obvious—there's a lot more to it when the surface under your tires is no longer smooth pavement. Off-road riding gives a new meaning to balancing, stopping and turning. Can you handle steep hills, big rocks, creeks, muddy bogs, loose sand, tree roots, deep gravel, sharp turns or radical washboards? These are the kinds of factors that differentiate mountain biking from street riding and demand balance and skills above and beyond those required to ride around the neighborhood. Practice is the key to acquiring the necessary abilities for cycling off-road—start easy and work diligently until you achieve a comfortable level of control of your bike, a level of control suited to the level of riding you intend to do.

1. BICYCLE

Your performance on a mountain bike can be dramatically affected by the bicycle you choose to ride. All mountain bikes are not created equal! Some bicycles marketed as "off-road ready" would do better to stay on the pavement. They have too much weight, are too long or too short (wheel base), have ineffective braking or shifting systems or poorly welded frames, are equipped with too-smooth tires, and so on. As a general rule, the mountain bicycles marketed by the discount store chains, department stores, and sporting goods stores are only suited to on-road, non-aggressive, non-abusive use. Bicycles from bike shops, excepting their least-expensive models, are usually designed and built for heavy duty, skilled off-road use—hence, the higher prices.

Mountain bikes, if they are to be used hard, should be relatively light (under 30 pounds), have a fairly short wheel base and chain stay (for agility), moderately steep head angle (again for agility), strong and dependable braking and shifting systems, well-made frames, and knobby/aggressive tires. There exist many subtleties in bicycle design (the shape and angles of the frame. The

Tony Quiroz

"geometry" affects both handling and comfort. In addition, the last decade has generated bikes with more specialized function such as either front or front-and-rear suspension (shock absorbers). Most bike store bikes over $500 now come with a front shock fork—it will improve both comfort (reduces jarring to the arms and shoulders) and keeps your front wheel from bouncing up and down on rough terrain, aiding both steering and balance. For cyclists who love the adrenaline rushes from high-speed downhilling, a bike with suspension front and rear is an amazing machine. For details on choosing the right bike for you and the kind of riding you intend to do, consult with the experts at your local bike shop. They can help you not only with selecting a bicycle, but also with various important secondary decisions such as suspension forks, bar ends, clipless pedals, gear ratio changes and, most critically, size.

Whatever bike you decide on, make sure you get the correct size. This is extremely important. Bicycle size will dramatically affect both handling and comfort. Most manufacturers of bike store bicycles offer four to six different sizes, usually represented by varying heights (14", 16", 18", 20", and 22" are common sizes). As a bike gets taller, its wheel base also increases. If a bicycle is much too big for you, you will never be able to properly handle it no matter how hard you try. If a bicycle is much too small, it can create a very uncomfortable riding position and feel very "twitchy" when put to aggressive cornering or downhilling. A general rule of thumb is: a rider standing flatfooted on the floor, straddling the top tube of a bike, should have 2 to 4 inches of clearance, crotch to bike. If you find yourself in-between sizes and plan to do serious off-road riding, opt for the smaller bike; when comfort is the primary concern, choose the larger size. Again, for assistance in this important aspect of bicycle selection, consult your local bike shop.

Once you choose the type and size of mountain bike that suits you, it's time for fine tuning. Occasionally, a rider's very short or very long torso will require a shorter or longer stem to get the proper "cockpit" length, but fine tuning is mostly done with the saddle. Most saddles can be adjusted for tilt and moved forward and back as well as raised and lowered. The tilt of your saddle affects how it impacts your bottom and can change your fore-and-aft balance on the bike. For example, if it is tilted down in the front, it throws your weight forward, straining your hands, wrists and arms. Saddles that are tilted up in the front tend to take the weight off your buttocks and put undue pressure forward onto the crotch. Forward and back adjustment affects the cockpit length and the centering of weight over the pedals. If you change your weight placement significantly by fore-and-aft saddle movement, it may affect the bike's stability when not on level ground.

For general cross-country riding, set your saddle height so that, when the pedal is in its lowest position, your knee is still slightly bent—this will give you maximum power without straining your knees or causing your hips to rock when pedaling. When you find the right height, mark the seatpost just above where it goes into the seat tube (bicycle frame), so if it is moved (for example, lowered for a tough downhill section of the trail), you can later return it to its optimal position. A saddle in the correct position for aggressive mountain biking is usually 2 or 3 inches higher than the handlebars. For riders using rise handlebars to emphasize either downhill riding or comfort, that measurement should be between 0 and 1 inch.

2. FUNDAMENTAL PRINCIPLES

There are some very general rules for off-road riding that apply all the time. The first—ride in control—is basic to everything else. Balance is the key to keeping your bike upright. When you get out of control, you may lose your ability to balance the bike and crash. Imagine a situation where a series of quick turns on loose sand among breadbox-sized rocks is required while you are flying downhill at over 30 miles per hour. This scenario foretells a nasty ending. Control is directly related to speed, and excessive speed for the conditions you are facing is the usual precursor to loss of control. When in doubt, slow down!

The second principle for off-road riding—read the trail ahead—is sometimes called "scanning." In order to have time to react to changes in the trail surface and obstacles, you should repeatedly scan the space from directly in front of your bicycle out about 10 to 15 feet. As your speed increases, you should read the trail out in front still farther ahead. You want to avoid being surprised by hazardous trail features such as rocks, logs, roots, ruts, water, holes, blind corners, and so on. If you see them well ahead, you can pick a line to miss them, slow down to negotiate them, or even stop and get off your bike and walk over or around them. The cyclist whose entire focus is immediately in front of his or her front wheel is going to wind up upside-down in rough terrain.

The third principle is to stay easy on the grips. One of the most common reactions by novices on difficult terrain is to tense up severely, most noticeably with a "death grip" on the handlebars. This level of tightness leads not only to hand, arm and shoulder discomfort, but markedly interferes with fluid, supple handling of the bike. If your current speed in current conditions frightens you, slow up! You want to keep enough pressure to maintain control. Hold the handlebar grips loosely and bend at the elbows a bit—don't fight your bicycle, work with it!

The last general principle is plan your shifting. If you are scanning the trail ahead, there should be no shifting surprises. Anticipate the need for lower gears. Downshift before or during your slowdown for negotiating technical sections of trail. Plan ahead when approaching hills, especially very steep ascents, and shift before your drive train comes under a strong pedaling load. Shifting under tremendous pressure puts extreme strain on your bicycle's drive train, especially the chain. Snap one chain as you are hammering the pedals; it will provide a hard lesson in shifting skills.

A general rule of thumb, even on flat ground, is to moderate your pedal pressure (ease up, just turn the gears without much powering of the rear wheel) during any shifting. A second general principle for using bicycle gears is to avoid chain crosses (extremely angled chain line). Not all of today's mountain bikes with 21 to 24 speeds offer 21 or 24 different gear ratios. Beginners who try to start in the lowest possible gear and then shift 20 or 23 times to progress through all the options (created by the three chain rings in the front and 7 or 8 cogs in the back) soon learn that there are overlaps/duplications in gear ratios. Avoid the situation wherein you have the lowest gear in the front (little chain ring) and the highest gear in the back (smallest cog) or vice versa. Essentially the same gear ratios can be achieved using the middle chain ring up front, with a much-less-angled chain line. Chain crosses create undue wear on the chain and all the gears involved. The problem is often audible, creating chain "rattle" or grinding sounds. Chain crosses also increase the probability of throwing the chain, especially as you shift. Develop the habit of using the middle ring up front with all seven or eight rear gears (a sharply-angled chain line is impossible with the use of the middle chain ring). When you "run out of gears" as you downshift or upshift, switch the front to either the smallest ring (for more lower gears) or the big ring (for higher gears). As soon as you finish your hard climb or high-speed run, shift the front back to the middle and leave it there until the next time you run out of gears. Cyclists who always leave the front in either the smallest or the biggest rings are most likely to chain cross. Mountain bikes have a lot of gears and their proper use will make any excursion easier and more enjoyable.

3. CLIMBING

Mountain bikes were originally single-speed, balloon-tired cruisers taken by truck or car to the top of a hill and used for an exciting and rapid descent. After a few years, some inventive rider suggested transplanting gears from road-racing bicycles to eliminate the necessity of a motor vehicle shuttle. Gears allowed these cruisers to be ridden slowly up the same steep hill they intended to descend at mach speed. Over the past decade, off-road bikes have been produced with lower and lower gears, so that strong riders now have difficulty finding hills they can't climb. If a hill has to be walked, usually it is because it is not only very steep but it is also very technical, most often with a very loose surface that makes traction difficult.

Climbing takes considerably more energy than riding along flat ground at the same speed, all other conditions (wind, trail surface, and so on) being equal. Some bicycles with rear suspension can make the job even harder as some of your pedaling energy is lost to "pogoing" (the bouncing up and down of the rear of the bike). One of the keys to long, difficult ascents is attitude—it's a mental thing. You need to be able to accept an extended, aerobic challenge with thoughts like "I can do it" and "this is fun." Use some visualization; imagine making it all the way to the top; see yourself cresting the hill.

Your bike is made with hill climbing in mind. Find a gear and a pace that is tolerable, not anaerobic, and try to maintain it. Pick a line ahead, stay relaxed, and anticipate shifting, as noted earlier. If the hill is very long, don't look to the top—focus on the trail in front of you. In addition, be alert to problems in weight distribution that occur when climbing. It is best to stay seated, keeping your weight solidly over the traction (rear) wheel if possible. However, if the slope is so steep that the front wheel lifts off the ground, you will have to lean forward and slide toward the front of the saddle. If you come upon an obstacle that you must ride over, re-center your weight and pedal the rear wheel over it. Constant attention to weight distribution will give you optimum traction and balance for a climb. When there is good traction, and obstacles are not a problem, you can get off the seat and stand on the pedals for a change of position and more speed. Off-the-saddle, aggressive pedaling, swaying from side to side, is called "honking;" most cyclists cannot sustain this high-energy riding style for long.

For long climbs, make certain that your saddle height is positioned so that, when your foot is at the bottom of a pedal stroke, your knee is only very slightly bent. A saddle too low or too high will significantly reduce both power and control on a steep, difficult climb. Finally, many mountain bikers feel that climbs are aided by attaching bar ends (perpendicular 4- to 8-inch long attachments) to their handlebars. Not only do they afford alternate grip positions to minimize hand and arm fatigue, but "pulling" on them opens your chest for easier breathing.

One of the difficulties mountain bikers routinely face is restarting after being forced to dismount during a climb. It is difficult to get initial forward momentum up a steep hill. If the track is wide enough, start off at an angle to lessen the grade. If your balance is good and a boulder, log or some other immovable object is handy, you can back your rear wheel into it before starting to prevent rolling backward as you mount up. Lock up the rear brake and position the pedal under your stronger leg at the top, ready for a downstroke, with the other foot planted firmly on the ground. Stand up on the pedal, simultaneously releasing the brake and pushing off with the other foot. Without an obstacle to hold you on a restart, resuming your riding is done exactly the same way, but it is more difficult. For all uphill restarts, you will find that you exhaust your power stroke (the initial downstroke) very quickly. It requires practice to get your push-off foot up from the ground and onto the pedal in time for the second stroke. If you ride with toeclips or clipless pedals, don't worry about getting clipped in—just make the stroke any way you can to maintain momentum. Clip in later, after you are comfortably in progress. No matter how you get restarted uphill, you must maintain good traction with the rear wheel. Keep just enough weight on the front wheel to graze the surface of the trail; just enough to allow you to steer. Uphill restarts on steep grades are tricky maneuvers. Novice riders should practice them on non-technical terrain to gain proficiency.

4. DESCENDING

This is where most serious mountain-biking accidents occur, primarily because a downhill lends itself to high speed. It is unquestionably the most exciting part of off-road riding—expert riders reach speeds well over 50 mph! For descents, the "stay in control" and "read the trail ahead" principles can be injury-saving. Know your ability and don't exceed it. Be certain your brakes are in excellent working order—don't believe the slogan "brakes are for sissies." On steep and difficult downhills, everyone has to use them. If you have any doubt about the ability of your brakes to perform properly, have them checked out at your local bike shop.

A general principle in braking: When you need only a little slowing, gently apply just the rear brake. However, if you need a significant increase in stopping power, you will have to use both front and rear. Another principle of bicycle braking: When you intend to use both, apply the rear brake before the front. This is most important in fast, steep descents where using the front brake first can cause you to "endo" (an ugly crash where you catapult forward over the handlebars). On modest descents, emphasis on the front brake will not lead to an endo but can cause steering problems. It is recommended that, whenever possible, use your brakes in spurts rather than "dragging" them. Extended application of the brakes will lead to overheating of the brake pads and rim, and to decreased performance. Mostly, mountain bike brakes are used to slow the bike down, not stop on a dime. Finally, be aware that if the rims and brake pads become wet, slowing is often the best they can do—you won't get the same performance you've come to expect when the brakes are clean and dry.

As was the case for steep uphills, steep descents require attention to weight distribution. Many riders lower their saddles an inch or two prior to descending to get a lower center of gravity and a more stable riding platform. All cyclists quickly learn to lift their weight slightly off the saddle and shift back a few inches to keep traction and to avoid the feeling of being on the verge of flying over the handlebars. Practice this weight transfer on smooth but steep downhills so later you can do it comfortably on obstacle-laden terrain. If it's extremely steep, position your rear clear back over the rear wheel. When braking, use both front and rear and avoid locking them up (except for an emergency stop). If you ever find yourself in the situation of having to use only the front brake due to rear brake failure, lock your arms to maintain steering and be certain your weight is on the back of the saddle.

It is possible to go too slow on a difficult downhill, so slow you can't "blast" over obstacles. Instead, because of lack of momentum, hazards can bring you to an abrupt stop or twist your front wheel; both of these can cause loss of control. Riders with suspension find that their bikes will absorb a remarkable amount of tough terrain. They can just ride over a large share of the obstacles they encounter on descents. Experience and practice will help you find that optimum speed, the pace that will allow you to maintain control but go fast enough over rough terrain.

5. TURNING

A particularly treacherous time for mountain bikers is high-speed or obstacle-laden cornering. A basic principle is: Don't enter a curve too fast. At higher speed, your bicycle wants to go straight ahead—this can be catastrophic when the trail doesn't. Turns often contain loose dirt and debris created by all the mountain bikes that preceded you. The optimal cornering model: Slow down as you approach a turn, evenly power through it, then accelerate out of it. Lean around the turn as smoothly as possible, always keeping an eye out for obstacles. As the corners get sharper, it is common for the rear wheel to skid. To take the fright out of that phenomenon, go find a gentle turn with soft dirt and practice skidding a few times to learn how you and your bike respond. Generally, you should keep skidding to a minimum when mountain biking. From an environmental perspective, it tears up the surface of the trail. From your bike's point of view, if you create a lot of lateral pressure on your wheels from sideways or angled sliding, you run a high risk of bending them.

6. OBSTACLES

If you get into the real spirit of off-road cycling, you will not ride just on smooth, groomed trails. You will encounter rocks, roots, limbs, logs, trenches, ruts, washboards, loose sand (or dirt or gravel), and water in a variety of forms from snow and ice to mud bogs to free-flowing springs and creeks. Obviously, the easiest means for handling an obstacle is to go around it; however, you can't always do that.

For raised obstacles (and narrow ruts), those you need to get up and over, you need to learn to "pop" the front wheel. To practice this, find a low curb or set out a 4x4 piece of lumber. Approach it and, just before the front wheel impacts it, rapidly push down then pull up the front wheel. The wheel lift is enhanced if you simultaneously lower and raise your torso and apply a hard pedal stroke. Most novices find that they can learn very quickly to pop the wheel 3 or 4 inches into the air; for most recreational cyclists, that distance is sufficient. After your front wheel clears the obstacle, shift your weight up and forward a little so the rear wheel can bounce over it lightly. This final step— "unloading" your weight from the rear wheel—is often overlooked by cyclists, and can result in high-impact shots to your rear rim which in turn can create unrepairable flat spots. Advanced riders, when encountering extreme conditions, can make some obstacles easier to negotiate by "hopping" the entire bike (popping both wheels at once) over them. Proper use of this technique minimizes the possibility of slamming the rear wheel into an obstacle. Depending upon the rock or log that confronts you on the trail, sometimes the best maneuver is to dismount and walk over or around it. As obstacles become larger or the trail less flat or less straight, maintaining balance while clearing them becomes harder. Obstacles on hills, turns, loose surface, and so on, should be approached cautiously. The tougher the challenge, the greater the chance of a nasty crash.

There are trail conditions that present numerous, closely-spaced obstacles, creating a washboard. You can't jump over all of them, so you must either ride through repeated bumping and constant vibration, or get off and walk. If the washboard doesn't create a safety hazard, stay on your bike and keep pedaling. Except for those riders with front and rear suspension on their bikes, the key to relatively-painless negotiating is to maintain a moderate speed and get into a shock-absorbing posture—slightly up and off the saddle, knees slightly bent, elbows slightly bent, loose grip on the handlebars (especially if you don't have a suspension fork); stay relaxed. You will get through the washboard faster and you won't feel so much like you're getting beaten up doing it.

Very common to many mountain biking trails are sections of loose surface material (sand, decomposed granite, gravel, and so on). Many cyclists, fearing loss of balance, abandon their bikes too soon when plowing into the loose stuff. Go slower, but not extremely slow, and "power through." Shift your weight back just a little to ensure traction, then keep your bike straight and keep pedaling. Maintaining momentum and a straight line is also important in mud holes; be certain to do any shifting you need to do prior to soft spots or bogs or you may lose momentum. Sharp turns can present a particular problem because you are more prone to losing the rear wheel to a slide-out, so be extra cautious when the trail surface is loose, If you ride a lot of loose surface trails, you can make it a little easier by having aggressive knobbies with a large "paddlewheel" tread on your rear tire.

Another type of obstacle often encountered when mountain biking is rideable ruts or trenches. Very small ones can be crossed by lifting the front wheel or flying completely over them, depending on their width. With a little practice, many of the wider ones can be ridden through. First, if possible, go through at an angle to make the up-and-down as gradual as possible. As you head steeply down into the rut, your weight must be back far enough to avoid flying over the handlebars (as for any steep descent). Just before you reach the lowest point, transfer your weight even further back so the front wheel gets "unloaded" of your weight. This weight shift is done to avoid the sudden stop that comes from bogging down the front wheel in the bottom of the rut or from slamming it into the abrupt uphill ahead. As your front wheel starts uphill, rapidly transfer your weight forward as you climb out—find that balance between good traction and "popping wheelies" with your front wheel. Like all mountain biking skills, it takes some experience and practice to learn what ruts to ride over, what ruts to ride through and, most important, what ruts are unrideable.

Going through water can be a lot of fun or it can be a rude awakening if you end upside-down in a creek or puddle on a cold February afternoon. Before any attempt to cross a waterway, stop and examine it first. Make sure it isn't so deep that it will stop you abruptly, then find the route that has the least obstacles. Look for deep holes, big rocks, and deep sand. Approach the crossing at a fairly low speed and, much like dealing with a loose trail surface, plan on pedaling through it (rather than coasting) for maximum traction and control. Slow down as you approach the water, then power through it. Most stream- and lake-edge beds feel like loose sand or gravel. Be aware of the potential for harmful effects that riding through water can have on your bearings, if they are not sealed, and on exposed moving parts. Plan on lubricating your chain, derailleurs, inner wires, and so on when you return home.

Ice or snow create unique problems for the mountain biker. As much as possible, stay away from ice. The effects of ice when riding a bicycle can be very unpredictable; almost always your braking and cornering are compromised. Ice feels a lot like pavement when you lose control and crash. Snow riding can be fun, but if it's deep, it can be very laborious. Maintaining momentum and avoiding buried obstacles are the two major tasks for snow riders. The difficulty of steep ascents and descents and cornering are significantly magnified by a few inches of snow. Most cyclists riding on snow prefer flat or nearly-flat terrain and don't plan high-mileage rides.

The Care & Feeding of a Mountain Bike

by R. W. Miskimins

ROUTINE CHECKUPS FOR YOUR BICYCLE

The key to years of fun and fitness from your mountain bike is giving it check-ups on a regular basis. You need to know how to clean it, lubricate a few places, make simple adjustments, and recognize when something needs expert attention. For the average rider, most bike shops recommend tuneups once a year and complete overhauls every two to three years. All of the maintenance in between your trips to the bike shop you can do yourself. Given below is a nine-step checkup procedure—a list to run through after every extensive ride—before you head back out into the hills again.

1. CLEANUP

Unless the frame is really filthy, use a soft rag and a non-corrosive wax/polish such as Pledge to wipe off the grime and bring the old shine back. If you need to use water or soap and water prior to the polish, don't high-pressure spray directly at any of the bearing areas (pedals, hubs, bottom bracket or head set). You should clean all your components, too (including the chain and the rear cogs), but use a different rag and a lubricant such as Tri-Flow or Finish Line for wiping them down. Do not use polish or lubricants to clean your rims—an oily film will reduce your braking ability. Instead, wipe off the rims with a clean dry rag. If you need to remove rubber deposits from the sidewalls of the rims use acetone as a solvent.

2. INSPECTION

After you get the grit and grime off, check out the frame very carefully, looking for bulges or cracks. If there are chips or scratches that expose bare metal (especially when the metal is steel), use automotive or bicycle touch-up paint to cover them up. Your inspection should also include the components. Look for broken, bent or otherwise visibly damaged parts. Pay special attention to the wheels. When you spin them, watch the rim where it passes the brake pads. Look for wobbles and hops, and if there is a lot of movement, the wheel needs to be trued at home (or take it to a bike shop) before using it. Look for loose or broken spokes. And finally, carefully check your tires for sidewall damage, heavy tread wear, cuts and bulges, glass and nails, thorns, or whatever.

3. BRAKES

Grab the brakes and make sure they don't feel mushy and that the pads are contacting the rim firmly (be certain the brake pads do not rub against the tires!). If the brakes don't feel firm, there are barrel adjusters at one or both ends of the wire cables that control the brakes—turn them counterclockwise to take up some of the slack. If you are unsure as to the dependability of your brakes, for safety's sake let a bike shop check them.

4. BEARING AREAS

Most cyclists depend upon professional mechanics to fix any problems in the pedals, hubs, bottom bracket or head set, but they should be able to recognize when something is wrong. Spin the wheels, spin the crankarms (and the pedals) and move the handlebars from side to side. If you feel notches or grittiness, or if you hear snapping, grating or clicking noises, you have a problem. Check to make sure each of the four areas is properly tightened. To check for looseness, try to wiggle a crankarm side to side or try to move a wheel side to side. Check your headset adjustment by holding the front brake, rocking the bike forward and backward, and listening for clunking sounds.

5. SHIFTING

Presuming your bike has gears, check to make sure you can use all of them. The most common problem is the stretching of the inner wire that operates the rear derailleur. If your bike is not shifting properly, try turning the barrel adjuster, located where the cable comes out of the derailleur. Turn it just a little; usually a counterclockwise direction is what you need. Unless you know what you are doing, avoid turning the little adjustment screws on the derailleurs.

6. NUTS AND BOLTS

Make sure the nuts and bolts which hold everything together are tight. The handlebars and stem should not move around under pressure, and neither should your saddle. And make certain that the axle nuts or quick-releases that hold your wheels are fully secure—when a wheel falls off, the result is almost always crashtime. If you have quick-release hubs, they operate as follows: Mostly tighten them by holding the nut and winding the lever, but finish the job by swinging the lever over like a clamp (it's spring-loaded). Do not wind them up super tight as you would with a wingnut—for safe operation they must be clamped, and clamped very securely, with considerable spring tension! If you are at all uncertain regarding the use of quick-releases, go by a bike shop and ask for a demonstration.

7. ACCESSORIES

Make sure all your accessories, from water bottles to bags to pumps to lights, are operational and secure. Systematically check them all out and if you carry flat-fixing or other on-the-road repair materials or tools, make sure you've got what you need and you know how to use what you carry. Statistics show that over 90% of all bicycle breakdowns are the result of flat tires, so it is recommended that you carry a pump, a spare tube, a patch kit, and a couple of tire levers with you whenever you ride.

8. LUBRICATION

The key to long-term mechanical happiness for you and your bike is proper and frequent lubrication. The most important area of lubrication is the chain—spray it with a Teflon-based or other synthetic oil (WD-40, household oil, and motor oil are not recommended), then wipe off all the excess. You can use the same lubricant for very sparsely coating the moving parts of your brakes and derailleurs.

9. INFLATION

You now are ready for the last step. Improper inflation can lead to blowouts or pinch flats. Read the side of your tires to see what the recommended pressure is and fill them up. If there is a range of pressures given, use the high figure for street cycling, the low figure or near it for off-road riding.

After going through these nine steps of getting your bike ready you've earned another good long ride!

Roadside Repairs

by R. W. Miskimins

Cyclists who take a little time to prepare for equipment failure before riding will get the most enjoyment out of their bicycle. Although there are dozens of things that can go wrong on a ride, especially if you crash, most of them happen so rarely that it doesn't make a lot of sense to worry about them. The chance that you will need to replace a bent axle or replace a wheel with a dozen broken spokes or tighten the lock ring on your cassette (rear sprockets) or replace a defective shift lever is always there, but thankfully these are not the common trailside problems. In these kinds of difficulties, most cyclists ride, carry or coast the bike back to their car and head for a bike shop.

It has been written that more than 95% of all trailside or roadside repairs involve either fixing flats or simply tightening something that has rattled loose. With this in mind, consider the following as insurance against long walks home.

PRE-RIDE PROTECTION

Bicycles arrive from the factory with regular tubes and no added protection to cut down on the possibility of flats. There are three different approaches to minimizing the possibility of air loss while riding your bicycle. The most popular over the years has been "thorn resistant" tubes (they used to be called "thorn proof"). They do help, but are not very effective against much of what might create problems for you. Two more effective products are tire liners (plastic or Kevlar and plastic strips that go inside the tire between the tire and the tube) and sealants (goo that goes inside the tube and seals the holes that thorns, staples, and so on make). Some cyclists employ two and sometimes three of these measures to minimize flat tires. Bear in mind that each of them adds a significant amount of weight to your bike, so it is best to select one and hope for the best. Short of using solid, airless tubes (which is not recommended), nothing is foolproof. Always be prepared to fix flats.

BICYCLE BAGS

Whatever you choose to carry in the form of tools and spare parts will require a comfortable means to haul them. Although you could carry what you need in a fanny pack or backpack or even in your pockets, the most popular kinds of bike bags are those that fit under the rear of your saddle (underseat bags). They do not interfere with mounting or dismounting or handling, and they carry a remarkable amount of gear. The best ones have some form of plastic clips, rather than just straps, to attach them to the bike. The extremely small ones are best suited to racing since they carry very little. The extremely big ones are best suited to slow, nonaggressive riding; they tend to bounce around on rough terrain and, when full, add too much weight. Other forms of bags include the frame pack, which doubles as a shoulder strap when carrying your bike; handlebar bags, which are suitable when off-road handling is not an issue; and bags that attach to racks (either on top or hanging down alongside the wheel), most often used for long-distance touring.

REPAIR KIT

Once you have chosen a bag for your bike, consider the following as essentials to pack: a spare tube (whenever possible, put patches on punctured tubes at home rather than in the outback), a patch kit to cover you if you get more than one flat on an outing, tire levers (plastic tools for getting the tire off and back on the wheel), and a set of Allen wrenches—especially 4mm, 5mm and 6mm—to tighten up loose stem, saddle, handlebar, shifters, and so on. Before you go riding, be certain that you know how to take your wheels on and off and how to replace a bad tube. A lot of people carry the right repair materials but don't know how to use them.

These suggestions will take care of a remarkable number of trail/road repairs. At many shops this is all that is recommended for the typical cyclist to carry. There are a few other tools, however, that some cyclists—especially mountain bikers who ride far from civilization—like to carry. Again, if you bring these tools along, be sure they will work for your specific bike and that you know how to use them.

Consider the following: crescent wrench (needed if both your wheels are not quick release), chain tool to repair damage to the chain by taking out a link or two, spoke wrench for straightening slightly bent wheels, crank wrench for tightening loose crankarms, small screwdriver for derailleur adjustments, cone wrench for tightening loose hubs, or socket wrenches (8mm, 9mm, or 10mm) to use for brake adjustments and the like. In addition, some long-distance cyclists carry spare parts such as cables, brake pads, and a rag to wipe their hands.

BICYCLE PUMPS

Since flat tires are the primary problem for cyclists, a pump becomes important. It doesn't do any good to replace a punctured tube with a new one if you cannot inflate it. There are basically three kinds of bicycle pumps.

Floor pumps are generally too awkward to carry on a ride; since they pump high volumes of air and fill tires rapidly, they are perfect for home and shop use.

For many years, most cyclists have carried frame-fit pumps on their bikes for emergency use. With the proper size, they can be squeeze-fit on to a bicycle frame with no additional hardware needed. However, if you use a frame-fit pump on a mountain bike and you like to ride rough terrain, consider a secondary velcro tie or something similar to ensure that the pump doesn't fly off the bike as you negotiate bumps. Also, consider placing the frame-fit pump behind your seat tube, rather than in the usual position below the top tube, so it is not in the way if you need to carry your bike.

Mini-pumps, the third type, have become most popular for mountain bikers over the past few years. They are very small and can fit into out-of-the-way places on your bike, such as alongside a water bottle cage. This requires special hardware but is a tidy application. The down side to these pumps is that they move very small volumes of air at a time. Many of them now are "double shot," meaning they move air when both pushed and pulled. Since pumps are for emergencies, inflating a tube beats hours of walking, no matter what size your pump.

Finally, be aware that there are two different kinds of valve stems on bicycles now. The "regular" ones, like those on cars, are called Schrader valves. The skinny metal ones are Presta or French valves, and they require that you first unscrew the little gadget on the top before applying a pump. All the standard pumps can be altered now to work for either type of valve. Also available at a very nominal cost are adaptors that allow you to use Presta valves at a regular gas station pump connection.

Below is a checklist for the most basic, inexpensive roadside repairs:

☐ tire liners   ☐ patch kit   ☐ mini pump

☐ underseat bag   ☐ tire levers   ☐ Allen wrenches

☐ spare tube   ☐ Presta adaptor *(if needed for your bike)*

Recommended Reading

Cycling

Friel, Joe, *The Cyclist's Training Bible*. Velo Press, 1996.

Nealy, William, *Mountain Bike! A Manual of Beginning to Advanced Technique*. Birmingham: Menasha Ridge Press, 1992.

Nealy, William, *The Mountain Bike Way of Knowledge*. Birmingham: Menasha Ridge Press, 1989.

Skillbeck, Paul, *Singletrack Mind*. Velo Press, 1996.

Smith, Jill, *The Mountain Bikers' Cookbook*. Velo Press, 1997.

Stuart, Robin and Cathy Jensen, *Mountain Biking for Women*. Waverly, New York: Acorn Publishing, 1994.

Zinn, Leonard, *Zinn and the Art of Mountain Bike Maintenance*. Velo Press, 1996

Backcountry Travel and First Aid

Graydon, Don, ed., *Mountaineering, The Freedom of the Hills*, 5th edition. The Mountaineers, 1992.

Lentz, M., S. Macdonald, and J. Carline, *Mountaineering First Aid*. The Mountaineers, 1990.

References

Dodd, K. *Guide to Obtaining USGS Information*. U.S. Geological Survey Circular 900, 1986.

Hall, Clarence A., Jr., Editor. *Natural History of the White-Inyo Range*. Berkeley and Los Angeles: University of California Press, 1991.

Irwin, Sue, *California's Eastern Sierra, A Visitor's Guide*. Los Olivos: Cachuma Press, 1991.

Little, Elbert L. *Audubon Society Field Guide of North American Trees*. New York: Alfred A. Knopf, 1980.

MacMahon, James A. *Deserts*. New York: Alfred A. Knopf, 1985.

Peterson, P. Victor, and P. Victor Peterson, Jr. *Native Trees of the Sierra Nevada*. Berkeley and Los Angeles: University of California Press, 1975.

Putman, Jeff, and Genny Smith, Editors. *Deepest Valley, Guide to Owens Valley*. Mammoth Lakes: Genny Smith Books, 1995.

Stegner, Wallace and Page Stegner, *American Places*. "There It Is: Take It." New York: Greenwich House, 1983. (A good reference for understanding the history of water problems in the Eastern Sierra.)

Stellenberg, Richard, *Audubon Society Field Guide of American Wildflowers—Western*. New York: Alfred A. Knopf, 1979.

Route Index

Outdoor Publications from Fine Edge Productions

RECREATION TOPO MAPS FROM MOUNTAIN BIKING PRESS™

(with Mountain Biking, Hiking and Ski Touring Trails, 6-color, double-sided, includes trail profiles & route descriptions)

Eastern High Sierra-Mammoth, June, Mono, 2nd Ed., ISBN 0-938665-21-9	$9.95
Santa Monica Mountains, ISBN 0-938665-23-5	$9.95
San Bernardino Mountains, ISBN 0-938665-32-4	$9.95
San Gabriel Mountains—West, ISBN 0-938665-13-8	$8.95
North Lake Tahoe Basin, 2nd Ed., ISBN 0-938665-34-0	$8.95
South Lake Tahoe Basin, 3rd Ed., ISBN 0-938665-35-9	$8.95

Laminated copies – $10 surcharge.

MOUNTAIN BIKING GUIDEBOOKS FROM MOUNTAIN BIKING PRESS™

Mountain Biking North America's Best 100 Ski Resorts by Fragnoli, ISBN 0-938665-46-4	$16.95
Mountain Biking Northern California's Best 100 Trails by Fragnoli & Stuart, ISBN 0-938665-31-6 (classic routes, 80 detailed maps, 300 pages)	$16.95
Mountain Biking Southern California's Best 100 Trails, 2nd Ed., Fragnoli & Douglass, Eds., ISBN 0-938665-53-7 (classic routes, 80 detailed maps, 352 pages)	$16.95
Mountain Biking The Eastern Sierra's Best 100 Trails, by Hemingway-Douglass, Davis, and Douglass, ISBN 0-938665-42-1	$18.95
Mountain Biking the Santa Monica Mountain's Best Trails, by Hasenauer & Langton, ISBN 0-938665-55-3	$14.95
Mountain Biking the San Gabriel Mountains' Best Trails with Angeles National Forest and Mt. Pinos by Troy & Woten, ISBN 0-938665-43-X	$14.95
Mountain Biking North Lake Tahoe's Best Trails by Bonser & Miskimins, ISBN 0-938665-40-5	$14.95
Mountain Biking South Lake Tahoe's Best Trails by Bonser & Miskimins, ISBN 0-938665-52-9	$14.95
Lake Tahoe's Top 20 Bike Rides on Pavement & Dirt by Miskimins, ISBN 0-938665-36-7	$6.95
Guide 4, Ventura County and the Sespe, 3rd Ed. by McTigue, ISBN 0-938665-18-9	$9.95
Guide 10, San Bernardino Mountains by Shipley, ISBN 0-938665-16-2	$10.95
Guide 11, Orange County and Cleveland N.F., 2nd Ed. by Rasmussen, ISBN 0-938665-37-5	$11.95
Guide 13, Reno/Carson Area by Miskimins, ISBN 0-938665-22-7	$10.95

OTHER GUIDEBOOKS

Up the Lake With a Paddle, Canoe & Kayak Guide, Vol. 1, Sierra Foothills, Sacramento Region, by Van der Ven, ISBN 0-938665-54-4	$18.95
Favorite Pedal Tours of Northern California, by Bloom, ISBN 0-938665-12-X	$12.95
Ski Touring the Eastern High Sierra, by Douglass & Lombardo, ISBN 0-938665-08-1	$8.95

To order any of these items, see your local dealer or order direct from Fine Edge Productions. Please include $2.50 for shipping with check or money order. California residents add 7.25% tax.

MOUNTAIN BIKING PRESS™

FINE EDGE Productions

Route 2, Box 303
Bishop, California 93514
Fax (760) 387-2286
Prices are subject to change.
© 1998 Fine Edge Productions
www.fineedge.com